W/P

William Morris and
his Earthly Paradises

Frontispiece 'Souls being Received into the Heavenly Paradise.'
Illustration by Burne-Jones for *The Golden Legend*,
Kelmscott Press, 1892.

William Morris and his Earthly Paradises

Roderick Marshall

Compton Press

For my family

© Mrs Roderick Marshall 1979

First published in Great Britain 1979
by The Compton Press Ltd
The Old Brewery, Tisbury, Wiltshire

Produced, designed and printed at
The Compton Press

ISBN 0 900193 71 9

Contents

List of Illustrations

Frontispiece 'Souls being Received into the Heavenly Paradise.' Illustration by Burne-Jones for *The Golden Legend*, Kelmscott Press, 1892.

Plate

1. Dante led by Beatrice through the Earthly Paradise. Woodcut facing opening of 'Il Paradiso' by Dante in an edition printed at Brescia, May 31, 1487.

2. William Blake's 'The Youthful Poet's Dream.'

3. Tibetan Mandala Thangka. At the centre of the mandala is the female deity Cunda associated with Vairocana, the white Buddha of the centre. 18th century.

4. Tibetan Thangka. Avalokitéshvara, the Boddhisattva of compassion, surrounded by attendant deities in his heavenly palace. 18th century.

5. 'The Earthly Paradise.' Illustration by Burne-Jones for *The Golden Legend*, Kelmscott Press, 1892.

6. Plaque of Morris by George Jack on one of the cottages in Kelmscott village.

7. From an edition of the *Cantica Canticorum* blockbook. (*The Song of Songs* as related to the Blessed Virgin Mary.) Netherlands, *c.* 1470?

8. 'Is this the Land?' Illustration by Walter Crane for *The Story of the Glittering Plain*, Kelmscott Press, 1894.

9. Detail from 'Allegory of Good Government' by Ambrogio Lorenzetti in the Palazzo Pubblico, Siena.

10. Detail from 'The Last Judgment: the Paradise' by Fra Angelico (1387–1455), San Marco Museum, Florence.

11. 'Friends in Need Meet in the Wildwood.' Illustration by Burne-Jones for *The Well at the World's End*, Kelmscott Press, 1896.

Acknowledgements. We are indebted to Dr. David Rogers of the Bodleian Library, Oxford, for identification of illustrations 1 and 7; to the Trustees of the Pierpont Morgan Library, New York City, for illustration 2; and to the Fratelli Alinari, Florence, for illustrations 9 and 10.

Preface

During the years when we lived in and loved Kelmscott Manor and showed its treasures to hundreds of people, my husband began to pull together the principal ideas which had been growing within him through a lifetime of thinking and teaching. These centred around Morris's name not only because we were occupying the home he loved but because Roderick could see the pattern of everyman's life as it was reflected in that of 'the poetic upholsterer.' Therefore it was William Morris about whom he chose to centre the struggle of man to integrate his personality and so to achieve the mandalic experience toward which Dr. Carl Jung saw his clients struggling through the stages of their psychoanalysis.

Thus the book becomes Roderick's testament to the faith that man need not be crushed by the blows of a loveless marriage nor beaten to earth by a world out of touch with beauty. He can eventually see through and beyond these dilemmas to a world in which all things do work together for good and in which tragedy does not define the end of man's life.

As in the case of Sophocles and Shakespeare before him, this mandalic vision of life found triumphant expression in Morris's later stories and underpinned the hope beneath his conviction 'I cannot believe that I shall be annihilated.'

MARGARET WILEY MARSHALL

Oxford 1978

Use of Sources

Such sources as I needed to quote from I have noted in the text as follows:

The volumes of William Morris's *Collected Works*, ed. May Morris, 24 vols., 1910–15, are indicated as follows: XXII, 265, which means Vol. XXII, p. 265.

May Morris's two supplementary volumes, *William Morris, Artist, Writer, Socialist*, 1936, are noted simply as Sup. I and Sup. II, followed by pagination.

The Letters of William Morris, ed. P. Henderson, 1950, is referred to simply as *Letters*, followed by pagination.

Some of Morris's works went through many editions and are still in print or easily come by; quotations from these are noted in ways useful to owners of any edition, thus:

(1) The tales of *The Earthly Paradise* are indicated by the story titles only;

(2) *News from Nowhere*, by chapter numbers, as Ch. XV;

(3) *A Dream of John Ball*, by chapter numbers;

(4) *Sigurd the Volsung*, by book numbers, as Bk. IV;

(5) *Poems By the Way*, by the poem;

(6) Morris's Lectures, collected in *Hopes and Fears for Art* and *Signs of Change*, by both the book and lecture titles.

For secondary sources I try to smuggle the name of the author, the title of the book, the date and the pagination into the text as unobtrusively as possible. Since so few secondary works were used, I saw no need for the usual apparatus of footnotes, *ibids.*, *op. cits.*, and bibliography. Mackail's *Life*, 1899, which appeared in two volumes separately paginated, is referred to simply as Mackail I, 243 or II, 303; Georgiana Burne-Jones's *Memorials of Edward Burne-Jones*, 1904, which also appeared in two separately paginated volumes, is referred to as *Memorials* I or II with pagination.

R.M.

Mandala

For those for whom the references to the mandala throughout this book are not precisely clear and for those who may wonder about its appearance in other times and places throughout the history of man this explanation is provided.

Jung's definition of the mandala in *Memories, Dreams, and Reflections* is as follows: Mandala (Sanskrit), Magic circle, symbol of the centre goal, or of the self as psychic totality; self-representation of a psychic process of centring; production of a new centre of personality. Represented by circle, square, or the quaternity, by symmetrical arrangements of the number four and its multiples. In Lamism and Tantric Yoga, the mandala is an instrument of contemplation (*yantra*), seat and birthplace of the gods. No European mandalas known to me ... achieve the conventionally and traditionally-established harmony and perfection of the Eastern mandala.

The oldest form of the mandala is the paleolithic 'sun wheel' discovered in Rhodesia. The Jews later made use of talismans, derived from the Arabic word *tilsam*, which means 'capable of insuring protection to the person wearing it or passing on powers which he did not possess at birth.' See visions of Ezekiel, Daniel, Enoch.

Later, the rose gardens of the philosophers were often conceived to have had a mandalic form. In the mythology and folklore of many peoples certain motives repeat themselves in almost identical form. Jung calls these motives archetypes and by them understands forms or images of a collective nature which occur practically all over the earth as constituents of myths and at the same time as autochthonous; individual products of unconscious origin. Mandalas are birth places, vessels of birth in the most literal sense, lotus flowers in which a Buddha comes to life. Sitting in the lotus seat, the yogi sees himself transfigured into an immortal. The mandala is a magic circle, the wholeness of self, as when the Egyptians portrayed Horus and his four sons in the form of a mandala. They also made use of the hieroglyph of the *uroboros*, the serpent with its tail in its mouth. From whatever source, this mandalic form was used by the author of the *Song of Solomon* and by the author of *Ecclesiastes*.

The Hindu and Buddhist mandalas, which represent a withdrawing from maya, become subjectively avidya, nescience, complacent abandonment to life; all this is represented by the lotus flower with four or eight petals. Royal palaces in the East, such as Angkor Wat, are built on a mandalic plan, with paradises in the centre and at four cardinal points of one's heart. In the West, the *tetraktys* was the fundamental member in the Pythagorean system. The Platonic man was round on all sides and united the two sexes within himself. The Aztecs and the Pueblo and Navaho Indians of Taos identify themselves with the sun, whose sons they are. This arrangement provides the pattern for many of their sand paintings.

In the Middle Ages there are Dante and his mystic rose and also the rose windows of European cathedrals. The *hortus conclusus* or enclosed garden is often used as an image of the Virgin Mary in medieval hymns. The rosa mystica is one of her attributes in the Litany of Loreto. The crusaders, when they returned from the Middle East, brought with them the concept of an enclosed garden, which poets made use of in the *Romaunce of the Rose*. In China the Golden Blossom represents the mandala and in the Occident the rose and the golden flower. With Buddha, the mandala is Siva in the lotus; with Christ it is in the rose, in Mary's womb. In the Western Christian mandala of the Middle Ages, God is enthroned in the centre as the triumphant Saviour, with four symbolic figures of the evangelists. In Christian cathedral art, there are floor mandalas before the high altar and beneath the transept. Occidental cloisters are often designed with a well or fountain in the garden, just as the court of a mosque has a ritual wash house in the centre. Later there were the cabalistic mandalas and Boehme's 'philosophical eye' or 'mirror of wisdom,' containing the summa of secret knowledge. Even today, the Amish farmers in Pennsylvania have mandalic signs painted on their barns – to ensure good crops and therefore prosperity.

M.W.M.

Foreword

After the handsome rehabilitation (1964–1967) of Kelmscott Manor, for twenty-five years (1871–1896) the summer home of William Morris, by the Society of Antiquaries of London, many people have come to enjoy the beauty of the 'old house by the Thames' and honour the 'poetic upholsterer' in his handiwork. Some also have come to ponder on the spot 'the ideas of Morris and the example of his life' as these have, so the William Morris Society of Great Britain believes, 'the most value for the present-day world.' Since the restoration, my wife Margaret and I have had the good fortune to spend much of our time at the Manor and have done our best to answer the questions of the eager visitors. Besides their specific questions about what they see – wallpapers, chintzes, embroideries, a tapestry, rugs, furniture, the shelves of blue and white china, the *grès de flandres* mugs and pitchers, and the pictures, mostly Rossetti's, with his *Mrs Morris in the Blue Dress* still presiding over the Manor – they nearly all end with the same question: 'Which is the best biography?'

Unfortunately, this is the question hardest to answer. Morris's life does not easily lend itself to a well-rounded story, unified, moving chronologically to a well-prepared climax. Of his childhood we know only that he was at first sickly; then liked, clothed in a miniature suit of armour, to chink about Epping Forest on a pony; finally that he had read all Sir Walter Scott's novels by the age of seven. When old enough, he went to Marlborough School, using the school as headquarters for exploring British antiquities like the Avebury Circles, the Wansdyke, and Uffington White Horse. While at Exeter College, Oxford he made a close friend of Burne-Jones and others, wrote poetry, and visited the cathedral towns of Northern France. Soon he married Jane Burden, whom he met when helping Rossetti decorate the Oxford Union, built Red House with his friend Philip Webb as architect, and, finding nothing with which he was willing to furnish it, discovered his life's work in combating ugly Victorian interiors, designing wall papers, textiles of all kinds, rugs, carpets, furniture, etc. He organised his artist friends into a firm to fight this battle on every front, and became the father of two daughters. Forced to leave Red House by the winters on Bexley Heath, he found Kelmscott Manor in the southwest corner of Oxfordshire on the banks of the Baby Thames as a summer place in 1871, and settled down (1878) in Kelmscott House on the Embankment at Hammersmith as his town house. Without showing many symptoms, he was nevertheless driven to distraction

by an affair carried on between his wife and his friend Rossetti from 1867
to the latter's death in 1882. In 1871 and 1873 he took trips to Iceland, of
which he left stirring accounts in *Journals* kept for Lady Burne-Jones.
During the 1880s he was instrumental, though mostly by thinking otherwise, in developing early British Socialism and in the 1890s he founded
the Kelmscott Press, cutting fonts and designing magnificently decorative
borders, floriated capitals, etc. He published resplendent editions of his
favourite authors and a number of the romances he had written during
his last years (*d.* 1896).

Thus we can see at a glance that Morris's life as an artist and craftsman was full of literally thousands of facts. On the other hand, what letters he wrote were largely about the weather or travels in Europe. Nor
did he share his inner life, it is said, with his nearest friends. In each of
the arts and crafts there is at least one book devoted to what Morris
accomplished and, taken together, they constitute a kind of workaday
biography. Lately, too, a book has been written about him in which each
chapter is devoted to one of the arts or crafts he practised, usually to its
improvement. However, such 'biographies' are not what most of our
visitors have in mind. There are books about the role he played in building British Socialism in the 1880s. That by E. P. Thompson, *William
Morris, Romantic to Revolutionary* (1955) is very thorough in quoting
from his letters and essays, but covers a period of his life that does not
fascinate those who want to know about the mind which produced the
lovely things they see about them, about Jane, and the drive that never
gave up trying to remould the repulsive indoor face of Britain and the
world.

Those books which seek to tell his *whole* story chronologically, usually
in chapters consisting of five- or six-year chunks with every known fact
or so-far reported legend thrown in, do not seem to help our enquiring
visitor either. These biographers from Mackail (1899) to Henderson
(1967) have troubles all their own caused by Morris's simultaneous practice of half-a-dozen arts and crafts while he was at the same time leading
a full poetic, business, political and domestic life. Though Morris is
necessarily the catalyst of the many-fronted action described, little effort
is made to find the centre from which his energy emanated or the central
unity toward which it fought its way. It is rather unlikely that a convinc-
ing human being will emerge from books bearing such bizarrely entitled
chapters as 'Red House – Formation of the Firm – The Fall of Troy' or
'A Dream of John Ball – the Odyssey – Bloody Sunday,' especially when
these chapters are neither inwardly unified nor shown to relate to a cam-
bium point from which a growing tree of life is seen to be spreading.
Thus treatments of Morris in terms of a single art or a dozen, or of all
the facts verified and unverified, leave him without a centre, without

coherence or true humanity. Marooned among a thousand facts, he seems to shrink rather than grow. For most who write about Morris there is such a harvest of accomplishments to be rehashed that the superficies easily come to push the underlying inspiration even further under.

The result of all this fact-hounding is two erroneous notions, which threaten Morris's very life. One: that this Renaissance-rounded master of arts and trades, needing little help from any except hired workmen, was inhumanly chilly, sexless and friendless – Mackail's adjectives are 'isolated, self-centred, almost empty of love or hatred' (II, 349) – a lion-maned beast of a man who walked on his own. Two: that behind his watery light-blue eyes, which seldom looked directly at you, worked a complicated and inscrutable mind which only psychologists with far subtler insights than any available at present will be able, some day in the far-off future, to elucidate. As Fridolf Johnson wrote about Morris in *American Artist* (December, 1968), 'His personality was so complex that it will take many more years for the experts to sort it out.' This claim implies that his personality – the motivated man we can understand – may remain stuck behind wallpaper or squashed between the pages of a well confected book forever.

Extrapolated further, this line of unreason suggests that perhaps we should not bother to look for the man even in his works. As long ago as 1899, Mackail, the biographer par excellence, said that Morris's 'work ... gives only partial glimpses' of his personality 'nor does it bear any trace at all of what made his personality ... unique' (I, 214). Are we being asked to stop trying to conjure a personality from what seem like hoarded clues, especially in the poems and imaginative prose? We know that his daughter May wrote, 'No glimpse of the inner life of Morris was ever vouchsafed even to his closest friends – *secretum meum mihi*' (Sup. I, 441), but we can't let even her deprive us of the pleasure of relating Morris's imaginative work to whatever we can discover about his life. Many years ago W. H. Hudson wrote, 'poetry is most valued and loved when it is made to seem most human and vital; and the human and vital interest of poetry can be most surely brought home to the reader by the biographical method of interpretation.' If we won't use what we can discover about Morris's life to motivate his poetry or his poetry to illuminate his life, we will lose our hold on his vital humanity just as surely as we would have lost much of that humanity if the Antiquaries had decided not to revivify Kelmscott Manor.

The last step along the road of Morris's complete disappearance as a human being – as when he vanished from Kelmscott Church at the end of *News from Nowhere* – was now prepared and took place, it seems, when S. D. Harris pontificated in a lecture 'Evaluating William Morris' delivered in the Stanford University Library in May 1967; the very day, one might say, when the rehabilitation of the Manor was completed and it was handed back – a unique example of Morris's arts and crafts when practised at their best for his own joy – to England and the world, for theirs. In that lecture Harris laid it down, mincing no words, that 'Morris's achievement is ... not to be sought among the direct results of his manifold labours. It is hardly in this sense tangible at all. Morris's real importance is rather as an influence, a key figure in the intellectual history of the nineteenth century, and therefore of the twentieth century.' In other words, let's give up the happiness his books and textiles and furnishings afford us and seek to assess – on the basis of what? – his penumbral influence on historical tendencies and movements!

I doubt that May or Mackail would have liked this sorry subsidence, these last slow raindrops of the tempest called William Morris, and it will never satisfy the pilgrims to Kelmscott who *know* there stands behind everything they see, a man – unusual but not inhuman. It is for their sakes that I have written this book.

I cannot explain to the visitors why existing books about Morris (some fifty so far) do not satisfy me, but I felt that perhaps a fresh and quite different approach might help to make a more coherent account of a coherent man. Where in Morris's writings, imaginative and all the others, can one avoid the phrase 'Earthly Paradise?' The notion is almost obsessional with him quite apart from the great collection of poems which bear this title. And here were my wife, myself and our questioners talking together in Kelmscott Manor – alias Nowhere – alias Utopia – alias the Earthly Paradise. On such an occasion a unified theme began to emerge from all his books, all his arts, all his acts. I found myself thinking that it might be possible to use his poems, stories, Icelandic translations and travels, with the romances written toward the end of his life, to find – well-hidden, of course – those biographical facts which Hudson says give richness and vitality to an artist's work. I experimented here, there, everywhere among his works. The experiment was like that of helping to extract Morris from agony on that day during the decoration of the Oxford Union in 1857 when he got caught in a tailor-made suit of armour and could have passed literally for the Man in the Iron Masque. The casque which he had instructed a blacksmith to make for the sake of pre-Raphaelite *verismo* in the painting of Arthurian scenes, once clamped over his face, could not be pried open without the help of half a dozen friends, but it was no poetic fantasy they brought to light. They found Morris himself, screaming for the 'back-rung bells' of that Paradise once recaptured at Camelot. Though May, Mackail and others have long been trying to hide Morris behind prudish petticoats of chain mail, I believe that he will curse himself free with the help of sympathetic readers and clarify the life-style to which he firmly adhered.

At the Manor here we have a complete Morris library, including all important related material – a bequest to the Manor by Ney MacMinn of the contents of his houseboat on the Seine. (MacMinn was one of those professors who do not quite trust Oliver Wendell Holmes's assurance that all good American professors when they die go to Paris, and sought to anticipate the blessed event by as long as possible.) Since I am convinced, with Hudson, that imaginative literature is most lovable and vital when the lights of biography can be seen flashing through the art, I have read and reread everything and searched between the lines of poetry and prose for the seeds of biography that sometimes lie buried under the hundreds of facts about what Morris did, when, where, how much, etc. About all I found in this secondary material was just more of the crack-browed fellow – little of the man of high haemoglobin, the artist of the considerable solar plexus, that virile centre from which interknotted strengths are said to ray out in indefatiguable creative warmth.

In spite of May's dogmatic 'never a word vouchsafed to his closest friends,' it is impossible for a creative writer to keep from revealing his hidden life and frustrated impulses. In fact, he more than often writes to relieve these strains by externalising them in exaggerated or muted forms. Nowhere is the intimate life of Morris presented to us as an open book, but if we will open *all* his books and read carefully, especially between the lines, we will often find revealed at a stroke both his not infrequently sorry life *and* the glory he made of every shattering experience. It is in the poems, stories, Icelandic translations and travels, along with the romances written toward the end of his life – the books most frequently ignored, denounced and out of print – that one can find, I believe, the man to match the house here. Morris has been called one of our best unread writers. It has been years, or rather forever, since any writer on him has quoted from the rich material so neglected, but so needed if we are to get a just idea of what he was, of what he wanted to tell his readers, of what is relevant to us today; that is, of the art of living.

From first to last, like most of us, he sought to make life yield its keenest happiness, a quest which always leads to looking for a Paradise on earth. The difference between Morris and the rest of us was perhaps a more highly strung set of nerves, more highly attuned to pain even than to pleasure. He had to pursue happiness unceasingly if he was to avoid unceasing pain. Except for Thoreau, perhaps, Eden is dreamt of as inhabited *à deux*. Heaven on earth and its *anima loci* are, accordingly, at the very centre of Morris's thought and work. Because he needed such an Eden so badly, to find or fashion viable paradises became the goal of nearly all his speculations and efforts. In time he became an adept of heavens on earth, an expert on Golden Ages, an habitué of Nowhere.

The most important of these Nowheres or Utopias which he partly found, partly created, for his solace and delight was Kelmscott Manor. What his impassioned researches and dreams turned up on the subject of earthly happiness is possibly the heart of his enduring fascination. Here lie his 'ideas,' here the source of his 'influence,' here the 'example of his life, of which his admirers make so much. His paradisal probings are hardly something which, if we knew more about them, we would care to ignore. Fortunately, we can know as much about them as we please, for everything Morris thought, wrote or did was concerned with little else. In all his writings no phrase occurs more frequently than 'Earthly Paradise'.

After living for the last half-dozen years in Kelmscott Manor, among the things Morris made, designed, or collected, among the books he wrote and printed, the birds and flowers and trees he loved, near the villages he venerated, beside the river he fished in, I cannot resist the temptation to try to re-upholster the frayed elbows of the poetical craftsman. I hope this story, told as it appears to me, may be worth something to people plagued like Morris himself by blighted towns and cities, blighted loves, blighted projects, blighted health. I hope it may, without neglecting his effect on 'intellectual history,' recapture in his words some of the genuine feeling that, coming from the heart, is always said to go to other hearts. The life and work of Morris, seen in all their interplay, present today's sufferers with a classic lesson about survival in the modern world, about 'making the best of it,' which is unlike anything I have come across elsewhere. He may have spread his artistic energy thinly at times, but when what we can discover of his life is related to his manifold creations, and vice versa, he emerges as a figure of truly impressive proportions, a man, as Bernard Shaw said, great 'not only among little men but among great ones.' Without the interplay of life, poetry and art, you reduce him to a machine; perhaps half a dozen machines. They may have been prodigious in output, but Morris gets stuck under wallpaper or flattened between beautiful books. He becomes a picture of Nobody sequestered in Nowhere, rather than a beleaguered soul battling for happiness – Utopia, if you will – against disappointment, pain, fear and boredom with a superb armoury of highly differentiated weapons all self-forged. No biography of Morris, including Mackail's, has ever given me the sense of a living man meeting Life's dilemmas with a supply of ripostes that do, indeed, have 'relevance to our time.'

In fact, Morris has been said to have brought into English life a note of kindness, calmness, balance, and even happiness which is still working in us unconsciously. W. B. Yeats, writing of Morris, said that 'if some angel offered me the choice, I would choose to live his life, poetry and all, rather than my own or any other man's' (*Autobiographies*, 1955,

141). Yeats had the feeling that in some inscrutable way Morris, in spite of hyperaesthesia and a nagging empathy for others' misery, in spite of his deathly disgust with the sooty, stock-jobber century in which it had been his supreme misfortune to be born and meet Jane Burden – that somehow Morris had lived the happiest life possible to a human being. Elsewhere (*Fortnightly Review,* March 1903) Yeats hailed Morris 'as the greatest of those who prepare for the last reconciliation when the cross shall blossom with roses.' If the reader will bear these words of Yeats continually in mind, he will see in the following pages how Morris sought to make bale, heartbreak, anxiety and dread bear fruits of beauty. According to Yeats he actually found ways of turning our present afflictions to affections. In his poetry, prose and art he offers us a healing, consolatory, countervailing Eden. He is the pioneer of as much of heaven as we are likely to get on this earth.

I cannot, of course, tell my opinion of the biographies of Morris to the curious people who stream to Kelmscott with their questions, nor does it matter. But I would often like to tell them about the chapters that follow. After all, they know what it is that makes an old house, no matter how lovely both inside and without, live – people – and they are right to keep on trying to find out what the complex and mysterious inhabitants were and did in this Earthly Paradise. To make the record complete and easily understandable I have tried to draw together here everything Morris thought on the subject nearest his heart – that of building heaven on earth. Here one can use the chronological approach fruitfully because we have a single theme in which biography and literature dovetail to make a modest study, which I think of as a calling-card left on the tray at Kelmscott Manor to show that Margaret and I were here once and tried to understand.

1 Gathering Building Blocks for Paradise

The first thing we hear about the baby born at Elm House, Waltham-stow, in 1834 is that young William Morris was sickly. He could hardly digest food and was a thoroughly irritable infant. However, beef tea and calves-foot jelly kept life's delicate child from perishing, and throughout his early boyhood, spent largely in the open air in and around Epping Forest, he grew healthy and even robust in body. As much cannot, per-haps, be said for his inner life. Throughout his boyhood and youth he is reported to have been nervous and excitable. Stories of early temper tan-trums are many, and while these are said to have been of short duration, it is also clear that as he grew older they became fiercer, and with the breaking of his childhood pipe more strident. For years he is referred to as shouting rather than speaking. 'Strange fits of passion' led him to beat his head against stone walls or kick in door panels – if eruptions of such ferocity ever really happened, as several of his friends were given to col-ourful embroidery. However, the tropical proliferation of their anecdotes makes these episodes seem so 'strange' that many people have been tempted to interpret 'fits' in a medical sense. It is probably not necessary to go so far.

However, the stories of Morris the sickly infant, the petulant child, the Marlborough boy with the 'fearful temper' and murderous single-stick, the compulsive netter, the indefatigable reader and tale-teller, all point to a painful restlessness engendered by something other than the redundant health which he claimed to have picked up riding his pony through long days in Epping Forest. Neither can it be attributed wholly to what A. Clutton-Brock (*William Morris*, 1914, 9) and others have called 'aesthetic discontent,' which they conceive of as a peculiar disease resulting from the degradation of workmanship and the desecration of nature caused by the Industrial Revolution at the acme of capitalist exploitation. It was a long time before Morris became aware that he was afflicted by this essen-tially Ruskinian form of neurasthenia. Something like aesthetic unease plagues us still when we shrink hopelessly from growing hideousness while cowering with inferiority before the glories of the past. Actually, some kind of hyperaesthesia, perhaps affecting the senses of taste, touch and hearing as well as of sight, may have kept Morris's nerves stretched to the breaking point. From childhood through university – and indeed to the end of his life – no adjective was more often used of him than 'fid-gety.' He could not sit still for more than a few moments even at meals, when, it is said, he relieved his restlessness by chewing the tines of his fork out of shape or jumping up spasmodically to fling distasteful food from the window. Fortunately the acute sensitivities which made the world in its frequent ugliness an almost unbearable trial to Morris furnished also the means of surviving in it. The beauty which he discovered in nature and (some) art or found he could fashion for himself made up to him for every thin-skinned pain and panic alarm. Nevertheless, he was often worried by 'the instability which he found, or thought he found, in his own character' (Mackail I, 137), and from an early age he was aware of wishing to be unruffled, genial, magnanimous. 'O how I long to keep the world from narrowing me, and to look at things bigly and kindly.' (Quoted in Mackail II, 268). To achieve something like this jovial serenity entailed a life-long battle against a 'complex' which made him more afraid of death, of being ugly and unlovable, of living in a civilization on the edge of doom, than was natural or conceivable in a child or, for that matter, in a young man of much less than the 'roaring health' he had acquired in the forest.

When twenty-two he published a story called 'Frank's Sealed Letter' which possibly gives us some notion of the trepidations he suffered as a child. In this a deformed boy, Hugh, the narrator, is terribly hurt when a little girl called Mabel refuses to crown him with flowers because he is 'too ugly.' Similar words spoken to Morris in his youth – ' "I want a man who is brave and beautiful. You are a coward and a cripple" ' – haunt him like a nightmare from which he tries vainly to awake

as often, when a child, I used to wake from a dream of lions, and robbers, and ugly deaths and the devil . . .

But for Frank's letter, Mabel's words would have left Hugh a

vanquished man; and really without any object in life, not desiring death more than life, or life more than death; a vanquished man though no coward; forlorn, hopeless, unloved, living now altogether in the past.

This story seems to embalm experiences or hallucinations of a hectic kind not uncommon to Morris in his childhood.

What the child seems to have wanted from his world was consolation for some unknown loss, steadiness for an uncommonly delicate balance-wheel, the alleviation of indefinable fears. The boy had his mother, Emma Morris, to comfort him but she was very busy bringing children into the world. There had been three before William, the first of whom, the only boy, had proved too fragile to survive; then after William, in as quick succession as she could manage, six more: four boys and two girls. There were finally four girls in the family. It seems as if William, even if his hard-pressed mother could find little time for patting her sensitive child, could have found a mother-surrogate or so in his two slightly elder sisters. In fact Emma, named after her mother, is said to have been 'very close' to her baby brother but may have been so alarmed by the infant's dangerously poor health that she infected him with fear of death at an age when such fear is largely unheard of. She may even have tried to discourage the growing child's adventuresomeness with constant reminders of the days when his very survival was considered doubtful; also, of the death of the family's first-born male. Somehow, at any rate, he acquired a fear of death quite unnatural in a child and not much more natural, later on, in a young man of good health. While there is little doubt that he had in the two Emmas women who were quite ready to love and even to 'spoil' him, it seems that only the sister had the time and talent to satisfy his appetite for sympathy and adoration. Emma was the sister with whom he used to read 'tales of terror' on the edge of the forest near Woodford Hall, the house the family moved to when he was six – read till darkness overtook them and they had to retreat, 'half-dead with terror,' to the shelter of the Hall. It was Emma with whom he carried on an animated correspondence from Marlborough, and he agonised over her marriage to a man of the cloth. The loss of the one woman who understood and loved him for what he knew himself to be upset him thoroughly and John le Bourgeois thinks he never recovered. He thinks it was the memory of Emma when set side by side with the realities of Jane Burden that soured Morris's marriage in the first place and drove his wife into the arms of Rossetti. It is probably unnecessary to find so much of Orestes and Electra in this childhood affair – if it is necessary to use such a darkling analogy at all.

Not only was the danger of imminent death instilled in the boy, but he was apparently also plagued by the feeling that he was distasteful to girls (deserted by his sister?), probably ugly, and possibly unlovable. The latter fear is perhaps attested in 'Frank's Sealed Letter,' while the preoccupation with early death crops up in even his most juvenile – no one knows how juvenile – poems in such lines as,

> What is the bottom of the river like?
> O! green it is with swinging weeds,
> O! yellow with bright gravel,
> O! blue with the water overhead . . .
>
> I said 'the water overhead'
>
> For I lie here a-dying.

Another very early poem contains lines like

> Ah! all things die, and come again,
> Ah! all things but the feet of men . . .

So weepeth he, so weepeth he
Beneath the boughs o' the beechen tree
So weepeth he – so dieth he.

(Sup. I, 531, 523)

Even when he first came to Oxford he was writing juvenile verses in his maudlin vein:

O! my lost love moaned there
And her low moans in the air
Sleepy startled birds did hear . . .

When I lifted up her head
And I softly to her said,
Blanche, we twain will soon be dead.

Let us pray that we may die
Let us pray that we may lie
Where the softening wind does sigh. . . .

There I kissed her as she lay
O! her spirit passed away
'Mid the flowers her body lay.

And of course the 'poet' followed her so that

. . . over them over them ever
The long long wind swept on . . .

(Mackail I, 60–61)

That the dead boy managed to record all this seems to be due to resurrection or waking up.

One of the more remarkable instances of Morris's youthful – this time not juvenile – fear of early death occurs in the story 'Golden Wings' printed in the *Oxford and Cambridge Magazine* for December 1856. Though less suggestive of autobiography than 'Frank's Sealed Letter.' it is a prime example of his claim of 1856 that 'my work is the embodiment of dreams in one form or another' (*Letters*, 17) – a slight paraphrase of Poe's 'The business of my life is to dream.' Perhaps both Morris and Poe suffered from frightful nightmares which they disguised in weird feats of high-wire fiction. 'Golden Wings' ends with a scene in which the hero's lover is kissing his feet while his enemies are closing in. Finally,

She sprung up from my feet with a low, bitter moan, most terrible to hear, she kissed me once on the lips, and then stood aside, with her dear head thrown back and holding her lovely loose hair strained over her outspread arms . . .

Then one thrust me through the breast with a spear, and another with his sword, which was three inches broad, gave me a stroke across the thighs that bit to the bone; and as I fell forward one cleft me to the teeth with his axe.

And then I heard my darling shriek.

Since the victim here is also the narrator, this bloody tale can have come to us only as the memory of a horrible death-dream or a pastiche of nightmare fears. In the second chapter we will follow Morris, now a young poet, through several such incidents, each more grisly than the preceding. It is not impossible that similar dreams, though less sophisticatedly ghastly, had haunted him since childhood. However brought on, by ghost stories, tales of terror, cramps in the neck, midnight memories of Rob Roy's ghoulish wife, or fearful headaches, such dreams, added to his hyperaesthesia, made pretty gruesome baggage for a lad to carry into life. However, young William, activated by a remarkable battery of talents and tutelary instincts, began at an almost phenomenally early age to seek out ways of neutralising his midnight dreads.

By the time he was seven Morris the child, according to Morris the man, had read all the novels of Walter Scott – had, so to speak, tucked the lot of them under the toy armour he wore as he galloped his pony through Epping Forest. About all we know of him in those early days when he lived near Walthamstow on the borders of Epping, first at Elm House (from birth to six years), then at Woodford Hall on the far side of the forest (until he was fourteen), is that he bolted Scott whole by seven. All his life he never tired of boasting, in his mild way, of this feat and was always grateful to Scott for the pleasure and store of insights, or rather of unforgettable images, with which the novels had filled his imagination then – and if then, as always with Morris, forever after. On 24 June 1896, Morris – not far from his end and staying at Folkestone on doctor's orders – was visited by Wilfred Scawen Blunt, to whom he gave what seems to have been the last happy lecture of his life. He 'talked a great deal about his boyhood, said he had read the whole of Scott's novels before he was seven, and had gone through the phase of *Marmion* and the *Lady of the Lake*.' (W. S. Blunt, *My Diaries*, 1-fol. ed., 1932, 231). If anything could revive, even if only for a few moments, the sparkle of life in the dying man, it was, apparently, to remember the often gorgeous pre-Raphaelite imagery of Scott and especially a configuration of nature and architecture which Dr Carl Jung, taking the word from ancient Buddhist and Hindu usage, calls a mandala and considers symbolic of healing and restoration. In *Mandala Symbolism* (extracted and translated by R. F. C. Hull, Princeton UP, 1972) Jung says that

In the sphere of religious practices and in psychology it denotes circular images, which are drawn, painted, modelled, or danced. As psychological phenomena they appear spontaneously in dreams . . . Very frequently they contain a quaternity or a multiple of four, in the form of a cross, a star, a square, an octagon, etc.

Both the circle and the square, especially in combination (they can be arranged inside each other *ad infinitum*) seem – by constructing a central

point or concentric field around or within which disordered or irreconcilable elements can be peacefully arranged – to lessen confusion, heal division, bring order out of inner chaos. The pattern imposed by a circular or
square scheme, or a combination of the two, acts to tame, neutralise or
conterbalance disorder or chaos in the psychic state. Jung says the appearance of mandalic forms in dreams and art or art-like forms is an *'attempt
at self-healing* on the part of Nature, which does not spring from conscious reflection but from an instinctive impulse.' (4) A fundamental
schematisation existing everywhere is turned to instinctively and used all
over the world by the tortured psyche in search of peace. Such patterns or
pictures (Jung distinguishes half a dozen or more) he calls archetypes.
The mandala he is inclined to call the *'archetype of wholeness'* (4) for the
quaternity of the One, the squaring of the circle 'is the schema for all images of God' – that is, of peace, rest, joy, that passes understanding. In a
typical mandala we find circles of trees or monoliths; streams and
gardens enwreathing castles or churches which have at their centres –
called temenoi by Jung – fountains of life or altars draped with embroidered female saints. The mandala with its sacred centre or temenos,
whether dreamed of, painted or otherwise created, seems to allay apprehension and bring a soothing sense of peace, of self-healing to minds
made irritable by disorder and panicky by irreconcilable elements in
experience.

Morris was haunted by an unusual share of his misgivings and there is
reason to believe that even in childhood, depression was always lurking
for him around every corner of Woodford Hall. That Scott was his prized
psychiatrist can be deduced, perhaps, from the fact that when asked by
the *Pall Mall Gazette* in February 1886 for a list of the Best Hundred
Books, he nominated nearly all of the master's novels, adding in a note
on modern fiction, 'I should like to say here that I yield to no one, not
even Ruskin, in my love and admiration for Scott.' (That Ruskin's admiration was considerable can be gathered from the fact that from childhood he had found relief in Scott from the yearly cover-to-cover reading
of the Bible which his mother had forced on him, and at the end of his
life was collecting material for a work to be called *Walter Scott and Epic
Art.*) Among Morris's hundred books, Scott contributed massively to a
roster notable for the Hebrew Bible, Homer, Froissart, Dante, Chaucer,
Malory, Shakespeare, More, Keats, Ruskin and Carlyle (*Letters, 245–7*),
so great was his gratitude to his doctor.

We may assume then, though of course we can never know, that while
the boy in his custom-made armour chinked about the great forest
famous for its hornbeam trees, he was really seeing in his mind's eye
magically be-fountained Scottish glens, mysterious stone circles or forest-
surrounded castles filled with chambers a-rustle with green tapestries.

Since there is evidence in at least one signal instance that his reading of Scott shaped his way of apprehending the world, we may speculate a little on Sir Walter's influence on the boy urging his pony from grove to glade in Epping. Though Poe, Browning and others came to influence his way of seeing life, Scott was clearly the first power to shape Morris's own remarkable power of imagination.

One of the simplest forms of mandala (the Sanskrit word for circle) is a forest glade or grove set around a well-watered open space and itself sometimes surrounded by mountains or hills. The water – of life – occupies the centre of the composition and may take the shape of a spring, stream, tiny river (like that of the Earthly Paradise), small lake or, more sophisticatedly, fountain, either natural or man-made. The centre may also be a building, a palace or temple with a fountain in its central court. The space enclosed by the trees and surrounding the sacred centre or temenos is customarily embroidered or enameled (these are the favourite adjectives of writers of many lands and eras) with bright flowers. Birds sing in the trees and summer weather prevails. In addition, and now we come to the heart of the mandala experience, the whole is presided over by the spirit of the fountain – a numinous female that crystallizes out of the fresh-scented water, called variously a nymph, mermaid, 'messenger from Heaven' (Dante's Beatrice), benignant Eve, 'Queen of Faërie,' 'embodied Romance' or a goddess identified as Proserpine, Diana, Venus, or the Virgin Mary in the West and with a dozen female deities in the Orient (often White Tārā dancing at the heart of the sacred centre). Such is man's (at least, articulate man's) oldest dream of a place of rest and refuge. The whole mandalic concept, with its circles of woodland and flowers surrounding a fountain or architectural centre, itself round or square, is a dream of country peace and retirement, the kind of spot to nourish the happier contemplations of men fed up with the discord, dirt and frenzy of life in cities. Such is the kind of spot likely to resolve tensions, reestablish joy, and nourish larger, richer loves. This is a picture and belief which flares up in human consciousness from time to time as if from forgotten sources of truth or, less ponderously, from free-darting, firefly fidelities that play hide-and-seek with the conscious mind. From time to time writers and painters have pinned down the vision in forms that turn out to be almost identical, naming the hallowed spot Eden, the Terrestrial Paradise (even Dante's elaboration of the picture goes very little beyond the essentials sketched above, see Plate 1), Tempe, Arcadia, the Elysian Fields, the Mead of Enna, the Happy Valley, the Locus Amoenus or Great Good Place, the Garden of Adonis, the realm of Saturn, the Isle of Venus (Camoens), the Flower-Heaven of Amida. All these constitute what Jung calls an archetypal dream, a vision flashing in the hidden depths of consciousness to relax, steady and reinvigorate tortured nerves. Prosaically, it is the sustaining if only vaguely imaged vision of a holiday home in Connecticut or a cottage in the Cotswolds.

I suggest that the boy Morris, dashing on his pony from end to end of Epping Forest in search of sunlit glades watered by trickles from the River Lea and surrounded by handsome hornbeams, was looking for forest mandalas with their immense measure of peace. The almost furious urge to find and enjoy these oases among extraordinary trees which, once frequently pollarded, have often thrown four or five new polls straight up from a branch in the form of an Aeolian harp for the winds and birds to sing in – this would have been inexplicable to the boy but irresistible. And what of the female spirit of the forest sanctums? Morris was *very* young. Yet it is also true that his surviving juvenilia are haunted by a longed-after lost love. Did Epping have a resident goddess? Well, there was in fact Boadicea, whose putative burial mound is located near some of the boy's favourite clearings. He undoubtedly felt the wonder of his solitary forest adventures and the relief they brought him. Later he introduced into his poetry and prose romances literally hundreds of descriptions, some slight, others highly developed, of just such wooded sanctuaries. These are, in fact, one of the hallmarks of Morris's literary work, and all his life he was grateful to the Epping glades for their solace and inspiration.

In the year before his death he wrote two letters to the editor of *The Daily Chronicle* (*Letters*, 363–7) to protest against 'the danger of further ruin' to this beloved woodland. On 23 April 1895:

I venture to ask you to allow me a few words on the subject of the present treatment of Epping Forest. I was born and bred in its neighbourhood (Walthamstow and Woodford), and when I was a boy and young man knew it yard by yard from Wanstead to the Theydons, and from Hale End to the Fairlop Oak. In those days it . . . was always interesting and often beautiful. . .

The special character of it was derived from the fact that by far the greater part was a wood of hornbeams, a tree not common save in Essex and Herts. It was certainly the biggest hornbeam wood in these islands, and I suppose in the world. The said hornbeams were all pollards, being shrouded every four or six years, and were interspersed in many places by holly thickets; and the result was a very curious and characteristic wood, such as can be seen nowhere else. And I submit that no treatment of it can be tolerable which does not maintain this hornbeam wood intact.

In May 1895 he followed this letter with another, further praising the 'romantic' beauty of the hornbeams and arguing for their protection against the prejudices of a verderer called Buxton:

About Monk Wood there had been much, and I should say excessive felling of trees apparently quite sound. This is a very beautiful spot, and I was informed that the trees there had not been polled for a period long before the acquisition of the forest for the public: and nothing could be more interesting and romantic than the effect of the long poles of the hornbeams rising from the trunks and seen against the mass of the wood behind. This wood should be guarded most jealously as a treasure of beauty so near to 'the Wen.' . . . it has a peculiar charm of its own not to be found in any other forest; in short it is thoroughly *characteristic* . . . Mr Buxton declares in so many words that he wants to change the special character of the forest: to take away this strange, unexampled, and most romantic wood, and leave us nothing but a commonplace instead. I entirely deny his right to do so . . . I assert, as I did in my former letter, that the hornbeams are the most important trees in the forest since they give it its special character . . . in spite of all disfigurements, the northern part of the forest, from Seardsone Green to beyond Epping, is still left to us, not to be surpassed in interest by any wood near a great capital.

For three quarters of a century Epping was saved from being turned into spears (unpolled) timber for sawmills or into golf courses, but in this decade (*The Times*, 5 April 1971) we hear again that 'Epping Forest, in Essex, needs a champion if it is not to disappear as a refuge for man and wildlife.' This warning was first given in the April issue of the *Ecologist*, in a report which says that 'the forest is threatened by massive road building.'

That Morris loved the forest of 'sacred clearings' so deeply was due, above all, to an instinctive search for his own salvation, but it seems to me that he could easily have had his scent for such refuges, for Mother Nature's boudoirs, as Thoreau more lightly called them, sharpened if not formed by his omnivorous reading of Scott. I will mention only one instance, probably lodged, though unconsciously, in the boy's mind from the minute he first came across it. The consecrated glen I have in mind is described in considerable detail in *The Monastery* and its companion novel *The Abbot*. It is the valley of Glendearg as described in *The Monastery*. This glen, imprisoned in purple hills, was watered by a stream not

void of beauty. The turf which covered the small portion of level ground on the sides of the stream, was as close and verdant as if it had occupied the scythes of a hundred gardeners once a fortnight; and it was garnished with an embroidery of daisies and wild flowers.

The steep hills or *braes* which overshadowed the glen were covered with thickets of oak, birch, mountain-ash, alders, and quivering aspens, which enclosed the velvet-turfed stream. We are told that though not 'strictly . . . sublime or beautiful,' Glendearg or Red Valley was rather awe-inspiring because of its extreme solitude. As in all Scott's novels of life above the border, superstition plays a role, here peopling one wild recess of the glen called *Carrie non Shian* (corrupt Gaelic for 'the Hollow of the Fairies') with a 'White Maiden' dwelling by a fountain or mountain spring who was thought to guard the decaying fortunes of the House of Avenel. This 'mystic being' certainly helps in adventures which are much more outlandish than eerie to reerect the tottering family that bore her White Shape on their arms. This is the proper role of the female figure in the temenos at the centre (of Beatrice, for instance, in Dante's Earthly Paradise, who both reproves and rewards, soothes and animates). As the soul of the natural scene, the White Maiden might be called the Psyche or Anima of both nature and man (without seeking to identify her with Jung's complicated concept of the Anima).

In *The Bride of Lammermoor* Scott seems to be going to use this same device for restoring the fortunes of the ancient family of the Ravens-woods. Here the White Lady of the central fountain is a mermaid who lives, or lived, in it, but this 'naiad' had long ago been alienated from the Ravenswoods. Though Lucy Ashton, after being saved from the wild bull by Edgar Ravenswood, was carried for recovery to the 'plentiful and pellucid fountain' in the mountain glen in which Ravenswood Castle was set, and later had meetings with her lover there, the mermaiden offered the lovers no real help, as everyone familiar with Italian opera knows.

'I like this spot,' said Lucy . . . 'The bubbling murmur of the clear fountain, the waving of the trees, the profusion of grass and wild-flowers, that rise among the ruins [of its ancient coping], make it a scene in romance. I think, too, I have heard it is a spot connected with the legendary lore which I love so well.'

'It has been thought,' answered Ravenswood, 'a fatal spot to my family . . .'

(Ch. XII)

Just so, for this time the *anima loci* (long since murdered?) could not play her customary role, and the Houses of Ravenswood and Ashton both went down amid scenes of horror.

Young Morris did not soon forget either of these stories with their evocation of picturesque Scottish scenes and superstitions. From them he probably became acquainted with the notion that certain landscape configurations were almost sacred. Their comfort and peace goes so far beyond understanding that we tend to postulate indwelling guardian spirits as their inhabitants. These are usually imagined as female, partly because their historians are male and partly because nature and all her hills, trees, flowers and waters have almost invariably been personified as girls or women. Moving from India to the Indians of the New World, or vice versa, we find that still, or up to fewer than a hundred years ago, earth was called Mother; mountains her breasts, waters her blood, trees and all the growth of the soil her hair. Spots such as Scott described have always, as far as I can find out, been treasured by human beings, set apart as the haunts of deities, and called, once man had found a word for them, paradises. When 'paradise' was made interchangeable with 'heaven,' they were called earthly paradises.

The word 'paradise' derives from the Old Persian word *pairidaëza* – formed on *pairi* (around) and *dis* (to mould, to form) which meant the royal park, enclosure or orchard of the Persian king. Even at its origin, the word signified a specific natural place with a special (in this case royal) character. The subsequent history of the word has two branches: it becomes Hebrew *pardēs*, and and it is adapted by the Greek [*paradeisos*] and, through Latin, French, and Middle English, becomes our word 'paradise.'

   (A. B. Giamatti, *The Earthly Paradise and the Renaissance Epic*, 1966, 11)

   Hebrew *pardēs* meant in the beginning a park or garden (but not Eden) as did *paradeisos*, first used by Xenophon to mean a royal park, though the Greek word was soon used to mean (1) the Garden of Eden and (2) Heaven or the Abode of the Blessed Dead, these meanings being attributed later to *pardēs* too, so that early uses of 'paradise' mostly mean an 'earthly paradise' with blooming parks or gardens planted 'around' a splendid building. This picture was seldom forgotten, it seems, for in much medieval illustration a gorgeous house or temple (God's? Solomon's?) was pictured at the centre of a roundabout garden called Eden. The flower garden was itself invested by a forest and the forest by a wall. Here you have circles within circles sweeping about a predominantly square bit of architecture, royal or ecclesiastical, and this, we may say, is the essential form through the ages, and in nearly all countries, of the earthly paradise. It is what is often called an archetypal picture which haunts the depths of the perhaps unconscious mind, but one which can be dredged up into consciousness without much effort and actually brought into physical existence by a king or a gardener. The configuration is that of a highly elaborate and stylised – and finally conventionalised – form of the mandala described above. It is from Hinduism and Northern Buddhism that this arrangement of square and circle gets the name of mandala and pictures of mandalas are drawn by Nepalese and Tibetan monks in search of serenity, soothfastness, internal unification, luminous equipoise, spiritual royalty, beyond trepidation or shadow of disturbance. We shall have a little more to say about mandalas, their construction and uses, later in this chapter. All I wish to stress here is that they would seem to offer what a somewhat haunted, driven, frustrated boy – or man – like Morris was always in search of.
   And what of Sir Walter Scott? It is with him in mind that I have introduced this discussion of the mandala, for I think young William Morris may first have thrilled to this archetype in Scott's fiction, where it occurs so often. At the beginning of the second chapter of *Quentin Durward* we read:

It was upon a delicious summer morning, . . . while the dews yet cooled and perfumed the air, that a youth . . . approached the ford of a rather large brook, tributary to the Cher, near to the royal castle of Plessis-les-Tours, whose dark and multiplied battlements rose in the background over the extensive forest with which they were surrounded. These woodlands comprised a noble chase, or royal park, fenced by an enclosure, termed in the Latin of the middle ages, *Plexitium*, which gives the name of Plessis to so many villages in France. The castle and village of which we particularly speak, was called Plessis-les-Tours . . . and was built about two miles to the southward of the capital of ancient Touraine, whose rich plain has been termed the Garden of France.

Here the boy Morris encountered, without knowing it, a perfect picture of the original earthly paradise, the palace around which was moulded an extensive royal park (*pairidaëza*) composed of woodlands watered by tributaries of the Loire and fenced at the periphery by a boundary wall.

To make the paradise somewhat sombre in keeping with the character of Louis XI and the atmosphere of his novel, Scott did not dwell at length on the terraces and gardens that usually tie a chateau of the Loire to its hunting preserve and form the typically mandalic circles of the *plexitium*. Actually, Plessis-les-Tours in Scott's time was perhaps as ruinous or non-existent (a couple of rooms) as it is today. However, the triple-walled and well battlemented castle which Scott describes at length contains many memories of the visit to the Loire chateaux which he made in search of pictures for his novel. In fact, he invents in the 'Introduction' another imaginary castle, Hartlieu, whose picturesque ruins he describes as the headquarters of his sojourn by the river. Between his two imaginary castles he manages to divide the most 'romantic' details of most of the great fifteenth- and sixteenth-century French castles, landscape gardens and forests. Most of his details, however, he seems to have taken from Chambord and Blois, behind both of which it is still possible to distinguish traces of a 'grim old fortress.' During the eighteenth century Chambord was inhabited by a violent man, the Maréchal de Saxe, who, like Scott's Louis XI, hung men for the least failure in discipline from the branches of an old elm. Chambord's once royal park (now called the Parc National d'Elevage et Réserve Cynégétique) is even more immense than that ascribed by Scott to Plessis-les-Tours; it covers 13,600 acres of which 11,000 are woodland (*vd.* Michelin *Green* or British *Blue*). The wall which encloses this huge *plexitium* is actually twenty miles long, with six gates leading to the Renaissance pleasure-palace whose plan is, nevertheless, still feudal, consisting of a central keep with four round towers connected by curtain-walls – a study, from the air, in squares, parallelograms and circles. It is not likely that Morris, having penetrated at a stroke into mankind's earliest and never-forgotten, if sometimes neglected, conception of the Earthly Paradise, ever forgot it or

ceased to be grateful to Scott for the dozens of castles he described from
Coningsburgh to Kenilworth. Years later, in his lectures on *Hopes and
Fears for Art* (1882) he was still lamenting that Scott 'thought himself
continually bound to feel ashamed of, and to excuse himself for, his love
of Gothic architecture; he felt that it was romantic, and he knew that it
gave him pleasure, but somehow he had not found out that it was art
...' By 'romantic' Morris meant, as we do not always remember, that
effect of art or beauty which soothes and solaces. It was for this 'rest'
above all that he loved the Middle Ages:

From the first dawn of history till quite modern times, art, which nature meant
to solace all, fulfilled its purpose; all men shared in it; that was what made life
romantic, as people call it, in those days; that and not robber-barons and in-
accessible kings with their hierarchy of serving-nobles and other such rubbish.

The fact is, as Morris learned, that every room of a castle, or any building, can be a little mandala in itself if adorned by Sir Walter's bright,
pre-Raphaelitish imagination. Such a small fane – sacred by reason of
form, colour, restfulness, reassurance – can be found even in Saxon
Rowena's boudoir:

The walls were covered with embroidered hangings, on which different-col-
oured silks, interwoven with gold and silver threads, had been employed with
all the art of which the age was capable, to represent the sports of hunting and
hawking. The bed was adorned with the same rich tapestry, and surrounded
with curtains dyed with purple. The seats had also their stained coverings, and
one, which was higher than the rest, was accomodated with a footstool of ivory,
curiously carved.
    No fewer than four silver candelabras, holding great waxen torches, served
to illuminate this apartment.

(Ch. VI)

This 'apartment' was possibly a bit more self-flaunting than any room
Morris was ever to decorate, but we can easily imagine the first impact of
such a picture on the seven-year-old whose declared aim in life was to be:
'rebellion against sordid ugliness, especially in the domestic arts, whose
harvest should be the chief part of human joy, hope, and consolation ...'
('Making the Best of It,' *c.* 1879, printed in *Hopes* and *Fears for Art*,
1882). I will not describe the fecundity of Scott's genius for verbal interior decoration including gorgeous tableware as well as carpets, bedsteads,
chairs, tapestries, pictures, etc., but will stress a well attested example of
its impact on Morris the boy.
    In a lecture on 'The Lesser Arts of Life' (given in 1882; first printed in
Lectures on Art and Industry, 1902) he says,

How well I remember as a boy my first acquaintance with a room hung with
faded greenery at Queen Elizabeth's Lodge, by Chingford Hatch, in Epping

Forest . . . and the impression of romance that it made upon me; a feeling that
always comes back on me when I read, as I often do, Sir Walter Scott's *Anti-*
quary, and come to the description of the green room at Monkbarns, amongst
which the novelist has with such exquisite cunning of art embedded the fresh
and glittering verses of the summer poet Chaucer.

The scene in Scott's *Antiquary* occurs when young Lord Lovel is lodged
in a bedroom

hung with tapestry, which the looms of Arras had produced in the sixteenth
century . . . The subject was a hunting-piece; and as the leafy boughs of the
forest trees, branching over the tapestry, formed the predominant colour, the
apartment had thence acquired its name of the Green Chamber. Grim figures,
in the old Flemish dress, with slashed doublets, covered with ribbands, short
cloaks, and trunk-hose, were engaged in holding greyhounds or staghounds in
the leash, or cheering them on upon the objects of their game. Others, with
boar-spears, swords, and old-fashioned guns, were attacking stags or boars
whom they had brought to bay. The branches of the woven forest were
crowded with fowls of various kinds, each depicted with its proper plumage.
It seemed as if the prolific and rich invention of old Chaucer had animated the
Flemish artist with its profusion . . .

(Ch. X)

Oldbuck, the antiquary to whom the house called Monkbarns belonged,
had accordingly had certain lines from Chaucer embroidered in Gothic
letters on a border which he added to the tapestry. On most of the tapestries which he was later to design Morris too gave a prominent place to
Gothic-lettered mottoes and poems – not by Chaucer but by his loyal dis-
ciple William Morris. It could be argued that his fondness for tapestry,
including the Samson hangings of the Tapestry Room at Kelmscott
Manor, probably dated back to the combined effect of seeing Elizabeth's
Hunting Lodge in Epping and reading *The Antiquary*. In *Kenilworth*
both a Samson tapestry (in the castle) and a Samson bas-relief (in the
summer-house at Cumnor) are mentioned. While aware that the Samson
tapestries at Kelmscott in their faded glory were probably more handsome 'than they were meant to look,' Morris was genuinely fond of them
because 'they give an air of romance to the room which nothing else
would quite do' (Mackail I, 230). The word 'romance' carries us at once
back to Morris's conception of that quality in art which is mainly dignified, healing, consolatory. In other words, the Tapestry Room at Kelmscott and the dozens of gorgeous or gorgeously dilapidated rooms in
Scott's novels were, indeed, small sacred spots with surrogate altars
within buildings which might, or might not, stand within grand mandalic convolutions. In Scott the virtuoso reader was finding building blocks,
if we may put it this way, for many an Earthly Paradise, and in Epping
Forest with Elizabeth's Lodge, real examples of an earthly Eden.

Besides castles with their sacred inner shrines there is another type of structure well fitted to be the centre of successive girdles of walls, forests, and flowers. I mean, of course, ecclesiastical buildings, large or small. Though he has much to say of Melrose Abbey in *The Monastery* and *The Abbot* and of a dozen other fanes, real or invented (like the ruinous one in *The Antiquary* or the palatial 'Sanctuary of the Lord' in *Quentin Durward*), Scott, possibly because of a strong Protestant bias, seldom described a Catholic structure with his usual amount of affectionate detail. A form of sacred structure which seems to have fascinated him more than churches was the henge or mysterious ring of standing stones which be usually associated, as in *The Betrothed*, with 'the Druids ... deemed not unacquainted with the arts of sorcery, which they practised when they offered up human sacrifices among those circles of unhewn and living rock ...' (Ch. XV). It is near the beginning of *Ivanhoe*, actually, that we have the most loving elaboration of such a structure, encircled by a primitive park to give us the numinous feeling of the mandalic scheme.

Hundreds of broad-headed, short-stemmed, wide-branched oaks, which had witnessed perhaps the stately march of the Roman soldiery, flung their gnarled arms over a thick carpet of most delicious green sward; in some places they were intermingled with beeches, hollies, and copsewood of various descriptions, so closely as totally to intercept the level beams of the sinking sun ... A considerable open space, in the midst of this glade, seemed formerly to have been dedicated to the rites of Druidical superstition; for, on the summit of a hillock, so regular as to seem artificial, there still remained part of a circle of rough unhewn stones, of large dimensions. Seven stood upright; the rest had been dislodged ... (Ch. I)

That the boy who loved Scott was always intrigued by these ageless open-air temples is not surprising though it was not till he went to school at Marlborough that he had an opportunity to indulge his taste for British antiquities. There he learned, as he told Blunt in the last year of his life, 'nearly everything he knew about architecture and medieval things, running about the country.' (*My Diaries* 1932, 232) Among 'medieval things' he must have included the remarkable prehistoric remains with which Berkshire and Wiltshire abound, including the largest of all opentemple stone circles, at Avebury. This consists, in fact, of two large circles which almost intersect, surrounded by an enormous circle. Morris did not, and could not, understand the topography of the great shrine as we do today, but his enthusiasm was unbounded, as he revealed to his favourite sister Emma in an unpunctuated letter of 1849, written when he was fifteen:

On Monday I went to Silbury Hill which I think I have told you before is an artificial hill made by the Britons but first I went to a place called Abury

where there is a Druidical circle and a Roman entrenchment both which encircle the town originally it is supposed that the stones were in this shape first
one large circle then a smaller one inside this and then one in the middle for
an altar but a great many in fact most of the stones have been removed so I
could [not] tell this. On Tuesday morning I was told of this so I thought I
would go there again, I did and then I was able to understand how they had
been fixed; I think the biggest stone I could see had about 16 feet out of the
ground in height and about 10 feet thick and 12 feet broad the circle and entrenchment altogether is about half a mile; at Abury I also saw a very old
church the tower was very pretty indeed it had four little spires on it of the
decorated order, and there was a little Porch and inside the porch a beautiful
Norman doorway loaded with mouldings and the chancel was new and was
paved with tesselated pavement ...

(Letters, 4–5)

Years later he wrote of this same scene, this time including Stonehenge:

The man must be hard to move indeed who is not moved as he turns the
corner of one of our commonplace English highways and comes suddenly across
that marvellous hedge of grey stones that our Saxon ancestors called Stonehenge: or looks from the great circular earthwork of Avebury – looks down
on the little old village that lies within it, where the cottages are cheek by jowl
with the few remaining stones of the ancient temple there: lying close by the
huge barrow of Silbury, the hills about all dotted with graves of the early
chieftains; the mysterious Wansdyke drawn across the downs at the back ...
a familiar place to my boyhood; yet a holy place indeed.

(Quoted in E. Meynell, Portrait of William Morris, 1947, 194)

His enthusiasm for such circles, especially when set in great forest clearings (Savernake Forest replaced Epping for almost weekly excursions
while he was at Marlborough and acted as a backdrop for the prehistoric
treasures of the neighbourhood), never waned, as we can see from these
letters and the late romances, especially the Doom Ring of *The House of
the Wolfings*.

I included Morris's description of the old church at Avebury in the
quotation from the early letter because it points to an interest in church
architecture which is relevant to the question of mandalas and which
may have been stimulated by the Scott's detailed descriptions. Old
English churches seem to have drawn the boy like a magnet from as far
back as he could remember or we can discover. They were the first
ancient buildings which he could really finger and caress, his first friends
in the Valley of the Lea, daughters of what he came to call the queen of
arts, Architecture, a tangible embodiment of the sanctuary which he
always needed in order to soothe his fears and insufficiencies. As Mackail
writes,

. . . the old Essex churches within reach of Woodford and their monuments and brasses, were known by Morris at a very early age; and a visit which he made with his father to Canterbury when only eight years old left on his mind an ineffaceable impression of the glory of Gothic architecture. On the same holiday they saw the church of Minster in Thanet. It is characteristic of his extraordinary eye and even more extraordinary memory, that just fifty years later, never having seen the church in the interval, he described it in some detail from that recollection. No landscape, no buildings that he had once seen did he ever forget, or ever confuse with another.

(Mackail, I, 10)

On 19 July 1895 Morris wrote to Lady Burne-Jones about another church which he remembered in detail after years of absence:

On Wednesday I went a journey into Suffolk for the S.P.A.B., a pretty journey all through my native Essex. . . . Blyborough was what we went to see . . . with the ruins of a small religious house and a huge 15th century church built of flint after that country manner: a very beautiful church, full of interest, with fine wood-work galore, a lovely painted roof, and some stained glass; the restorations not much noticeable from the inside . . . I was there some twenty-five years ago; and found I remembered it perfectly.

(*Letters*, 369)

These quotations make it clear that good old churches had for Morris as boy and man a very special message, speaking a language his whole nature always craved to hear. To him they were never quaint or queer but expressed in their lovely dignity and stillness the state of mind he always aimed at but seldom achieved. He felt that the men, the whole society, which had produced these buildings must have been lovable, and he loved them as if they were still alive, as they were in Scott's novels.

At the university, where he arrived in 1853, Morris found what Mackail calls 'the old Oxford, the stronghold or sleeping-place of a belated yet still living Mediaevalism' (I, 28), almost intact though on the verge of capitulating to 'modernity,' with 'its tramways and electric lighting, its whirlwind of building up and pulling down, its tragi-comedies of extension and modernisation' (I, 31), its 'meshes of suburb hideous in gaunt brickwork and blue slate' (I, 29).

one still approached it as travellers had done for hundreds of years, and saw its towers rise among masses of foliage straight out of the girdle of meadow or orchard. 'On all sides except where it touched the railway,' writes Sir Edward Burne-Jones, 'the city came to an end abruptly as if a wall had been about it, and you came suddenly upon the meadows. There was little brick in the city; it was either grey with stone, or yellow with the wash of the pebble-cast in the poorer streets, where there was still many old houses with wood carving, and a little sculpture here and there.'

(I, 29)

The Oxford of 1853, 'girdled' with meadows and trees and surrounded by its old walls, however invisible, was almost a temenos-centre itself. It 'breathed from its towers the last enchantments of the Middle Ages' (I, 30), which meant to Morris that he was free to haunt some of the loveliest ecclesiastical buildings extant and read on fine days in the garden of New College cloister, which probably reminded him of the great cloister of Canterbury, unforgotten since his childhood visit. Both these cloisters are rectangular mandalas with their fountain-temenos gone, but still filled with ancient peace and 'the sound of many bells.' In Oxford Morris was actually living the life he had once lived in imagination with Sir Walter as guide.

This fascination with sacred stone reached its apex in visits which Morris made to Northern France in the Long Vacation of 1854 and the summer of 1855. There, in Amiens, Beauvais, Chartres and Rouen he found what he held to be the finest achievements of the noblest human ideals. He loved not only these mandalic arrangements but the very soil of France from which they seemed to him to have sprung like incredible stone flowers. He planned to write for *The Oxford and Cambridge Magazine*, published in monthly instalments throughout 1856, a series of articles on 'the Churches of North France,' but completed only 'No. 1 – Shadows of Amiens,' which appeared in the February issue. From this article I will patch together a few quotations which may help us to appreciate how deeply he felt the 'romantic' – that is, the tranquil, consolatory, ataraxic – appeal of a beauty of the Middle Ages first called to his attention by Sir Walter Scott.

. . . I will say here that I think these same churches of North France the grandest, the most beautiful, the kindest and most loving of all the buildings that the earth has ever borne; and, thinking of their past-away builders, still surely living, still real men, I love them . . . for this . . . upraising of the great cathedral front with its beating heart of the thoughts of men, wrought into the leaves and flowers of the fair earth; wrought into . . . stories of the faith and love of man that dies not . . .

After mentioning 'the twined mystery of the great flamboyant rose window with its thousand openings, and the shadow of the flower-work carved around it,' he describes the huge arches of the nave and every architectural detail till he comes to the sculptured figures of the Virgin Mary who are, as it were, the temenos-hearts in this great mandalic arrangement of squares and circles. It is the Madonna in the southernmost porch of the west front that he likes best.

The Virgin's face is calm and very sweet, full of rest – indeed the two figures [of mother and child] are very full of rest; everything about them expresses it from broad forehead of the Virgin, to the resting of the feet of the Child . . .

in the fold of the robe that she holds gently, to the falling of the quiet lines of her robe over her feet, to the resting of its folds between them.

Here at the age of twenty, Morris throws himself with an audible sigh of relief before deified Rest as if it were for him already the longest-lost, the most eagerly sought, the most precious recompense life can yield. We cannot help thinking of the 'Epoch of Rest' which the hero of *News from Nowhere* enjoyed with the virginal Ellen in the fane of Kelmscott. Thus we understand why for Morris this tutelary goddess of the great fane of Amiens is the most 'romantic' of the Virgins of France – she who guarantees her lovers rest, hope, faith, the power to imagine and the strength to accomplish.

It is difficult to say just how much of his enthusiasm for church architecture Morris owed to his early reading of Scott but there is no doubt that his love of both Scott and churches was born and grew simultaneously. In Morris's fondness for describing churches there are echoes from the whole range of the Waverley novels. Of course the child enjoyed the adventure stories but it was Scott's descriptions of castles, palaces, abbeys and the like which helped him to see and treasure the world about him. It was this side of Scott which helped the unusual boy to become father to the remarkable man. Usually writers about Morris have little to say of the early years except that he rode his pony about the forest and read all of Scott's novels by the age of seven. Perhaps these two bits of information, if closely examined and interrelated, tell us more about him, then and later, than any dozen teething-tales on record.

Before we go on to describe how Morris used the mandala with its temenos-centre in two of his early stories – the climax of a chapter intended to suggest how he first moved, as we would now say unconsciously, into the ambience of the Earthly Paradise he would never cease trying to find – we must take a little time to say something more about this archetypal structure and its psychic use and value.* Of all the pioneering physicians who have explored the bosky and neglected jungles of the unconscious, Carl Jung seems to me to have returned with the most fascinating report, verifiable, he claims, in the dreams of his patients, and verified, if we may use the word, in an extant body of art and literature stretching over more than four thousand years before Jung was born. Archetypal figures (as he calls them) such as the Puer Aeternus, the Wise Old Man and the Anima, though buried under nine Troys of repression, he finds still living and working, even in the most derailed of us, to heal and integrate the splits, frustrations, and fears which keep us from living

---

* See MWM's explanation of Mandala, page ix.

forceful, affirmative, joyous lives. The integration toward which these
symbolic archetypes or actors, themselves all fragments of our own dis-
jointed personalities, urge us – the recovery from mind-rending fears and
insecurities – is achieved, according to Jung, with the aid of dream pictures, the chief of which is the mandala encircling its sacred centre. Let
us suppose that the fractured personality has been trying to pull itself
together; the success of the effort would be represented by dreams reaching some kind of centrepoint which Jung finds described in Eastern trea-
tises as 'the heavenly heart,' the 'terrace of life,' the 'realm of the greatest
joy,' the 'square-inch field of the square-foot house,' the 'purple hall of
the city of jade,' the 'dragon palace at the bottom of the sea.' Having got
this far, it is only necessary for the dreamer, depending on his need, to
surround this centre, characterised by diamond-like light and strength,
with defensive circles of flowers and trees, with protective furrows and
towered walls, to get an arrangement which Jung calls a mandala. This,
he says, is 'a Sanskrit word [which] means circle or magic circle. Its
symbolism embraces all concentrically arranged figures, all circular or
square circumferences having a centre, and all radial or spherical arrangements.' (*The Integration of the Personality*, tr. S. Dell, 1940, 95n.) In
the West this elaborate dream pattern may be drawn by the dreamer on
awaking in order to hold on to its beneficent effect; in the East such
mandalas are drawn on the ground or painted on cloth, as in Nepal or
Tibet today, in order to build up, quite consciously and according to age-
old specifications, personality-strength. Commenting on his patients' pictures of this kind, made many years before he had ever heard of the
Eastern practice or seen a sample of such a mandala, Jung says:

One source is the unconscious, which spontaneously produces such fantasies;
the other source is life, which, if lived with complete devotion, brings an in-
tuition of the self, the individual being. ... the mandala symbol is not only a
means of expression, but works an effect. It reacts upon its maker. ... it derives
originally from the 'enclosing circle,' the 'charmed circle,' the magic of which
has been preserved in countless folk customs. The image has the obvious purpose of drawing ... a magical furrow around the centre, the *templum* or
temenos (sacred precinct), of the innermost personality in order to prevent
'flowing out. ... by means of these concrete performances ... the interest is
brought back to an inner sacred domain, which is the source and goal of the
soul, and which contains the unity of life and consciousness.'

(*The Secret of the Golden Flower*, tr. from Chinese into German by R.
Wilhelm with a Commentary by C. G. Jung, and from the German by C. F.
Baynes, 1962, 102–3.)

When this unity, now lost, is found, the inner kingdom recovered,
Jung calls the achievement 'the integration of the personality.' He has a

book, as we have seen, with this title in which he describes and analyses several dreams of a patient who seems, by the help of his dreams, to have regained his lost union of life with consciousness. The dreams are filled with every conceivable image suggesting roundness and squareness; as the dreams unfold, these images tend to arrange themselves into the mandalic form of circles encompassing squares with, at the heart of the innermost geometry, a holy structure (church, castle, golden city – sometimes elaborate enough to be a mandala itself) which is the paradisal place of wholeness characterised by almost blinding light. Usually the place of light materialises in the form of a fountain, tree, flower or mysterious woman. True, flower and fountain are described as themselves symbols of the woman or goddess, and all represent the water of life or holy of holies, the cosmic source of energy around which the mandala is protectively constructed. In Tibetan or Nepalese mandalas, of which I have a couple, the power at the centre appears as a god or goddess, preferably the White Goddess of Buddhism known as Tārā (Sanskrit for 'star'). She is often, appropriately to a symbol of the free-flowing lifeforce, dancing. In his 'Commentary' on *The Golden Flower* Jung says that 'deep introspection, or ecstatic experience, reveals the existence of a feminine figure in the unconscious; therefore the feminine name, anima, psyche, or soul' (116) which, in the West, we often give to Tārā.

I do not claim that William Morris, as child or man, ever saw or heard of a mandalic picture though he seems to have thought a good deal about the integration of the personality. It must have been something like this he was forever in search of when he spoke of wanting to be at peace with himself, fearless, inviolable, magnanimous, noble. However, if this configuration is, in both its simple and complicated forms, an archetypal dream, not properly remembered, not entirely forgotten, but submerged through lack of use for many centuries, it is likely to surface anywhere in the world when needed by a sufferer in search of a stilled mind – especially among poets and artists on the neurasthenic side. This at any rate is the belief of Dr Jung.

In the stories Morris wrote when only twenty-two or younger for *The Oxford and Cambridge Magazine* (1856), we find two really remarkable uses of the temenos-centre surrounded by an almost Oriental luxuriance of mandalic imagery. In what he calls 'The Story of the Unknown Church' in the January issue we have a dream of dreams, narrated in the present by a man six hundred years dead, about a fane which vanished from the earth two hundred years ago! 'No one knows now even where it stood.' Besides, there is practically no story, only the account of the construction of what is so much a mandala that no other word will des-

cribe it. Of course, Morris was not the first to write a so-called story with
no narrative interest except the gradual movement from a periphery toward a centre. I need not stress the difficulty of giving such a 'narrative'
general interest or, indeed, of executing it at all. A few great poets had
accomplished something like this in the past; in the present perhaps, and
in what he called a tale in prose, only Edgar Allan Poe. In fact Poe is the
master of elaborate descriptions whose only 'story' consists of adding to
splended details, details still more gorgeous until he manages, we can
hardly tell how, a climax of interest filled with a sunburst of light. It
must have been at least partly from Poe, whom he read and much
admired, that young Morris caught the notion of constructing such an
eventless tale as 'The Unknown Church,' – especially from 'The Domain
of Arnheim' and 'Landor's Cottage.' 'Arnheim' tells of a certain fabu-
lously rich man in whose brief existence Poe has, he fancies, 'seen refuted
the dogma that in man's very nature lies some hidden principle, the anta-
gonist of bliss.' That brief existence had been devoted to constructing,
through incredible gardening – and then enjoying – a wondrous, never
quite completed mandala-landscape. The centre of Mr Ellison's mandala
has to be approached in a boat which, as it travels along a confined
stream of shining water, seems at times to be 'imprisoned within an
enchanted circle, having insuperable and impenetrable walls of foliage, a
roof of ultramarine satin, and no floor' until it reaches a circular basin
surrounded by low hills, which form with the crystal water a stunning
mandalic effect, the reader seeming to sit enchanted at the centre of a
suspended ball. The sides of the hills

sloped from the water's edge at an angle of some forty-five degrees, and they
were clothed from base to summit – not a perceptible point escaping – in a
drapery of the most gorgeous flower-blossoms [while seen] far down in the
inverted heaven [shimmered] the duplicate blooming of the hills. On these
latter there were no trees, nor even shrubs of any size. The impressions wrought
on the observer were those of richness, warmth, colour, quietude, uniformity,
softness, delicacy, daintiness, voluptuousness, and a miraculous extremeness of
culture . . . but as the eye traced upward the myriad-tinted slope, from its sharp
junction with the water to its vague termination amid the folds of overhanging
cloud, it became, indeed, difficult not to fancy a panoramic cataract of rubies,
sapphires, opals, and golden onyxes rolling silently out of the sky.

From here it is not far for the seeker of the centre to float until

the whole paradise of Arnheim bursts upon the view. . . . there is a dream-like
intermingling to the eye of tall slender Eastern trees – bosky shrubberies –
flocks of golden and crimson birds – lily-fringed lakes – meadows of violets,
tulips, poppies, hyacinths, and tuberoses – long intertangled lines of silver
streamlets – and, upspringing confusedly from amid all, a mass of semi-Gothic,

semi-Saracenic architecture, sustaining itself as if by miracle in mid air; glittering in the red sunlight with a hundred oriels, minarets, and pinnacles . . .

the temenos itself.

'Landor's Cottage' Poe wrote as a pendant to 'The Domain of Arnheim,' to give the idea that a simple structure could be as sacred a place as a castle, provided it were set in a circle of blue slopes or hills, the amphitheatre thus formed being floored with 'green Genoese velvet' and inlaid with a small lake reflecting tall tulip trees bearing innumerable perfumed blossoms and having at *its* centre a small island on which stood un 'utterly unpretending cottage' in the New York-Dutch fashion. And in it – a lovely young woman who led the traveller to say to himself, 'Surely, I have found the perfection of natural, in contradistinction from, artificial grace. The second impression which she made upon me, but by far the more vivid of the two, was that of *enthusiasm*. So intense an expression of romance, perhaps I should call it, or of unworldliness . . . had never sunk into my heart of hearts before.' At last: the goddess, of which there had been none in 'Arnheim' except Ellison's beautiful bride, who is not firmly anchored anywhere in the gorgeous ambience. With her appearance in Landor's cottage we have reached the climax and conclusion of our 'tale.'

And now for the 'story' of 'The Unknown Church.' The Abbey grounds where the now defunct narrator, an architect and sculptor, built the Church were 'not girt by stone walls, but by a circle of poplar trees . . .' This circle of trees surrounded a complex of buildings, at the centre of which stood the Church and Abbey

joined . . . by a cloister of round arches, and in the midst of the cloister was a lawn, and in the midst of that lawn, a fountain of marble, carved round about with flowers and strange beasts; and at the edge of the lawn, near the round arches, were a great many sun-flowers that were all in blossom . . . and up many of the pillars of the cloister crept passion-flowers and roses.

Beyond this centre, surrounding all the holy buildings and uniting them to the poplar trees at the periphery was a 'great garden' with trellises covered

with roses and convolvolus, and the great-leaved fiery nasturtium; and specially all along by the poplar trees were there trellises, but on these grew nothing but deep crimson roses; the hollyhocks too were all out in blossom at that time, great spires of pink, and orange, and red, and white, with their soft, downy leaves. I said that nothing grew on the trellises by the poplars but crimson roses, but I was not quite right, for in many places the wild flowers had crept into the garden from without; lush green briony, with green-white blossoms, that grows so fast, one could almost think that we see it grow, and deadly nightshade, La bella donna, O! so beautiful; red berry and purple, yellow-spiked flower, and deadly, cruel-looking, dark green leaf, all growing together in the glorious days of early autumn. And in the midst of the great garden was a conduit, with its sides carved with histories from the Bible, and there was on it too, as on the fountain in the cloister, much carving of flowers and strange beasts.

In a passage like this Poe is certainly out-Poed.

In the midst of the cemetery which, one more circle among so many, surrounded the Church stood a stone cross carved on one side with the Crucifixion and on the other with 'Our Lady Holding the Divine Child,' who is perhaps the goddess-centre of this 'story' though a competing centre of holiness is the elaborate tomb which the sculptor raises to his beloved sister and her betrothed, who had been his best-loved friend. The friend having been killed in war, the sister has died of grief, and the rest of the 'tale' tells how the sculptor, working for twenty years, raised over their bodies in the nave of the church a last centre, carved and painted with many flowers and once-loved faces before he died, chisel in hand, 'underneath the last lily of the tomb.' The agony of life in the world and the peace and consolation of work at the centre are both well conveyed by our young author in this entirely impressionistic evocation which, following Poe, he called a 'tale.'

A story which, though again conveyed through elaborate impressions rather than preachments, contains much sound narrative and impressive psychology while unfolding the hero's search for the girl-haunted temenos is Morris's 'The Hollow Land' (October, 1856). This begins with the words, 'Do you know where it is – the Hollow Land?' There 'I saw my love first.' The storyteller, Florian de Liliis, seeking to understand the long-flouted peace of the centre – for this is a moral tale – says,

> Yea, in my ears is a confused noise of trumpet-blasts singing over desolate moors, in my ears and eyes a clashing and clanging of horse-hoofs, a ringing and glittering of steel; drawn-back lips, set teeth, shouts, shrieks, and curses.
> How was it that no one of us ever found it till that day? for it is near our country: but what time have we to look for it, or any good thing . . .
> Lives past in turmoil, in making one another unhappy; in bitterest misunderstanding of our brothers' hearts, making those sad whom God has not made sad, – alas, alas! what chance for any of us to find the Hollow Land?
> Yet who had not dreamed of it? Who, half miserable yet the while, for that he knows it is but a dream, has not felt the cool waves round his feet, the roses crowning him, and through the leaves of beech and lime the many whispering winds of the Hollow Land?

The Hollow Land is then, rather obviously, the Happy Valley or Earthly Paradise or, to use Jung's Greek and Sanskrit words, the mandalic schema enclosing the temenos or sacred point. This is too good a tale, in the real sense, to be burdened with analysis. Florian remembers how Queen Swanhilda, infuriated by his brother stumbling and allowing the canopy he was holding over her to bow her proud neck,

smote my brother across the mouth with her gilded sceptre, and the red blood flowed all about his garments; yet he only turned exceeding pale ... though he was heir to the House of the Lillies: but my small heart swelled with rage, and I vowed revenge, and, as it seems, he did too.

Sixteen years later, on Christmas Eve, Arnald summoned Florian with many knights to help him wreak his long-nursed fury on the queen. After praying to God to give Swanhilda into their hands, they rode through the falling snow to her capital. One of Morris's most lovely poems, a Christmas carol sung from the battlements of Swanhilda's city, causes the furious onrush to pause for a moment:

> Queen Mary's crown was gold,
> King Joseph's crown was red,
> But Jesus' crown was diamond
> That lit up all the bed
> *Mariae Virginis.*

And another stanza:

> Ships sail through the Heaven
> With red banners dress'd,
> Carrying the planets seven
> To see the white breast
> *Mariae Virginis.*

But having sliced off the queen's 'tiger head,' the whole House of the Lillies, pursued by the counter-vengeance of Red Harald, the fierce son of Swanhilda, met its doom in a battle where most of the liegemen surrendered after 'spitting, cursing, and shrieking, as they tore away like a herd of wild hogs.' Florian and Arnald, now the sole and hopeless hope of the Lillies, were prodded back to a cliff's edge which cut short one side of the battle-moor. At the foot of the cliff lay a country rife with 'wild tales of glamour' for it was

... oh such a land! not to be described by any because of its great beauty, lying, a great *hollow* land, the rocks going down on this side in precipices, then reaches and reaches of loveliest country, trees and flowers, and corn, then the hills, green and blue, and purple, till their ledges reached the white snowy mountains at last.

Both the brothers were prodded over the edge to what seemed like inevitable death, but Florian at last regained consciousness in what 'seemed to be a cool green light ...' where it was sweet to hear a glorious voice ringing out,

> Christ keep the Hollow Land
> Through the deep spring-tide,
> When the apple-blossoms bless
> The lowly bent hill side.

'Thereat my eyes were slowly unsealed, and I saw the blessedest sight I have ever see before or since: for I saw my Love. . . . She was so lovely and tender to look at, and so kind, yet withal no one, man or woman, had frightened me half so much.' She tells him she has been waiting for him for a long time, but, though 'strange knowledge, strange feelings were filling my brain and my heart,' he cannot answer a word. Though she lulls him to sleep with the songs of 'all the poets I had ever heard, and of many others too, not born until years long after I was dead,' he could not bring himself on awaking to touch her. Finally, they come together in untellable happiness for a moment after she had denounced the cowardly murder of Swanhilda, whose sobbing shade, dressed in scarlet and gold, seems somehow to plague the Hollow Land. After encountering this ghost, Florian is mysteriously separated from the woman of pity and peace.

After fighting fierce duels with his brother, who has been saved like himself, in the family Castle of the Lillies, 'its towers blackened now and shattered' yet maniacally painted scarlet and yellow within, he awakes from a deep sleep, unarmed and blissful, to hear a beloved voice singing:

> Christ keep the Hollow Land
> All the summer-tide;
> Still we cannot understand
> Where the waters glide:
>
> Only dimly seeing them
> Coldly dimly seeing them
> Many green-lipped cavern mouths
> Where the hills are blue.

' "Then," she said, "come now and look for it, love, a hollow city in the Hollow Land." ' Florian kissed the singer and they went in search of a palace in a yellow city, a place 'cloistered off' from the other houses, with 'its own gaiety, its own solemnity apart from theirs; unchanged, unchangeable were its marble walls . . .' Before the gates of this centre within a centre, they paused, trembling as they opened the portals upon the innermost sacred place – 'and no man gainsaid us. And before us lay a great space of flowers.' And in the centre of this, we may say with certainty that Florian embraced forever Margaret, his soul, having learned that all's lost by violence.

There is perhaps no story in any language which points so well as 'The Hollow Land' to the sedative meaning and value of making mandalas. It seems to be the masterpiece of a process working in Morris since earliest childhood. Remember the fidgety, death-haunted, anxious, easily angered boy flitting through Epping Forest in search of an indefinable but deeply craved stillness. Recall how, probably with the help of Scott, he found in hornbeam glades, in an old green tapestried hunting-lodge, and in ancient churches, alleviation, if only partial, of his nebulous but always nagging need. Think how at Marlborough he held his doubts and fears at bay by hikes to prehistoric stone circles which he identified, quite correctly, as open-air temples, of which the greatest in England, Avebury's, were at his doorstep. At Marlborough he also fell to telling endless tales to his fellow schoolboys. We have no idea what these tales were about but we may surmise that they contained echoes of Sir Walter Scott and especially since he was reading Poe about this time – intimations of the luxurious images of *Oxford and Cambridge* stories to come. Psychologically, the college student was little different from the bedevilled boy, but during the first two decades of his life he had learned a technique of assuagement. He had learned how to use his hands and head to quiet his fears and soothe his beating brain – how to work at, as he put it, the art of living. 'The Hollow Land' is a milestone, with mandala and temenos and a ghastly depiction of the insane red violence that the making of mandalas is held to assuage.

These discoveries were to go on perfecting themselves and branching from one field of self-expression to another all his life. The art of constructing sacred enceintes in dream and in fact, outdoors and indoors, in poetry and prose, wallpaper and chintz, tile and tapestry, calligraphy and book design, was to go on to the very end. He called it the art of living. Had he had the word, he might have described it more specifically as the art of making mandalas. Though as yet a tiro, he had begun, powerfully, to deliver his most valuable lectures on how to live in the disoriented world we inhabit today. He had begun to build up the heritage of art and ideas he was to leave us.

II Paradise Picked up at the Theatre 1857-1859

I have suggested that one of the causes of Morris's anxieties and fears, felt from a very early age, may have been the feeling that girls did not, perhaps could not, like him. In the surviving juvenile verses he continually bemoans unreturned affection or beweeps the lost love of a vanished or perished (also imaginary?) sweetheart. He wails for unrequited affection or echoes Scott's melancholy dwarf: 'Lost! lost! lost!' In the year before he met Jane Burden, he described in one of his *Oxford and Cambridge* (1858) stories ('Frank's Sealed Letter') a woman who not only rejects but scorns the man who adores her:

She sat by the cold hearth, with her back to the window, her long hands laid on her knees, bending forward a little, as if she were striving to look through and through something that was far off – there she sat, with her heavy, rolling, purple hair, like a queen's crown above her white temples, with her great slumberously-passionate eyes, and her full lips underneath. . . . Except that the wind moved a little some of the folds of her dress, she was as motionless and quiet as an old Egyptian statue, sitting out its many thousand years of utter rest, that it may the better ponder on its own greatness . . .

It is impossible not to find in this description something weirdly prescient of the Oxford girl he persuaded (apparently with some trouble) to marry him in April 1859. In 'Praise of My Lady' we have the same pale face, heavy hair, 'slumberously-passionate eyes' focused on something 'far off,' 'full lips,' 'long hands.'

> My lady seems of ivory
> Forehead, straight nose, and cheeks that be
> Hollow'd a little mournfully.
> > *Beata mea Domina!* . . .
>
> Not greatly long my lady's hair,
> Nor yet with yellow colour fair,
> But thick and crisped wonderfully:
> > *Beata mea Domina!* . . .
>
> Beneath her brows the lids fall slow,
> The lashes a clear shadow throw
> Where I would wish my lips to be.
> > *Beata mea Domina!*

Her great eyes, standing far apart,
Draw up some memory from her heart,
And gaze out very mournfully;
—*Beata mea Domina!*—

So beautiful and kind they are,
But most times looking out afar,
Waiting for something, not for me.
Beata mea Domina! . . .

Her full lips being made to kiss,
Curl'd up and pensive each one is;
This makes me faint to stand and see.
Beata mea Domina! . . .

Of her long neck what shall I say?
What thing about her body's sway,
Like a knight's pennon or slim tree
—*Beata mea Domina!*—

Set gently waving in the wind;
Of her long hands that I may find
On some day sweet to move o'er me?
Beata mea Domina!

Morris first met Jane Burden in the early autumn, probably in September, of 1857 and published *The Defence of Guenevere* about seven months later. He met her either at the theatre in Oxford where he had gone with Rossetti, Burne-Jones and Arthur Hughes or in the temporary Oxford rooms of Rossetti after the painter-poet had found her sitting behind him in the theatre and persuaded her to pose for him and his friends and pupils. Rossetti was in Oxford during the Long Vacation of 1857 to decorate the large bays between the gallery windows of the octagonal clerestory of the Oxford Union. This was a voluntary job for which he had enlisted the services of six friends including Burne-Jones and Morris, both now living in London in Rossetti's old quarters in Red Lion Square. Jane, whose father is said to have been a livery-stable keeper or perhaps an employee at Simmonds' stables in Oxford, was a tall, slender girl with a great mop of crinkly black hair, heavy-lidded large blue-grey eyes, very full lips – said to curl easily if not to be themselves positively curly – a towering neck, and a rather swarthy or gold-brown complexion, which has led to the conjecture that, though coming of Cotswold stock, she had gipsy blood. However, her face is never referred to as nut-brown or ruddy, but usually as pale-gold, and so Rossetti represents it in most of the canvases he devoted to her. He was very aware, however, of Jane's Italian-like complexion, an olive colouring often taking on tints of brown. A portrait of Mrs Morris made in 1871 which he at first intended to name *Twilight* he ended by calling '*Perlas-cura* (i.e. dark pearl, as an Italian female name). ... The name is exact for complexion.' (*Letters*, quoted by V. Surtees, *Paintings and Drawings of Dante Gabriel Rossetti, Text*, 1971, 127) Of another picture of Mrs Morris, dated 1878 but begun ten years earlier, Rossetti wrote, presumably to Jane,

I did not want it to be talked about among strangers by your name so have christened it *Bruna Brunelleschi*, of course bearing on the dark complexion; I did think of calling it *Vittoria Colonna*, who I find was certainly the original of those heads by M.A. which are portraits of you but I thought it would not do to tackle Mike.

(Quoted by V. Surtees, *Ibid.*, 148)

Her hands and feet were long like those of Botticelli goddesses, those pre-Raphaelite girls par excellence much treasured in England in engravings of *Primavera* like that which hung in Morris's study at Kelmscott House and now hangs here in the attic of the Manor.

Rossetti's first study of her head, done in pencil and now here at the Manor, is inscribed, 'J. B. Aetat. xvii, D. G. R. Oxoniae primo delt. Oct. 1857,' which was probably about the time when Morris met her. It was also about this time that Morris did a similar but softer sketch of her (now in the Morris Gallery at Walthamstow); began painting her as Guenevere (his only surviving oil painting, definitely dark-skinned, now in the Tate); and fell desperately in love. It seems, also, that Rossetti himself was much attracted to Jane; some fifteen years later (when more deeply infatuated and free of the old commitment to Lizzie Siddal) he wrote a parable, 'The Cup of Cold Water,' suggesting that Jane had almost died of love for him in 1857/8, and that it was only through his intercession that she had agreed to marry Morris. The marriage took place in April 1859, more than a year and a half after Morris and Jane had first met. What the lovers felt for each other during the first six months after meeting (toward the end of which time they became engaged) we may reconstruct a little, I think, from some of the poems published in *The Defence of Guenevere* in March 1858. Several of the poems in *The Defence* seem, like 'Praise to My Lady,' to have been written in the months after Morris fell in love at first sight.

That Morris in 1857 was still nagged by the fear that women might not or could not love him is evident, I think, in his choice of an Arthurian subject for his fresco at the Union: 'How Sir Palomydes loved La Belle Iseult with exceeding great love out of measure, and how she loved not him but rather Sir Tristram.' This fresco faded so quickly that all anyone seems to remember of it was the head of Tristram rising over a row of sunflowers. Above the window of the bay must have appeared Iseult extending one hand to Tristram on the right while with the other she dismissed Palomydes on the left – the whole sorry scene being half-smothered in Blakeian sunflowers that longed, like 'the youth pin'd away with desire,' for 'that sweet golden clime where the traveller's journey is done.' The round sun, the perfect mandala, the disappointed effort to approach it, and the love death – this is perhaps the world's shortest short story. The feeling of Palomydes's frustration was so acute with Morris in the Oxford days that the knight's sobbing stole, however inappropriately, into nearly all the poet's Arthurian poems. One of the discarded poems of the *Guenevere* time, entitled 'Palomydes' Quest,' tells of the dreamt-of capture of the Beast Glatysaunt. Palomydes imagines a great ovation for himself at Camelot:

> Abroad from thence the bruit shall go of me,
> And many a lord shall say, 'Hold we high feast;
> Tomorrow an uncouth sight shall we see:
> Here commeth Palomydes and his beast.'

> And so to Cornwall shall I come at last –
> But saying this he sighed, for well he thought,
> When all this noble fame has been compassed,
> Shall Iseult's love be nearer to me brought?
>
> (XXIV, 71)

This question accompanied him relentlessly across lovely forests and fields alive with thrushes and poppies and the chime of far-off bells, and the answer was always, 'She loves me not.'

In the *Guenevere* volume, however, we have a slightly more cheerful view of Palomydes's predicament. In 'King Arthur's Tomb' Guenevere thinks of him as one of the glories of Camelot's jousting days. True, he fought bravely because ' "he fear's a scoff/So overmuch," ' yet what genuine knight would have dared

> To mock that face, fretted with useless care,
> And bitter useless striving after love?
> O Palomydes, with much honour bear
> Beast Glatysaunt upon your shield, above

> Your helm that hides the swinging of your hair,
> And think of Iseult, as your sword drives through
> Much mail and plate . . .

Further, in 'Sir Galahad, a Christmas Mystery' Morris makes the ascetic boy compare his God-inspired quest of the Grail unfavourably with Palomydes' Iseult-inspired quest of Glatysaunt:

> And what if Palomydes also ride,
>   And over many a mountain and bare heath
> Follow the questing beast with none beside?
>   Is he not able still to hold his breath
>
> With thoughts of Iseult? doth he not grow pale
>   With weary striving to seem best of all
> To her, 'as she is best,' he saith? To fail
>   Is nothing to him, he can never fall.
>
> For unto such a man love sorrow is
>   So dear a thing unto his constant heart,
> That even if he never win one kiss,
>   Or touch from Iseult, it will never part.
>
> And he will never know her to be worse
>   Than in his happiest dreams he thinks she is:
> Good knight, and faithful, you have 'scaped the curse
>   In wonderful-wise; you have great store of bliss.

Farther along in the poem, however, Christ, 'sitting on the altar' of the winter-wind-swept chapel 'as a throne,' condemns Palomydes for 'fretting out his soul' about a woman. However, a last twist is given to the frustrated knight's tale when Sir Bors, in the speech that ends this 'Christmas Mystery,' does *not* list Palomydes among the knights who 'come foiled from the great quest,' that is, entirely disappointed in their search for a symbol of holiness on earth.

This clutch of Palomydes pictures and poems seems to show Morris slowly working up a little amorous confidence and in the *Guenevere* poem, 'A Good Knight in Prison,' he represents himself as rescued from self-doubt and love-fears by Lancelot himself (Rossetti?). It is possible that Rossetti gave Morris confidence that he had manly appeal for women and (mischievously?) the strength to carry to the marriage climax his love of Jane Burden, who from 1857 had become Morris's favourite model for Guenevere in art and, perhaps, in poetry. But first Jane, under the name of Rapunzel-Guendolen, had to be rescued, it seems, from a witch's tower. The poem in which she appears as Rapunzel seems to celebrate a turning point in Morris's emotional development. At last, he is sure of himself sexually, so sure he is willing and anxious to take on the daily companionship and responsibilities of marriage.

'Rapunzel,' a longish, dramalike poem, tells how a prince is drawn from mere dreams of love into the reality of marriage. Spurred by his councillors, Prince Sebald tells us,

> I put my armour on,
>   Thinking on what they said:
> 'Thou art a king's own son,
>   'Tis fit that thou should'st wed.'

Solid significance is slowly built into the fairy tale of the girl with extra-ordinary hair (Jane's was unusual too, but in a different way from Rapunzel's!). Sebald realises that so far he has lived only in a 'wretched way,' exposed to the scoffing 'of any knave or coward.' But when he has set himself seriously to find – and give – love

> ... then I saw my real life had begun
> And that I should be strong quite well I knew.

> For I was riding out to look for love,
>   Therefore the birds within the thickets sung,
> Even in hot noontide, as I pass'd; above
>   The elms o'erswayed with longing towards me hung.

Rapunzel's real name was Guendolen, the first being the name of her demon-captor – 'eh! not so sweet?' – who had her taunted by fiends who periodically tortured her. When Sebald finds the lovely girl impri-soned in the tower, anguished by foul 'witches' sabbaths,' frozen for lack of love, cowering under 'a great loneliness that sicken'd me,' he read the riddle of life:

> What other work in all the world had I
> But through all turns of fate that face to follow?

When he came 'where/The piled- up arms of the fighting angels gleam,' he knew himself

> Not born as yet, but going to be born,
>   No naked baby as I was at first,
> But an armèd knight, whom fire, hate and scorn
>   Could turn from nothing: my heart almost burst ...

References to 'her face quite pale,' her 'thin feet bare,' and the 'lines of care' that 'Had sunk the cheeks and made the great eyes hollow' suggest Jane hiding under the masses of Rapunzel's yellow hair. Besides, Jane herself, in the Oxford days probably as well as later, was tortured like Rapunzel by repulsive dreams of fiends and dreary presentiments that her 'weak heart' could hardly bear –

> The crayfish on the leaden floor,
> That mock with feeler and grim claw.

Was the real Jane disgusted with livery-stable life? Did she fear the sodden undergrowth? Did she hate wrangling and yelling? Did she get on badly with her father? Probably we shall not know. At any rate, Sebald, now king, finds the strength and joy by which men live, through rescuing Rapunzel-Guendolen and setting her on the throne beside him. Drawing the temenos girl from the mandala tower makes much play with our Paradise symbolism. True, her last words of the playlet are ambiguous:

> Nothing wretched now, no screams;
> I was unhappy once in dreams,
> And even now a harsh voice seems
> To hang about my hair.

Did the Rapunzel side of Guendolen have confessions to make to her rescuer before marriage? Had the devils' ugly rumours involved her in those witches' sabbaths? In Morris's poem 'The Defence of Guenevere,' the title-piece of the 1858 volume, there sounds under the queen's long monologue a *continuo* of hectic strain so immediate and moving that many have felt that something more than clairvoyance or psychological insight almost incredible in a poet of twenty-four must have stung Morris into miracle. Such a fever of self-flagellation, self-contradiction, self-vindication by Guenevere as she stumbles about 'like one lame' before judges trying her for adultery was never milked out of Malory's account of the incident. Such deficient, baffled, broken speech clattering from the tongue of a woman wrenched and skewered with pain – well, it is impossible to believe there was never anything like this in the the young poet's experience of life. I believe all important poetry springs from personal glory or grief so deep that its pressure must be staunched and stabilised by the artist's utmost effort. No one hesitates to use almost any good poet's verses to illuminate his life and vice versa. Byron, Keats and Shelley are probably the poets most freely exploited in this way – Morris said the poetry of his time still danced to the tunes of these three. As we saw in the Foreword, it has been said that Morris never revealed one iota of the inner man in anything he wrote or made, whereas, it seems to me, the very opposite is true. Personally I cannot get the most out of anything he did without finding in it at least as much relation to some actual experience as we customarily insist on detecting in *Endymion, Don Juan* or *The Revolt of Islam*. It is quite true that most self-styled critics of Morris seldom find anything but faded tapestry or stale marzipan in his poetry and romances, probably for the simple reason that they will not put the same effort into appreciating him that they give to other poets. If I find more correlations between his life and his art than others, it may be because I am abstracting for whole generations of voiceless readers.

Certain things in 'The Defence' point to a possible partial identification of Guenevere with Jane. The most superficial of these are the physical traits the poet gives the queen: 'the great eyes,' 'her full lips,' 'the hair like sea-weed,' her 'long throat,' and 'the tenderly darken'd fingers' of her 'long hand' where

> The shadow lies like wine within a cup
> Of marvellously colour'd gold . . .

Nothing striking here, of course, except perhaps the aureate brown skin. Yet the awkward, broken, somewhat angular movements – these also suggest the early Jane, who was too tall and thin to be willowy-gracile. In addition, the strangeness of her self-defence against Gauwaine's charges of adultery is as openly opaque, firmly capricious, innocently seductive, as any the real-life Jane can ever have been called on to invent. She readily admits to garden and bedroom love-making – but not adultery. Once in spring

> I was half mad with beauty on that day,
> And went without my ladies all alone,
> In a quiet garden walled round every way;
>
> I was right joyful of that wall of stone,
> That shut the flowers and trees up with the sky,
> And trebled all the beauty . . .
>
> Came Launcelot walking; this is true, the kiss
> Wherewith we kissed in meeting that spring day,
> I scarce dare talk of the remember'd bliss,
>
> When both our mouths went wandering in one way . . .
> Nevertheless you, O Sir Gauwaine, lie . . .

Each of her confessions is followed by a denunciation of Gauwaine as an unholy liar. Then finally, she turns to reprove Gauwaine's churlish, yelling invasion of her bedroom privacy and the present attempt to burn her at the stake. Of course, she had asked Launcelot to come to her

> In my quiet room that night, and we were gay . . .
>
> Nevertheless you, O Sir Gawaine, lie,
> Whatever may have happened these long years,
> God knows I speak truth, saying that you lie !
>
> All I have said is truth, by Christ's dear tears.
> She would not speak another word . . .

At last Sir Launcelot-Morris rescued her both from fire and from drowning in her ambiguities. It is possible that Guenevere-Jane had never, in fact, committed adultery, but it seems significant that Rapunzel-Guendolen's rescuer had also to be a knight 'whom fire, hate, and scorn/ Could turn from nothing . . .'

That the question of a woman having adulterous or extra-marital relations was much on Morris's mind when writing these poems is shown also in 'The Judgment of God,' in which Roger, the defender of Ellayne, fears he will lose the fight to establish her innocence. Only the Christmas before he had, like Launcelot, rescued the already condemned girl from the fire, but he, unlike Launcelot, is called a 'recreaunt knight' and stoned and 'spat on.' 'The Judgment of God' is one of the 'grinds' read by 'Top' in Rossetti's Oxford rooms to the group painting the Union frescoes. The time seems to have been shortly after Morris first met Jane, and already he seems to have been dreaming of clearing her from charges of infamy and glorying in the thought of suffering every kind of indignity for her. The poem begins,

> 'Swerve to the left, son Roger,' he said,
>   'When you catch his eyes through the helmet-slit,
> Swerve to the left, then out at his head,
>   And the Lord God give you joy of it!'

Yet Roger scarcely hopes to win even in his father's 'crafty way' and many hold he cannot expect divine help, not being 'God's knight any longer.' In other words, 'Top' seems to have given himself every possible handicap in seeking to vindicate a woman from charges of something. A variant of the theme of the probably virginal, possibly unvirginal girl enters for a moment into 'The Haystack in the Floods' when the villain threatens to charge the anguished heroine with fornication before the already suspicious people of Paris:

> Do you know, Jehane, they cry for you,
> 'Jehane the brown! Jehane the brown!
> Give us Jehane to burn or drown!' . . .
> This were indeed a piteous end
> For those long fingers, and long feet,
> And long neck, and smooth shoulders sweet . . .

There is also a trace of the question of 'sin' in 'Concerning Geoffray Teste Noire.' Here John of Castel Neuf, the Browningesque monologuist, is moved by the sight of two lovers murdered long ago to apostrophise the woman. He seems driven by the bones, 'shapely still and tall,' to recreate the living woman in a description which strikes me as being in some ways a finer and subtler tribute to Jane than the 'Praise of My Lady' quoted above.

> O most pale face that brings such joy and sorrow
>   Into men's hearts – yea, too, so piercing sharp
> That joy is, that it marcheth nigh to sorrow
>   For ever – like an overwinded harp.
>
> Your face must hurt me always; pray you now,
>   Doth it not hurt you too? seemeth some pain
> To hold you always, pain to hold your brow
>   So smooth, unwrinkled ever; yea again,

> Your long eyes where the lids seem like to drop,
>   Would you not, lady, were they shut fast feel
> Far merrier? . . .
>
> Or say your mouth — I saw you drink red wine
>   Once at a feast; how slowly it sank in,
> As though you fear'd that some wild fate might twine
>   Within that cup, and slay you for a sin.
>
> And when you talk your lips do arch and move
>   In such wise that a language new I know
> Besides their sound; they quiver, too, with love
>   When you are standing silent; know this, too,
>
> I saw you kissing once; like a curved sword
>   That bites with all its edge, did your lips lie,
> Curled gently, slowly, long time could afford
>   For caught-up breathings . . .

This sensitive poem leaves us wondering, perhaps, what 'sin' it was that condemned the sword-lipped lady to her wild fate.

In 'The Wind' Morris dreams ('My work is the embodiment of dreams,' remember) of a 'wild fate' for Jane brought about by sin, perhaps, but rather his than hers. The poem is poised like a dentist's drill on the point where suppressed doubts and desires blend with a live nerve to produce first-rate nightmare pain. The dreamer walks with his love on 'the highest hill in the land' where

> I held to her long bare arms, but she shudder'd
>   away from me,
> While the flush went out of her face as her head
>   fell back on a tree,
> And a spasm caught her mouth, fearful for me to
>   see;
> And still I held to her arms till her shoulder
>   touch'd my mail,
> Weeping she totter'd forward, so glad that
>   I should prevail,
> And her hair went over my robe, like a gold
>   flag over a sail.

They kiss and then she 'lay down on the grass, where the mark on the moss is now,/And spread her arms out wide . . .' Afterward the dreamer gathered 'great sheaves of the daffodil' which he piled high on her – 'How they were caught and held in her loose ungirded vest' – but when he removed this flower robe,

Alas! alas! there was blood on the very quiet breast,
Blood lay in the many folds of the loose ungirded vest,
Blood lay upon her arm where the flower had been prest.
I shriek'd . . .

Not wounded by anything sharper than daffodil stems, she was never-theless dead and the dreamer's wits glimmered away. There is some puzzling, unhelpful symbolism of bleeding oranges, wizard's jars and lily-seeds, but the purport of the poem seems clear enough: before he had really won Jane, Morris, perhaps because of his self-doubt, the rumour of some shadowy 'sin' of hers – there must have been some kind of 'talk' – and her tendency to shudder away from him, had taken to possessing the girl in dreams and thereby lost her – horribly – forever.

At one point he may have gone home to tell his mother about Jane. Some time in 1857 there are, says Mackail (I, 136), 'traces of him at his mother's new house at Leyton . . .' Almost certainly she objected to the groom's daughter as a wife for William and may have tried to keep him away from Oxford for as long as possible. If this opposition inspired 'Spellbound,' the visit must have occurred in late October or early November of 1857.

How weary is it none can tell
    How dismally the days go by!
I hear the tinkling of the bell,
    I see the cross against the sky.

The year wears round to autumn-tide,
    Yet comes no reaper to the corn:
The golden land is like a bride
    When first she knows herself forlorn – . . .

In this day-dream, Jane (?) 'sits and weeps' though

He is not dead, but gone away.
    How many hours did she wait
For me, I wonder? . . .

Did she with the coming of darkness hurry to lay on her bed

The wedding samite strewn with pearls:
    Then sit with hands laid on her knees,
Shuddering at half-heard sound of girls
    That chatter outside in the breeze?

Did 'her poor heart throb' and was she dragged

. . . sternly down before
People who loved her not? in prayers
    Did she say one name and no more?

Is the poet wondering whether she called for help on God and William –
or on god and Gabriel? From this question he retreats into a night
dream in which hands are prest

> *About my forehead, and thy lips*
>   *Draw near and nearer to mine own;*
> *But when the vision from me slips,*
>   *In colourless dawn I lie and moan,*
>
> *And wander forth with fever'd blood,*
>   *That makes me start at little things,*
> *The blackbird screaming from the wood,*
>   *The sudden whirr of pheasants' wings.*

He remembers how, after 'that wild time' of their first acquaintance, he
had at last folded her in his arms, never thinking 'those days could die.'

> Yet now I wait, and you wait too,
>   For what perchance may never come;
> You think I have forgotten you,
>   That I grew tired and went home.
>
> But what if some day as I stood
>   Against the wall with strained hands,
> And turn'd my face toward the wood,
>   Away from all the golden lands;
>
> And saw you come with tired feet,
>   And pale face thin and wan with care,
> And stained raiment no more neat,
>   The white dust lying on your hair: –
>
> Then I should say, I could not come;
>   This land was my wide prison, dear;
> I could not choose . . .; at home
>   There is a wizard whom I fear . . .

Was this wizard in fact a witch? Yet now that the forsaken girl has
sought him out, his 'heart upswells' and he grows bold to break his
'silken chains' but she must show more enthusiasm for the wedding than
she has – more energy, less languidness. Yes,

> . . . I shall die unless you stand,
>   – Half lying now, you are so weak, –
> Within my arms, unless your hand
>   Pass to and fro across my cheek.

'Golden Wings' is another poem of a deserted girl, but apart from her
name – Jehane – and a few traits like her 'long throat,' 'thin' feet, and
awkward movements of despair, she suggests Jane less vividly than do

Guenevere and the others we have been considering. When Golden
Wings is too long returning, Jehane kills herself.

> She took a sword within her hand,
>   Whose hilts were silver, and she sung,
>   Somehow like this, wild words that rung
> A long way over the moonlit land: –
>
> Gold wings across the sea!
> Grey light from tree to tree,
> Gold hair beside my knee,
> I pray thee come to me,
> Gold wings!
>   The water slips,
> The red-bill'd moorhen dips.
> Sweet kisses on red lips;
> Alas! the red rust grips,
> And the blood-red dagger rips,
> Yet, O knight, come to me!

Perhaps it was only after some such nightmare as this that Morris hurried back to Oxford and the dear 'feet ... cold and thin,' where the marriage was held but not until April 1859.

It is pleasant to be able to report that before *Guenevere* was published in
1858 Morris enjoyed a modicum of happy dreams (see Plate 2). Like
Lionel in the *Oxford and Cambridge* prose romance of 'Golden Wings,'
he seems, soothed by increasing friendliness and caresses, to have grown
surer of being 'beautiful and brave and true ...' Temporarily at least he
moved from under the cloud that had shadowed him since childhood, decided that women really could love him, no longer felt his character was
falling apart, began to feel his way with some confidence into what had
up to now been a wavering or even blank future. Again like Lionel, 'all
doubt and sorrow went away from me; I did not even feel drunk with
joy, but rather felt that I could take it all in, lose no least fragment of it
...' At about this time one of his friends, according to Mackail (I, 137),
declared in a curious phrase that Morris has lately taken a strong fancy
for the 'human'.

A jolly poem with lots of action – lady-inspired of course – is 'The Gilli-
flower of Gold,' which needs no commentary.

> A golden gilliflower to-day
> I wore upon my helm alway,
> And won the prize of this tourney.
>   *Hah! hah! la belle jaune giroflée....*

Although my spear in splinters flew,
From John's steel-coat my eye was true;
I wheel'd about, and cried for you,
 Hah! hah! la belle jaune giroflée.

Yea, do not doubt my heart was good,
Though my sword flew like rotten wood,
To shout, although I scarcely stood,
 Hah! hah! la belle jaune giroflée.

My hand was steady too, to take
My axe from round my neck, and break
John's steel-coat up for my love's sake.
 Hah! hah! la belle jaune giroflée. . . .

The Sieur Guilaume against me came,
His tabbard bore three points of flame
From a red heart: with little blame –
 Hah! hah! la belle jaune giroflée.

Our tough spears crackled up like straw;
He was the first to turn and draw
His sword, that had nor speck nor flaw, –
 Hah! hah! la belle jaune giroflée. . . .

Once more the great swords met again,
'*La belle! la belle!*' but who fell then?
Le Sieur Guilaume, who struck down ten; –
 Hah! hah! la belle jaune giroflée. . . .

Such medievalism, if that's what it is, seems to outdistance Tennyson's by a destrier's leap.

Another of the grinds which made such a deep impression on Val Prinsep (letter quoted by Georgiana Burne-Jones in *Memorials* I, 161–2) when read by Morris to Rossetti's group that autumn evening in 1857 was 'The Eve of Crecy,' whose hero was the impoverished Sir Lambert de Bois.

Gold on her head, and gold on her feet,
And gold where the hems of her kirtle meet,
And a golden girdle round my sweet; –
 Ah! qu'elle est belle La Marguerite. . . .

If I were rich I would kiss her feet,
I would kiss the place where the gold hems meet,
And the golden girdle round my sweet –
 Ah! qu'elle est belle La Marguerite. . . .

And sometime it may hap, perdie,
While my new towers stand up three and three,
And my hall gets painted fair to see –
 Ah! qu'elle est belle La Marguerite.

That folks may say: 'Times change, by the rood,
For Lambert, banneret of the wood,
Has heaps of food and firewood: –
    Ah! qu'elle est belle La Marguerite.

'And wonderful eyes, too, under the hood
Of a damsel of right noble blood;'
St. Ives, for Lambert of the wood! –
    Ah! qu'elle est belle La Marguerite.

Here all the strain, apprehension and actual horror of so many of the *Guenevere* poems have drained away and the ruddy, undiscourageable knight that the boy Morris had always wanted to be, shines through.

Another such vigorous poem is 'Two Red Roses Across the Moon,' in one breath hearty, relaxed, mysterious and charming.

There was a lady lived in a hall,
Large in the eyes, and slim and tall;
And ever she sung from noon to noon,
Two red roses across the moon.

There was a knight came riding by
In early spring, when the roads were dry;
And he heard that lady sing at the noon,
Two red roses across the moon.

Yet none the more he stopp'd at all,
But he rode a-gallop past the hall;
And left that lady singing at noon,
Two red roses across the moon.

But when he returned victorious,

I trow he stopp'd when he rode again
By the hall, though draggled sore with the rain;
And his lips were pinch'd to kiss at the noon,
Two red roses across the moon.

When someone asked Morris what *'Two red roses across the moon'* meant, he gave the foolish question a foolish answer, 'But it's the knight's coat-of-arms of course!' I suppose he thought that if the knight's mouth was 'pinch'd' or puckered to 'kiss' the two red roses at noon, the most unimaginative reader would divine that they stood for the two full, curly lips of a girl with orange-brown-yellow skin suggesting the glow of an English moon through mist. And what a mandala!

We have now come, I think, to the lovers' overt engagement and have no literary material to carry us through the year that was to elapse before the marriage. We know that in 1858 Morris completed as much of his

Queen Guenevere painting as he was ever to finish. It seems that he gave it to Madox Brown to touch up and then to Oliver Brown, the painter's painter-son, who died young but not before passing the picture on to Rossetti, who is said to have offered him £20 for it in 1874. After Rossetti died, this now quite famous picture was catalogued among the dead man's pictures as *La Belle Iseult;* however, it was finally restored by Rossetti's brother William to the original Guenevere and hung at Kelmscott Manor till given, years later, by May Morris to the Tate Gallery in exchange for Rossetti's first oil of her mother, the well known *Blue Dress*, which now hangs here in the alcove opening off the White-panelled Room. The *Guenevere* stresses the brownness of Jane's skin while in *The Blue Dress*, as in nearly all Rossetti's pictures of Jane, the tone is highlighted to pale gold.

In August Morris made another trip to Northern France with Faulkner, an Oxford friend, and Philip Webb, whom he had lately met while studying to be an architect in G. E. Street's offices in Oxford – an ambition he quickly relinquished but not the friendship of Webb, who became a life-long colleague in all his decorative works. In fact, he became the architect of Morris's first home, the famous Red House on Bexley Heath in Kent, which was discussed and partly planned during a rowing trip down the Seine. In October Morris returned to France, this time to buy old manuscripts, armour, and decorative iron work and enamel, all with a view, probably, to furnishing his home-to-be. Already, it seems, he had begun to think of it as that 'small "Palace of Art" of my own,' which he now peopled in imagination with Jane and their possible children. Finally, on Tuesday 26 April 1859, Jane and William were married in the old parish church of St Michael's in Oxford when she was nineteen and he twenty-five. Faulkner, Burne-Jones and a few of his Oxford friends were present but not his mother. Perhaps she disapproved or was ill at the time; in any case it is not necessary to go so far as to declare, like a recent writer, that his 'parents' rejected Jane as 'a working-class girl, the daughter of an ostler,' who 'had been picked up at a theatre.' (T. Hilton, *The Pre-Raphaelites*, 1970, 169) At the time of the marriage his father had been dead for twelve years. It has often been said that the general attitude of the Oxford Group toward the marriage was summed up in a letter which Swinburne wrote to Edwin Hatch on 17 February 1858, in which he says he likes to think of Morris 'having that wonderful and most perfect stunner of his to – look at and speak to. The idea of his marrying her is insane. To kiss her feet is the utmost men should dream of doing.' (Henderson, *William Morris*, 50). Actually, Morris was to enjoy years of wonderful happiness with her and their children and friends in the Red House 'Palace of Art.'

Whether his sometimes bedeviled courtship followed by a period of happy marriage has any lessons for our time I cannot say.

III Paradise Domesticated in a 'Palace of Art', 1860-1866

That Morris married Jane on 26 April 1859 at St Michael's, Oxford, that the honeymoon was passed in a tour of Paris, Belgium and the Rhineland, and that the pair lived in furnished rooms in Great Ormond Street till the house built for them by Philip Webb was ready for occupation toward the end of the summer of 1860, we have often been told. That is all we know or in all probability are likely to know of their transition into wedded life. Whether his mother disapproved of the marriage of her son to the daughter of a father who signed the marriage register 'Robert Burden, groom,' we do not know or need to care. Nothing in Morris's life up to this time indicates class-consciousness on his part, and it is unlikely that it began to worry him now that he was warmly married to a girl whose fulgurous pre-Raphaelite beauty made her the wonder, and him the envy, of his friends. With her curly black hair projecting stiffly from the right, left and back of her head, with her low forehead and thick black eyebrows, with a nose not exactly straight and a too-short upper lip, with lips 'deep-freighted' (as Rossetti wrote), with her prominent chin and overlong, slightly goiterous neck, with her tall, rather lean figure, Jane was certainly the polar opposite of a petite, blond Raphael madonna whose features resembled those of tinted Greek sculpture. She was more nearly Botticellian, but even among the willowy shapes of the *Primavera* she would have been unique because of her extraordinary features. What more natural than that Morris should have sought to protect her from possible social snobbery by building, somewhat off the beaten track, 'a small "Palace of Art" of my own,' worthy of her looks, her eagerness, her natural dignity – an 'actual home,' as Mackail wrote, 'in which life and its central purposes need not be thwarted by any baseness or ugliness of immediate surroundings,' (I, 137) physical or social.

Red House, dreamt up by Morris and Philip Webb on the brief visit to France in 1859, was built in an orchard of apple and cherry trees on the plateau of Bexley Heath near the village of Upton, about ten miles from London in those days. Morris seems to have been very happy designing and directing the decoration of Red House by himself, Jane and a fairly large circle of friends including the Burne-Joneses, married in 1860, and

Rossetti, who by now had wedded Lizzie Siddal. Just about everything for the house had to be invented and made by the group of week-enders because hardly a stick of furniture or a shred of textile worthy of Morris's vision of a 'Palace of Art' was to be found, he said, in all of London. To be sure, he didn't waste much time searching, for the vacuum merely repeated that encountered in 1857 when he had sought to furnish his first studio in London. Then, as now, the cupboard-bareness had driven him to make or design furnishings of his own, awakened him to what he now began to recognise as somewhat peculiar talents and powers. The result was that he welcomed the problem as a frolic. His friends, too, were almost instantly infected by the decorative visions which had haunted 'Top', he now said, since childhood. The drawing-room on the first floor was to be, by Morris's own claim, the most beautiful room in England. Rossetti himself was drawn into the vortex of creative enthusiasm, writing to Charles Eliot Norton in 1862, 'I wish you could see the house which Morris . . . has built for himself in Kent. It is a most noble work in every way, and more a poem than a house.' Burne-Jones agreed that by 1862 'Top' was slowly making Red House, both inside and out, 'the beautifullest place on earth' (Mackail I, 159).

What 'Top' was seeking to do at Red House was, obviously, not to sketch in sand the outlines of a stylised Buddhist dream but to create with real flowers, trees, water and building materials a tangible mandala with a tangible goddess, his bride, at the temenos-centre. The house was not so much a medievalising escape from the current stucco square box covered by a slate lid, (so it struck all who saw it for the first time) as an original creation whose formal elements seemed not only to grow upon the beholder but actually to expand into a magnificent lodging for the spirit, which was tempted thereby to spread new wings. It was an effect as of magic though the plan was very simple, the house being merely a two-storied L-shaped building of red brick with a high-pitched roof of red tile. As Mackail wrote, 'the two other sides of this half-quadrangle' made by the limbs of the house 'were masqued by rose-trellises, enclosing a square inner court, in the middle of which rose the most striking architectural feature of the building, a well-house of brickwork and oak, with a steep conical tiled roof.' (I, 142) Lady Burne-Jones tells of how 'we sat and talked and looked out into the well-court, of which two sides were formed by the house and the other two by a tall rose-trellis. This little court with its beautiful high-pitched brick well in the centre summed up the feeling of the whole place.' When we recall that this 'square inner court' with its temenos-well was produced by a half-house, half-garden structure which was itself 'surrounded' by a rich apple orchard, we begin to sense the source of the magic of Red House. What Mackail calls the 'rose-trellises' which extended the north- and east-running limbs of the house into a square edifice should be recognised as a peculiarly Morrisian touch. So, too, the garden in front of the house (that is, to the north), which was a great square composed of four small squares. According to a principle announced years later in 'Making the Best of It,' Morris thought that 'a garden should be divided and made to look like so many flower-closes in a meadow, or a wood.' Each of the four closes at Red House was fenced with live hedges, wattle or stout trellises. Together they extended Morris's 'Palace of Art' into still nobler proportions. Each of these closes seems to have specialised in different flowers or kinds of roses. Thus the gardens of Red House, both front and back, were rightly considered to be, as Mackail says, as original and unique, simple and dignified, as the house itself. They did in fact, as Morris required of every garden, 'look like a part of the house.' They must have been ex-tremely colourful if they contained memories of 'The Unknown Church' with its 'trellises covered over with roses and convolvulus and the great-leaved fiery nasturtiums.' Some northern closes may have contained holly-hocks, 'great spires of pink, and orange, and red, and white, with their soft, downy leaves,' while others were dominated by sunflowers of the single kind, 'beautiful with ... sharply chiselled yellow florets relieved by the quaintly patterned, sad-coloured centre clogged with honey and beset with bees and butterflies.' Each enclosed square must have suggested a redoubt of gaily uniformed soldiers on the alert to guard what Rossetti called, prematurely, 'the towers of Topsy.' (Remember how eagerly Sir Lambert, banneret of the wood, looked forward to the day when 'my new towers stand up three and three'?)

There was, as there still is, only one tower, which rises in the garden-facing corner of the L. This solitary tower of Red House is simply the enclosing wall of the magnificent staircase which leads from the great north entrance hall to the first floor. Its roof is less steeply pitched than that of the magic well in the garden, though the well-cone carries one's eyes inevitably to the louvre in the tower, open but charmingly umbrel-laed by a steep-pitched little roof of its own, which sings antiphonal res-ponses to the song of the well-cone.

Though modern buildings crowd Red House today, though the north gardens no longer exist and the surrounding orchard has practically dis-appeared, a visitor to Red House can still detect the restful mandalic pat-tern which underlay Morris's original conception. It is probable that he intended to replace the high rose-trellises with brick wings, raising at least three more towers, something like the one over the staircase, at the new corner angles. The result would have been a miniature chateau of wondrous simplicity and repose. From the very beginning he was dream-ing of an east wing to accommodate the Burne-Joneses. By 1861, Philip Webb had already drawn a plan for it, and Morris was ready to set to work on it by 1864. This wing was to have been half-timbered and vine-covered. A scheme for enlarging a brickwork castle with a half-timbered wing can be seen, as Paul Thompson points out, in Morris's designs for his St George Cabinet of 1860, now in the Victoria and Albert Museum.

As Red House stood in 1862, we have in the orchard-surrounded square of house and gardens with the charming well of fresh water as the fountain-centre a trimness of plan which reminds us of the '*holy mathematicks*' of 'Upon Appleton House,' where Marvell so described landscape and edifice as to make us think once again of Tibetan or Jungian pictures. In the old poem we hear much of 'The *Circle* in the *Quadrature*' and the *Square* [that] grows *Spherical*.' Marvell's garden closes, perhaps like Morris's wattled squares, congealed 'In the just Figure of a Fort,' and tulips, pinks and roses arranged themselves in platoons, each under its regimental colours, to guard the sacred centre. Beyond and about Appleton House and its flowers were rose trees which, like the military flowers, constituted another line of defence, this time immense and serving as a personal body-guard:

> How safe, methinks, and strong, behind
> These Trees have I incamp'd my Mind ...
>
> (See Plate 4)

All this Morris's Red House makes us think of, I say, and we recall also Marvell's '*Blest Nymph*,' the pole around which Appleton's small but perfect world turned. Maria Fairfax endowed the whole configuration with her beauty, sweetness and protective might – was the White Goddess by whose '*Flames*, in *Heaven* try'd,/*Nature* is wholly *vitrifi'd*.' In a word, Marvell's Maria was Morris's Jane of the early '60s, and Red House, like Appleton,

> ... *Heaven's Center, Nature's Lap,*
> *And Paradice's only Map.*

Making sport of Tennyson's poem of that name, Morris called Red House his 'Palace of Art,' a name given by the older poet to an edifice erected by

> A sinful soul possess'd of many gifts, ...
> A glorious Devil, large in heart and brain,
> That did love Beauty only

in an art-for-art's sake way. For Morris, on the other hand, the craving for lovely things was instinctive and imperious – a condition of the good life. A house in which every sight was pleasing – where every table, chair, bed, chest, settle or cabinet, every paper or chintz for the walls, every tile for the fireplaces, every window curtain and drape, every candlestick, wine-jug or drinking glass was handsome both in itself and in relation to its surroundings – was the first condition of his well being. Surely it was not Tennysonian 'serpent pride' or 'slothful shame' which made him undertake to supply out of his own untrained but inexhaustible invention and seething energy the decor of his 'Palace of Art.' Tennyson's edifice is inflated with would-be gorgeous effects but obviously no one could live in it for a moment. For the 'sinful soul' that built it as a 'palace of strength' there was nothing to do but die of aesthetic horror at Tennyson's megalomaniac architecture. Nothing like it could have been dreamt by a spirit in search of inner peace through outer works. There is hardly a trace in Tennyson of the mandalic structure, mankind's immemorial prescription, as Morris had long divined, for protection, rest, refreshment, solace, and even analgesia. If for a moment the oriental pattern is suggested, the effect is immediately ruined by Tennyson's un-house-broken imagination:

> Four courts I made, East, West and South and North,
>   In each a squarèd lawn, wherefrom
> The golden gorge of dragons spouted forth
>   A flood of fountain-foam.

I imagine that for Morris the only detail of the description which did not seem hopelessly artificial or impossibly overblown was an 'arras green and blue,'

> Showing a gaudy summer-morn
> Where with puff'd cheek the belted hunter blew
> His wreathèd bugle-horn.

This may have made him think of Elizabeth's hunting-lodge at Chingford or the Green Bedroom at Monkbarn's in *The Antiquary*. Otherwise, Tennyson's creaking poem gave Morris nothing but a nick-name, adopted in playful irony, for his lovely home. (See Plate 5.)

As I have said, nothing available in the London market would do for Morris's castle. We should, of course, except some Persian carpets, blue-and-white China, and a few odd chests, Elizabethan and European, carved or inlaid, examples of all of which are here in Kelmscott Manor today, some having come from Red House by way of Kelmscott House in Hammersmith. More pertinent to our theme are a number of textiles, also here, which Morris patterned to cover the nakedness of Red House walls till they could be frescoed by his painter friends. As he later recalled,

what a rummage there used to be for anything tolerable in the way of hangings, for instance, and what shouts of joy would be raised if we had the luck to dig up some cheapish commonplace manufacture which, being outside the range of fancy goods, had escaped the general influence of the vacuity of the times. On the whole, I remember that we had to fall back upon turkey-red cotton and dark blue serge.

The embroidered blue serge hangings now attached to the seventeenth-century oak screen which divides the North Hall from what we call the foyer to the White-panelled Room at Kelmscott were made for the Red House bridal chamber and are generally thought to be the first of their kind devised by Morris. The flower pattern in red, white and yellow wool, laid on the serge and stitched down, apparently by Jane, is simple yet delightful. It was taken from an illumination in Froissart (British Museum, Harl. MAA. 4379/80) and became the inspiration for the first Morris wallpaper to be produced commercially, the 'Daisy' of 1864. Another hanging, now in the Green Room at Kelmscott and used at Red House, was made entirely by Morris himself about 1857, when living in Red Lion Square, as an experiment in reviving a method of embroidery. On a frame made for the purpose he embroidered on linen, using the old-fashioned 'darning' stitch and covering the canvas completely, a hanging which Mackail described as consisting of 'green trees with gaily-coloured birds among them, and a running scroll emblazoned with his motto in English 'If I can,' adopted from Jan van Eyck's '*Als ich kan*' and also used by Morris in its French form, '*Si je puis.*' Actually, the green trees and the whole hanging, apart from the raised red fruits (pomegranates?), are now faded to an almost uniform dun-brown. There is no running scroll but over each tree – there are thirty-five tiny trees arranged in five soldierly rows – is a small scroll with the words ' + If + I + can + .' The 'birds' are arranged between the rows of trees, their unavian bodies being about as long as the tree trunks and six times as thick! The importance of this hanging is nine-tenths historical. In embroidering these 'trees' and 'birds' on linen in long parallel stitches in so far as the pattern allowed, Morris revived an art which he was only too happy to teach to any women-folk he could lure into this kind of web. Customarily, the embroidery they did for him consisted of figures, flowers and trees which, unlike those of the experiment, were first worked on linen and then cut out and appliquéd on velvet or serge. The success of the 'Tree and Bird' gave Morris a brilliant idea for decorating the walls of an entire room at Red House with silk-and-wool-embroidered female figures mounted on different couloured velvets and serges. These figures are often called 'Illustrious Women' but why Morris chose them from among hundreds of others and what inner need the scheme was designed to satisfy are unanswered questions which tease the imagination.

Before considering these women – the most original of the Red House emblazonries – we should look for a minute at the crisis which drove

Morris to invent or reinvent nearly all the furnishings for his 'Palace of Art.' Though it is not uncommon to belittle his achievement in furniture, chintz, papers, tapestry and other forms of design, we must remember the ugliness and pointlessness of the decor that nauseated him. As a young man of seventeen or eighteen he is said to have stared aghast at the tasteless banality of everything he found in the Great Exhibition of 1851. There he saw the stock-in-trade of the London house-furnishers magnified into gigantic forms that crushed him: great stuffed chairs with curly legs and wavy backs; towering plate-glass mirrors in sprouting ormolu frames; curtain-rods of thick mahogany tipped with metal battering rams which held aloft festoons of drapery heavy as lead; fat bronze clocks supported on lion-legs or the severed heads of boa-constrictors; monstrous stuffed birds or weird exotic plants (dried, of course) under glass domes of every shape, colour and height; wooden fire-place surrounds painted to look like green marble and topped with stippled mantelpieces muffled in embroidered velvet which was hung with tiers of cotton balls; bull-heart pincushions so solidly beaded with coloured glass that there was no room to insert even a needle; perhaps the ancestor of Swinburne's 'Chinese' daybed, built to emerge from a cupboard lacquered to simulate crocodile jaws. In short: a chaos of artifice, atrocious to look at whether painted, gilded, padded, carved into curlicues or decorated with marquetry of ivory, mother-of-pearl and seven different woods. These were the things Morris could have bought for his Palace, and to set them off to advantage he could have painted his walls bottle green or chocolate-brown or papered them with nosegays tossed on a buff ground, cabbage-size roses crushed on fern-green, or four-inch vertical stripes, black and white, red and blue, what he willed, so long as he successfully distorted the dignified proportions of the room under attack. It was not at a stroke, then, that Morris mastered the many arts needed to make Red House correspond to the deep-seated, instinctive demands that were not to be evaded. When he had to leave the beloved building, he had not half-completed its inner embellishment nor mastered half the needed arts. Before he moved, however, he had with his artist friends launched a movement in which, as Walter Crane wrote (*William Morris to Whistler*, 1911, 19–20):

Plain white or green paint for interior woodwork drove graining and marbling to the public-house; blue and white Nankin, Delft, or Grès de Flandres routed Dresden and Sèvres from the cabinet; plain oaken boards and trestles were preferred before the heavy mahogany telescopic dining table . . .

One of Morris's ideas for decorating walls was to have his wife and women friends embroider in wool and silk, as described above, a group of famous women. Worked on linen, the figures were usually cut out and appliquéd on serge and velvet grounds measuring about four (or fewer) feet in width by five and a half in length. Like most of the other blazonries of Red House, the series was not completed when Morris left in 1865, but five heroines were finished, one more than half done, another painted for copying in wool, and still another beautifully drawn in outline. Twelve, it is said, intended probably to cover the walls of the dining room, were projected, and of these we have knowledge of eight. Nearly all the books about Morris call them 'Illustrious Women' and they are said to represent the figures in a famous poem by Chaucer. Yet only one of the eight is celebrated by Chaucer in *The Legend of Good Women*; thus the literary source of Morris's inspiration, if he had one, remains a mystery. But the mystery of where these Red House girls came from is probably more psychological than literary. Both aspects of it are worth probing though we may not be able to pluck out its heart.

In his interesting though often highly opinionated book on Morris (*The Work of William Morris*, 1967) Paul Thompson points to G. F. Bodley as the man who gave Morris the idea of hanging a whole room with female figures. Bodley was a well known church architect who gave considerable orders for stained glass and ecclesiastical cloths and clothes to the young friends who, having tried their prentice hands on Red House, formed a partnership of interior decorators known as Morris, Marshall, Faulkner and Company in April 1861. It seems likely that the Morris group had come into contact with Bodley through the Hogarth Club organised by Rossetti in 1858 and consisting of painters, poets and architects. They made glass for Bodley's new churches at Selsey, Gloucestershire, in 1862, Scarborough, 1861, and Brighton 1862. It seems that about 1860–61 Bodley himself was designing rather large-scale embroideries for altar frontals and sedilia hangings in these churches, where Morris would have been likely to see them. The embroideries showed, as Thompson says, 'sweet graceful female saints ... remarkably close in style to the first surviving Morris work [of this kind], the panels of Chaucer's Good Women made for Red House by his wife.' (109) Though Mackail simply says that for the Red House dining-room, 'embroidered hangings of a ... splendid nature were designed and partly executed ... of twelve figures with trees between and above them, and a belt of flowers running below their feet' (I, 159), nearly all who have ever commented on these 'figures' afterward have said they were inspired by Morris's devotion to Chaucer. Obviously the poem meant is Chaucer's *Legend of Good Women* though the embroidered figures are frequently referred to as 'Illustrious,' as in Henderson's *William Morris* (60–61), where he writes of the 'elaborate series of figure embroideries in wool, silk and gold thread on woolen twill, designed to imitate tapestry and based on Chaucer's Illustrious Women ... Seven of these splendid figures out of the original twelve were completed by the time Morris left Red House in 1865.' Three of these women, made into a screen for Lady Carlisle, are now in the Morris Room (formerly the Green Dining Room) of the Victoria and Albert Museum. One bears a great torch and is named 'Fiamma Troiae' (Helen of Troy) but the other two have never been identified by the art experts of the Museum. One wearing mail, carrying both a sword and spear, and crowned with a conqueror's garland, may possibly represent Joan of Arc. The third, swathed in queenly robes and wearing a great crown, holds a sword in the right hand while she tests its sharpness with her left. Her face registers dramatic determination. She could, quite possibly, represent Dido of Carthage. If so, she is the only one of the eight known heroines of Red House who could have been inspired by a Chaucerian Good Woman. I am tempted to believe she is Dido, for the Burne-Jones illustration of her in the Kelmscott Chaucer (made years later, of course) shows her in the same sword-assessing pose.

Besides Dido and Helen, the six other figures known to have been designed for Red House are Venus, Diana, Penelope, the heavily armed and garlanded warrior-girl who, as I have suggested, might be Joan of Arc, Guenevere, and St Catherine. A painted cartoon for 'Venus' is at present in a gable room at Kelmscott Manor while 'Penelope' and 'St Catherine,' both finished, along with an unfinished 'Guenevere,' hang in or near the foyer to the White-panelled Room, in which I am writing. We know what the Diana panel was to have looked like because May used her father's carefully finished drawing for the frontispiece of Volume IX of *The Collected Works*. It would be pointless to speculate about the four figures never, so far as I know, mentioned or in any way sketched or worked at. The eight we know are a strange enough collection of flower-bed sisters to make us wonder why Morris chose them from among all the world's females to preside over his dining-room. Surely they were odd heroines to have been inspired by the 'sweet graceful female saints' of Bodley's church cloths. One wonders whether there was some other literary source besides Chaucer to which Morris went for his assemblage. I find none in Ovid or other classical authors. However, among the week-enders at Red House was young Swinburne, who was scribbling sometime before 1862, that is, when the wall hangings were being conceived and embroidered, his 'Masque of Queen Bersabe.' This poem is crammed with women illustrious in their kind, twenty-three to be exact, including Herodias, Cleopatra, Semiramis, Pasiphae, Sappho, and Messalina, but it could have had no influence on the wall decoration. Swinburne's women are smiting, biting, men-eating viragos – lesser versions of Dolores or Faustine of sisters of the blond Amazons of St John's

Wood who flagellated the poet half out of his wits – not at all Morris's tutelary types. I note them here simply because they show the taste of the time for collections of famous (with Swinburne, infamous) women. The whip that drove Algernon to collect his imaginary 'dames' was much more a literal instrument – much less an inner goad – than the spur that drove Morris to conjure up his unusual body-guard of beautiful girls.

We know that Morris purchased from F. S. Ellis in the early 60s a copy of the 1473 Ulm edition of Boccaccio's *'De Claris Mulieribus'* with the famous woodcuts. In *De Claris Mulieribus, of* which Morris probably talked much to his week-enders, even calling it – just possibly – 'my *Illustrious Women*,' we may have the source of many of the hieratic females projected for Red House. 'Claris,' meaning 'famous,' is even more exactly translated as 'illustrious,' and Morris was a good Latinist. Now if he told his noisy week-enders that he was getting ideas for his hangings from the *Illustrious Women* of an author much admired by Chaucer, the misunderstanding that Topsy's famous figures originated in his favourite poet could have taken root at an early date, lived on underground, and surfaced later in so many (unreading) writers. That at least some of Morris's women may have come from Boccaccio is suggested by the fact that three or four of the eight we know of appear in *De Claris Mulieribus*. This is a high score for Boccaccio when compared with any other likely source. First, the Italian gives finely conceived accounts of Helen and Penelope. Second, he treats Venus as a one-time earthly queen in the best euhemeristic manner – a manner which suggests a possible reason for Morris showing no hesitation in planning to hang goddesses like her and Diana among the 'illustrious women' on his walls. Boccaccio also has various warrior queens among his illustrious females, notably Penthesilea and 'Brunchilde Francorum regina.' The latter, Morris was to come to admire extravagantly, as we know. Practicing euhemerism on his own, he idolised or deified her in his 'Icelandic period,' making her the heroine of his most ambitious and probably finest poem. However, since this tragic Valkyr cannot appropriately wear the conqueror's wreath which we find twisted round the red hair of Morris's heavily armed figure, Joan of Arc must for the time remain our best guess. It is intriguing to think that Boccaccio, that medieval Italian Euherus turning goddesses into queens, may have been the first to introduce Morris to the Valkyr who became in time his own 'Illustrious Woman' par excellence.

Not having been able to find a clear-cut literary source for *all* of Morris's women, one which might have established definitively the meaning and value which he attached to them as a group, we must ask what inner craving, what psychological need, their presence on his walls would, or might have satisfied. We can only speculate, of course, but we can speculate along lines, guidelines, already pondered in Chapter I. There we saw how certain Hindu, Buddhist and Tibetan groups seek to mitigate if not conquer what seem to be 'inevitable and innate anxieties,' fears and disappointments which are inescapable drawbacks of the human condition, by means of a construct which, though largely inner, can also be presented outwardly by a traditional pattern of squares in circles incised or heaped on the earth, or by pictures of circles of fire, water, trees and flowers surrounding a square castle, at the heart of which is an animating deity – more often than not White Tārā dancing on a pink lotus. The goddess is said to dance in the inch-square space within the human heart which is identified as a man's life-source or essence. The whole construct, which may also be found or created, as we know, in scenery united with architecture, is an elaborate fortress designed to protect essential being from the erosions of anxiety, misery, fear, pain and death. The flashing, ineffable peace in the inch-square space is the object of all man's searching and may be *compelled* to light up inside him by his making mandalas. (See Plate 3.) It may also be kept alight by the care he takes to beautify these structures with guardian figures. Besides Tārā, the pictured mandalas are often filled with protective deities. More often than not these deities are female or female manifestations (personified energies) of gods. Often, it is said, as in a well known Tantric text, that Tārā, called simply 'the Goddess,' stands at the hub of psychocosmic pattern, the mandala, whence ray out spokes to the farthest rim: 'Then imagine that all the spokes assume the aspect of the Goddess: As eternally the rays shine forth from the sun, thus also the Goddesses arise from the body of the "Great Goddess." ' (G. Tucci, *The Theory and Practice of the Mandala*, tr. A. H. Brodrick, 1961, 26) These deities guard the doors of the heart and ward off evil – that is, dark powers that undermine man's precious moments of omniscience, omnipotence, all-lovingness, creation in the beautiful, unalloyed joy – by vigorous dancing, but they may also, and usually do, carry weapons. I remember seeing carved in the central dome of a Jain tample on Mt Ābū in India a great marble flower composed of goddesses armed with swords and spears – a miracle of art which made the heart leap, rejoice and then relax.

By the discussion above I have been trying to lead the reader, none too subtly, to the notion that Morris's famous women were meant to finish off the fine mandalic structure which he had created at Red House among its orchards and gardens. These were 'the Guardians of the Doors,' the multiplication of the deity at the centre – as indeed they were, for each woman has the features of Jane and the long red hair she coveted. At the same time they were emanations of the artist's creative imagination suggested by cogitations or impulses only more or less conscious. As we read in a Tantric text quoted by Tucci (27), 'O son of noble family, ... these shapes come from no other place; they are solely the fabric of thy mind.' Even in their unfinished state, Morris's panels constitute a remarkable collection of tutelary figures. Though we may make various guesses as to why and how he came to choose his Good Women, the impulse to surround himself with a dozen protective tychés in what he seems to have considered a very important room of Red House must have sprung to some degree from unconscious depths and seems to have represented the last step taken, after the orchard, gardens, and walls, to protect Red House's temenos or sacred centre. It is quite possible that the female saints of G. F. Bodley's pulpit hangings may have stimulated Morris to create a hagiology of personal but profane (apart from St Catherine) figures much as *The Golden Legend,* with its roster of monotonously pious female martyrs, is generally supposed to have tempted Chaucer to write his *Legend of Good Women* about pre-Christian girls who died for Eros. With the example of Bodley's Christian and Chaucer's pagan saints before him, it is interesting that few of Morris's figures have ever been associated with martyrdom of any kind. It should also be noted that Joan of Arc (if it is she) and St Catherine in her shining goodness (reinforced by the largest sword conceivable) have shed all odour of death and have become 'Guardians of the Doors' par excellence. Therefore, of Morris's eight figures none can be associated with any one role or theme so easily as that of protector of the sacred centre.

This centre originated, we remember, in a real Persian palace located at the heart of circles and squares of trees and flowers – the whole complex being called a *pairidaēza* or paradise. Flattened into a picture, this arrangement, known in ancient Indian religion and to modern psychiatry as a mandala, was usually provided with protective deities, usually female (Tārā multiplied), who guard the four palace gates, the four directions (corners of the structure) and the four-sided holy-of-holies at the centre. Hence twelve tutelary figures (sometimes only four or eight; sometimes as many as twenty-eight) are frequent in Mahayana Buddhist mandalas, from which we know the configuration best. If, as Jung believes, the mandala is a universal dream flashing in the depths of the unconscious mind when in search of, or enjoying, happy healing, we can begin to understand the profundity of this unique scheme of decoration. Not all the women are armed but Diana, Dido, Joan, and St Catherine with her great sword are perfectly weaponed. Besides these, Helen brandishes the great torch which burned Troy like a defensive weapon, and Penelope carries her web over her right arm like a shield for the defence of Morris's palace against suitors. Only Venus – after all, she is rising naked from the waves – and Guenevere have no bows, swords, spears, shields or other material of war. But is it accurate to think of these two heroines as powerless to guard the centre? In Homer, Venus fought at Troy and in

Virgil she appeared in arms to her son Aeneas; in a famous myth she disarmed Mars and subdued him thoroughly, though not in conventional warfare. Vague memories of all these stories may have lain behind Morris's choice of this woman-goddess to head the procession on his walls. Besides, he was in love! The Guenevere here at Kelmscott carries nothing in her hands but a (never embroidered) flower, yet Morris may have chosen her because she, rather than Arthur, had power to galvanise the physical force of the Round Table (and especially that of the world's strongest knight) to beat down evil. She was the catalyst of campaigns to protect the weak and rescue beleaguered goodness – a battalion in herself. That the tutelary powers of all these women were never far from Morris's mind I shall try to show whenever they surface in our examination of his art or books of poetry and prose.

Lest the reader should think the dining-room unworthy to figure as the heart of Morris's essentially spirit-centred structure, all I can say is that the master seemed never happier than when he came beaming among his guests with bottles of wine in either hand and as many more tucked under his arms. He was a gourmet of sorts and a good cook. When in 1867, the Firm of 1861 being pretty well established, Morris and Co. were called on to decorate the Dining Room of the South Kensington Museum (now known as the Morris Room of the Victoria and Albert), Morris immediately had the idea of running around the large room a frieze of twelve hieratic women, painted by Fairfax Murray after designs of Burne-Jones on panels interspersed with others of leaves and flowers on a background of gold. These are still in situ, 'renewed' by Murray toward the turn of the century though again somewhat dingy. They represent the twelve signs of the zodiac, Cancer, Leo and Virgo being attractively plump nudes in Burne-Jones's earlier manner. Thus tutelary women and good food seem to have been definitely linked in Morris's mind and perhaps in that of his time. The association was not, we may be sure, of women with appetite but with the fruits and grains needed for life. These zodiacal girls presided over the growth of the soil throughout the year and in this role continued the symbolism of the three graces of antiquity or of the Hindu zodiacal signs. Tucci tells us (82) that, for certain passionate persons, Mahayana Buddhism permits the substitution of the Hindu planetary and constellation figures (considered deities and usually represented as females) for the more orthodox guardians of the temenos. This fact, though of course unknown to Morris, may help in the mysterious way of the collective-unconscious to explain Morris's devotion to groups of females in his decorative schemes and to these zodiacal girls in particular. It seems that he treasured Burne-Jones's charcoal cartoons for them (so much brighter and more clean-cut now than the darkening paintings in the V. and A.) and kept them about him when at work. They are now, all but one, in the foyer to the White-panelled Room here at Kelmscott, making that small space into the temenos-centre of Morris's mandalic refuge by the Thames. Similar collections of girls were used by Morris and Burne-Jones (1874–1882) for an embroidered frieze at Rounton Grange (now at The William Morris Gallery in Walthamstow) which, though depicting a garden-scene from *The Romaunce of the Rose,* recalls the slender Graces and other females in Botticelli's *Primavera.* This famous picture of gracile girls scattered among gracile trees by a real 'pre-Raphaelite' was beloved, it seems, by the nineteenth-century anti-Raphaelites beyond all other old Italian pictures. Even Morris, who did not much enjoy his trips to Italy because he resented the 'calculated geometry' and 'tiresome idealisation' of high-Renaissance art, brought home a small black-and-white reproduction of the *Primavera*, which now hangs in one of the Kelmscott attics. Burne-Jones designed a fine *Primavera* tapestry (an enlarged duplicate of the original picture) which was woven at the Merton Abbey workshops. Another arrangement of girls and trees recalling the beloved Italian painter appears in the *Orchard* tapestry, woven in 1890 but designed much earlier, probably by Morris alone, which is now in the V. and A. Here four lovely women, positioned against different fruit trees, hold a scroll containing a poem by Morris which suggests something of what is symbolised by any group of tree-spirits if we remember that 'growth of the soil' is often used as synonymous with 'growth of the soul.'

> Midst bitter mead and acre shorn
> The world without is waste and worn;
> But here within our orchard close
> The guerdon of our labour shows.
> O valiant earth, O happy year,
> That mocks the threat of winter near,
> And hangs aloft from tree to tree
> The banners of the spring to be.

Thus groups of women, armed or unarmed, treading on flowers and interspersed among trees, were used by Morris from the beginning of his career as a decorator to symbolise fruitfulness and peace, abundance and safety, luxuriance and rest – all we can imagine of beauty, healing, solace, numinosity and resurrection. Of such is the experience of the centre of the mandala. Such was the ambience and such the centre of Red House. Life at Red House, like the structure itself, was a thing apart, and can give us living today some idea of how a home set among its trees and gardens can be more a poem, as Rossetti said, than a house.

It is not hard to see why Red House was, while good weather lasted, a literal Earthly Paradise. (See Plate 9.)

IV 'The First Earthly Paradise' and the Quest of Jason

Meanwhile, long before his protective angels could be hung at Red House, Morris's great goddess, his white Tārā, had descended into the centre of the lotus, where she danced hypnotically or, more probably, hypnotically reclined on a chaise longue recently designed by her husband. Having taken up her position at the heart of the mandala, the traditional Tārā, say the old texts, must be 'imprisoned' there, forever if possible, as the mainstay of the poised, protected, magnanimous life which the successful creator of the mandala has attained. We are warned, however, that when the mandalic structure is created of natural materials, not just painted on cloth or drawn in sand, and Tārā Śakti ('almost always a sixteen-year-old girl' – Tucci, 123) is led to her place 'at the centre,' where she blesses the artist-initiate with unearthly union with her gold-pure, naked beauty – when this happens, there is danger! As Tucci ponderously observes, 'All human institutions are subject to corruption and this applies in particular to the Schools which have chosen so audacious a symbolism and which daringly make use of sexual imagery to express their mystical aspirations' (123). In Morris's case, the *sakti* being his wife and the mandala having been unconsciously constructed to make the ritual ceremony at the centre as sacred as possible, we can hardly blame him for the spiritual peril into which he was so confidently rushing. Only Swinburne with his no-man-should-go-further-than-to-kiss-Jane's-feet attitude may have had any realistic idea of what might happen to the Red House bliss.

Pretty clearly, Morris was moving quickly in the direction of confusing a spiritual pattern or archetypal vision – an inner-apprehended map of the healed and integrated personality – with a literal Earthly Paradise. To be sure, factual experiences corresponding to the deepest human needs may have contributed to the earliest Edens and most regal Persian *pairidaëzas*, but the mandalic design is always more visionary than real, an ecstasy sprung from, ministering to, and carried about in the mind. To seek to realise it in detail in the actual world is, almost immediately, to tempt the immemorial dualisms – spirit and matter, heart and reason, quiet and movement, the sacred and the secular – to clash. However, Morris was so happy with his new house, his new wife, and his new-found power of designing and making all the furniture and drapery necessary for a sacred enclosure, from enormous painted settles to the

smallest of bedroom altar-cloths, that Mackail did not hesitate to declare
the Red House years the happiest of Morris's life. It was then that his
two daughters were born, that the Firm was founded, as has often been
stressed, and that, as has not been sufficiently stressed, he conceived and
wrote several portions of a poem to be called *The Earthly Paradise*.

May Morris possessed early versions of the prologue and eleven stories
of the paradise poem, contained in quarto manuscript books numbered 1
to 6 in 'my father's writing' and therefore throwing 'light on the order in
which the poems were written' (III, xv). The order in which the poems
were written and published is important for there were really two
Earthly Paradises, one reflecting the happy Red House days, the other
the personal tragedy that followed. Roughly, the first two volumes com-
prise the 'First Paradise,' the third and fourth the 'Second Paradise,'
though this division cannot be relied on at all times. After the first draft
of the prologue (changed entirely when volume I of the only published
Earthly Paradise appeared in 1868) came 'Cupid and Psyche,' 'The Lady
of the Land,' 'The Palace East of the Sun,' and others ending with 'The
Deeds of Jason.'

This last story, outgrowing many notebooks in itself as Morris worked
on it, was published in book form in 1877 as *The Life and Death of
Jason*. Much of it must have been completed in or before 1866, the year
after Morris left Red House, a fact which argues that the other stories in
the sequence of manuscript quartos were written during the Red House
period. In other words, there never was a ten-year break (between the
Guenevere of 1858 and the *Jason* of 1867) in Morris's poetic activity. This
hiatus in publishing is often confused with a suspension of writing
because the atmosphere of *Jason* is rather placid and amiable compared
with the fevers of much of *Guenevere*. It is widely declared that in both
Jason and *The Earthly Paradise* Morris, uxoriously gorged with Jane,
surfeited with the orchard apples that came tumbling in at the open windows of Red House on summer nights, filled with flagons and friendships to spare, exulting in fatherhood and craftsmanship, reduced poetry
to one interminable, languorous, sensual lullaby. When not called the
longest soporifics in the language, *Jason* and *The Earthly Paradise* (all
four published volumes) are often accused of being mere embroideries,
tapestries, tiles or wallpapers in verse meant to decorate married life with
mythic images arranged in repetitive patterns. Above all, these books are
blamed as escapist literature, ignoring tragedy, never piercing below the
surface psychologically, and meant to do no more than help Morris's
countrymen forget the dull and pointless lives they lived among the
sordid squalor they were every day compounding for themselves and for
the world. Actually, there may be a grain of truth in these charges. If so,
the short-comings of *Jason* and the tales composed at Red House (mostly

those published in the early volumes of *The Earthly Paradise*) are probably to be traced to the fact that for those five years Morris's fidgets, for the first time in his life, were becalmed, his fears, especially of death, toned down, and the whole range of his talents brought to bear on a meaningful, heart-felt enterprise. The trouble was, perhaps, that things did go too well for us to expect more *Guenevere* poetry with, as Pater said, 'its accent falling in strange, unwonted places with the effect of a great cry.' In fact, the creation of his protective mandala progressed so well at Red House and proved so effective, at least for the time being, that Morris became for a while confused about the essentially spiritual nature of the cosmograph and thought he had really achieved at Red House man's ancient dream of a literal return into Eden.

Here I would like to describe briefly the poetry I take to have been written, in whole or in part, at Red House: the 'Prologue' and the ten first-written stories of *The Earthly Paradise* in their early form, and *The Life and Death of Jason*. A few of the early stories were used almost verbatim in the published *Earthly Paradise,* but most were changed rather radically to bring them into harmony with Morris's somber if not tragic mood of 1868 to 1870, when volumes III and IV were brought out. There were, then, really two *Earthly Paradises*; the one published between those dates and the one written between 1861 and 1866, of which enough remains to give the reader the clearest notion he can get of what was on the poet's mind in the Red House years.

First there is the prologue, entirely different from that printed in 1868, which gives us a good notion of Morris's early conception of the Earthly Paradise. Here we have a sense that Eden is materialising on Bexley Heath, that Saturn is throning it down in the orchard, that the spiritual topography of the mandala is turning into the palpable landscape of the Golden Age. Suddenly natural bowers and groves, garden enclosures dedicated to Venus, brilliant roses, lilies and begonias, springs of fresh water, perfumed breezes, eternal springtide, beautiful girls (no old women allowed) unfailing in kindness and passion, jewel-bodies impervious to sickness, age or impotence – suddenly all these paraphernalia of the classical Golden Time or Elysian Fields replace the visions of the inward eye. The earlier, more geometric, more spirit-spun and more healing mandala configuration has turned under the spell of Morris's new happiness into a loosely arranged, perfume-drenched Garden of Armida filled with unclothed bathing beauties. That Morris was well acquainted with the Earthly Paradise literature of the Renaissance (Ariosto, Tasso, Spenser, *et al.*) is doubtful, but he probably knew a good deal about the classical writers from whom the western idea of the Golden Age derives. I mean Homer (*Odyssey* IV and VII), Hesiod (*Works and Days*), Pindar (*Pythian* X and *Olympian* II), Virgil (*Eclogue IV* and *Aeneid VI*), Ovid

(*Metamorphoses* I), Theocritus (*Idyll* VII) and Claudian (*Epithalamium de Nuptiis Honorii Augusti*). Like the components of the mandala, those of the Elysian Fields or the Garden of the Hesperides have an atmosphere of the archetypal about them but constitute more a surface daydream than an inner-directed vision welling up from unconscious depths to restore health and sanity.

I will just recall the dominant characteristics of the day-dream, so well known to most of us either from reading or direct experience, in order to give a notion of what Morris had in mind when he sent the Wanderers of the early prologue in search of the Fortunate Islands in the West, and later devised stories of Earthly Paradises won or sometimes, through the cowardice, wickedness or folly of the seekers, lost. Ovid sums up the dream somewhat as follows: no laws, no wars, no lack of harmony among men or between them and the soil, which yields multiple births of fruit, grains and flowers of her own volition in an eternal springtime while her breasts stream with milk and nectar; there are no fortifications, no hatreds, no insecurity, no fear, no injustice in this dew-drenched country ruled by Saturn and pervaded by Astraea the Virgin, deity of equity for all. Ovid is here expanding Virgil's famous projection of the happy after-life upon the earthly future, but he does not go so far as to assert that in the *coming* Golden Age it will no longer be necessary even to dye wool, for sheep will grow it in all the colours used for clothing. Besides, nothing is said by either of the Roman poets about the absence of sickness and death or incursions of boredom. A modern evocation of the Earthly Paradise, put in the wounded Arthur's mouth by Tennyson and undoubtedly enjoyed by Morris, locates it in

> . . . the island-valley of Avilion;
> Where falls not hail, or rain, or any snow,
> Nor ever wind blows loudly; but it lies
> Deep-meadow'd, happy, fair with orchard-lawns
> And bowery hollows crown'd with summer sea,
> Where I will heal me of my grievous wound.

Early in the Red House days Morris had the notion of gathering into a book a number of the world's oldest tales, Greek, Near Eastern and Teutonic, to show how men everywhere, yearning always for the same immortality in the same Happy Valley, have recorded the adventures of the search. The old stories that Morris loved to retell are gathered from myths, fairy-tales, and apologues, already often retold but still full of valid encouragement or warnings for those trying to beat a path to a Red House of their own. Paradisal landscapes, often close to mandalic imagery but acclimatised to recognisable English scenery, are the stock-in-trade backgrounds of Morris's tales. More often than not the stories begin with a lovely description of wold and meadow, birdsong and country peace, and proceed to tell how the hero lost and regained this Good Place or (not often) sacrificed it forever through his shortcomings. Morris did not entirely side-step those old tales in which the hero is harassed or even crushed by the positive evil of others. These seem to have so distressed him in his new-found happiness that he felt bound to reveal that all life did not move to the sweet canticles and bold marching songs of Red House. Still, there was such happiness and hysterical horseplay among the young people there at week-ends that the joviality rubbed off on most of the early paradise poems, especially the prologue (later entirely rep-placed).

The Wanderers here, the seekers of perfection, unlike those in the later prologue who flee from a raging plague, are tempted to leave their northern homes in search of unfailing health and immortality merely on hearing their captain recount a dream of happy young people on an island where

> Rose up a temple of green stone
>   Like glass : therein were images
> As of Diana, burd-alone,
>   Trim-shod, with dainty naked knees. . . .
>
> And midmost there, with wings that met
>   Over his head, was mighty Love,
> And there beside was Venus set,
>   Fresh, soft, and naked, with her dove . . .

(XXIV, 89)

In his dream the captain had heard one youth telling another

> 'That every man grows young again
> That underneath our gates doth go,
>   And never after suffers pain;
>
> No war, no winter, no disease,
>   No storm or famine reach us here,
> Ever we live 'mid rest and ease
>   And no man doth another fear ! . . .'

(90)

Though set far ' "apart/From all the world," ' this land is

> 'Not altogether hard to find
>   If still you steer west hardily
> Beseeching Venus to be kind.'

Here the first of many suggestions for illustrations to be made by Burne-Jones – 'Kneeling to Venus (big)' – is entered opposite these stanzas which continue to describe the captain's dream:

> 'Down fell I straight upon my knees,
>   And holding Venus by the feet,
> "I pray thee give me rest and peace
>   And fearless life, my lady sweet . . ." '

(90)

Keeping tight hold of the image, the captain continued to utter prayers till suddenly, as once with Pygmalion, ' "The stone my hands were laid upon/Grew into soft flesh" ' and 'the fair leg' was a little retracted as the goddess granted his wish. It is not hard to detect the youthful fun in Morris's requiring his friend to draw this picture 'big.' In fact, nearly all the scenes of the prologue which were to be shown 'big' included unclad girls. These scenes are so many and so important that merely to list them will give a good idea of the prologue – also, of the fact that the *Śakti* dancing on the Red House lotus had become an almost obsessive image!

After finding one Edenic island to the west inhabited by head-hunters and another by black-skinned savages, the Nordic Wanderers begin to think they have 'sinned Adam's sin' of thinking to become gods, but conclude there is still a good chance of finding the 'very Earthly Paradise' the captain had dreamed of. They push on to an adventure meriting at least seven '(big)' pictures! This occurs on an island to which both the Greeks and Amazons of pre-history have somehow found their way and are continuing their ancient animosity. The patriarchs, who hold the great city of the women in subjection, demand of its queen a yearly offering of ten girls, each more lovely than Andromeda, whom they sacrifice, not to a sea-monster, but to lions. From a well chosen hiding-place the Wanderers watch the preparations for the ghastly sacrifice. At a command from the pitiless priests the girls threw off their ceremonial crowns and golden copes and 'set their fair hands to their gowns':

> Then on the green grass piteously
>   The silken garments down did rain,
> The soft smocks slipped from breast and thigh
>   They never now should hide again. . . .
>
> And then came forth four sturdy men
>   With brazen chains that foot and hand
> They did upon the damsels ten;
>   And when so bound they all did stand,
>
> Unto the rock they made them fast.
>   And when we saw them side by side
> Wailing and naked, then at last
>   Scarce in our place could we abide.

(117, 118)

Here occurs the direction to Burne-Jones: 'Ladies chained to rocks, lions coming (big).'

Fortunately the patriarchs withdraw before the feast begins, leaving our heroes free to slay the lions and save the girls:

> Then from rock all tenderly
>   We loosed those ladies; and full oft
> Deliciously our hearts beat high
>   At touching the round limbs so soft . . .
>
> (120)

When Amazons in black armour come to collect the bones of their sisters, there floats

> Over their heads a great banner,
>   Wherein was painted royally
> Diana, with her snooded hair
>   And fair legs naked to the knee.
>
> (122)

This is the very modelling of the Diana whom Morris designed as a Red House guardian and we may feel this whole espisode sprang from his fondness for dreaming of a military *Śakti* who, oriental-fashion, had lost her clothes. The love-struck Wanderers, not expecting to find 'a fairer sight/In any hall of Paradise,' married the Amazons, broke the power of the patriarchs and settled down to raise families after a love scene glorified by one of Morris's tenderest poems, to be itself glorified by a picture of 'Two lovers with music (big).'

> SHE
> In the white-flowered hawthorn brake,
> Sweet, be merry for my sake;
> Twine the flowers in my hair,
> Kiss me where I am most fair,
> Ah! kiss me, love, for who knoweth
> What thing cometh after death?
>
> HE
> Love, hold back the golden hair,
> That hides you where you are most fair,
> Let me kiss the rose-tinged snow.
> Ah! the time goes, fast or slow —
> Kiss me, my sweet! for who knoweth
> What thing cometh after death?
>
> (138)

Only years later, themselves now old, did the Wanderers' old dream return to drive them farther and farther west. The next island adventure is notable for Morris's use of a situation which was mildly obsessive with him. He had already used it in the *Oxford and Cambridge Magazine* story of 'Svend and His Brethren' in 1856. With uncanny power Morris could conjure up pictures of people in apparently suspended animation though really, in spite of their fresh complexions and vigorous-seeming gestures, dead – overwhelmed, as he here suggests, by divine 'blows/That kill without destroying men.' (147) From an early age he seems to have seen the conventional activities of most men as a kind of life-in-death, though the scene he most frequently freezes in flesh tones is that of banqueting royalty. Here we pass through a whole city of workmen and traders on permanent strike, to the climactic banquet in the great castle. On the way we come on certain sights that Morris seems to have thought Burne-Jones might like, in the spirit of Red House high-jinks, to record, though he did not demand large illustrations – merely 'Ladies bathing (small)' and 'Lovers (small).' Passing through a soldier-guarded door, the Wanderers

> . . . found a court of marble white,
>   Set round with pots of orange-trees,
> And midmost, open to the light,
>   A clear green pool, where three ladies
>
> Naked, but covered to the knee
>   By the thin water, stood bathing;
> While on the brink lay daintily
>   Their clothes with many a chain and ring.
>
>   (149)

After leaving the city of life-in-death, the old Wanderers lose their 'lust to live on earth' and are prepared to give up at the very moment when they sight the green-glass temple to Venus and Diana, those Red House deities, the dream of which had catalysed the quest. With its fair fields, burdened orchards, painted palaces, white homes, cunning workmen, grave philosophers, gentle laws and loving people, the object of the long search certainly seemed to have materialised, but the presence of storm and frost, decay and inevitable death, showed the Wanderers that their last island was simply a remarkable simulacrum – alas, alas! – of the captain's original dream – not an impregnable Golden Age garden filled with unfading nudes. Of necessity they settle down in this pleasant geriatric refuge and exchange Earthly Paradise stories with their elderly hosts, whose ancestors, luckily, had come centuries before from Greece, the home of so many *loci amoeni*, and had left them many tales to swap with the Northmen. The stories told by both groups gave them (and Morris) ample opportunity to retrace again and again the beloved features of the paradise complex while they waited for death 'with little pain.' Though the passion for the earthly Eden conceives the elements of the mandala – groves and gardens clustering around a central palace at the heart of which dances a goddess or fountain – as real rather than symbolic, traces of archetypal serenity and joy cling about the old story-tellers' efforts. To describe the mandalic scenery, temple and almost ubiquitous half-clothed girls as real pleases the elders and seems to be appropriate geriatric 'work.' They dream without hope but are still true to Morris's motto that the business of his life was to dream. Morris's last humorous directive to Burne-Jones for an illustration to the Prologue reads, 'Old chaps telling tales (big) no women.' (170)

The first ten stories of the collection were composed, May Morris believed, in the following order: 'Cupid and Psyche' – 'The Lady of the Land' – 'The Palace East of the Sun' – 'Story of Adrastus' – 'The Doom of Acrisius' – 'The Proud King' – 'The Watching of the Falcon' – 'The Hill of Venus' – 'The Writing on the Image' – and 'The Deeds of Jason,' which was published by itself as a full-scale book in 1867. When the stories named above, plus fourteen others, appeared between 1868 and 1870 as *The Earthly Paradise*, what we may call the apologues or moral pieces were kept almost intact while the love stories became something like tales of terror. It is the Red House versions of these latter which interest us because the sombre published versions of them, to be discussed in another chapter, can be traced to changes in Morris's life. I find no reason for discussing the merely didactic tales and shall say more at once, after a word about 'The Writing on the Image,' of the early form of the love tales.

In 'The Writing' where Morris tells in what May called his 'minstrel metre' of a 'poor scholar' who, having pierced the secret of the laconic words on the statue's upheld hand, dreams of becoming 'the richest man in all the land,'

> And some unheard-of palace have;
> As if my soul I may not save
> In heaven, yet here in all men's eyes
> Will I make some sweet paradise,
> With marble cloisters, and with trees
> And bubbling wells, and fantasies . . .

Driven by his vision of an Earthly Paradise, he works his way underground in the direction of the treasure, only to come on

> A goodly hall hung round with gold,
> And at the upper end could see
> Sitting, a glorious company:
> Therefore he trembled, thinking well
> They were no men but fiends of hell . . .

And drawing nigher did behold
That these were bodies dead and cold
Attired in full royal guise,
And wrought by art in such a wise
That living they all seemed to be,
Whose very eyes he well could see . . .
Shining as though alive they were.
And midmost of that company
An ancient king that men could see . . .
And next beside him sat his queen . . .
On either side of these, a lord
Stood heedfully before the board,
And in their hands held bread and wine
For service . . .

Once again, the banquet image of the dead-alive that seems to have fascinated Morris all his life either as symbolic of regal inanition or, perhaps, of the only immortality possible even for those who have managed
to discover or create an Earthly Paradise. It is possible that such images
first took hold of Morris's imagination when, as May Morris, following
M. C. Irwin, suggests (Sup. I, 405–4) her father may have read, as he
well may have, the Abbé Huc's *Voyage en Tartarie et Thibet* (ed. 1850, I,
115–17). Here Tartar kings are said to have been buried underground in
great brick-work tombs with their gold, jewels, precious robes and some
of their subjects, usually beautiful children 'suffocated by huge doses of
mercury,' by which means the freshness and colour of their faces was
preserved to the point of making them seem forever alive. These were
placed upright about the body of their master and given his pipe, fan and
favourite dainties to hold for his ghostly use. To guard these treasures,
bows fitted with arrows were placed about the burial cave, all tautly
drawn and aimed at the cave's door, which could not be moved without
releasing deadly darts at the would-be robber. This ingenious defence is
made still more ingenious by Morris. His underground tomb is lit by a
huge red carbuncle suspended from the roof and his dead-alive royalty,
dressed in a treasure of jewels and golden robes and still fingering their
gold goblets, are guarded by

An image made of brass and wood,
In likeness of a full-armed knight
Who pointed 'gainst the ruddy light
A huge shaft ready in a bow.

When the scholarly robber, after filling his bag with loot extracted from
the helpless heads and bodies of the red-cheeked cadavers, tries to pry a
last precious stone from the cave floor, a mechanism causes the knight to

discharge his arrow at the carbuncle, leaving the banquet-hall in darkness
and closed forever to escape.

Such are Morris's didactic tales, of which I thought I should mention
this one because of the poor scholar's longing for a paradise on earth and
his encounter with the dead-alive.

Apart and differing in spirit from these apologues, 'The First Earthly
Paradise,' as we may call it, retold a number of the world's famous love
tales. Several of these stories, in the collection's final form, turn out
badly. The interesting thing for us is that some of the most harrowing
tales in the printed volumes are revisions of pieces treated almost de-
bonairly in the quarto manuscripts. Before sketching the early versions of
stories like 'The Palace East of the Sun and West of the Moon' and 'The
Hill of Venus,' I must say something about 'The Story of Cupid and
Psyche,' which stood at the head of the stories in May Morris's leather-
bound manuscripts and was believed by her to be the first of *The Earthly
Paradise* stories written. This must date back, then, to about 1860, for
May's first drafts of 'The Proud King' and 'The Watching of the Falcon,' perhaps the sixth and seventh stories to be composed, occur in a
notebook dated by Morris himself 'June 1861.' 'Cupid and Psyche' was
also intended, in all probability, to establish the atmosphere and trend of
the love stories in the collection as Morris first conceived them. It seems
also that he planned to publish 'Cupid and Psyche' separately as a book
with a hundred woodcut illustrations by Burne-Jones. (See J. Dunlap's
The Book That Never Was and a modern edition of all that ever was,
edited by A. Richard Dufty.) That this story was to a degree paradigmatic is shown by the central role in it of the Earthly Paradise, here very
elaborately treated by the poet, and made the centre of action. Aphro-
dite, jealous of Psyche's reputation for being more beautiful than the
goddess of love herself, sends her son Eros or Cupid to torture and kill
her. Instead, he carries her to refuge in his more than heavenly palace set
among more than Edenic scenery. Of course, Psyche loses Love's love
and Olympus-on-earth by succumbing to the advice of malicious sisters.
She breaks Cupid's taboo, forfeits his protection, and is tormented by
Venus herself. After this purgation, however, she marries Cupid and is
translated to a paradise beyond the least breath of bad sisters, bad
weather, bad pain, bad age, bad death (Cupid's set-up on earth had been,
it seems, far from offering full protective coverage) on Mt Olympus. The
scenarios of the early 'Palace East of the Sun and West of the Moon,'
'The Watching of the Falcon' and 'The Hill of Venus' are quite similar
to that of 'Cupid and Psyche' inasmuch as the protagonists (now all
males) begin like Psyche in distress, meet a divine or fairy-like being, live
with her in an Earthly Paradise, lose her through violating a taboo, and,
if fortunate, recover their vanished bliss.

When Psyche is rescued from torture and death by the invisible god of love, she finds herself in distinctly Poe-esque country:

> A lovely grassy valley could she see,
> That steep grey cliffs upon three sides did bound,
> And under them a river sweeping round,
> With gleaming curves the valley did embrace,
> And seemed to make an island of that place;
> And all about were dotted leafy trees,
> The elm for shade, the linden for the bees . . .
> The pomegranate, the apple, and the pear,
> That fruit and flowers at once made shift to bear,
> Nor yet decayed therefore; and in them hung
> Bright birds that elsewhere sing not, but here sung
> As sweetly as the small brown nightingales
> Within the wooded, deep Laconian vales.
>   But right across the vale, from side to side,
> A high white wall all further view did hide,
> But that above it, vane and pinnacle
> Rose up, of some great house beyond to tell;
> And still betwixt these, mountains far away . . .

Psyche makes her way to this 'love heaven,' timidly approaches a door in the high white wall, and (I use printed *Paradise* text)

> . . . raised the latch, and her sweet sinless eyes
> Beheld a garden like a paradise,
> Void of mankind, fairer than words can say,
> Wherein did joyous harmless creatures play
> After their kind, and all amidst the trees
> Were strange-wrought founts and wondrous images;
> And glimmering 'twixt the boughs could she behold
> A house made beautiful with beaten gold . . .

Inside the house were 'golden hangings' and 'silver mirrors' and oriental rugs. Toward evening Psyche, casting off her clothes (a scene for Burne-Jones?), refreshes herself in a room-sized bath before retiring to a bed of gold and ivory and strange embroideries which made her feel she had 'wandered heedlessly/Into a bower for some fair goddess made.' Such descriptions go on till Morris has exhausted the richest Paradise Palace he can conceive. Then he allows Psyche to lose Cupid and the ineffably embroidered bed at the temenos-centre. Of course, she regains him, as everyone knows, along with a celestial home on the mountain of the gods and immortality. Psyche's encounter with Venus gave Morris an opportunity to describe at length one of the guardian goddesses of Red House, cartooned in oils but never to be embroidered. I give a few lines from his picture of the enthroned queen:

> A crown there was upon her glorious head,
> A garland round about her girdlestead,
> Where matchless wonders of the hidden sea
> Were brought together and set wonderfully;
> Naked she was of all else, but her hair
> About her body rippled here and there,
> And lay in heaps upon the golden seat,
> And even touched the gold cloth where her feet
> Lay amid tresses – ah, how kind she seemed!

Some pattern like that of 'Cupid and Psyche' Morris intended, I think, for his retelling of all the old love stories planned for *The Earthly Paradise*. Though, in the Red House days, he did not hesitate to retell some pretty dismal love tales, he smoothed them to happy endings. It is often claimed that the stories of the published *Earthly Paradise* show a complete turn-about from the vivid violence, fevers and glooms which dominate *Guenevere*, and I am prepared to agree that this is more or less true of the versions of the love tales written, but unpublished, at Red House. The revision of these for the printed *Earthly Paradise*, along with the new love tales like 'The Man Who Never Laughed Again,' are seldom open to this 'versified tapestry' charge, however often it is made.

'The Lady of the Land,' which ends tragically, is not essentially a love story, though it may be mentioned here. It is a tale of wonder; also an apologue of a knight who fails in bravery – in knighthood. We cannot be sorry for him though we may enjoy Morris's description of the ruined castle which he chanced upon with its Tārā 'throned on ivory.'

> Naked she was, the kisses of her feet
> Upon the floor a dying path had made
> From the full bath unto her ivory seat;
> In her right hand, upon her bosom laid,
> She held a golden comb, a mirror weighed
> Her left hand down, aback her fair head lay
> Dreaming awake of some long vanished day.

We have seen in 'Cupid and Psyche' how a bed could be the temenos-centre of an Earthly Paradise; here the centre is close to being a bath-tub. The trouble is that this medieval Helen –

> Backward her heavy-hanging hair she threw
> To give her naked beauty more to sight –

is most of the time a dragon who, after a convention well known to Arthurian romance and Sir John Mandeville, must be kissed to be reconverted forever to her human shape. When the knight's nerve fails him, he deserves no pity. He has broken the first rule of chivalry.

The third story in May's manuscript collection in 'The Palace East of the Sun and West of the Moon.' This well known fairy tale of the Swan-Maiden who visits earth from time to time with her six sisters in order to dance a naked *pas de sept* would, of course, have offered a challenge to Burne-Jones's pencil. However, the folk versions of the tale treat the capture and wooing of the swan-girl crudely, and Morris from the first swept away most of the legendry, substituting for it a mortal's love for a half-goddess, a period of bliss in the temenos-bed of a palace in the heart of 'a marvellous land/Fruitful, and summer-like, and fair,' located east of the sun and west of the moon. When he breaks a taboo connected with revisiting his homeland, he loses her, suffers, seeks, and finally persuades her to make another appearance on earth. None of the men in these tales are so fortunate as Psyche, but they consider their sojourn in an Earthly Paradise, however brief, ample recompense for their lonely years. They are ready, in accordance with an old tradition, to endure death itself for one night of love, which is precisely the attitude of the adventurous king in 'The Watching of the Falcon,' who eyed the unblinking bird unblinkingly for seven days and nights in a gorgeously tapestried room at the centre of a four-square castle made additionally remarkable by a paradise garden:

> Within the bounds of that sweet close
> Was trellised the bewildering rose;
> There was the lily over-sweet,
> And starry pinks for garlands meet;
> And apricots hung on the wall
> And midst the flowers did peaches fall,
> And nought had blemish there or spot,
> For in that place decay was not.

His reward – a night with the castle 'fay' to be followed by a life of frustration and defeat – he accepted quite jocularly, it seems, and his battle with the Soudan [*sic*] who destroyed his power was planned and carried out with great zest by Morris, who seems to have had more interest in the battle of St Michael's Bridge than in the king's night with the 'fay.'

The last of these early-told love stories that May had in her father's manuscripts, 'The Hill of Venus,' was modelled on Tieck's tale of Tannhäuser, and the immortal for whom the German knight threw his soul away was no other than the foam-born deity who, had her panel ever been embroidered, would have hung in Red House as the first of Morris's illustrious women. In the early version of this poem (there are three or four manuscripts all differing considerably, even in the name of the hero – Lawrence, Amyot, Walter) the Venus country into which the knight bursts is not a forbidding and foreboding woodland but a paradisal spot where

> . . . as he looked along the slope he saw
> Not many yards away a damsel stand
> Her dainty feet nigh touching the rough paw
> Of a great lion, and her slim right hand
> Laid on his wrinkled brow; a silken band
> Hung to her left arm, and its end was bound
> About a white fawn laid upon the ground.
>
> (Sup. I, 435)

From this paradise-garden the Tannhäuser-figure moves on to a paradisal city where

> . . . gilded spires and vanes were borne aloft
> From the fair walls by carven turrets high,
> And doves and pigeons in their fluttering soft,
> With bright unknown birds thereabout did fly
> And from the windows came melodiously
> The sound of music that made all things seem
> Half dim and fleeting, like a happy dream.
>
> (VI, xviii)

The streets swarm with lovers on the way to the temple of Venus to
whom they sing a hymn of praise, another of which occurs later at a
tournament. This latter Morris preserved through all the many rewritten
versions though its joy and innocence hardly fit the published form of the
tale:

> *Before our lady came on earth*
> *Little there was of joy or mirth; . . .*
>
> *Unkissed the merchant bore his care,*
> *Unkissed the knights went out to war,*
> *Unkissed the mariner came home,*
> *Unkissed the minstrel men did roam.*
>
> *Or in the stream the maids would stare*
> *Nor know why there were made so fair;*
> *Their yellow locks, their bosoms white,*
> *Their limbs well wrought for all delight,*
> *Seemed foolish things that waited death . . .*
>
> *Therefore, O Venus, well may we*
> *Praise the green ridges of the sea*
> *O'er which, upon a happy day,*
> *Thou cam'st to take our shame away . . .*
> *O Venus, O thou love alive!*
> *Born to give peace to souls that strive!*

It is possible that Morris composed this song, or parts of it, to be embroidered on the Venus panel. He may have intended to write verses for all

his Red House heroines, as he did later for his 'Flora' and 'Pomona' tapestries.

For Burne-Jones's inspiration there was a long description of Venus at her bath. Born of the sea, she often felt its call and one night deserted her lover. 'Left naked of her love, and growing old,' Walter-Tannhäuser left the Hill, went with a band of pilgrims to Rome, confessed his sin to the Pope, ending with a mad boast that he belonged to the Hill after all (an episode not in Tieck), was cursed for as long as the Pope's dry staff should fail to put forth fruit and flowers, and returned to Venus. May had three fragmentary versions, from stanzas of which I reconstruct Walter's return, which hardly seems to have been distressing.

> What hope in her turn to? There between
> The blossoming trees she stood, in such a shade,
> That e'en the very air seemed well-nigh green,
> With one hand on a smooth stemmed sapling laid
> The other on her white breast, where there played
> From over-head a thin bright flickering ray
> Upon the place whereon his head once lay. . . .
>
> And what is fair beside her? the first day
> When o'er the ruined winter blithe birds sing,
> The summer eve when storms have passed away,
> The blossomed boughs of happy dying spring,
> The meadows in the May-tide flourishing –
> All these we have, and lose with little pain
> And nigh forget them till they come again.
>
> But who can e'er forget her, having seen
> Her beauty once, or ever take delight
> In aught but her, or be as he has been,
> Or rest in peace a moment day or night,
> For thinking of the tremor of his sight,
> When, like a man who gazes on the sun,
> He scarce beheld her as he might have done?
>
> (VI, xxiii–iv)

Finally, Venus puts in a few good words for herself:

> 'Be wise, come back if for a while again!
> I am the thing that thou didst cry to have,
> That rest and refuge from dull common pain
> For which within the world thou didst so crave:
> Whence came I, where I wend, what thing shall save
> My beauty from the swift decay of earth
> I know not; but my heart is full of mirth:

'My heart is full of mirth, and all is good;
Good the slow creeping longing and the ruth
That grows to restless fever of the blood,
Good the sweet blindness, good the flash of truth
That dies and comes again; and good the growth
Of half regret and half forgetfulness
That as the days wear the worn heart doth bless.'

(VI, xxii)

And then news comes from Rome: the Pope's long-dead staff has blossomed as a sign that to one who loves rest and refuge from the vulgar world all is likely to be forgiven.

Before leaving these early forms of some of Morris's finest love stories, I would like to stress once again their pattern – misery or boredom relieved by a more of less supernatural creature in an Earthly Paradise sweeping round a central Palace of Art, who imposes conditions or taboos which cannot be broken without disaster, but usually are. This pattern fitted quite well what Morris had to say in 'The First Earthly Paradise.' To include them in the second, he had to alter the tone, change the atmosphere, modify the moral, which meant to revise them out of recognition.

Meanwhile, Morris's ideas on the Earthly Paradise were maturing and in a single but not short poem he played out the whole gamut of his thoughts on this fascinating subject. *The Life and Death of Jason*, if not envisioned while Morris was still at Red House, was written between the time he left that paradise in 1865 and 1867, when it was published. The voyage of the Argo contains stopovers at every Great Good Place (or Great No-Place) imagined by the Greeks and Romans, who, after all, invented all those Elysian spots which continue to haunt the imagination of Western man. More than ever, shall we say, now that Homer's literal delights have mingled with the mandala's metaphysical overtones. In Jason's day flourished the classic Golden Age in its every nuance and Morris was careful not only to describe but to assess from his maturing point of view every shade of Golden Age meaning and value.

In September 1864 menacing clouds began to gather over the idyll at Red House. Burne-Jones's little son caught scarlet fever; when his mother caught it, the result was a drawn-out dangerous illness frightening to her husband, himself poorly, and the Morrises. Next Morris himself 'caught a chill on a wet, cold journey between London and Upton, which brought on a severe attack of rheumatic fever. For some time he was wholly crippled.' (Mackail I, 163). Suddenly, the more or less daily trip from Red House to London became for both the 'ailing' old friends unbearable either to perform or think about. Red House, begun during the hot summer of 1859, faced north and was made more than ordinarily cold by the gales which swept Bexley Heath in winter. Burne-Jones was forced to take his family to London in order to be near doctors and his daily work, and the dream of building a new wing to Red House had to be dropped. Giving up the old plan for a joint home was a deep disappointment to Morris, now bed-ridden, and the prospect, slowly forcing itself on his mind, of having himself to abandon the scene of so much creative fun and friendship was devastating. When beginning to recuperate a bit toward the end of October he wrote a letter to Burne-Jones dated 'In bed, Red House' which gives an idea of his misery:

As to our palace of art, I confess your letter was a blow to me at first, though hardly an unexpected one: in short I cried, but I have got over it now; of course I see it from your point of view but I like the idea of not giving it up for good even if it is delusive. But now I am only thirty years old; I shan't always have the rheumatism, and we shall have lots of jolly years of invention and lustre plates together I hope.

(Quoted in Mackail I, 164)

However, the 'lustre plates,' as brightly arranged as possible over his wound, could not effectively hide, let alone cure it. Once Morris had finally tugged himself loose from Red House, which was not until November 1865, he 'never set eyes on it again, confessing that the sight of it would be more than he could bear.' (Mackail I, 165) His illness, which he must for a time have feared was mortal, and which ended in the forced abandonment of his 'Palace of Art' with its gorgeous gardens and freighted orchards, seems to have put an end to his ever-increasing hope that an actual Golden Age could be revived in a truly Earthly Paradise. He eased his heart-break in *The Life and Death of Jason*, which he probably began during the last sad months at Red House and finished in 1867.

Jason strikes me as one long farewell to Red House or, rather, a dozen separate farewells piled one on another. With the help of these Morris seems to have convinced himself at last that the Golden Age is only a dream – a dream born of man's unconquerable unease, anxiety, inadequacy, laziness, physical afflictions, and fear of death – while the Earthly Paradise is essentially a mental pattern of repose from care which can be 'realised to a point in the decorative arts he practised but not in nature for more than a summer day.' The thoroughness with which in *Jason* Morris canvases and tests, as it were, all the classical concepts of the Earthly Paradise is tinged, for all the easy beauty of the verse, with desperation. Looked at this way, *Jason* is often deeply moving and not a little pitiful. How writers on Morris like Dixon Scott, Clutton-Brock,

Philip Henderson and Mackail himself can harp on the notion that *Jason* is a poem of mere escapism – not a losing battle for hopes indispensable to Morris's well-being – escapes me entirely. Not to see that the power which drives the great river of song forward is scourged hope, even despair, is obtuse. Only persons who had never read what Morris wrote or had not read it with sympathy and attention could conclude that every vestige of the painful reality of life is rejected in *Jason*, every chance of facing facts refused. The most eloquent exponent of such condemnation is probably Dixon Scott in an essay in *Primitiae* (1912, 232–3), who holds that Morris quite consciously aimed at nothing in his post-*Guenevere* poems but word-woven textiles and rhetorical ceramics. In the interval between *Guenevere* and *Jason,* says Scott, 'he had married, had built himself a house, had laid out his life like a garden, and had settled down into a smug social philosophy.'

To have lashed himself, fought for a strange poignancy struggled and burned in the throes of creative desire, would have been to have broken the precepts of his own kingdom absurdly; to write smoothly and easily, to make versification a sunny aid to his enjoyment of the visible world and the untroubled play of his senses (which was the secret sum of his desires) was established as his honest duty. . . . Surely no poet ever wrote so much with such a small outlay of fatigue. . . . The act of creation for him was simply a jolly recreation : he would not allow it to become anything more. He resolutely refused to enter those dark inner chambers of the mind where the last efforts of the imagination take place in torment, and the supreme revelations are received. He never wrought himself into a fever or indulged in any spiritual wrestlings; rather, he used his art as a source of relief, to relax the pressure of real life.

It hardly needs to be pointed out that most art is used to relax the pressure of real life, and no poetry more so, perhaps, than Morris's own *Guenevere* volume.

Most poets are not born 'lisping in numbers;' and that odd activity begins only after lone 'crying in the night.' In *Jason* Morris simply drops the high-wire contortions of the early volume for a new stance: steadier, larger, more relaxed, and elegiac as befits this monumental farewell to his Palace of Art and its never-to-be-repeated happiness. In deciding to leave his home, he had wandered through many dark chambers of the mind and driven his imagination to those efforts that take place in torment. If Red House itself was built as an escape from the industrial ugliness of London and the class-conscious ugliness of Victorian society, *Jason* represents Morris's renunciation of this refuge – a misery which hardly deserves to be belittled. The poet had every right to complain and collapse. Instead, he faced his fate, reviewed past joys, and pondered at length why Golden Age conditions achieved in Earthly Paradises cannot be prolonged. Perhaps they should never even be dreamt of – except that the Happy Garden dream is hopelessly embedded in human nature.

It is just possible that Morris, recovering strength after his dangerous illness, had a superstitious reason for retelling the story of Jason. Perhaps the ancient dream would not altogether die, and *Jason* itself, which told of the sacrifice of one Good Place after another, was whimsically intended to promote an instauration. After all, we know Morris never stopped trying to create with his many arts and ideas various approximations to an earthly enceinte stuffed with Gold-Age blessings. Though Blake and so many other idealists back to Plato had held that 'All Forms are Perfect in the Poet's Mind but these are not abstracted or compounded from Nature, but are from the Imagination,' Morris had had too near a success to quite believe this. Most of us tend to overlook, I think, a preposterous reason for his writing about Jason besides the elegiac. He was perhaps impressed by a passage in Virgil's Fourth Eclogue, which so eloquently prophesies the return of the lost Golden Age simultaneously with the birth of the son of Virgil's friend, the consul Pollio. For centuries readers have been so bemused by this prediction of the Golden Age to come that Pollio's baby has been identified with figures as disparate as Augustus Caesar and Jesus while Virgil's preconditions for the return have been overlooked. Before man and nature will be reborn together and in perfect chime with one another, Virgil insists that battles must cease and ships stop ploughing the tender breast of the ocean. This will not happen, however, until another Trojan War has been fought and a second Argo launched to suffer the disillusions of the paradise islands. Jason must sail and suffer again if he is fully to digest the lessons of his first wanderings. Perhaps the second Trojan War and the new voyage of the Argonauts were intended to give later poets a chance to draw the philosophy and symbology hidden in the old story. Only after they have been thoroughly understood will all things be well, the earth yielding her fruits unforced, trees sweating honey, herds grazing in peace, men enjoying infinite leisure through termless lives. Back in the *Guenevere* days Morris had written several scenes of a Greco-Trojan cycle which still exist. Was it only necessary now to send Jason a-voyaging once more to fulfill Virgil's conditions for something like instant paradise on earth? Perhaps such a hidden hope kept Morris from collapse and made *Jason* a poem too sober, epic-like, and philosophical for inclusion in *The Earthly Paradise,* as that book was first conceived. *Jason* is at once a farewell to the paradise Morris has lost, a description of all lost paradises, and yet ... perhaps ... possibly ... a prelude to fresh and different paradisal experience.

It is time to give a brief review of the paradises Jason lost and emphasise their loss in relation to that of Red House. To begin with, Jason was reared by the centaur Chiron on the lower slopes of Mt Pelion in a wood

where his unhappy father prays his son may be forever spared the burden
of a crown. He would have him know only

> 'The garments of the spotted leopard's hide,
> The bed of bear-skin in the hollow hill,
> The bath within the pool of some green rill;
> There shall the quick-eyed centaurs be thy friends . . .
> And when the spring brings love, then mayst thou find
> In some fair grassy place, the wood-nymphs kind,
> And choose thy mate, and with her, hand in hand,
> Go wandering through the blossoming sweet land;
> And naught of evil there shall come to thee,
> But like the golden age shall all things be . . .'
>
> (Bk. I)

This passage, which reflects Morris's early days in Epping Forest and
Woodford Hall, is not an elaborate *pairidaëza*, but suggests here, at the
very beginning of the poem, the simple moral which a survey of Jason's
life and death leaves with us at the end. Ignoring his father's prayer for
him, he is soon off to bring home the Golden Fleece and recover his lost
kingdom. In Colchis, chief city of the realm of Medea's father, the
Argonauts find a unique mandalic enclosure:

> In such a hall as there has never been
> Before or afterwards, since Ops was queen.
>   The pillars, made the mighty roof to hold,
> The one was silver and the next was gold,
> All down the hall; the roof, of some strange wood
> Brought over sea, was dyed as red as blood . . .
> Midmost the hall, two fair streams trickled down
> O'er wondrous gem-like pebbles, green and brown,
> Betwixt smooth banks of marble, and therein
> Bright-coloured fish shone through the water thin. . . .
>
> (Bk. VI)

Lightly clothed girls move and sing among the pillars, but the Argonauts,

> O'er-burdened with delight, still dreaded death;
> Nor did they think that they might long draw breath
> In such an earthly Paradise as this,
> But looked to find sharp ending to their bliss.
>
> (Bk. VI)

They knew that inside the great structure, 'within the brazen temple
gates/The guardian of the place forever waits.' Luckily, Medea, a white
witch who can be-spell even the dragon-protector of the Fleece, falls in
love with Jason and helps the Argonauts escape with their loot. She is the
larger-than-life woman who dances at the centre of her father's Earthly
Paradise. With her help Jason is destined to win back his father's king-

dom; also, to lose his life when he breaks a taboo-like promise to love her alone.

During the long voyage back to Greece every facet of Earthly Paradise lay-out, intertwined with every nuance of Golden Age bliss, is lovingly encountered and reluctantly abandoned. It is crucial to note that this canvassing of classical paradises, occupying almost half of Morris's story, does not occur in his classical sources for Jason's adventures, neither Hyginus, Ovid nor the others. It was added, I can only suppose, to give the poet ample space to mull over and assess the meaning of the Red House experience – also, to bid a fitting series of mournful farewells to that abandoned Eden. It seems to have been at this time that he perceived that the mandala structure is a projection into consciousness of a configuration treasured in the unconscious psyche, while the Golden Age is a mere dream born of discontent, laziness, frustration and fear of death. The first is helpful to a mind in search of reassurance, poise and imperturbability; the second debilitating and dangerous because untrue and impossible. This distinction is pointed to by Morris when Jason, piloting the strayed Argo, seeks to cheer his followers in the only way he can think of by declaring that they are approaching cliché Golden Age country – not

> '. . . bound for Pluto's kingdom drear,
> But for fair forests, plentiful of beasts,
> Where, innocent of craft, with joyous feasts
> The wise folk live as in the golden age,
> Not reddening spears and swords in useless rage;
> Nor need they houses, but in fair-wrought cave
> Their bodies from the winter's cold they save;
> Nor labour they at all, or weave, or till,
> For everything the kind land bears at will.
> Doubt not at all that they will welcome us
> As very Gods, with all things plenteous.'
>
> So spake he, knowing nought of that same land . . .
>
> (Bk. X)

The country they stray into actually drives them hysterical with fear:

> All seemed as in a dream, where deadly fear
> Is mingled with the most familiar thing;
> And in the cup we see the serpent's sting,
> And common speech we answer with a scream.
>
> (Bk. X)

Actually, the wild folk they encountered, though naked, 'houseless and lawless,' were relatively gentle and had, as Medea explains, a religion of sorts with groves for temples in which 'They offer strangers up in sacrifice' – a doom the Argonauts escaped. Not too strangely, it was in their country that Orpheus, the minstrel of the expedition, began a 'hear-piercing "Alas! for Saturn's days of gold" ' when there was no toil, no war, no pestilence, no biting frost in winter (though the season was so-called),

> 'And on the crown of July days,
> All heedless of the mid-day blaze,
> Unshaded by the rosy bowers,
> Unscorched beside the tulip flowers,
> The snow-white naked girl might stand;
> Or fearless thrust her tender hand
> Amidst the thornless rose-bushes . . .

> 'Alas! what profit now to tell
> The long unweary lives of men . . .
> Unbent, unwrinkled, beautiful,
> Regarding not death's flower-crowned skull . . .
> In such love as leaves hope behind.
>   'Alas, the vanished days of bliss!
> Will no God send some dream of this.
> That we may know what it has been?'

(Bk. X)

This can hardly be other than a knell for the passing of the Golden Age side of the Red House dream which illness, bleak winds and the threat of death had overshadowed and destroyed. According to Orpheus (and his creator) the only recourse from agony like this is the gift of Bacchus, whom he calls upon to

> ' . . . think of us
> And drive away these piteous,
> Formless and wailing thoughts, that press
> About our hour of happiness.'

The poet ends this elegy with eyes shining in 'the red torchlight with unwilling tears' like those which Morris shed more than once on giving up what he considered an actual, if momentary, taste of Golden Age experience at Red House.

From here on, Orpheus-Morris undertakes to refute such delusive Golden Age songs as those the Sirens sang – usually considered beyond recall! – to the Argonauts. To the Sirens' boasts of their fadeless beauty Orpheus repostes sarcastically,

> O fair as the doomed victim's wreath,
> O fair as deadly sleep and death,
> What will ye with them, earthly men,
> To mate your three-score years and ten?
> Toil rather, suffer and be free,
> Betwixt the green earth and the sea.

(Bk. XIV)

To which the Sirens, who are mermaids with their well known passion for submariners, beg them to come to their underwater gardens and the pillared palace surrounded by woods of chrysolite.

> Poor souls, ye shall not be alone,
> For o'er the floors of pale blue stone
> All day such feet as ours shall pass,
> And, 'twixt the glimmering walls of glass,
> Such bodies garlanded with gold,
> So faint, so fair, shall ye behold,
> And clean forget the treachery
> Of changing earth and tumbling sea.

There are about ten pages of these antiphonal chanties, ending when Orpheus, sounding like a true-born Englishman, bullies the oarsmen into rowing past the temptresses' field of magnetism. The gravamen of his last song is simple: rather than live half-dead forever with nereids, Orpheus would rather be truly dead and dreaming, if the dead can dream, of the Red House mandala –

> . . . those fresh joys that once were mine,
> On this green fount of joy and mirth,
> The ever young and glorious earth;
> Then, helpless, shall I call to mind
> Thoughts of the sweet flower-scented wind,
> The dew, the gentle rain at night,
> The wonder-working snow and white,
> The song of birds, the water's fall,
> The sun that maketh bliss of all,
> Yea, this our toil and victory . . .

Or did the Sirens have the last word metaphysically as well as actually?

> Ah, will ye go, and whither then
>   Will ye go from us, soon to die,
> To fill your three-score years and ten,
>   With many an unnamed misery?
>
> And this wretchedest of all
>   That when upon your lovely eyes
> The last faint heaviness shall fall
>   Ye shall bethink you of our cries . . .

However, the lesson of Red House – that unalloyed Golden Age bliss is an illusion while the true paradisal experience, of inner equilibrium and peace, tends to occur where circles and squares have crystallised around a sacred centre for which a deity is desirable but dangerous if too humanly feminine – is clarified beyond doubt in the encounters with

Circe and Glauce. In contrast to the Argonauts, Medea has perfect genius for assessing the falseness of Golden Age promises. Beating about in the Mediterranean at night, the Argonauts see a light shining as from some great palace among trees and at dawn

> Their longing eyes beheld a lovely land,
> Green meadows rising o'er a yellow strand,
> Well-set with fair fruit-bearing trees, and groves
> Of thick-leaved elms, all populous of doves,
> And watered by a wandering clear green stream;
> And through the trees they saw a palace gleam
> Of polished marble, fair beyond man's thought.
>   There as they lay, the sweetest scents were brought
> By sighing winds across the bitter sea,
> And languid music breathed melodiously . . .
> The young men well-nigh wept, and e'en the wise
> Thought they had reached the gate of Paradise.
>
> (Bk. XIII)

Medea tells them to look on the uneasy animals that stalk the shore – once heroes like themselves but now forever condemned to moan in vain for women. Circe lives in

> A lovely pleasance, set with flowers, foursquare,
> On three sides ending in a cloister fair
> That hid the fair feet of a marble house,
> Carved thick with flowers and stories amorous,
> And midmost of the slender garden trees
> A gilded shrine stood, set with images,
> Wherefrom the never-dying fire rose up
> Into the sky, and a great jewelled cup
> Ran over ever from a runlet red
> Of fragrant wine . . .

Its geometry makes this enclosure sound very mandalic but not its inmates, half-naked girls who, seizing an unwary traveller, would lead him into a 'dark cool cloister' from which he emerged 'uncouth with spots and dangerous of claw.'

Medea runs the gauntlet of these despairing beasts to be shriven of past sin and advised about the future by her kinswoman Circe, the deathless sorceress of this temple,

> Upon whose knees an open book did press,
> Wherein strange things the Gods knew not, she read;
> A golden vine-bough wreathed her golden head,
> And her fair body a thin robe did touch
> With silken folds, but hid it not so much
> As the cool ripple hides Diana's feet . . .

Having learned from Circe how to guide them home, Medea orders the
Argonauts away from this paradise-garden (so much more like Tasso's or
Spenser's than like Homer's).

> With that they left the fair death-bearing shore,
> Not gladlier than some fair young man may leave
> His love, upon the odorous summer eve,
> When she turns sighing to her father's house,
> And leaves him there alone and amorous,
> Heartsick with all that shame has let him see,
> Grieved that no bolder he has dared to be.

On the other hand, the Garden of the Hesperides seems more lovely,
mandala-like and topographically peaceful, while the girls at the centre
are no sirens.

> But in the midst there was a grassy space,
> Raised somewhat over all the flowery place,
> On marble terrace-walls wrought like a dream;
> And round about it ran a clear blue stream,
> Bridged o'er with marble steps, and midmost there
> Grew a green tree, whose smooth grey boughs did bear
> Such fruit as never man elsewhere had seen,
> For 'twixt the sunlight and the shadow green
> Shone out fair apples of red gleaming gold.
> Moreover round the tree, in many a fold,
> Lay coiled a dragon, glittering little less
> Than that which his eternal watchfulness
> Was set to guard; nor yet was he alone,
> For from the daisied grass about him shone
> Gold raiment wrapping round two damsels fair,
> And one upon the steps combed out her hair,
> And with shut eyes sung low as in a dream;
> And one stood naked in the cold blue stream . . .
>
> (Bk. XIV)

All seems arranged for an amorous garden party, but Medea assures the
sailors that these are ' "the wise Hesperides," ' who preside over the only
spot of authentic Golden Age life that remains.

> 'And where the while they watch, scarce can a God
> Set foot upon the fruit-besprinkled sod
> That no snow ever covers? therefore haste,
> Nor yet in wandering your fair lives waste;
> For these are as the Gods, nor think of us,
> Nor to their eyes can aught be glorious
> That son of man can do . . .'

Once more the Argonauts row reluctantly away while the priestesses of the centre dance round their orange-tree singing,

> 'Lo, such as is this garden green
> In days past, all the world has been,
> And what we know all people knew
> But this, that unto worse all grew.

> 'But since the golden age is gone,
> This little place is left alone,
> Unchanged, unchanging, watched of us.
> The daughters of wise Hesperus.'

Here Morris definitely gives up the Golden Age. Lovely female influences had hung over Red House too but had been no more willing than the Hesperides, it seems, to save their men from strife, regret and fear.

> 'Neither from us shall wisdom go
> To fill the hungering hearts of men,
> Lest to them threescore years and ten
> Come but to seem a little day,
> Once given, taken soon away.
> Nay, rather let them find their life
> Bitter and sweet, fulfilled of strife.
> Restless with hope, vain with regret,
> Trembling with fear, most strangely set
> 'Twixt memory and forgetfulness;
> So more shall joy be, troubles less,
> And surely when all this is past,
> They shall not want their rest at last.'

Arrived back in Greece at last and having taken, with Medea's indispensable aid, possession of his father's stolen kingdom, Jason, just as Circe and the Hesperides had darkly hinted, ' "wearies of his great felicity,/Like fools, for whom fair heaven is not enough ..." ' (Bk. XVII) From the beginning Medea has been presented as the golden girl incomparable, lovely, wise, resourceful, determined to make the most of the human life to which she has condemned herself far from her native land. After ten years she is still hopelessly in love with Jason while he has decided to supplant her with a young Greek wife. Wearied with mortals, the beautiful barbarian witch from Colchis decides to let his life follow the dreary course of earthly men's. Accordingly she lets him pursue Glauce to the very temenos-centre of a forest-surrounded marble fane,

> Not great indeed, but builded cunningly,
> And set about with carven images,
> Built in a close of slim young apple-trees;

A marble fountain was there nigh the door,
And there the restless water trickled o'er
A smooth-hewn basin coloured like a shell,
And from the wet pink lip thereof it fell
By many a thin streak into a square pool . . .

All goes well till his wedding day when the Greek princess, as everyone
knows, was burned to a cinder and Medea vanished forever. Broken in
health and spirit, Jason wandered about muttering things like

'Once did I win a noble victory,
I won a kingdom, and I cast it by
For rest and peace, and rest and peace are gone.
I had a fair love, that loved me alone,
And made me that I am in all men's eyes;
And like my hard-earned kingdom, my fair prize,
I cast my tender heart, my Love away . . .'

until the sternpost (often the female figure-head) of the long-beached
Argo, loosening when he was underneath it, put him out of his misery.
It would be hard to link these episodes with events in Morris's life, but
the forced abandonment of Red House, with his guardian goddesses still
unhung, may have made him feel that he had betrayed the sacred centre
of his 'created' mandala while the Golden Age atmosphere had simultaneously evaporated. Apparently he felt the tragedy was not only his but
of his own making.

Jason, more than any poem composed before 1867, seems to examine and
criticise the premises of Morris's plan, conceived in the early days at Red
house, for a collection of many-times-told tales to be called *The Earthly
Paradise*. From the first he probably intended these stories, often dressed-
up fairy-tales, not only to please his children when older or to challenge
Burne-Jones's winsome way with nudes, but to present his growing ideas
about human life and values. At first the core stories were a number of
apologues stressing the notion that man's search for peace, security and
completeness can be satisfied through the practice of bravery, honesty,
humility, and kindness. Then there enters the tales a Palace of Art where
all things are made, preferably by oneself, rich, restful, and impertur-
bably lovely. The general plan of the palace and its surroundings I have
called mandalic though the word was unknown to Morris and has been
popularised only in our own day by the Swiss psychiatrist Jung as, of the
many 'archetypal' dreams by which man lives and keeps his sanity, the
culminating glory. Jung stresses the essential inwardness of this dream,
the form of which is held to derive from unconscious levels of the mind.

How it got there might be partially explained in terms of man's long pre-history if only we knew enough about it. At the centre of the mandala is a female figure, but to identify her with a real girl or woman can place the healing power of the dream in considerable jeopardy. The trouble becomes even worse when the centre is placed in the Elysian Fields, Fortunate Isles or Unfallen Eden where Golden Age conditions of unremitting youth, love, ease, concord and springtime are conceived of as real or quite possible. Actually, the mandala formation is more or less present in every enclosed orchard-and-garden which swirls in blossom and flower around a well built house, and can be helpful to the fidgety, afflicted or simply tired. Such an Earthly Paradise has been the heart of every dream of country retirement for hundreds of years, shadowed only by bad weather and winter sadness. It is the installation at the centre of the paradisal mandala of a real girl in the role of Tārā, Goddess of Mercy, that brings trouble. This real-life deity, far from guaranteeing endless peace and bliss, can introduce confusion and strife. There is some evidence, even before Morris left Red House, that Jane was beginning to play this latter role. Then came the severe illness which drove Morris from his 'Palace of Art.' It was this blow, combined with growing experience of what may be expected from life, that led to *The Life and Death of Jason*, a tale which so thoroughly, however reluctantly, discredited the Golden Age ideas that it turned into a modest epic not only in size but in thoughtfulness.

There is little doubt that the conclusions reached in *Jason* influenced the ideas and working-out of the *Earthly Paradise* as published between 1868 and 1870. Drawing a line of demarcation between Golden Age and mandalic paradise concepts, though this can never be thorough or even desirable, led to the recasting of several of the early tales, the abandonment of some projected ones, and the choice of new tales to be included. Generally, the Golden Age is given up while the mandala, the healing dream half-in, half-out, of reality – half in the world, half creatable in art – becomes more important. However, there is usually trouble with the goddess at the sacred centre – such trouble as was to be the source of great personal calamity to Morris at this time and therefore the overriding concern of the whole published *Paradise* – the catalyst of his most abysmal failure in life and of his most imposing success in poetry.

V Paradise Disarrayed by a 'Belle Dame Sans Merci', 1866-1870

The crisis in Morris's life with Jane is expressed in many stories and lyrics in *The Earthly Paradise*; in *Poems By the Way* (published in 1891, but much of it written in what Mackail in 1899 called 'those stormy years of *The Earthly Paradise* time and the time following it'); in the collection of MS. poems in the British Museum called *Short Poems and Sonnets* and known, more or less revised, in May's *Collected Works* (XXIV) as 'Poems of the Earthly Paradise Time about 1865-70'; and, finally, in a group of verses edited by May as Volume I of the two Supplementary Volumes of 1936 as 'Poems of the Earthly Paradise Period.' Everyone has heard of the hopeless (for all parties) triangle that developed among Morris, Jane, and Rossetti between, say, 1865 and 1874, the year Rossetti left Kelmscott Manor – hopeless enough to cause Morris distress from which he (or at least his marriage) never recovered, to put Rossetti through two nervous breakdowns, and subject Jane to a series of backaches that threatened to turn her into an incurable invalid.

But, first of all, what did love mean to Morris before 'the stormy years'? We remember the small boy devouring volume after volume of Walter Scott in opening after opening of Epping Forest. But Scott's love stories were conventional or even banal. Unlike Shelley before him or Charlotte Brontë later, Sir Walter seems to have been little influenced by the love story that dominated European literature for more than a hundred years: Rousseau's *Julie; ou, La Nouvelle Héloïse*. In this novel, love is conceived of as a union not only of bodies but of tastes, mental powers, ideals and ideas so peculiarly congruous as to make the lovers, apart from a few primary characteristics, indistinguishable halves of a perfect whole. Shelley summed up this conception, which dominated most of his own eroticism, in quaintly 'scientific' language: 'The intellectual faculties, the imagination, the functions of sense, have their respective requisitions on the sympathy of corresponding powers in other human beings.' To find these 'requisitions' united in a beautiful woman was to know love; to miss finding them was to suffer the fate of a Werther, Manfred, or Alastor. With Scott, bluffer than his fellow romantics and certainly no metaphysician, love was love. Something that everybody just naturally knows about. Of course Dy Vernon would have enchanted Shelley himself with her wit and bravery and beauty but we are never told what attracted Frank Osbaldistone to her, while Edward of Ravenscrift, Scott's most Byronic figure, apparently loved the pale wraith of Lammermoor because he had saved her from a bull. With women half educated, if educated at all, Victorian dreamers of a Shelleyan 'affinity' (not much different, really, from Milton's 'speaking help,' failing to find whom a man 'may despair even unto madness') were at a great disadvantage. For them love almost had to consist of sexual attraction plus, well . . . good nature.

By contrast, one Victorian who married an almost Shelleyan affinity was Browning, whose *Men and Women* was much admired and touchingly reviewed by Morris in *The Oxford and Cambridge Magazine* for March, 1856. In fact Browning, who adored Shelley, writes rather little of the shared life of body, intellect and spirit, though he may have insisted on it in everyday intercourse with E.B.B., as is suggested in 'A Woman's Last Word,' which Morris quotes as 'perfect in thought as in music.'

> Be a god and hold me
>   With a charm –
> Be a man, and fold me
>   With thine arm !
>
> Teach me, only teach, Love !
>   As I ought
> I will speak thy speech, Love,
>   Think thy thought.
>
> Meet, if you require it,
>   Both demands,
> Laying flesh and spirit
>   In thy hands ! . . .

It is, strangely, in his comments on 'Childe Roland,' a young knight thrown, in almost Icelandic isolation, into the jaws of horror, that young Morris had most to say about what Browning (or at least his reviewer) meant by love.

In my own heart I think I love this poem the best of all in these volumes.

And yet I scarcely know; for this and all the others seem to me but a supplement to the love-poems . . .

And in these love-poems of Robert Browning there is one thing that struck me particularly; that is their intense, unmixed love; love for the sake of love, and if that is not obtained, disappointment comes, falling-off, misery. I suppose the same kind of thing is to be found in all very earnest love-poetry, but I think more in him than in almost anybody else.

'Any wife to any husband,' 'The last ride together,' – read them, and I think you will see what I mean. I cannot say it clearly, it cannot be said so but in verse; love for love's sake, the only true love, I must say. – Pray Christ some of us attain to it before we die !

Browning's most beautiful poem on 'love for love's sake' was, for Morris, 'Evelyn Hope.' In this piece the poet says he claims the dead girl for his own love's sake:

> Delay'd it may be for more lives yet
> Through worlds I shall traverse, not a few:
> Much is to learn and much to forget
> Ere the time be come for taking you.

One must love in death as well as life, in rejecting as well as embracing, eternity as well as time, if he is to stretch his grasp of life to the furthest. In other words, Browning's 'love for love's sake' was Shelleyan affinity thrilling off into infinite universes throughout endless incarnations. This idea entranced young Morris and later he sometimes wrote, in frustration, of being willing or even anxious to pass through the 'jaws of death' in order to get perfect rapport with a loved woman in worlds purified of modern dross. Pray God, indeed, that he should find Browning-esque love on earth!

As we know from previous chapters Morris was scourged, as it were, from childhood with a fear of death generated, it would seem, by early weakness, rheumatic illness, stories of a baby brother's demise and his father's death when William was only thirteen. Such fear of, or at least preoccupation with, death, hardly conceivable by most of us at any age, is said when it occurs to be associated with feelings of self-doubt, insecurity, misgiving, – of blind alleys, hidden enemies, hostile wastes – all of which may in desperation be blamed on some fault or self-imputed sin. Bearing all this in mind, it will not be hard for us to understand that more than, or perhaps in addition to, Shelley-Browning love Morris needed from women something which perhaps he had never obtained in full measure from his mother or sisters. I mean the protection of a goddess like Tārā – a beautiful Jane – to enclose him in her arms forever in the throne-room of a castle set among gardens, encircled by non-existent walls surmounted by armed female angels, with the orchard of Eden swirling all around. It is exactly in this shape, really, that Eden was often presented in the 'painted' medieval books which were Morris's favourite reading at many times during his life. It was something as nearly as possible like this immemorial dream that Morris had sought to recreate for himself at Red House. Recall the great sanctuary he had planned for his domestic ceremonials among a dozen women from Venus to St Catherine, armed with the invincible power of love.

It is no wonder, then, that Morris's first full-length portrait of a woman was Medea of the *Jason* poem. Partly, or largely, I think, it was on her account that what was planned as simply one more earthly paradise story grew into an epic-like volume. His master Chaucer had of course presented Medea most sympathetically and even made 'Duc Iasoun' the villain of her story in *The Legend of Good Women*. (It seems to have been Euripides who began the exoneration of the barbarian princess.) Morris did not, like Chaucer, suppress the episode of the murdered children altogether, but he left no doubt of her surpassing wisdom, worth, and beauty. After all, Medea had saved Jason's life from wild beasts and the dragon at Colchis, delivered the Fleece to him, and forsaken her native land to protect him and the Argonauts from multitudinous physical and spiritual dangers among the paradise islands that strewed the way back to Greece. Finally, by bringing about the death of the usurping King Pelias, she had restored Jason to his inheritance. In a word, she had herself provided all the wisdom, done all the work, achieved for Jason and the Argonauts all the glory of the immortal voyage. When Pelias is disposed of and Medea hurries back to tell Jason that the voyage and its purpose are indeed complete,

> . . . for one moment did he start aback,
> As if some guardian spirit of the land
> Had come upon him; but the next, his hand
> Had caught her slim wrist, and he shouted out:
> "Ashore, O heroes! and no more have doubt
> That all is well done we have wished were done;
> By this my love, by this the glorious one,
> The saviour of my life, the Queen of Love . . ."
>
> (Bk. XVI)

Later on, just before betraying Medea's faithful love by seeking to marry Glauce, he ponders how the gold-haired barbarian, 'not the least of goddesses,' has filled his kingdom with joy, causing folk to forget pain and making even 'Death and Fear' but 'idle words.' Here we have what had been, were, and would continue to be key words in Morris's conception of love. More than ten years earlier, in 'Golden Wings,' a story published in the *Oxford and Cambridge Magazine* in 1856, the hero had told how the self-surrender of a loving woman cancelled all his fears: 'then all doubt and sorrow went quite away from me; . . . then at once I felt that I was beautiful and brave and true . . .' Love is the only power on earth that can cancel the gnawing of self-doubt, the dread of villainy in ambush, of plague that steals through the night – in other words, the fear, and especially the fear of death, that for Morris was life's least bearable torment. Thus 'love for love's sake' was for him really 'love for fortification's sake.' Love gave him self-confidence and a vocation – a vision of what the world should be (that is, something worthy of the beloved's poised sword and goodness and beauty) along with the zest and power to work at building such a world. It gave him renewed strength when tired, solace when afflicted, strong round arms to shield him from his foes.

Most of all, it naughted in lovers' bliss the mere thought, not to mention the terror, of death. Here was the sovereign salve for neurasthenia with its crippling worries, fatigues and undermining attacks of inadequacy – the cave lighted to its depths, and now seen to be monsterless, by a woman's eyes. Of course most men – and women – must have found some such salvation and fortification of the personality in love, and it is possible that it is largely the loss of these gifts of love which causes the caved-in breast, the dried-out mind, the inner and outward collapse known only by stereotyped expressions such as disappointment in love or heart-break.

Medea, as her character unfolded through the long poem, seems to have become Morris's lover par excellence right down to the tips of 'the fair fingers' that brought Jason 'such mighty aid.' (Bk. XVII) In his heart Jason knew himself a fool to cast off for pretty Glauce the stunning beauty of a face lighted by ' "clear-seeing wisdom, better than a host/ Against ... foes," ' and filled with ' "truth and constancy/Thou wilt not know again ..." ' (Bk. XVI)

> 'For me she gave up country, kin, and name,
> For me she risked tormenting and the flame,
> The anger of the Gods and curse of man;
> For me she came across the waters wan
> Through many woes, and for my sake did go
> Alone, unarmed, to my most cruel foe, . . .
> Making me king of all my father's lands . . .'
>
> (Bk. XVII)

Had Morris designed the tutelary goddess for Red House six years later than he did, one of them, and perhaps the most important, would surely have been Medea the great witch-princess of Colchis in whom both Euripides and Chaucer had already divined a superb human being. I hardly think that Morris could have based her portrait on any woman in the Red House circle though there may be in her touches of both Jane and Georgiana Burne-Jones. Mainly, however, she is surely an elaborate and loving dream-picture of Morris's perfect or quintessential woman. She is the dancing Tārā of Red House elaborated in Morris's mind in the years after Jane, languorous and unable to keep up with the rush of her husband's proliferating work, had failed to play that divine role. Medea taught him how to say farewell again to the Kentish Eden disguised in one classical paradise after another. Long before 1867, when *Jason* was finished and published, Jane, once the mistress of the Red House revels, had drifted away from Morris and was on the point of subjecting him, for he still loved her deeply, to every nuance of pain, every sting of inadequacy, inferiority, fear and failure which, precisely, he 'was not made' – that is, was not born or in any way prepared – 'to bear.'

(Sup. I, 539)

As everyone knows, what is called a 'triangle' had developed over the years, with Morris, Jane, and Rossetti marking the sharp elbows. Ever since the move from Red House to London, Rossetti had been sketching, drawing and painting Jane at his studio in Cheyne Walk and Jane, it seems, had been growing apart from her husband. It was when Morris began to flesh out *The Earthly Paradise* with a view to completion and publication that we get, from his own pen, some idea of a crisis developing, not fast perhaps but fatally, with something like steam-roller speed and sureness. It is not till the latter half of the *Earthly Paradise* (covering the months from 'September' through 'February') that we get introductory lyrics, revisions of early tales like 'East of the Sun' and 'The Hill of Venus,' and new stories like 'The Death of Paris,' 'The Man Who Never Laughed Again,' 'The Lovers of Gudrun' and 'The Ring Given to Venus' which indicate the full range of his suffering.

It must have been some time in 1868 that the marriage bed fell completely apart. At first, Morris cannot understand when or how or why he has lost Jane, but he becomes steadily less hopeful of regaining her, even in night-dreams. He has lost, or is fast losing, not merely the prop of his roof-tree, the mother of his children, but his diademed queen of love and beauty – a great tutelary being about whose husband a dozen Jane-personae bearing the arms and insignia of saints from Venus to Catherine were to have performed a protective sword-dance. As the dream of Medea faded, Morris was left defenceless against the complete loss of Jane, once the pivot of the most 'real' paradise he had known. Now that Red House with its gardens was gone, he had to recreate, somehow, that sacred ambience, but creation without a centre was impossible. The experience was dreadful, overwhelming, filled with despair, and sometimes seemed to be leading him to the brink.

His eventual salvation came, probably, from the fact that he could pour his despair into the collection of poems he was already writing or revising when he first became fully aware of the terrible emptiness in his life, the unquenchable ache in the breast. Of course, there was his art work for the Firm but it was probably his lyric gift which helped him most. Some lines from the sad songs he wrote at this time will give an idea of Morris's condition in 1869 and '70. Apparently the lovers had had quarrels of a sort before the long and horrible dichotomising began. For instance, in the lyric for 'July' (one lyric poem precedes each month's pair of narratives in *The Earthly Paradise*) Morris, recalling how happy they had been on waking one morning, begs Jane to 'be happy now!'

> Peace and content without us, love within
> That hour there was, now thunder and wild rain
> Have wrapped the cowering world, and foolish sin
> And nameless pride, have made us wise in vain!
> Ah, love! although the morn shall come again,

> And on new rose-buds the new sun shall smile,
> Can we regain what we have lost meanwhile?
>   E'en now the west grows clear of storm and threat,
> But midst the lightning did the fair sun die –
> – Ah, he shall rise again for ages yet,
> He cannot waste his life – but thou and I –
> Who knows if next morn this felicity
> My lips may feel, or if thou still shalt live
> This seal of love renewed once more to give?

It is hard to imagine what 'foolish sin' they had committed except, perhaps, some quarrel or in what lay their 'nameless pride' except in refusing to forgive each other immediately. The last lines are filled with
Morris's apparently unremitting concern with death, including Jane's,
though I do not think the last lines contain a murder threat! Their
alienation had hardly progressed beyond a spat or squabble.

However, the song for 'September,' preluding 'The Death of Paris'
and the revised 'East of the Sun,' lands us right in the middle of the
domestic disaster.

> Look long, O longing eyes and look in vain!
> Strain idly, aching heart, and yet be wise,
> And hope no more for things to come again
> That thou beheldest once with careless eyes!
> Like a new-wakened man thou art, who tries
> To dream again the dream that made him glad
> When in his arms his loving love he had.

In the song for 'October' the death-fear or rather -wish rises strongly to
the surface but he tells us he cannot cease loving though he now knows
love's high hope will never be fulfilled. The important tale for 'October'
is the really terrible 'Man Who Never Laughed Again.' The 'November'
poem, in which he addresses himself, tells of a home 'hung with pain'
from which he is too full of inner loneliness to flee to the lonely moon
outside:

> Yea, I have looked, and seen November there;
> The changeless seal of change it seemed to be,
> Fair death of things that, living once, were fair;
> Bright sign of loneliness too great for me,
> Strange image of the dread eternity,
> In whose void patience how can these have part,
> These outstretched feverish hands, this restless heart?

In 'December's' lyric, again addressed to himself, he mourns 'kindness
lost,' apparently forever, but cannot bring himself to curse what he has
once loved, and continues to hope, however despairingly, for the new day
that the New Year bells are supposed to ring in.

Ah! through the hush the looked-for midnight clangs!
And then, e'en while its last stroke's solemn drone
In the cold air by unlit windows hangs,
Out break the bells above the year fordone,
Change, kindness lost, love left unloved alone;
Till their despairing sweetness makes thee deem
Thou once wert loved, if but amidst a dream.

O thou who clingest still to life and love,
Though nought of good, no God thou mayst discern, . . .
Yet since thy weary lips no curse can learn,
Cast no least thing thou lovedst once away,
Since yet perchance thine eyes shall see the day.

January's stories, containing 'The Ring Given to Venus,' are introduced
by a mournful lyric lightened for a moment by what seemed a flash in
her loved eyes of the old affection. This is followed by a plea that she
'come back' bearing 'strange rest and dear among the long dull pain.'
But the flash was just that, and Morris's lost 'rest' still lost; those 'eyes of
heaven' were not destined, as he now felt confident, to fill his future day
'with utter rest.'

From this dull rainy undersky and low,
This murky ending of a leaden day,
That never knew the sun, this half-thawed snow,
These tossing black boughs faint against the grey
Of gathering night, thou turnest, dear, away
Silent, but with thy scarce-seen kindly smile
Sent through the dusk my longing to beguile.

There, the lights gleam, and all is dark without!
And in the sudden change our eyes meet dazed –
O look, love, look again! the veil of doubt
Just for one flash, past counting, then was raised! . . .

Whose doubt? Probably his but it could well have been Jane's bewilderment at finding her simple self married to this incomprehensible Renaissance genius. The 'February' lyric, introducing the climactic 'Hill of
Venus,' depressed and grey-shrouded beyond any story in the collection,
yields nothing more than a dreary gale which the poet sees sweeping
ahead into May itself, when he will still be wondering distractedly 'that
it liveth yet,/The useless hope, the useless craving pain . . .'
    This is all we can learn about Morris's marital crash from the poems-
of-the-months though Mackail tells us that 'in the verses that frame the
stories of *The Earthly Paradise* there is an autobiography so delicate and
so outspoken that it must be left to speak for itself.' (I, 210) However,
other lyrics written about this time (some published in 1891 in *Poems By*

the Way) make it clear that hope was 'long a-dying.' He simply could not forget 'the time that was not long ago' when 'Beneath my lips thy cheek did burn . . .'

> Wilt thou be glad upon the day
> When unto me this love shall be
> An idle fancy passed away,
> And we shall meet and smile [and] say
> "O wasted sighs of long ago!"
>
> Wilt thou rejoice that thou hast set
> Cold words, dull shows 'twixt hearts drawn close,
> That cold at heart I live on yet,
> Forgetting still that I forget
> The priceless days of long ago?
>
> (XXIV, 365)

For months she seemed often on the point of relenting:

> She wavered, stopped and turned, methought her eyes,
> The deep grey windows of her heart, were wet;
> Methought they softened with a new regret
> To note in mine unspoken miseries,
> And as a prayer from out my heart did rise
>   And struggled on my lips in shame's strong net,
>   She stayed me, and cried 'Brother!' Our lips met,
> Her dear hands drew me into Paradise.
>
> Sweet seemed that kiss till thence her feet were gone,
>   Sweet seemed the word she spake, while it might be
>   As wordless music – But truth fell on me,
> And kiss and word I knew, and, left alone,
> Face to face seemed I to a wall of stone,
>   While at my back there beat a boundless sea.
>
> (Sup. I, 538–9)

After several experiences of this kind, hope died indeed but not passionate longing:

> Strong are thine arms, O love, & strong
> Thine heart to live, and love, and long;
> But thou are wed to grief and wrong:
> Live, then, and long, though hope be dead! . . .
>
> (*Poems By the Way*)

Later in this poem, 'Hope Dieth, Love Liveth,' he addresses his own passion which shows no sign of deserting him, however long the road:

> I bless thee, O my love, who say'st:
> 'Mock not the thistle-cumbered waste; . . .
> The long years wear our hearts in vain . . .
> Our eyes gaze for no morning-star . . .
> Behold with lack of happiness
> The master, Love, our hearts did bless
> Lest we should think of him the less:
> Love dieth not, though hope is dead!'

He tells Jane that, no matter how inhumanly and irresponsibly she acts, his love will not entirely die, 'for fear and mockery/And shame' will not entirely kill it –

> Then hearken! thou who forgest day by day
>   No chain, but armour that I needs must wear
>   Although at whiles I deem it hard to bear,
> If thou to thine own work no hand will lay,
> That which I took I may not cast away,
>   Keep what I give till Death our eyes shall clear.
>
> (XXIV, 359)

Temporary release from pain sometimes came in dreams, but awakening, with its slow reassertion of empty, pointless pain, made him hate the day.

> O many-voiced strange morn, why must thou break
>   With vain desire the softness of my dream
>   Where she and I alone on earth did seem?
> How hadst thou heart from me that land to take
> Wherein she wandered softly for my sake
>   And I and she no harm of love might deem?
>
> (XXIV, 356)

The definitive realisation that 'Thy love is gone, poor wretch, thou art alone' (XXIV, 355) was dreadful. Often, now, his dreams filled his nights with almost as much horror as his days, as in 'The End of May' poem –

> Ah, through the tangled dream
> Where others have no grief
> Ever it fares with me
> That fears and treasons stream
> And dumb sleep slays belief . . .
> Until the hopeless light
> Wakes at the birth of June
> More lying tales to weave,
> More love in woe's despite,
> More hope to perish soon.
>
> (*Poems By the Way*)

What wonder that the May winds were howling when he awoke for it was only to his own solitary 'unlonged-for face!'

At times he felt the hand of death reaching for his lonely heart, as in 'Lonely Love and Loveless Death,' so beautifully and ironically illuminated with flowers and full-fruited trees in the *Book of Verse* he wrote out for Georgiana Burne-Jones in 1870. In this poem a dream of 'enfolding/Arms blessing the lover' carries him not to green pastures but to the very edge of 'The dark void.'

> O have I been hearkening
> To some dread new-comer?
> What chain is it bindeth,
> What curse is anigh,
> That the World is a-darkening
> Amidmost the summer,
> That the soft sunset blindeth
> And Death standeth by?
>
> Doth it wane, is it going,
> Is it gone for ever,
> The life that seemed round me,
> The longing I sought?
> Has it turned to undoing
> That constant endeavour
> To bind love that bound me,
> To hold all it brought? ...
>
> Beaten back, ever smitten
> By pains that none knoweth,
> Did love ever languish,
> Did hope ever die?
> I know not, but listen
> By the light that love showeth
> I beheld her through anguish
> Never lost, never nigh.

Waking always brought her back – 'never/The day was without her' – but now as a sinister herald of death, no longer as the centre of the sacred dance – rather as a newcomer threatening the health-giving properties of the mandalic pattern itself. Had he been able to speak, what words would he have used? The answer to this rhetorical question was,

> Words meet for the hearkening
> Of Death the new-comer,
> For the new bond that bindeth,
> The new pain anigh:

> For the World is a-darkening
> Amidmost the summer,
> Death sickeneth and blindeth,
> No love standeth by.

'Lonely Love and Loveless Death' marks the nadir of his anguish over Jane. He did not die, of course. In fact, he grew willing to settle for a little abatement of tension though by this time he knew the world to be a place of 'acted lies' and 'gainless eld,'

> Of love well trusted turned to shame
> And then the change we may not name . . .
> Unto the dark whence all things came.

What, if any, satisfaction did life have to offer before that actual end?

> Go cry aloud, 'A little rest
> Before the end, is all the best.'

This sounds like a tortured fore-echo of the last 'Lines for the Bed at Kelmscott':

> And for worst and best
> Right good is rest.

Actually, he wanted enough oblivion to forget the sharp distress of love but not its potential bliss – enough stillness to enjoy freedom from longing but not freedom from the power to long. He wanted numbness from shame but not enough numbness to make him think.

> The words a shame that once we spake
> 'For love and truth & honour's sake' . . .

Nevertheless, in the search for imperturbability

> Choose, choose the best, the pain, but pray
> If thou hast breath to cast away
> For somewhat of a better day;
> A rest with something good to gain
> More than dead love & wasted pain;
>   Cry bitterly, to draw anigh
> One heart at least, & cry in vain.
>
> (Sup. I, 540)

The bitter twist in the last line does not mean that Morris was never again to seek for a woman's love and understanding. In fact it may refer to a real heart which offered 'A rest with something good to gain,' but for which he had to cry, if honour was to be kept, in vain. There was something more than wasted pain – there was even 'rest' (note how often this word has occurred in these lines I have been quoting from 'What All Men Long For and What None Shall Have').

Throughout this tiny anthology we have found almost no attempt to account for Jane's growing estrangement: no references to the triangulation on which almost everyone nowadays (at least among those who come on 'pilgrimages' to the Manor here) seems to be an instant expert; no attacks on the rival who had once been Morris's beloved teacher and mentor. Mackail, writing when Jane was still very much alive, says nothing of the three-cornered combat. Rossetti had 'discovered' Jane, so to speak, in the Oxford theatre long ago and made a sketch, not very ingratiating, of her face in 1857. After Morris married her he was a frequent sojourner at Red House, both with Lizzie Siddal, whom he married in 1860, and after her death in 1862. It was not, however, till the Morrises moved to their Queen Square house in London in 1865 that he began to sketch and paint Jane until gradually, he became almost obsessed with her strange beauty, exotic enough for any painter in the days when Morris married her but now matured into a peculiar splendour of non-Raphaelite features lighted by blue-grey eyes and shadowed by great shelves of crinkly black hair. It must have been about 1867 that Rossetti began to work up what was to end as a frenetic attachment to Jane. I gather this from the fact that it was in this year that he began writing passionate poems to her and doing large oils instead of small charcoal or pastel pieces. To be sure, Rossetti had used Jane for the Virgin in the altar-piece of Llandaff Cathedral (1858–64) but from 1860 to '64 his 'housekeeper' Fanny Cornforth sat for most of his important canvasses including *Lilith*, Alexa Wilding for the *Monna Vanna* of 1866 and Ellen Smith for the coy *Joli Coeur* of 1867. Only in 1868 did Jane take the centre of the canvas in *The Blue Dress* (or *Mrs William Morris*), a place she held in most of Rossetti's important paintings until the end. Along the top of *The Blue Dress* canvas he inscribed a Latin couplet of his own which may be translated, 'Famed by her poet husband and surpassingly famous for her face,/Henceforward may she be famous for this my picture.' He also wrote a sonnet for the painting in which he represented himself as taking, here and from now on, the unique privilege and right of presenting her, body and soul, to the world.

> O Lord of all compassionate control,
>   O Love! let this my lady's picture glow
>   Under my hand to praise her name, and show
> Even of her inner self the perfect whole; . . .
> The very sky and sea-line of her soul.

Lo! it is done. Above the enthroning throat
The mouth's mould testifies of voice and kiss,
The shadowed eyes remember and foresee,
Her face is made her shrine. Let all men note
That in all years (O Love, thy gift is this!)
They that would look on her must come to me.

This is the picture of which Henry James, who visited the Morrises at their Queen Square home 'over the shop' in 1869, wrote to his sister in Boston, 'On the wall was a large nearly full-length portrait of her by Rossetti, so strange and unreal that if you hadn't seen her you'd pronounce it a distempered vision, but in fact an extremely good likeness.' This is the best answer I can give to the many visitors to the Manor who claim that no woman who ever lived could possibly have looked like the lady in blue. James' description of her – it precedes his mention of the picture – runs:

Oh, *ma chère*, such a wife! *Je n'en reviens pas* – she haunts me still. A figure cut out of a missal – out of one of Rossetti's or Hunt's pictures – to say this gives but a faint idea of her, because when such an image puts on flesh and blood, it is an apparition of fearful and wonderful intensity. . . . Imagine a tall lean woman in a long dress ... with a mass of crisp black hair heaped into great wavy projections on each side of her temples, a thin pale face, a pair of strange, sad, deep, dark Swinburnian eyes, with great thick black oblique brows, joined in the middle and tucking themselves away under her hair, a mouth like the 'Oriana' in our illustrated Tennyson, a long neck, without any collar, and in lieu thereof some dozen strings of outlandish beads – in fine, complete.

Some visitors to the Manor seem to be repelled by Rossetti's realistic picture, or at least by the woman it portrays, and I remember a 'pilgrim' writing, a month or so after seeing it, to ask whether it was not true that she had detected a trickle of blood issuing from the right side of the mouth! I could only reply that Jane may have been a vampire but not of the type she had in mind.

It seems to have been while Rossetti was working on *The Blue Dress* and another picture, apparently started in 1867 – *La Pia de 'Tolomei* – that he began squiring her about London to studio parties at the houses of various painters where in secluded corners he could feed her strawberries and they could find blissful oblivion of all but each other. Edmund Gosse reports a party held in Madox Brown's house in Fitzroy Square where Jane sat on her model's throne like a queen in her ivory-coloured velvet dress with Rossetti on a hassock at her feet. This was in 1870. Rossetti had held a party of his own at Cheyne Walk in April 1868 to celebrate the near-completion (or so it seemed at the time) of *La Pia*, a picture inspired by Dante's brief reference in *Purgatorio V* to a young wife unjustly accused of infidelity. Either the savage husband shut her up in a dungeon where the malaria of the Maremma, an infamous marshland south of Rome, destroyed her or had her hurled to her death from the battlements of the castle where she was imprisoned. Rossetti painted the picture (we know only the canvas finished in 1881 and now at the University of Kansas Museum of Art) so as to stress two points: Pia's fearful depression at being incarcerated in her husband's castle and the barbarous cruelty of the man. That she is faithful to the ruffian seems to be indicated by the symbolic ivy that covers the turret and perhaps by the fact that she keeps his letters along with her breviary and rosary at her side. However, there billow below her the husband's blood-red banners while a flight of rooks adds raucous horror to the scene. Crushed with melancholy, La Pia waits to be tossed from the battlements. This is the fate Rossetti's picture calls for rather than death by malaria though he annotated the picture with a translation of Dante in which the wife, now in Purgatory, says:

> "Ah! when on earth thy voice again is heard . . .
>   Remember me who am La Pia; me
> Siena, me Maremma, made, unmade,
>   This in his inmost heart well knoweth he
> With whose fair jewel I was ringed and wed."

For all this stress on the husband, it seems that at Rossetti's *La Pia* dinner in 1868, 'given,' says Madox Brown, 'in honour of the Topsies,' Morris had to be sent off to bring Faulkner because there would otherwise have been only thirteen at table. When he returned, there were fifteen. From the beginning Morris had been present as the fourteenth guest, but Rossetti, when counting up the feasters, had overlooked him! That the Morrises were persuaded to stay on at Cheyne Walk for a week so that Jane would always be available to sit for the master shows La Pia's husband more as victim than as victimiser.

Almost simultaneously Rossetti was at work upon a picture of Jane as Pandora, meant perhaps to threaten La Pia's tormentor with clouds of devils or at least to frighten him by showing 'in Venus's eyes the gaze of Proserpine,' goddess of hell. This picture is almost literally hair-raising, especially in the 'sanguine' version now in Buscot Park across the river from Kelmscott, made perhaps in 1869. The Princeton Art Museum has a water colour version of about 1870 which is hardly less menacing while an oil of 1871, which shows Pandora wrapped not only in masses of black hair but in a dark garment, emphasises her funereal threat to a man well known for his death-fears. Probably the weirdest version is in tones of muddy copse-green, in the Fogg at Harvard. The sestet of the sonnet which the painter wrote for *Pandora* ran:

> What of the end? These beat their wings at will,
> The ill-born things, the good things turned to ill, –
> Powers of the impassioned hours prohibited,
> Aye, clench the casket now! Whither they go
> Thou mayst not dare to think; nor canst thou know
> If hope still pent there be alive or dead.

Apparently Rossetti was warning Jane of the devilish dangers of frustrated passion, of the terrible turn it might take with her husband, especially if he still had a hope of regaining her. Of course, the warning may have concerned Rossetti himself – *his* impassioned hours prohibited, which with all hope dead might drive him to madness or suicide.

The final important picture of these years was *Mariana*, finished in 1870. 'Mariana in the moated grange,' is a character in *Measure for Measure* and a famous lute-song is sung by a boy to ease her woe. She is also the subject of a well known poem by Tennyson. Never did a picture better catch the note of weary futility with which Tennyson ended each stanza:

> She only said, 'My life is dreary,
>   He cometh not," she said;
> She said, "I am aweary, aweary,
>   And would that I were dead!'

the neurasthenic dejection in the eyes, the lifeless curl of the lips, the caving out rather than in of the columnar throat, the slump of the shoulders, the uselessness of the drooping hands – all are unbearable. It is as if Rossetti had plunged his model into hopeless longing for him and then reproached her for her longing. On the lower edge of the frame he inscribed a line from Shakespeare's lute-song: 'Take, O Take those lips away . . .' This picture may have upset Morris more than *La Pia* or *Pandora* for it suggested that he was married to life-in-death.

The four pictures of Jane painted between 1866 and '70 amount, I think, to high-powered psychological warfare, not only against the cruel husband of the model but also against the cruel model. Jane was often melancholy but whether because oppressed by William or merely pestered by Rossetti is not clear. She could pose for hours almost without moving, probably because she was by nature sluggish and languorous rather than because she was anxious to please the Master. Usually the one to conquer in love, the painter must have been not only intrigued by Jane's mysterious passivity but often infuriated. Rossetti was a complex person, intelligent, subtle, usually irresistible, handsome though short and stout, the most 'romantic' painter of the time, the most irresponsible man-of-the-world with an air of bearing all before him – which he usually did. But now he had genuinely fallen in love with his model and was determined to have her for himself before he was sure he could get her. From youth he had been fascinated by the notion of two men fighting for a woman who watched the hand-to-hand combat with horrified intensity. It is of interest here to note that Rossetti's most effective portrayal of this theme, *A Fight For a Woman* (Detroit Institute of Arts), dates from 1865, when the Morrises left Red House for London and Rossetti set out to conquer the self-absorbed 'Sphinx.'

He had little difficulty in attracting Jane to come from her house in Queen Square and model for him at Cheyne Walk. Life above the shop in 1866 and '67, where a dozen men were noisily concocting all kinds of decoration for the Green Dining Room of the South Kensington Museum and the Armoury and Tapestry Room at St James' Palace, must have been irritating and exhausting to a degree. We are told that the boisterous voice of her husband dominated the house not only during the work-day but in the evenings, complaining about meals, wrenching handles off doors that stuck, strumming on table-tops as he composed fresh lines for *The Earthly Paradise* or falling into fits of rage which he could not explain and of which he later felt ashamed. His outbursts, fidgets, and over-time labour (lasting to any hour of the night and usually beginning again at five in the morning), all of which seem to have been more stimulated than assuaged by the three bottles or more of wine which he is known to have drunk each day, seem to have left Jane more than glad to flee to the quiet of Cheyne Walk. There, however, another kind of stress often afflicted the refugee.

Rossetti, after what he called years of tongue-tied waiting, began to talk openly of his love and frequently to 'rave' about her beauty. Jane could quiet him, it seems, only by complaining that the 'mystical' poet of 'The Blessed Damoiselle' cared more for her body than her soul. How far the mingling of bodies went between 1865 and '70, no one can say. In 1870 Rossetti published a famous volume of *Poems* and it is easy to discern those written to Jane. There were passionate kisses, of course, but there is always, it seems to me, a very large and open question about the extent to which the robes of remoteness and unattainability in which Jane wrapped herself were ever dropped. She basked in the adoration of famous men, but remembering the rough conduct of her father, the groom, who was only too eager give her to Morris, she seems never to have really trusted masculine affection. Actually, she would seem, after bearing Morris two children, to have avoided passionate conclusions. The 1870 poems which suggest consummation have a slight odour of blackmail about them, but Jane, pleased with the adoration they showed, may have attributed everything to poetic license or mere delusion for, as she wrote to Theodore Watts-Dunton years later (1883), 'That Gabriel *was* mad was but too true, no one knows that better than myself . . .' (Quoted by R. C. H. Briggs in 'Letters to Janey,' *The Journal of the William Morris Society*, Summer, 1964.) Also, mad or not, Rossetti, being the complicated – spiteful?– person he was, may have spread the passion quite heavily over his sonnets in order to embarrass Morris, who had promised to review the *Poems* on their appearance. It is quite possible, however, that Rossetti was dealing with souls so transparent, or opaque, that his barbs drew nothing but ichor from wounds that closed the moment they were inflicted. Morris undoubtedly knew better than Jane what was up, but he produced his over-laudatory review of Rossetti–Shakespeare as promised. Then, without laying down his pen, he wrote to Mrs Coronio, 'I have done my review, just this moment – ugh!'

All through Rossetti's whirlwind wooing of 1868, '69 and '70, if that is what it should be called, Jane's backaches grew worse until in July 1869 Morris had to take her to the spa at Bad-Ems in Hesse-Nassau for help, not that any good came of the waters. Perhaps some came from Rossetti's letters, always solicitous of her health and bursting with gratitude that she had in some degree responded to his passion before her collapse. The extent of her response is questionable, for the painter-poet was himself on the verge of a breakdown. A significant passage in Rossetti's letter of 30 July runs:

I can never tell you how much I am with you at all times. Absence from your sight is what I have long been used to: and no absence can ever make me so far from you again as your presence did for years. For this long-inconceivable change, you know more what my thanks must be. But I have no right to talk to you in a way that may make you sad on my account, when in reality the balance of joy and sorrow is now so much more in my favour than it has been, or could have been hoped to become, for years past.

Jane wrote back frequently and Rossetti sought to enliven her tedium in Germany by concocting a cartoon called 'The Ms at Ems.' This shows Jane in her bath with seven glasses of spa water on one side of the tub and seven manuscript volumes of *The Earthly Paradise* on the other while her jailer-husband stands over her declaiming from still another volume. A note reads, 'This will prepare you for the worst – whichever that may be, the 7 tumblers or the 7 volumes.' Some time before this (or so it seems) Rossetti with the connivance of Jane (or possibly without it) had drawn her dozing over *The Defence of Guenevere*. Such were the Master's visual jibes.

After the Morrises' return to London in September of '69, both were as on edge as before and each sought relief in his characteristic way: Morris by writing more *Paradise* stories and Jane by sitting for pictures of herself as Pandora or Mariana and listening to the painter's hundred ways of saying, 'You are the noblest and dearest thing the world has had to show me,' as he wrote in a letter of 4 February 1870. (Henderson, *William Morris*, 111) In January he had written her that 'For the last two years I have felt distinctly the clearing away of the chilling numbness that surrounded me in the utter want of you . . .' (Henderson, ibid., 110) In March and April Jane joined Rossetti at a studio-sanatorium he had set up at Scalands near Robertsbridge (about twelve miles northwest of Hastings) in Sussex. On 18 April Rossetti wrote to his mother that 'Janey Morris is here and benefitting greatly. Top comes from time to time.' (Henderson, ibid., 110) From 1868 to '70 there seems to have been not a steady growing together but ups and downs, the ups catalysed by Rossetti, the downs by Jane. (In the 'noblest . . . thing' letter quoted above, the painter had buttered over some kind of estrangement 'I would . . . rather have had this to endure than have missed the fullness of wonder and worship which nothing else could have made known to me . . .')

I will quote from a few of the poems which Rossetti wrote to or of Jane by 1870 both to give some notion of their 'affair' and also of the dismay and anger which Morris must have felt when he came to review the 1870 *Poems*. The best known sonnets from the time when, though often together, they (or was it just Jane?) could not or would not speak of tender feelings fearfully suppressed, are probably those of the tiny 'Willowwood' sequence. This is a silent cry of frustration rising from a wood where a form stands by every tree,

> All mournful forms, for each was I or she,
> The shades of those our days that had no tongue.

However, the tree-spirits move together at last in one

> . . . soul-wrung implacable close kiss;
> And pity of self through all made broken moan
> Which said, 'For once, for once, for once alone!'

But Love sang,

> 'Alas! the bitter banks in Willowwood,
> With tear-spurge wan, with blood-wort burning red . . .'

This was written in 1868. By 1869, though Rossetti was close to a breakdown, a poem like 'The Stream's Secret' indicates, but certainly not explicitly, some kind of union:

> Oh sweet her bending grace
> Then when I kneel beside her feet;
> And sweet her eyes' o'erhanging heaven; and sweet
> The gathering folds of her embrace;
> And her fall'n hair at last shed round my face
> When breaths and tears shall meet.

> Beneath her sheltering hair,
> In the warm silence near her breast,
> Our kisses and our sobs shall sink to rest . . .

The future tense, as in 'shall meet' and 'shall sink,' does not assert that love has been consummated. Another poem of 1869 tells of the lover's starved soul (body?) sent supperless to bed.

> What shall be said of this embattled day . . .
> Of these thy vanquished hours what shalt thou say, –
> As every sense to which she dealt delight
> Now labours lonely . . .

> Stand still, fond fettered wretch! while Memory's art
> Parades the Past before thy face, and lures
> Thy spirit to her passionate portraitures:
> Till the tempestuous tide-gates flung apart
> Flood with wild will the hollows of thy heart,
> And thy heart rends thee, and thy body endures.

Poems like this make it difficult to decide just how literally we should take others like 'Nuptial Sleep' or 'Supreme Surrender.' One is tempted to think that the sleep and dream element in these poems may be more real than it is intended to be taken. When the poet awakes she is by his side but what has happened between the kisses and waking of these 'wedded flowers'?

> At length their long kiss severed, with sweet smart:
> And as the last slow sudden drops are shed
> From sparkling eaves when all the storm has fled,
> So singly flagged the pulses of each heart . . .
> Sleep sank them lower than the tide of dreams,
> And their dreams watched them sink, and slid away . . .
> Till from some wonder of new woods and streams
> He woke, and wondered more: for there she lay.

In its opening, 'Supreme Surrender' is an even dreamier poem. Only the poet and the 'spirits of love' who roam the fields of sleep know what happens, though the images that follow seem pretty explicit.

> To all the spirits of love that wander by
> Along the love-sown harvest-field of sleep
> My Lady lies apparent; and the deep
> Calls to the deep; and no man sees but I.
> The bliss so long afar, at length so nigh,
> Rests there attained . . .

However, the lady's husband, though suffering fearfully from Jane's coldness, did not find enough offense or warning in these sonnets to keep him from taking a joint lease with Rossetti on a house in the country, where he frequently left the couple alone with his children. He seems at times to have thought he had failed Jane in some way – but also that Rossetti was not the man to make up that deficiency. When, in 1964, fifty years after the poet-painter's death, his letters to Jane were opened to public inspection by the British Museum, R. C. H. Briggs wrote in *The Journal of the William Morris Society* (Summer, 1964) that 'the nature of Janey's stimulus for Rossetti is a mystery which these letters do nothing to solve, but that the stimulus was real and essential for him they establish beyond doubt.' (22) That Jane stimulated the painter and even the phantasising poet in Rossetti, Morris does not seem to have minded. He was not at this time jealous, or was only a little jealous, of Rossetti. Something quite different stung him and drove him almost to desperation as can be seen in the last two volumes of *The Earthly Paradise*.

That was Jane's ever-increasing indifference, not to say hostility, to him, a silent pool of resentment which had been icing over for years. She shrank, apparently, from his caresses and slowly but surely sealed up almost every pore through which communication could take place. This may have been in part because, as Morris's expertise widened almost daily to include art after art, craft after craft, she felt he was seeking to shut her out of his life. Partly it may have been due to his rather rough and boisterous ways. Oddly, perhaps, she suffered from a form of neurasthenia little different from her husband's but made worse by the fact that she did not have the background and talents to fight feelings of social inferiority, fatigue, and sensitivity to noise. She had less power to deal with work and blamed it on her indefatigable husband. Her humble view of herself can be seen in the postscript she added to a letter sent by Morris to Philip Webb 15 August 1869. It was written from her bed of pain – she could hardly sit up – at Bad-Ems:

My finger-tips are sound – as you see by this – and fit for much more hard labour – I feel that I have not much else about me that is good for anything – but I have a sort of presentiment (though of course you don't believe in such things) that I may make a rapid turn – and feel myself well all of a sudden – and then I have another presentiment that should this change come all those I now call my friends would also change – and would not be able to stand me.

(*Letters*, 104)

Of all this William seems to have had little inkling. When writing the two last volumes of *The Earthly Paradise* he was so preoccupied with frustrated passion that he had no time to try to understand his wife's quite real troubles. Sometimes what must be described as the poet's self-pity is embarrassingly excessive, and there is nothing like self-pity to block the operation of empathy and understanding.

It was not that Morris did not try desperately to explain Jane's coldness, but the idea that she may have been trying in her fashion, just as
hard as he in his, to save her sanity could hardly have occurred to him.
He was no subtle psychologist. To him she seemed simply to have abdi-
cated her responsibilities as the mistress of his home, and there came a
moment in 1868 or '69 when he could only decide that she had turned,
for some totally incomprehensible reason, not merely cruel but madly
malicious. She was set on a course, it seemed, deliberately calculated to
destroy their happiness forever. He could only conclude that she had
never loved him, never understood him, but only exploited his deep passion. Something, some peccadillo, some gesture of love she found re-
pugnant, she suddenly and unexpectedly turned into an excuse for
forbidding Morris her bed, perhaps to the extent of locking her door
against him. Perhaps she resented his turning for understanding to a
woman more capable of furnishing it – Georgiana Burne-Jones? Whatever happened, she made the most of it and remained adamant in her
decision. That her husband, thinking that both had extramarital feelings,
pleaded 'we two are in the same box and need conceal nothing – don't
cast me away – scold me but pardon me' (Henderson, *William Morris*,
94) did not alter by one jot what congealed into an iron-clad decision.
The crucial poem throwing light – or just more darkness – on this tragic
moment is called, in May's edition, 'Song'! Some 'little word,' some
hesitant kiss, some prayer gave Jane the excuse for an act she had probably been working up to for some time.

> Twas one little word that wrought it,
> One sweet pang of pleasure bought it;
> Long 'twixt heart and lips it hung
> Till too sore the heart was wrung,
> Till no more the lips might bear
> To be parted, yet so near –
> Then the darkness closed around me
> And the bitter waking found me
> *Half forgotten, unforgiven and alone.*
>
> Hearken: nigher still and nigher
> Had we grown, methought my fire
> Woke in her some hidden flame
> And the rags of pride and shame
> She seemed casting from her heart,
> And the dull days seemed to part;
> Then I cried out, Ah, I move thee
> And thou knowest that I love thee –
> *– Half forgotten, unforgiven and alone.*

Yea, it pleased her to behold me
Mocked by tales that love had told me,
Mocked by tales and mocked by eyes,
Wells of loving mysteries;
Mocked by eyes and mocked by speech
Till I deemed I might beseech
For one word, that scarcely speaking
She would snatch me from that waking,

Half forgotten, unforgiven and alone.

All is done – no other greeting,
No more sweet tormenting meeting,
No more sight of smile or tear,
No more bliss shall draw anear
Hand in hand with sister pain –
Scarce a longing vague and vain –
No more speech till all is over
Twixt the well-beloved and lover

Half forgotten, unforgiven and alone.

(XXIV, 360–61)

I have quoted this poem in full not only to tell us all that can be known about this 'one little word,' the faltering kiss, the prayer, but to stress a side of the couple's love hardly ever mentioned. What the 'word' was, what the pang of pleasure, what the prayer, we will never know, but that Jane had 'mocked' Morris with professions of love, in speech as well as looks, and that she had deliberately misled him because it gave her some perverse pleasure – this is perhaps the only place in his sad lyrics where he dwells on such double-dealing – such flagrant treachery. It is a moving poem though marred somewhat by the obtrusive music of Poe. What was building up slowly in Morris's mind was, apparently, a concept of Jane as a Keatsian *'belle dame sans merci'* or, to use the phrase popular in his time, *'femme fatale.'* The image of the fatal woman had been etched in sanguine, to say the least, on the blue Victorian heavens by Morris's good friend Swinburne: the merciless *belle dame* who seeks deliberately to inflame her lover while refusing to satisfy him because she loves to see him writhe in frustrated pain. Her look is invariably and unchangeably angry, resentful, crushing. She is not merely an enigmatic sphinx or Gioconda but, like Mary Stuart in Swinburne's *Chastelard* (1865), one who seeks to turn her lover's passion to 'a sort of curse/Made,' as he says, 'for my plague' and death. At this point we can hardly help recalling with a slight shiver Swinburne's judgement of 1858 that for Morris to marry Jane was 'insane. To kiss her feet is the utmost men should dream of doing.'

Though Morris seems to have taken no interest in the Swinburnian sadists of the *Poems and Ballads* of 1866 (though among his books here at Kelmscott is a copy which he seems to have bought and inscribed in 1868) – no interest in, for example, Faustine, Dolores, Sappho or the goddess of 'Laus Veneris' – he was fond of *Atalanta in Calydon* (1865), the Kelmscott edition of this poem being among the Press's most lovely volumes. The virgin huntress of the poem is frigid and the cause, if involuntary, of Meleager's death. She is

> . . . the strong woman, she the flower, the sword,
> Red from spilt blood, a mortal flower to men,
> Adorable, detestable.

When the dying Meleager asks for a touch of her 'rose-like hands,' a 'bitter kiss,' she brings the drama quickly to an end with 'I must away'! Though the women of Swinburne's 'Masque of Queen Bersabe,' Herodias, Semiramis, Pasiphae, Sappho, et al., could never have been candidates for tutelary Red House hangings, certain lines may have haunted Morris's tortured mind in the late 1860s. I mean lines like these from Messalina's self-description:

> These were the signs God set on me:
> A barren beauty subtle and sleek,
> Curled carven hair, and cheeks worn wan . . .

or these from Erigone's:

> My large lips had the old thirst of earth,
> Mine arms the might of the old sea's girth . . .
> Within mine eyes and in mine ears
> Were music and the wine of tears . . .

(Think of Jane as she appears in Rossetti's *Astarte Syriaca*!) Although it is preposterous to find Swinburnian vapours clouding Morris's essentially healthy though, as he admitted, sometimes melancholy mind, it must be said that the artistic atmosphere of the 1860s and '70s was alive with Medusas, Delilahs, Shebas (Flaubert-style) and Helens (as in the pictures by Moreau which Morris could have seen in France) – fiends masked as females. Even Burne-Jones was now painting pictures of a mermaid pulling a strong man to his death or a heavy-limbed Venus Discordia brooding over a bloody scene in the spirit of Dolores or Faustine, who

> . . . loved the games men play with death,
> Where death must win;
> As though the slain man's blood and breath
> Revived Faustine.

It is little wonder, then, that Morris's final attempt to understand Jane – now turned to a Mona Lisa Sphinx like the one sketched by Walter Crane – ran like this:

> Why dost thou struggle, strive for victory
> Over my heart that loveth thine so well?
> When Death shall one day have its will of thee
> And to deaf ears thy triumph thou must tell.
>
> Unto deaf ears or unto such as know
> The hearts of dead and living wilt thou say:
> A childish heart there loved me once, and lo
> I took his love and cast his love away.
>
> A childish greedy heart! yet still he clung
> So close to me that much he pleased my pride
> And soothed a sorrow that about me hung
> With glimpses of his love unsatisfied –
>
> And soothed my sorrow – but time soothed it too
> Though ever did its aching fill my heart
> To which the foolish child still closer drew
> Thinking in all I was to have a part.
>
> But now my heart grown silent of its grief
> Saw more than kindness in his hungry eyes:
> But I must wear a mask of false belief
> And feign that nought I knew his miseries.
>
> I wore a mask, because though certainly
> I loved him not, yet was there something soft
> And sweet to have him ever loving me:
> Belike it is I well-nigh loved him oft –
>
> Nigh loved him oft, and needs must grant to him
> Some kindness out of all he asked of me
> And hoped his love would still hang vague and dim
> About my life like half-heard melody.
>
> He knew my heart and over-well knew this
> And strove, poor soul, to pleasure me herein;
> But yet what might he do some doubtful kiss,
> Some word, some look might give him hope to win.
>
> Poor hope, poor soul, for he again would come
> Thinking to gain yet one more golden step
> Toward Love's shrine, and lo the kind speech dumb
> The kind look gone, no love upon my lip –

> Yea gone, yet not my fault, I knew of love
> But my love and not his; how could I tell
> That such blind passion in him I should move?
> Behold I have loved faithfully and well . . .
>
> (XXIV, 362–3)

Though it is difficult to tell when Morris wrote any given lyric in *Poems By the Way* (not published till 1891), certain poems seem to date from 1868–70 or just a little later. They show him suffering from a few aftertwists of the knife not recorded before and are superbly ironical. 'Echoes of Love's House' runs:

> Love gives every gift whereby we long to live;
> 'Love takes every gift, and nothing back doth give.' . . .
>
> Love turns life to joy till nought is left to gain:
> 'Love turns life to woe till hope is nought and vain.' . . .
>
> Love burns up the world to changeless heaven and blest,
> 'Love burns up the world to a void of all unrest.' . . .
>
> Ah! I praise thee, Love, for utter joyance won!
> 'And is my praise nought worth for all my life undone?'

In 'Hope Dieth, Love Liveth' the poet addresses his own power of love, which will not die along with hope:

> Weep, though no hair's breadth thou shalt move
> The living Earth, the heaven above
> By all the bitterness of love!
> Weep and cease not, now hope is dead!
> Sighs rest thee not, tears bring no ease
> Life hath no joy, and Death no peace:
> The years change not, though they decrease,
> For hope is dead . . .

Nevertheless, since 'Love dieth not,' Eros may have gained honour by thus testing its survival power, but it is not at all clear what benefit has accrued to the poet. In 'Earth the Healer,' dating from about 1873, he cannot do anything with the reality of Jane's conduct but

> Think of the thankless morning,
> The gifts of noon unused;
> Think of the eve of scorning,
> The night of prayer refused.

The echoes of love's house will do nothing but modulate through endless variations into one shocking, lonely pain.

How, then, can we sum up Jane's role, if not in life, at least as it was in her husband's mind? The best that can possibly be said of her is that she was, like her beauty, somewhat supernatural – an ice-queen, a witch, a snake- or swan-girl, a pagan empress fond of incomprehensible taboos who had strayed into the modern world to make tragic trouble for men. In the light of the last five or six years' experience of Jane which drove him to the character-analysis so pathetically yet decisively set forth in the 'Why dost thou struggle?' poem, many of the love stories written in the early '60s for *The Earthly Paradise* took on a new, malignant dimension. Other tales, more malignant still, suggested themselves to a mind which aimed always to tell the truth about life. These were now added. Some of the fairy-tales and apologues were kept, of course, but the overriding sense of the collection of tales to be published as *The Earthly Paradise* was now dark if not murky and required much revision. Morris was a man who could not help doing this, at whatever cost in pain and poems discarded. Thus by the sad route traversed in this chapter we have lost much of 'The First Earthly Paradise' and come to what must be called, from its chief stories, the second, or contrary, or little-short-of-infernal one. Yet in spite of all, the book was not the swan song of '*The idle singer of an empty day*' but a groping ahead toward fresher, wider deeper conceptions of paradise on earth.

VI 'The Second Earthly Paradise' 1868-1870

The ordeal which began for Morris in 1865 and reached its climax (though with many anti-climaxes still to come) in 1868–70 altered the whole conception of *The Earthly Paradise* as planned about 1861 and half worked out in its early form during the days at Red House. In those days it was thought of as a collection of stories exchanged between old gentlemen-mariners from Scandinavia and patriarchs of a people who strayed or were driven from Greece two or more millennia before. The Greeks had formed a kind of Atlantis in the Western Sea which the Northmen stumbled upon after the ordeals related in the first prologue. To recapitulate: from young manhood they had been in search of a Golden-Age paradise – no work, no winter, no pain, no death – of which their leader had had a peculiarly vivid dream with which he had infected his comrades. During their search they had encountered noble but stupid savages and fierce wild men including cannibals; had saved beautiful Amazons from lions and a frightful male tyrant, married them, raised families, grown old, and once more embarked on their original quest; had visited a great city inhabited by wonderfully life-like corpses; and after another dream by their leader – this one of the horrors of immortal life on earth – had reached the isle of 'Greeks,' which corresponded precisely to their captain's long-ago dream in nearly all details but the most important – there was no eternal summer, no reprieve from death. As we have seen, it is difficult to find profundity or even purpose in the adventures of this first form of the prologue, and it is little wonder that Morris, before sub-titling it 'The Wanderers,' called it 'The Fool's Paradise.'

The general tone of the early paradise tales was rather jaunty, as we can see from the moral apologues written early and used practically unchanged in the volume published in 1868. Usually a kind of earthly paradise is conferred on the main character and then quickly lost to the tune of the author's 'I could have told you so,' especially when the tale is

> Of kings, who in their tyranny
> Were mighty once, but fell at last;
> Of merchants rich as men could be,
> And yet one day their wealth was past.

(XXIV, 170)

The stories of lovers are somewhat differently conceived, for the loss of their Edens is less deserved and more often made up for at the end. However, 'the People of the Shore' who invite the Wanderers to spend their last years with them in the pleasantest site yet found on earth are well aware

> ... how vain it is
>   To strive against the Gods and Fate,
> And that no man may look for bliss
>   Without an ending soon or late.

They stress the shortcomings of their Atlantis to the point where we begin to wonder just what moral Morris had in mind when bringing these stories together. From the title it seems that he must have intended to celebrate the Red House apogee of human happiness. This was probably the case, but we know, on the other hand, that the poet, however happy, probably continued to be plagued by the fear of death, to which he had added at some period in his development a horror of sickness and old age, perhaps at the time of his father's mortal illness in 1847 when Morris was thirteen. Possibly the depression which used to lie in wait for him around every corner had lessened, but these old bugbears, always hovering in the background, kept Morris from silly optimism even when working out the early version of *The Earthly Paradise*. The Wanderers find their dreamt-of-isle at last, full of peace, plenty, gentle laws and trustworthy physicians – 'the crown of lands' – yet its venerable patriarch makes clear that at last these unusually favoured people die:

> O masters, here as everywhere,
>   All things begin, grow old, decay;
> That groweth ugly that was fair,
>   The storm blots out the summer day.
>
> The merry shepherd's lazy song
>   Breaks off before the lion's roar;
> The bathing girls, white-limbed and long,
>   Half-dead with fear splash toward the shore
>
> At rumour of the deadly shark ...
>
>   (XXIV, 167–8)

The patriarch suggests that the 'old chaps' from abroad join those of the island in swapping tales which will make them realise that their lives are

> ... but a story too,
>   So that no more your hearts shall ache
>   With thoughts of all ye might not do.
>
>   (XXIV, 170)

It was an interesting idea of Morris's that only by much story-telling and -hearing can a man be made to realise that his own life – and death – repeat a precious, universal pattern which it would be cowardly, were it possible, to evade. To make us realise that our own stories can be compared with typical tales from all lands and thereby mitigate remembered pain and grief, soften frustrated hope and transitory joy – that is what the narrators in both versions of *The Earthly Paradise* have in mind.

The prologue to the published *Paradise* was not just a revision or re-casting but an entirely new work from an almost new author. It is an appropriate introduction to tales of Edens missed, mislaid, misunderstood or mistakenly clasped. It reiterates the No-Golden-Age-Possible wisdom of *Jason*, which makes one wonder why Morris retained the early title and especially why he said on one occasion that the name of *Earthly Paradise* was the best thing about the whole book. By this time Morris had begun to think of himself, as in the poems which introduce and conclude the volumes, as '*The idle singer of an empty day*' with no ability to rescind man's universal condemnation to fear, grief, frustration and death.

> *Of Heaven or Hell I have no power to sing,*
> *I cannot ease the burden of your fears,*
> *Or make quick-coming death a little thing,*
> *Or bring again the pleasure of past years,*
> *Nor for my words shall ye forget your tears,*
> *Or hope again for aught that I can say,*
> *The idle singer of an empty day.*

However, like the 'old chaps' telling the tales to each other – and there is only one old chap of course: Morris himself – he claims to do nothing but seek to relieve for a little while the tensions and defeats which life inflicts on all. By carrying people 'out of themselves' through his art as a story-teller he can perhaps carry them deeper into themselves, to that psychic region where, eased or purged of pain by empathy with a sad story told in soothing verse and lovely images drawn from the procession of the seasons, they can enjoy an unlooked-for stillness. To lodge his readers, even if only for a short time, in this joyful region was all that Morris, at the time, thought he could do to relieve his suffering countrymen.

> *Dreamer of dreams, born out of my due time,*
> *Why should I strive to set the crooked straight?*
> *Let it suffice me that my murmuring rhyme*
> *Beats with light wing against the ivory gate,*
> *Telling a tale not too importunate . . .*
>
> *Folk say, a wizard to a northern king*
> *At Christmas-tide such wondrous things did show,*
> *That through one window men beheld the spring,*

> *And through another saw the summer glow,*
> *While still, unheard, but in its wonted way,*
> *Piped the drear wind of that December day.*

> *So with this Earthly Paradise it is,*
> *If ye will read aright, and pardon me,*
> *Who strive to build a shadowy isle of bliss*
> *Midmost the beating of the steely sea,*
> *Where tossed about all hearts of men must be . . .*

Understood in relation to the majority of the stories he is about to tell, the wizard-poet's invitation to leave winter's sadness is not proof, as it is always said to be, of escapism. In reality, he is inviting the reader to build an island of fruitfulness within to serve as a fortress against the storm of coal-and-iron ugliness that threatens to hammer our hearts to pieces. The island within is the only Eden possible and only when this is understood can the title of *Earthly Paradise* have real meaning. It signifies that the only possible heaven on earth comes from accepting the human condition and trying to make it bearable by setting forth the *whole* experience in the colours of art and consoling rhythms of poetry.

In all but one or two cases the incidents of the new prologue differ from those of the old. While the only catalyst of the quest in the first prologue is a master mariner's dream, that of the second is a fearful plague in a Scandinavian city. A flight from the plague which devastated Europe in 1348 furnishes what is always called a 'frame' for Boccaccio's *Decameron*, but the stories of that book in no sense add up to a criticism or commentary on the emotions which must have devastated the human mind in that awful period. However, the frame of *The Canterbury Tales*, which Morris so much admired and sought to emulate, did provide adequate motivation for Chaucer's stories: the pilgrims in search of shriving regale each other with tales of virtue and vice which act as clues to the changing health of their souls. In Morris the fear of death rather than damnation catalyses the Wanderers' search for a paradisal refuge while, later, fear of death from old age causes the disappointed heroes to retell, as part of their garnered wisdom, the world's great stories of how all men seek and sometimes find, but always lose at last their terrestrial Edens. Thus Morris's *Earthly Paradise* in its printed form does have inner coherence though the inclusion of some of the first-draft stories in the volume of 1868 (covering the months from March through August) keeps the poet from hitting his full stride before the September through February sequence (in two volumes, both published in 1870).

The new prologue begins

> Forget six countries overhung with smoke,
> Forget the snorting steam and piston stroke,

> Forget the spreading of the hideous town;
> Think rather of the pack-horse on the down,
> And dream of London, small, and white, and clean,
> The clear Thames bordered by its gardens green . . .

Morris then reminds his readers that the Thames he is thinking of would contain certain merchant vessels bearing pointed jars of oil from Greece, Eastern spices, gold-woven textiles from Florence,

> And cloth of Bruges, and hogsheads of Guienne;
> While nigh the thronged wharf Geoffrey Chaucer's pen
> Moves over bills of lading – mid such times
> Shall dwell the hollow puppets of my rhymes.

The moment the Wanderers reach their Greek Atlantis, they begin telling their hosts of the hardships they underwent on the long way hither. The first adventure, which corresponds to nothing in the first prologue, indicates a new seriousness in the author. The Wanderers from the plague had met 'Edward of England,' a monarch flaunting his mighty pirate-power in his old age but without point or purpose except to meet his death in battle. When Rolf the leader begs to be allowed to go on with his search for 'gardens ever blossoming/Across the western sea where none grew old,' Edward frees him and his men:

> 'Poor man, why should I stay thee? live thy fill,
> Of that fair life, wherein thou seest no ill
> But fear of that fair rest I hope to win
> One day, when I have purged me of my sin.'

In their second adventure in the new prologue the Wanderers come to a lovely island whose inhabitants are harmless and friendly; moreover, they are decorated with golden trinkets and have, somewhat like the Incas, a solid-gold god and burial customs which directly relate this adventure to that side of the Earthly Paradise theme having to do with immortality. Their kings and great men are clearly deathless – corpses. The people are skillful embalmers who can confer the semblance of life – a subject much favoured by Morris, as we know, to symbolise, among other things, the bitter height of man's most cherished self-deception.

> We saw indeed what things these figures were;
> Dead corpses, by some deft embalmer dried,
> And on this mountain after they had died
> Set up like players at a yule-tide feast . . .

This adventure, occurring so near the beginning of the North-men's wanderings, naturally shakes their hope of escaping the bitter quietus.

On another island they find that apparently noble savages are cannibals. This episode, otherwise somewhat like one in the first prologue, is

brought to bear on the paradise theme too. To be balked of their dream
of peace, dignity and immortality by sub-human barbarians lights in the
Wanderers a fierce fire of frustration which threatens to reduce them to a
sub-human status unworthy of candidates for any kind of paradisal life.

Escaping from this island, they quickly reach another whose people 'A
little of the arts of mankind knew.' Better still,

> . . . Now battered as we were,
> Grown old before our time, in worn-out gear,
> These people, when we first set foot ashore,
> Garlands of flowers and fruits unto us bore,
> And worshipped us as gods, and for no words
> That we could say would cease to call us lords,
> And pray our help to give them bliss and peace,
> And fruitful seasons of the earth's increase.

It seems that the coming of white saviours had been prophesied, and indeed these were needed to break the power of a neighbouring tyrant who
carried off from this people every fifth year ten youths and ten maidens
to be sacrificed on the golden altar. This episode echoes that in the first
prologue of the ten girls destined to be eaten by lions – but there is no
emphasis on female nudity. However, the Wanderers do settle down to a
life of endless gifts and adulation,

> And we had lived and died as happy there
> As any men the labouring earth may bear,
> But for the poison of that wickedness
> That led us on God's edicts to redress.

'Old and grey,' the remnant of the original band (in this new prologue
many had long before given up the quest and attempted to return to
Norway) are easily tricked into believing they can find eternal youth and
life on still another island. Here dying 'by slow decay' is made supremely
bitter for them – the punishment of their impious attempt to break the
law of God and kind in seeking immortality on earth – by their being in-
stalled with pomp in a temple whose architectural sophistication shows
an incredible mixture of the tower of Babel and Louis XI's chateau of
Plessis-les-Tours (as imagined by Scott). This overdone structure, mock-
ing the mandalic form which had sustained Morris before his anguish
over Jane and would do so again, shows the extent of his disillusion in
the late '60s. In a ziggurat enclosed by five circular walls, the Wanderers,
chained to golden thrones on a dais behind the altar and served meat and
wine by 'thin-clad' damsels who made the disabilities of age more than
usually intolerable, had ample time to savour the abysmal foolishness,
even sinfulness, of their quest. Given all the gifts that life can offer short
of unending youth, health, and life, they realised that they possessed

nothing but disgrace and degradation. Instead of love and accomplishment, they have only the service of incense-swinging girls and the 'ghosts of dead hopes' which demand in Carlylean accents,

'Where is thy work? how little thou hast done,
Where are thy friends, why art thou so alone?'

Needless to say, they are fortunate enough to escape from the temple of living gods to the idyllic Atlantic island where they spend their last days swapping Northland (and Eastern) stories with Greeks whose ancestors had been wrecked there two thousand years before.

All the books I have read about Morris record as a curious but otherwise unimportant fact that he was not content with revising the first prologue but manfully wrote an entirely new introduction. On the other hand, no commentator ever asks if he had a reason for doing this, or contrasts the prologues, or examines their relation to what we have called the two *Earthly Paradises*, or senses in the increasingly hopeless island-search the bitter tragedy of Morris's private life, or detects the wild despair in the farce of deified mortals imprisoned in a mock-mandala. Admittedly the poetry is usually not of the greatest and the moralising (when there is any) is pretty humdrum, but brilliant images stream past our eyes with the rapidity and power – and puzzlement – of a dream unfolding.

The two *Paradises*, the earlier preserved here and there in the second, were not wholly disparate. Most of the stories published in 1868 – the twelve tales told from March through August – are the same almost unmodified moral apologues we have already. To these have been added the very early (1861?) 'Man Born to be King' and fairy and folk-tale pieces such as 'Atalanta's Race,' 'Pygmalion and the Image,' 'The Love of Alcestis' and 'Ogier the Dane.' 'Atalanta' and 'Pygmalion' had been advertised at the end of *Jason* as destined for *The Earthly Paradise* and would seem to have been composed by 1867 or before. Most of these need no discussion, but three of the old stories, 'The Palace East of the Sun and West of the Moon,' 'The Watching of the Falcon' and 'The Hill of Venus' do. They appear in the published *Earthly Paradise* transposed into a tragic key relatable to Morris's domestic *débâcle*. All but 'The Falcon' appear in the 1870 volumes (September through February) where they are joined by a similar story, 'The Man Who Never Laughed Again,' also written before the crisis time but now changed out of recognition. There are pleasant early versions of 'Never Laughed' collected by May Morris and it too was advertised in *Jason* as perhaps ready, in one of its benign forms, for the press in 1867. Finally, there are two more tales deriving from the 'time of trouble'. Never mentioned before their appearance in the 1870 volumes, they must be mentioned here. These are 'The Death of Paris' and 'The Lovers of Gudrun.' All these love-trage-dies should be considered together, and immediately. After all, they are the very heart and *raison d'être,* it seems to me, of the printed collection.

In the previous chapter we looked at Morris's attempts to cope with the collapse of his domestic happiness – the world suddenly emptied of meaning, the desperate efforts to win Jane back, the still more desperate attempts to understand what had gone wrong with his Earthly Paradise. What had he done so unspeakable as to merit her unspeaking with-drawal; what could he do to make up for an unknown offense; why did she grant him at moments a Mona Lisa look of, say, melting background rocks; what psychological quirk, what weird urge to cause pain, lay (or so it seemed to him at last) at the bottom of her bizarre behaviour? Actually, we don't know much about her behaviour, but it is pretty clear that she would hardly speak to her husband and ended all sexual inter-course. Possibly she just didn't want to bear any more children, and if she was sexually cool or frigid, such behaviour would have come easily enough to her, but to Morris, who was normally and possibly even highly sexed, it would have been enough to drive him to distraction. If he attributed her coldness to love of Rossetti, and if he believed her unfaithful (guilty of a betrayal which Rossetti's *Poems* of 1870 seemed to flaunt like a matador's cape in the eyes of bull-Morris, whom he had asked to review the book), there must have been danger of physical, if not mortal, violence to Jane and Gabriel. Such horror might well have erupted in 1869 or '70 had not Morris found relief from his unbearable tensions in turning *The Earthly Paradise* from a collection of myths, fairy stories, fables and apologues into what is in nearly all its basic tales a tremendous vehicle for expressing his bewilderment, loathing, grief and despair at the fate which had overtaken him. By externalising the perilous stuff seething in his breast, by talking the symptoms out with himself and his reader, Morris was simply follow-ing the therapeutic procedure by which poets have immemorially held on to their sanity and humanity. Morris's self-cure, however partial, must be admired when we remember how outrageous his conduct over minor re-buffs and disappointments often was (or is said to have been). I will take up these basic tales, whether revised or new, one by one in the order in which they appear in the printed *Paradise,* reminding the reader of the innocuous or even half-jovial forms that many first had, and giving enough excerpts from the final forms to show how Morris, whose inner life has been called an impenetrable arcanum, revealed in them every facet of his suffering. He kept the early-adopted title for his collection, making its relation to the final form of the book intriguingly mysterious or devastatingly ironical by not adding the now appropriate and inevi-table last work, *Lost.* The seven stories I am about to consider seem to be facets – every possible facet – of the same story, or rather seven supports of an aqueduct large enough to carry off the poet's flow of pain. By enabling him to unburden his heart these stories proved indispensable to his mental health, and were not just, like most of the others, many-times-told tales.

May Morris had the first draft of 'The Watching of the Falcon' in 'a little leather account-book dated June 1861' (VI, xxvii), showing that it, along with 'The Proud King' and 'Cupid and Psyche,' was among the first *Earthly Paradise* tales to be written. May says that it was 'scarcely altered' for the printed book, but later (Sup.I, 406) she tells of 'insertions of fresh matter' as well as a good deal of revising and cutting. The love-making, altered, becomes 'more remote and mysterious and in due keeping with the spirit of the story; the last episode of an invasion by the Soudan and the King's defeat is all cut out.' Unfortunately, May's 'little leather account-book' along with the six leather quartos which contained the first prologue, the ten earliest stories and much of *Jason*, all discussed or mentioned in Chapter IV, seem to have perished or at least vanished for the time being. Without May's quotations from this early material, we cannot highlight what is peculiarly characteristic of the printed form as brightly as we would like. That the 'love-making' in 'The Falcon' was altered 'in due keeping with the spirit of the story' gives us nearly all we have to go on here, but it is enough. Since the first version was told in Morris's earliest 'minstrel metre,' as May called it – knockabout four-stress couplets better suited to convivial love-making than to 'remote and mysterious' love – we must assume much revision in imagery, chime and word-colour, designed to establish the atmosphere of bewilderment, doubt, fear, overhanging doom and death, which is so pronounced in the published tale. When we recall that Morris cut out entirely the elaborate battle-scene which was the climax of the first version of the story – a medieval war piece which must have delighted the hero of Red House highjinks in 1861 – we can realise the extent of the recasting.

In nearly all the stories we are about to look at, a supernaturally lovely lady warns the hero of the suffering that loving her will bring, but 'The Watching of the Falcon' is in this respect the most paradigmatic. Here the castle-fay actually gives the king a lecture in which she details step by step the mortal dangers he is courting. After the king has 'watched' the falcon for a week without falling asleep, – the prelude to winning a wish laid down in Morris's source, Mandeville's 'Castle of the Sperhauk' – the beautiful being appears to him on the seventh night in an aureole of brightness to grant the fulfilment of any desire. He chooses 'one night of love,' which she grants with quite enough reserve to make their love-making truly 'remote and mysterious.' Most of the passages I am about to quote could hardly have appeared in the account-book of 1861 for we

are now in the midst of the most painful phase (1868–70) of the collapse
of Morris's domestic happiness. Is it possible that a scene or scenes like
the following, repeated in nearly all of these stories, could have taken
place between Morris and Jane during his courtship? Could she have
warned him that as a wife, stricken by the cool passivity and depressive
introspection that she must have known in herself even if William
couldn't see them, she would bring him great pain and possibly the ruin
of his creative energy? Whether or not she ever made such a prediction
or threat, it is certain that by 1867 and for many years thereafter she
came close to making the sense of it come true. After a period of love the
fay withdrew, with the results to Morris already looked at in his lyrics.

In 'The Falcon' the supernal being begins her school-marmish lecture
by telling the king it is better to live the life of beasts enjoying sun and
grass than that of men, who 'needs must thirst/For what shall make
their lives accurst.'

> 'Therefore I bid thee now beware,
> Lest getting something seeming fair
> Thou com'st in vain to long for more,
> Or lest the thing thou wishest for
> Make thee unhappy till thou diest,
> Or lest with speedy death thou buyest
> A little hour of happiness . . .
>
> 'Alas, why say I this to thee?
> For now I see full certainly
> That thou wilt ask for such a thing;
> It had been best for thee to fling
> Thy body from a mountain-top,
> Or in a white hot fire to drop,
> Or ever thou hadst seen me here.'

The fay knows of herself what Swinburne knew so well of Jane, that no
man should dare more than kiss her feet. When the king presses for his
night of love, she goes on:

> 'Think well, because this wished-for joy,
> That surely will thy bliss destroy,
> Will let thee live, until thy life
> Is wrapped in such bewildering strife
> That all thy days will seem but ill –
> Now wilt thou wish for this thing still?'

Since the king presses his demand, she must perforce yield, but, sobbing,
offers to release him at the last moment, which she prefaces with a sad
homily:

> 'Ah, love,' she said, 'and thou art wise
> As men are, with long miseries
> Buying these idle words and vain,
> My foolish love, with lasting pain . . .'

After they have spent one blissful night together, she rejects him utterly. Fixing her 'solemn eyes . . ./Beneath her calm, untroubled brow . . . on his wild face and wan,'

> At last she said, 'Oh, hapless man,
> Depart! your full wish you have had;
> A little time you have been glad,
> You shall be sorry till you die. . . .
>
>   'Strife without peace, early and late,
> Lasting long after you are dead,
> And laid with earth upon your head;
> War without victory shall you have;
> Defeat; nor honour shall you save;
> Your fair land shall be rent and torn,
> Your people be of all forlorn,
> And all men curse you for this thing.'

When the king answers that he can bear all this if only she stays with him,

> . . . 'Poor man,' she said,
> 'Thou ravest! our hot love is dead,
> If ever it had any life:
> Go, make thee ready for the strife
> Wherein thy days shall soon be wrapped . . .'

As for the king, the further he passed

> From that strange castle of the fays,
> More dreamlike seemed those seven days,
> And dreamlike the delicious night;
> And like a dream the shoulders white,
> And clinging arms and yellow hair,
> And dreamlike the sad morning there . . .
> Yet why was life a weariness?
> What meant this sting of sharp distress?
> This longing for a hopeless love,
> No sighing from his heart could move?

Here Morris hits the centre, I think, of his agony over Jane: unbearable longing for her which turned his day-dreams into nightmares or his night-dreams, if touched with wish-fulfilment, into waking agonies which he could hardly bear in the new day. Like Morris, the king managed to live on through the loss of friends, family, battles and country for 'That fearful rest, that dreaded friend,/That Death' did not come quickly.

Comparatively little need he said about the next story, 'The Death of Paris.' The 'Argument' points to the story's relation to our theme: 'Paris the son of Priam was wounded by one of the poisoned arrows ... that Philoctetes bore to the siege of Troy; wherefore he had himself borne up into Ida that he might see the nymph Oenone, whom he had once loved, because she, who knew many secret things, alone could heal him: but when he had seen her and spoken with her, she would deal with the matter in no wise, wherefore Paris died of that hurt.' This story must have been written late in 1869, for it was at no time advertised as a tale planned for *The Earthly Paradise*, and appears to have been unpremeditated. It appeared as the first story of what we now call Volume III, printed at the beginning of 1870. It is short but, if we do not make too much of the fairy's one time desertion of Paris, we can detect the pattern of the supernal being who drives a hard bargain and persistently sticks to it even at the cost of the lover's frightful agony and piteous death. The chief stipulation which Oenone, like most nymphs or fays, had set for her mortal lover included unswerving faith, and this taboo he had broken. Whether she might have saved him but for his continued love of Helen which he cannot hide, is not clear. When he prays her to forgive his error and begs for life,

> As thunder laughs she laughed – 'Nay, touch me not!
> Touch me not, fool!' she cried. 'Thou grow'st a-cold,
> And I am Death, Death, Death! – the tale is told
> Of all thy days! of all those joyous days,
> When thinking nought of me thou garneredst praise.'

As Paris slowly expires to his wife's wild refusal to raise him to life even for 'a minute, ah, a minute' in order to enjoy a last kiss of the old kind, he reviews his life in

> That sudden flash, bright as the lightning-flame,
> Showing the wanderer on the waste how he
> Has gone astray 'mid dark and misery.
>
> Ah, and her face upon his dying face
> That the sun warmed no more! that agony
> Of dying love, wild with the tale of days
> Long past, and strange with hope that might not be –
> All was gone now ...

'The Death of Paris' seems to have been written as a filler, but it forcefully echoes the state of mind of the author tortured, deserted, and glee-

fully left to die by the only person who could have saved him! (To be
fair, we should note that Morris sympathetically presents the case of the
neglected wife, however it relates – if it does – to his own story.)

'The Land East of the Sun and West of the Moon' is the published
version, not very much changed, of the quarto 'Palace East of the Sun,'
except that now the swan-maiden of the fairy tale, whose feather dress
John sequesters in order to get her love, looms here as the supernatural
mistress or *femme fatale*. She is no Oenone; in fact she is quite sweet-
tempered, but she is as cruelly adamant about her imposed taboo as any
unearthly lover. Although the poet says she is won back at the end, he
does not convince us, as John feels such longing for the naked aerialist
whom he has captured that 'he thought he needs must die ...' The long
dialogue in which he tries to persuade her to live with him will make
some readers think of what may have passed between Morris and gipsy-
Jane when he proposed. She is reluctant; she foresees trouble as well as
some passing bliss:

> 'O hearken, hearken! – a poor prey
> Thy toils shall take, a thing of stone
> Amid your folk to dwell alone
> And hide a heart that hateth thee.'

That he adores her, has held her in his arms for a moment, has had a
whole world of wonder opened to him – is this not enough? she asks.

> 'Hast thou not cast thine arms round Love
> At least, thy weary heart to move,
> To make thy wakening strange and new,
> And dull life false, and old tales true; ...
> To quicken thee with wondrous fire,
> And make thee fairer with desire?
> Wilt thou, then, think it all in vain,
> The restless longing and the pain
> Lightened by hope that shall not die?'

However, John will not be put off:

> 'Thou knowest not the words thou say'st,
> Or what a wretched, empty waste
> This remnant of my life is grown,
> Or how I need thee all alone
> To heal the wound this morn has made!'

She admits that his 'fierce heart' has conquered, but alternatively, she
asks if he will

> ' . . . in mine own land be mine own?
> Live long, perchance, yet all unknown . . .
> Nor hope another lot to draw
> From out life's urn?'

He embraces the chance to leave a dead world governed by 'dead men's dreams.' Before accepting, however, she reminds him of 'lovers who outlived the love' they thought they could not do without, 'And so too it may be with thee.' If he has sense enough to leave her now, they will have a brave memory to live by; will never be quite so lonely as before – only 'sad, longing, loving, not accurst.' Nevertheless he insists that she carry him away to dwell, as it were, 'Upon the outer ledge of heaven.' During the translation she croons,

> ' – Alas, poor heart unsatisfied,
> Why wilt thou love? the world is wide
> And holdeth many a joyous thing:
> Why wilt thou for thy sorrow cling
> To that desire which resteth not,
> What part soever thou hast got
> Of that whose whole thou ne'er shalt gain?
> Alas for thee and me!'

In the swan-maiden's 'marvellous land,/Fruitful, and summer-like, and fair,' in a house or palace that recalls Red House, they live happily until he begins to hanker for his old home and relatives. It seems he is not quite sure of her love either –

> 'Would that I knew,
> If thou hadst ever loved me, sweet!
> Then surely all things would I meet
> With good heart.'
> Such a trouble came
> Across his face, that she, for shame
> Of something hidden, blushed blood-red . . .

She consents to send him back and says she will even come once more to redeem him from the dead-alive world of earth-dwellers, but on one condition – he must never call her back to his arms,

> 'For if thou dost, so strangely now
> Are we twain wedded, I and thou, . . .
> That at thy word I needs must come,
> Whereso I be, unto thine home; . . .'

– where love like theirs must perish. A scene like this suggests that Jane may have consented to Morris returning to his middle-class family provided he never called her into it. After a touching scene of reunion with his mother, John of course breaks the taboo. Through a terrible snow-storm she comes in her more or less invisible fairy garments to his family feast-hall, but after a night of bliss returns 'forever' to her eternal-summer home. John has no idea where it lies. Now indeed Morris indulges in reams of John- (or self-) pity, self-cursing, and prayers for mercy running to lengths equalled in no other story. I cannot give a tithe of a tithe of the passages drowned in this grey tide of tears. His breaking the taboo he now calls 'sin,' the word which Morris uses more than once in the lyrics to describe his offence, whatever it was, against Jane.

> 'Ah, woe betide, ah, woe betide,
> *East of the Sun, West of the Moon!*
> A land that no man findeth soon,
> The grave of greedy love that cries
> To all folk of its agonies . . .
> – O love, love, would thy once-kissed eyes,'
>
> etc., etc.

John seeks his swan-girl all over the earth (he has no means of sky travel) and at last comes to a perfect mandala of a land where, in the central court of a surpassing palace, he finds her as somnolent as the Sleeping Beauty. After managing to awake her with the magic phrase, 'East of the Sun' etc., they are united forever after. But *à quoi bon?* As Gregory the Star-gazer who dreams this story in the printed *Earthly Paradise* mutters in 'the pain of morn':

> *– Well, e'en so all the tale is said*
> *How twain grew one and came to bliss –*
> *Woe's me! an idle dream it is!*

The concluding lines of an earlier version, where there is no star-gazer, ran in the same vein:

> So twain were one and all is bliss,
> For lo, an idle dream this is.

None of the succeeding tales we are about to look at entice us to a happy ending which the poet then mocks. Of two of these, 'The Man Who Never Laughed Again' and 'The Hill of Venus,' May wrote,

In the case of both these poems a great deal of unused material exists which throws light on the thought and searchings and labour that went to the moulding of them . . . They are, as we know, both stories of wild, barren passion and are built up in an atmosphere of such an unquenchable melancholy that if my Father had written little else of note, and if they stood for an expression of himself (as a poet's work, however consciously fanciful, must do in some degree) you would say. Here is an inward-looking being with scarcely a hope in his life, cursed with a sense of the futilities of the world while keenly alive to its beauties.

(Sup. I, 433.)

Perhaps 'Never Laughed Again' presents us with Morris's most blood-curdling picture of a *belle dame sans merci* and her victims. The story comes from *The Arabian Nights* but, more clearly than ever, we can see Morris closing the pages of his source book – his usual procedure – and retelling the tale in such a way as to relieve the pressure of questions, doubts, horrors, and heart-break building up inside him in 1868–70. The tale begins with Bharam, an Eastern Timon, about to give up the ghost because he is absolutely disillusioned and disgusted with every human being. Yet the agony of his erstwhile friend Firuz, expressed in a chilling groan of 'helpless misery' – 'A dreadful prelude to a dreadful tale' – seems to be even more desperate than his own. Unexpectedly Firuz offers Bharam a fortune if he will perform a service for himself and six friends. At night they cross to a forest to

> . . . a fair and great abode
> Whereon the red gold e'en in moonlight glowed.
> There silently they lighted down before
> Smooth marble stairs, and through the open door

> They entered a great, dimly-lighted hall;
> Yet through the dimness well our man could see
> How fair the hangings were that clad the wall,
> And what a wealth of beast and flower and tree
> Was spent wherever carving there might be,
> And what a floor was 'neath his wearied feet,
> Not made for men who call death rest and sweet.

Obviously, Bharam was in the temenos-centre of a great mandalic sur-round which he discovered at daybreak to consist, as we might imagine, of gardens, 'thick-leaved trees,' and winding waters, the whole seeming to be the work of an artist 'who had a mind to mock eternity.' Imagine Bharam's horror to find the central hall inhabited, not 'by white limbs and glittering eyes,' but by six examples of 'man's accursed race,' 'out-worn with pain' and slumped on a kind of mourners' bench of marble. One of them, to be sure, is better off than the others for he lolls there 'Dead midst the living slaves of misery.' At this point Firuz explains to Bharam that he has brought him to this palace of pain to help bury these sufferers as one after another they collapse. Finally, Firuz will die, after which Bharam can plunder the palace of its interminable riches. Imme-diately, Bharam and the survivors carry the dead man through the sur-rounding gardens and forest to the shore of a stream which

> Was cleared of wood, in which space here and there
> Low, changing mounds told of dead men near.

On the far side of the river rose a dark-grey cliff, impassable but pierced low-down by a door apparently made of iron, with a key-hole, while moored by the grave mounds was a boat intended for 'Whoso had will such doubtful things to meet/As that strange door might hide ...' One by one the 'wretched mourners' were delivered from life and buried until it became the turn of Firuz himself, who died raving about a lost lover to whom he had 'prayed in vain' to relieve his 'ravening hunger' and 'quenchless thirst' for beauty.

Now Bharam, having taken a fortune from the centre of the deceitful mandala – where men were broken, not firmed, in spirit – finds he cannot enjoy it, but must needs, as Morris says, creep back to the place of horror. Past the now ruined palace, with its broken trellises and torn flowers, he is drawn to the field of tumuli and the cliff with the iron door. Crossing the river in the boat, he manages to step

> ... from out the fair light of day,
> Casting all hope of common life away.

In palpable darkness, he stumbles among visions of a world in which all things lovely, including women, are monstrously distorted till he falls into a 'sightless sleep' and awakes in – a not unpleasant land. In an early version of the tale (Morris may have begun it in 1866 or 1867: this oriental countryside is really charming, and May reproduces the description of it in the 'Introduction' to Volume V because of 'its particular English character.' A stream gurgles round a hill and young people are singing.

> But now they ceased, the happy notes of men:
> The reed-chat's warble and the late bee's drone
> The chuckle of the light-foot water-hen
> But made the lonely river yet more lone ...

Bharam found 'the level grassy spot of ground/Twixt stream and hill ... a very paradise' with its 'huge old trees .../And little closes hedged with trellis grey ...' The boys and girls, 'so far removed from death' strike up their song again, in which the boys complain about being parted from the girls, while the girls answer that the lads have nothing to fear. Much altered and enlarged, this was first published in *Poems By the Way* (1891). Cut out and never used was a lot of good advice proferred to Bharam by the village elders who seek to discourage him from sailing north in a black ship which always came to transport adventurous youths to their fate.' In the published tale the idyllic country scene is omitted altogether and Bharam goes straight from the iron door to the waiting ship, enticed by two 'lovesome' girls who promise him a queen who is also, incomparably, the queen of amorous arts. As they near her golden house, young men and women, echoed by the 'lovesome' enticers, substitute for the innocent duet of the country boys and girls a favourite ditty of their sovereign:

> *I think the sky calls living none but three:*
> *The God that looketh thence and thee and me;*
> *And He made us, but we made Love to be,*
>
> *Think not of time, then, for thou shalt not die*
> *How soon soever shall the world go by,*
> *And nought be left but God and thou and I.*

Made king in her house of gold, caught in the arms of the wondrous being – 'in the golden age they might have been' – Bharam lived for two years, not always so flushed as on the day he arrived,

> Yet still no less did love with him abide,
> Tempered with quiet days and restfulness;
> Desire fulfilled, renewed, this life did bless.

When he dreamed of living a more active life, he accused himself of swerving from singleness of heart though even 'in his love's arms he would feel the sting/Of vain desire and ne'er-accomplished bliss.' Then came a day when she told him that 'at the command/Of whose will I dare not disobey,' she was forced to leave him for a hundred days. This time the fairy's taboo required that during this period, though trusted with the key to their love-chamber, he must not enter it on pain of never seeing her again. With her gone, 'In agony he strove to cast from him/ Fresh doubts of what she was ...' How could anyone command her obedience? 'Was she his bane ...?'

> Then would he image forth her body fair,
> And limb by limb set before his eyes
> Her loveliness as he had seen it there;
> Then cry, 'Why think of these vain mysteries
> When still ahead such happy life there lies?
> And yet and yet, this that doth so outshine?
> All other beauty, is it wholly mine?'

Jealousy begins to take hold and there flits through his mind a memory 'Of men from some strange heaven of love outcast.' On the king's judgement seat he can 'think of nothing but her dear return' (from Scalands near Robertsbridge, perhaps, where Jane was alone with Rossetti during the last weeks of April, 1870).

> Love failed him not, but baneful jealousy
> Had scaled his golden throne and sat thereby.

He begins to think his wife's prohibition cannot have been seriously meant. Perhaps she wanted to test the power of his love-memories – wanted him to break the taboo. All within the forbidden room seems normal at first as he touches tenderly the clothes she had dropt by the bed as if stripping before leaving him. Then he sees a strange cup on her bed table with a message bidding him drink if he would sound ' *"all the depths of this hid thing."* '

> *'Drink then, and take what thou hast fairly won*
> *For make no doubt that thine old life is done.'*

Thinking that if he has sinned, 'she will forgive my sin,' he drains the cup. Then

> Did he think dimly of those mourning men
> And saw them winding the dark trees among,
> And in his ears their doleful wailing rung;
> His love and all the glories of his home
> E'en in that minute shadows had become.
>
> E'en in that minute; though at first indeed
> In one quick flash of pain unbearable,
> His love, his queen, made bare of any weed
> Seemed standing there, as though some tale to tell
> From opened lips; and then a dark veil fell
> O'er all things . . .

He awoke, of course, among the graves of his 'forerunners' opposite the cliff door, 'as one might wake in Hell.'

> Trembling awhile he lay, and scarcely knew
> Why he was sick with fear, but when at last
> His wretched soul unto his body drew,
> And somewhat he could think about the past,
> As one might wake to hell, around he cast
> A haggard glance . . .

Realising all he has lost, matchless wife, desire fulfilled, kingly days in a wondrous home – Jane, Red House, etc.? – he howled for her return. Crying, 'Come back to me'

> He cast himself adown, and hid his face
> Within the grass, and heeding no disgrace,
> Howled beastlike, till his voice grew hoarse and dim,
> And little life indeed seemed left in him.

However, he cannot die like his predecessors on the ruined mourners' bench in the shattered temenos, but 'must wander' till death. If he seemed to sleep, it was only to dream 'The worst of dreams' –

That he the fearful chain might never break;
And shameful images his eyes must make
That shuddering he must call by his love's name,
And on his lips must gather words of shame.

And when men saw

His changeless face drawn with that hidden pain,
They said, 'THE MAN WHO NE'ER SHALL LAUGH AGAIN.'

Surely the fay(?) of this tale is the most malignant and murderous of all those drawn in *The Earthly Paradise*. In English literature she is probably the *belle dame sans merci* par excellence, with Morris's other 'faeries' not far behind. How Mario Praz came to omit these destroyers from his long accounts of the baleful women who haunt large if sterile tracts of European literature of the nineteenth and early twentieth centuries is hard to see. Of course, Praz seems to miss most of the subtly cruel girls by indulging his taste for the banal type of tormenter who dances in frenetic nakedness through the pages of *The Romantic Agony*, attacking her lovers not only tooth and nail but with whips, daggers, drugs and drunkenness which leave them dead after a night of tedious massacre called love. Morris's *belles dames* owe practically nothing to his friend Swinburne either. They give themselves quietly and fully but then invent arbitrary taboos which, 'sinned' against, they punish adamantly by exiling the lover without reprieve. Somehow, these quiet *femmes fatales*, whose motivation is not to be looked for in the Marquis de Sade, strike us in their mysterious cruelty as more true-to-life than the French-Swinburnean stereotype. Can this be because they were founded on the author's experience of a languorous, self-absorbed, iron-willed real woman?

The next of Morris's inscrutable women differs from the others partly because her story is taken not from a fairy-tale but from a semi-historic Icelandic saga – the *Laxdaela*. Here the woman gets somewhat more attention than her lovers. Here at last we have open faithlessness (unintended?) in the woman and open jealousy in the man. Besides, the heroine of 'The Lovers of Gudrun' is not a witch in the usual sense of the word – just a *femme fatale*. Ineffably beautiful as any fairy-queen, she needs men pretty much in the human way and before meeting the Morris-persona, Kiartan, she has already had two husbands. One she divorced for striking her because, sneering and scornful, 'she ever gloomed before his eyes'; the other, whom she seems to have loved, was drowned 'By wizard's spells amidst a summer gale.' Gudrun, always 'fierce-hearted' when 'raging for her vanished bliss,' soon storms her way into the heart and arms of the handsome, gentle but in every way brave and heroic Kiartan. At the same time she makes a total though not flaunted conquest of Kiartan's great friend and foster-brother Bodli. These 'brothers' make a voyage to Norway in spite of Gudrun's disapproval, but she does not set up conditions for Kiartan's return which can be manipulated as an iron-clad taboo. In Norway, King Olaf Tryggvison holds Kiartan hostage until assured that all Icelanders will adopt his new state-religion, Christianity, while allowing Bodli to return to Iceland where he leads Gudrun to believe Kiartan faithless. Her 'long, slim figure' convulsed with anguish, she wails and throws her arms about until finally they encircle Bodli, whom she marries in revenge. When, shortly after, Kiartan returns unmarried and bearing gifts and honours for her, Gudrun becomes positively demonic, cursing Bodli for trying to imprison her in a 'hot-walled hell.'

> '— I curse thee now, while good and evil strive
> Within me, but if longer I shall live
> What shall my curse be then? myself so curst,
> That nought shall then be left me but the worst,
> That God shall mock himself for making me.'

Needless to say, she stirs up so much feuding among the hot-headed Icelanders that, when Kiartan marries another, he is soon killed by Bodli, who in turn is killed by Kiartan's family. After months of 'glooming,' Gudrun marries still again and lays another husband in the grave. At last, grown old, she tells one of her sons, curious to know which of his mother's lovers she had liked best, 'I did worst to him I loved the most' – an appropriate accolade from a woman who had never done any man good. Rossetti, who was apparently able to see himself as Kiartan betrtrayed by the foster-brother he had done so much to benefit, is said to have liked 'The Lovers of Gudrun' better than any other story in *The Earthly Paradise*! Morris, on the other hand, must have thought of the tale with which he ended the collection, 'The Hill of Venus,' as the most characteristic and powerful embodiment of what he had to express in the book which, in its final form, wears its first title so ironically.

'The Hill of Venus' was one of the first stories intended for inclusion in what was in those happy Red House days thought of, quite appropriately, as a collection of tales illustrating the attainment of heaven on earth by showing what paradise is, how it can be won, how lost, and how, if you take pains, recovered. True, the tale of 'The Hill,' Tieck's story of Tannhäuser, differed a little from the other early stories as the knight, apparently abandoned by Venus, determined to give up his tangible earthly paradise for the Christian heaven. However, in Rome he treated the Pope as cavalierly as only a cavalier could, and hurried 'home' to Venus while the Pope's dry staff bloomed in token of God's forgiveness of the sinner.

So much for the old 'Hill.' The new 'Hill' differs not only from the first one but also from the other tales of *femmes fatales*. Here the fairy or goddess has no desire, apparently, to reduce Walter (Tannhäuser) to misery or destruction. When he wishes to return to the 'vain, grasping, uncompassionate' everyday world, she imposes no veto, taboo, or punishment. He had entered her Hill by crossing a stream, piercing a cave into impenetrable darkness and fainting, thus reminding us inevitably of 'Never Laughed Again,' but, unlike Bharam, he was consciously fleeing from the world he had found deadening to the spirit. Walter had heard much of the dangers of the Hill but felt compelled to startle his numbed heart into life at any cost. Yes,

> . . . all the stories were at one in this,
> That still they told of a trap baited well
> With some first minutes of unheard-of bliss;
> Then, these grasped greedily, the poor fool fell
> To earthly evil, or no doubtful hell,
> Yet, as these stories flitted by all dim,

the knight's face softened, sweet they seemed to him –

> He muttered: 'Yea, the end is hell and death,
> The midmost hid, yet the beginning Love.
> Ah me! despite the worst Love threateneth,
> Still would I cling on to the skirts thereof,
> If I could hope his sadness still could move
> My heart for evermore.'

What has been left behind but ' "A world made to be lost, –/A bitter life 'twixt pain and nothing tossed" ' What he wakes to is a new life set at the centre of a lovely, mandalic schematisation of nature where he hears beautiful youths and maidens singing the song *Before our lady came on earth,*' which persisted from the earliest version to this last. And there he meets Venus, naked of course but as indescribable in her glory as Jane herself, offering 'No rest but rest of utter love' – ' "For this, for this/God made the world that I might feel thy kiss!" '

Here the poet pauses to exclaim, 'What, is the tale not ended then? Woe's me!' He recalls that so many stories end, do they not, with

> 'I longed, I found, I lived long happily
> And fearless in death's fellowship did wend?'
> –On earth, – where hope is that two souls may blend
> That God has made –

but Venus, like Jane, was not fashioned, it seems, with this hope in mind. Walter is plagued by questions with which he plagues her. How can it be that he will not die? Why should he alone have 'a love all perfect and his own'? Why has

'No heart my heart that loveth so ere found
That needed me? – for wilt thou say indeed
That thou, O perfect one, of me hath need?'

What of love's unique power to cancel the fear of life as well as of
death? Should he try to accomplish something worthy in the world? Is
he blindly seeking 'with ruin of his own life,/To ruin the world's ...?'
What of the fate of his immortal soul? Peace having fled, Walter himself
fled from Venus one night and joined pilgrims going to Rome for abso-
lution of their sins. However, he cannot confess to the Pope lest 'man's
hate,/Man's fear, God's scorn shall fall in all their weight/Upon my
love.' Venus, unseen by others, is standing near him defenceless, (like
Jane among middle-class philistines) in the Pope's garden. Well, he does
scorn Jane–Venus; he says,

'Yet is it so that evil dureth still,
Unslain of God – what if a man's love cling,
In sore despite of reason, hope, and will,
Unto the false heart of an evil thing?'

Being told by the Pope that ' "just so much hope I have of thee/As on
this dry staff fruit and flowers to see!" ' Walter retreats quickly back to
the Hill to enjoy with his irresistible paramour both 'horrors passing hell'
and joys by which all other 'joys are miseries.' 'No ignorance, no
wonder, and no hope/Was in his heart,' but self-analysis had saved his
soul. Because he loved much – that is, underwent much, gave much, got
little and expected nothing from Jane-Venus – he was forgiven. The
Pope's staff flowered.

However, the love ordeal of the man Bernard Shaw called St William
of Kelmscott was by no means ended. We have seen how he used what I
have called the second *Earthly Paradise*, the published one, to ease his
spirit of its most perilous pains. By externalising these in stories he could
indulge in bewilderment, anguish, horror, recrimination and self-pity to
any degree and extent which the distress of the moment dictated. There
is not so much denunciation of Jane and Rossetti, not so much jealousy,
as we might expect. In the preceding chapter we examined what his lyric
poetry had to say of his agony, but it is in *The Earthly Paradise*, especially in the stories we have just run through, that we get the clearest picture, probably, of what happened. Morris tends almost everywhere to
blame himself for Jane's conduct and never ceases to beg her to 'come
back' and even to 'forgive' him for some kind of offence or 'sin.' What
the 'sin' was we shall probably never know though the breaking of the
fairy mistress's 'taboo,' in almost every tale we have examined, is called a

'sin.' Though the taboos are always whimsical or arbitrary, their violation is in every case relentlessly and heartlessly punished by the fairy's disappearance. Her vanishings are treated quite realistically, to the actual locking of their chamber doors, as in 'Never Laughed Again.' Whether such incidents throw any light on Jane's actual behaviour, is impossible to say. One circumstance which may help to explain her actions is that the man to be punished often seems to be growing tired of his perfect love-life, or at least is longing to go back to his middle-class family for a visit. The supernal creature feels she cannot survive in the harsh sun and air (i.e., among the caste scorn and cruel innuendos) of that 'world.' Whether she 'really loves' the mortal is a question also raised in nearly all of the stories we have looked at. In 'The Hill of Venus' Walter has definitely tired of being linked forever to the acme of female beauty. Perhaps Venus does not need him either, but in those days of the promised Second Coming (A.D. 1000) Walter seems to feel he may be able to protect her from destruction and so, forgiving her for her former lovers, returns to the 'hell' of the Hill partly from a sense of duty. Was it this particular nuance of love in the knight, not entirely unlike that of the imminent Saviour, which caused the Pope's staff to blossom? That these *Earthly Paradise* stories reveal intimate secrets about Morris's life, he makes clear enough in a stanza of the *Envoi* which has two chief forms. In the first the poet addresses the Book he is sending into the world:

> Thou hast beheld me tremble oft enough
> At things I could not choose but trust to thee,
> Although I knew the world was wise and rough,
> Yet did I never fail to let thee see
> The littleness that each day was in me:
> Through all this while we dealt did I betray
> The idle singer of an empty day.
>
> (VI, xxxj)

In the second, the printed version, this stanza, somewhat modified, is supposed to be spoken by the Book on behalf of its author to Morris's master, Chaucer:

> *'I have beheld him tremble oft enough*
> *At things he could not choose but trust to me,*
> *Although he knew the world was wise and rough:*
> *And never did he fail to let me see*
> *His love, – his folly and faithlessness, maybe;*
> *And still in turn I gave him voice to pray*
> *Such prayers as cling about an empty day.'*

Probably there is no last word to be said about Jane and love (at least we shall say a good many more) and as for Earthly Paradises, they will spring up again and again in every form taken by Morris's creative work and thought. That this predominantly melancholy book should have kept the title of the first *Earthly Paradise* is due partly to conscious irony, and partly to the unquenchable hope of '*The poor singer of an empty day.*' When finally recasting 'The Hill of Venus,' he wrote to Jane in Torquay, less than six months after the Robertsbridge episode when she had been alone with Rossetti. Morris's despair over this can be surmised from 'Never Laughed Again.' He wrote,

For me I don't think people really want to die because of mental pain, that is if they are imaginative people; they want to live to see the play played out fairly – they have hopes that they are not conscious of – Hillao! here's cheerful talk for you. I beg your pardon, dear, with all my heart.

(Letters, 36)

The people who did most to keep Morris's spirits afloat during what Mackail called 'the stormy days of *The Earthly Paradise*,' were Aglaia Coronio and Georgiana Burne-Jones. In the letter to Jane quoted above he mentions visiting the former who always 'buttered him up so,' and the latter – Morris, who had known her so intimately during the Red House and *Paradise* decade, may have fallen in love with her as his relationship with Jane cooled. Many people think so and there is enough material in some of *The Earthly Paradise* poems and elsewhere to justify examining the possibility. Any analgesia which Georgiana may have spread over the hurt Jane caused which has held our attention for so long should be a relief to the reader too. Here another Earthly Paradise, not in irony, wholly in earnest, struggled into life.

VII A Friend in Paradise Lost
1868-1871

There are a number of tales in the printed *Earthly Paradise* which have a
lot to say about true love, but little or nothing, or at least nothing favour-
able, about Jane or the Jane-persona. When she appears in these stories her role is pretty much that of villainess. The heroines of the happier
tales, dainty but forceful, blonde rather than brunette, lively instead of
languorous, physically strong rather than just strong-looking, with clear-
grey eyes fixed in kindly concern on the world around rather than 'blue-
grey orbs' wandering off to some middle distance, and, finally, with a
determination to save their lovers from pain and death rather than torturing them for breaking whimsical taboos – these women were not
modelled on Jane. Many think the model was Georgiana Burne-Jones,
the wife of Morris's closest friend. Georgiana admired Morris though it
is hardly fair to claim, as has been done, that he is the real hero of the
biography she wrote (*Memorials of Edward Burne-Jones*, 2 vols., 1904).
Morris admired her too, to say the least, and she was not only a close
friend but his closest correspondent as long as he lived. That their relation was warmer than friendship must be considered pure speculation,
but Morris, as he himself said, could hide nothing from his 'book' or
lyrics, and he seems to have had a good deal to say about a lovely woman
who strongly suggests many things we know or think we know of Georgiana Burne-Jones. The first full-length portrait of her occurs in a late
romance. *The Well at the World's End*. Ralph of Upmeads, the hero,
has lost through murder a woman who may have been made out worse
than she was. He is lost in a black forest in the depths of still blacker depression when Ursula, armed *cap-à pie*, appears in the light of his bonfire. Morris persuaded Burne-Jones to illustrate this critical moment for
the Kelmscott edition. The picture is entangled with the words 'A
Friend in Need' – a heart-friend who watches over his life and furnishes
him with as much paradise and immortality as can befall a mortal. (Plate
11.)

Georgiana's *Memorials* of her husband naturally have much to say
about Morris because of their close and unbroken friendship, but they
also give the impression that Burne-Jones never paid a tribute to his
friend which she did not scrupulously store up and, when the time came,
glowingly set down. She did not recall where her husband's rooms at
Exeter College, Oxford, were but she remembered his speaking of Morris's as being ' "pleasant ones overlooking Exeter Garden and the

Schools, in a little quadrangle that was called Hell Quad. You passed
under the archway called Purgatory from the great quadrangle to reach
it." ' (*Memorials* I, 87) From a letter of Ned's to Cornell Price she
quotes,

Morris has a good deal of my time. He is one of the cleverest fellows I know,
and to me far more congenial in his thoughts and likings than anyone it has
been my good fortune to meet with . . . He is full of enthusiasm for things holy
and beautiful and true, and, what is rarest, of the most exquisite perception and
judgement in them. For myself, he has tinged my whole inner being with the
beauty of his own, and I know not a single gift, for which I owe such gratitude
to Heaven as his friendship. If it were not for his boisterous mad outbursts and
freaks, which break the romance he sheds around him – at least to me – he
would be a perfect hero.

(I, 95–6)

This was written in 1854 and writing home a little later he, to use Georgiana's paraphrase, 'exclaims that Morris still continues the most clever,
glorious fellow in or out of Oxford . . .' (I, 105)

   Though lamenting that no 'woman can hope to describe the life of
men at college since she can never have seen it as it really is' (I, 105),
Georgiana proceeds to tell us of Morris's custom, begun in 1854, of reading aloud to Burne-Jones, of the books thus read, and of the 'painted
books' and old chronicles devoured in the Bodleian. Jones, Morris and a
friend named Fulford visited France in the summer of 1855, and Georgiana gives such a circumstantial account of all they did and said that she
seems to have been with them. Actually she was simply recalling what
her husband-to-be later told her of the journey, in which 'Morris in his
wonderful way knew everything about every place they went to . . .' (I,
114). Meanwhile, Georgiana had met this paragon of friends, poets, and
men:

At the Royal Academy, where Wilfred Heeley had taken me, we saw him
standing before Millais's picture of 'The Rescue,' examining it closely: as he
turned to go away, Heeley said 'That's Morris,' and introduced us to each
other; but he looked as if he scarcely saw me. He was very handsome, of an
unusual type – the statues of mediaeval kings often remind me of him – and
at that time he wore no moustache, so that the drawing of his mouth, which
was his most expressive feature, could be clearly seen. His eyes always seemed
to me to take in rather than to give out. His hair waved and curled trium-
phantly.

(I, 111)

It was not easy for Georgiana to forget Edward's note from the Union-
time (1857) that 'Morris had a face always fit for Lancelot or Tristram,'
while Rossetti later chose his curly head for studies and pictures of young

King David. She selected another eulogy of Morris from a letter written by Edward (not yet her husband) in 1855 to an old friend, Maria Choyce:

'Watch carefully all that Morris writes. You will find one of the very purest and most beautiful minds on earth breathing through all he touches. Sometimes I even regret that he is my friend, for I am open to the charge of partiality by praising him so, and if he were a stranger I know I should detect him in a heap of others' writings, and watch for something very great from him, as I do now.'

(I, 123)

In 1856, when she was sixteen, Edward, then twenty-three, asked for Georgiana's hand. The chief effect of this in the *Memorials* was to increase the spate of stories about Morris, who now began 'a pleasant custom of running up [to London] from Oxford on Saturdays' to see his friend, who was at this time studying painting with Rossetti. She recalled how the latter, when recruiting painters to help him decorate the Oxford Union, would not let Valentine Prinsep beg off:

' "Nonsense," answered Rossetti confidently, "there's a man I know who has never painted anything – his name is Morris – and he has undertaken one of the panels and he will do something very good you may depend – so you had better come !" Rossetti was so friendly and confident that I consented and joined the band at Oxford.'

(I, 159)

This obviously was quoted from a letter of Prinsep's, and the tale of Morris's wonderful ingenuity and tireless energy at the Union Georgiana got from one of Edward's letters (to her?):

'Morris began his picture first and finished it first, and then, his hands being free, he set to work upon the roof, making in a day a design for it which was a wonder to us for its originality and fitness, for he had never before designed anything of the kind, nor, as I suppose, seen any ancient work to guide him. Indeed, all his life, he hated the copying of ancient work as unfair to the old and stupid for the present, only good for inspiration and hope. All the autumn though he worked upon the roof high above our heads . . .'

(I, 161)

According to Georgiana, Morris first saw Jane in an Oxford theatre, but this incident along with his marriage to her in April 1859 only receive a bare mention in the *Memorials*. However, once Georgiana and Edward were married and both began working to make Morris's Red House livable and lovely, we get from her the best description of the enterprise to be found anywhere. She more than anyone in the Morris circle seems to have divined what a personal Earthly Paradise meant to

Morris and the role that the mandalic pattern and atmosphere were to play in the whole of his creative life. Georgiana was perhaps more thrilled than her husband with Morris's plan of 1864 that Red House be enlarged to make a permanent home for the Burne-Joneses as well as the Morrises.

Edward says in the Notes: 'A lovely plan was made, too happy ever to come about. It was that Morris should add to his house, making it a full quadrangle, and Webb made a design for it so beautiful that life seemed to have no more in it to desire – but when the estimates came out it was clear that enthusiasm had outrun our wisdom and modifications had sadly to be made.'

The two sets of plans lie before me now, clean and unused, and it is curious to think how differently all our lives would have gone if this scheme had been carried out. We were not to have actually shared the house with the Morrises; there were separate entrances and rooms for the two families; but all was to have been under one roof with the garden in common. We looked forward to building in the spring of 1865 . . .

(I, 277)

The trouble was that Georgiana came down with a severe case of scarlet fever while Morris suffered such a recrudescence of rheumatic fever that both families had to give up not only the plan but the house itself. Both moved back to London, the Burne-Joneses settling at the Grange, North End Lane, Fulham, in 1867 and the Morrises gradually gravitating closer and closer to them until in 1878 they finally settled at Kelmscott House on the Embankment at Hammersmith. However, as Georgiana writes, 'Nothing ever interrupted the intimacy with Morris; that friendship was like one of the forces of nature.' When the Burne-Joneses went to live at the Grange, then quite far from Morris, who was living in Queen Square, Edward 'proposed that he and Webb should come every Sunday, to bind us together, and I remember . . . a letter he wrote in answer, more full of warm response . . . than he often permitted himself.' 'This,' says Georgiana,

was the beginning of the Sunday meetings of which mention will often be made. At first they were in the evening, but when Morris left Queen Square and came to live nearer the Grange the plan was altered, and he used to breakfast with us every Sunday and spend the morning in the studio with Edward. Before he left they always either invited me to join them for a little while or else sallied forth from the studio to pay me a call.

(II, 5)

Actually, some coolness seems to have developed between Jane and Georgiana about 1865, when it became clear that Jane cared nothing for the moulding of mandalas around a loved figure at the centre and was quite willing to wreck her husband's hundred-and-one plans to brighten the

face of England, as if to prove to him that love is *not* enough. The last
holiday the families, both with children now, spent together was in
Oxford during the Long Vacation of 1867, but Morris seldom missed his
Sunday call on his friends at the Grange or their seaside house at Rottingdean near Brighton. As Burne-Jones wrote in 1883, 'Morris never fail-
eth ...' (II, 133) A good thing too, for Morris was indeed a mainstay of
the painter's life and probably of his wife's too. A description of the
dreadful depression into which a retrospective showing of his work at the
New Gallery in 1892–3 threw Burne-Jones ends, says Georgiana, with 'so
beautiful a vision of the friendship between himself and Morris ... that
it may well be given here.' All I need to quote is the last sentence of
Burne-Jones' letter; 'This morning Morris brought fresh life to me – for
all the week my head had been low in the dust – and he talked of the
high things till I forgot my abasement.' (I, 214) In 1876 Morris, now rea-
sonably recovered from his troubles with Jane, also wrote a cheering letter to 'a friend,' usually conjectured to be Georgiana herself, who 'was
passing through one of those darknesses in which the whole substance of
life seems to crumble away under our hands.'

Sometimes ... I wish even that I were once more in trouble of my own, and
think of myself that I am really grown callous: but I am sure that though I
have many hopes and pleasures, or at least strong ones, ... I would give them
away, hopes and pleasures, one by one or all together, and my life at last, for
you, for my friendship, for my honour, for the world. If it seems boasting I
do not mean it; but rather that I claim, so to say it, not to be separated from
those that are heavy-hearted ... I wish I could say something that would serve
you, beyond what you know very well, that I love you and long to help you:
and indeed I entreat you (however trite the words may be) to think that life is
not empty nor made for nothing, and that the parts of it fit one into another
in some way; and that the world goes on, beautiful and strange and dreadful
and worshipful.

(Letters, 77–8)

In 1881 Edward summed up the role of Topsy in the life of the Burne-
Joneses in a letter to Charles Eliot Norton:

Towards evening Morris came – for it was Georgie's birthday – and you would
have found him just as if no time had gone by, only the best talk with him is
while he is hungry, for meat makes him sad... He is unchanged – little grey
tips to his curly wig – ... buttons more off than formerly, never any necktie –
more eager if anything than ever, but about just the same things; a rock of defence to us all, and a castle on the top of it, and a banner on the top of that ...

(Quoted in Henderson, *William Morris*, 186)

Even when Morris was ill with 'gout' in 1891, Sir Edward and his Lady
were still exclaiming over his incomparable energy of body and mind. As
Georgiana put it:

the labours of the Kelmscott Press had begun, and the time was come when they were to realise their old dream of making a beautiful book with beautiful pictures in it. Whenever I speak of the Kelmscott Press I think of its crowning glory, the Chaucer, and of the strength which carried the whole thing through – Morris' strength. Listen to Edward about this : 'Morris will be here tomorrow, strong, self-contained, master of himself and therefore of the world. Solitude cannot hurt him nor dismay him. Such strength as his I see nowhere.'

(II, 216)

Besides quoting most of the eulogies of Morris which her husband scattered over forty years throughout his own letters and 'Notes,' Lady Burne-Jones gave a pretty minute account of most of the art-work the friends had been engaged on together, added many 'Notes' of her own, and ended what the *Memorials* have to say about Morris by telling of a 'pilgrimage' she made the year after his death.

Quite suddenly things fell out so that, though Edward could not go, a chance was offered to me of visiting North France in most pleasant company, and on June 4th I started for a six days' pilgrimage to Abbeville, Beauvais, and Amiens. We were at Beauvais Cathedral on Whit Sunday morning, and all through the beautiful service the images of the young Edward and Morris of two and forty years ago were with me.

(II, 311)

Was Georgiana drawn on this pilgrimage by having lately read the article on Amiens which Morris published in the *Oxford and Cambridge Magazine* in February 1856, extolling the North-French churches as 'the grandest, the most beautiful, the kindest and most loving of all the buildings that earth has ever borne . . .'? Did she look with special interest at the deathbed of the Virgin in the great tympanum of the west front, where the beloved lies so quiet; according to Morris, 'with her hands crossed downward, dead at last. Ah! and where will she go now? whose face will she see always? Oh! that we might be there too!'

The *Memorials* give a clear indication that the Burne-Joneses were both in love with Morris throughout most of their lives. It is almost impossible that Edward's hero-worship should not have infected Georgiana. What, we may ask, must have been the effect on her when, putting the legendary son of Zeus to the test of day-to-day intimacy, she found him almost as noble-minded, high-spirited, multi-talented, kind-hearted, courageous, innocent and unbreakable as reported? Still, there did seem to be a gap in his dazzling armour, a dangerous hiatus. A woman he loved could wrong him miserably with indifference or drive him wild with scorn because he was not sure women found him attractive or could actually love him. We have come across this fear in many forms ever since 'Frank's Sealed Letter' with its remarkable divination, both physical and mental, of Jane in the person of Mabel, 'her heavy, rolling, purple

hair, . . . great slumberously-passionate eyes, and her red lips' – 'Quiet as
an old Egyptian statue' pondering its 'own greatness' except when pouring scorn on the inadequacies of a lover she had determined to 'cast'
from her heart forever with the imperious ' "I never loved you, never
shall . . ." ' Whether this story of 1856 was frequently read by Georgiana
one doesn't know, but she seems to have been among the first to realise
that Morris had married a woman like Mabel, who, even if she did not
break his geniality, enthusiasm, self-respect, ability to love and will to
work, would cause him years of misery. From a fairly early date, say
1866, Georgiana seems to have decided to do what she could to protect
and help and heal the vulnerable hero – that is to save his will to dream
of an Earthly Paradise.

Besides, she was not invulnerable herself. In 1868, perhaps earlier, her
husband became involved with one of his models, a Greek beauty of the
type affected by the pre-Raphaelites and employed also by Rossetti. It is
said that this woman, Mrs Marie Zambaco, who had possibly been de-
nied entrance to Burne-Jones's studio for a reason we can guess, began
haunting the Grange, wailing for her attenuated demon-lover until he
chased her, or she him, from his home. A characteristic letter from Rossetti to Madox Brown, dated 13 January 1869, imparts the dreadful news
that

Poor Ned's affairs have come to a smash altogether, and he and Topsy, after
the most dreadful to-do, started for Rome suddenly, leaving the Greek damsel
beating up the quarters of all his friends for him and howling like Cassandra.
Georgie stayed behind. I hear to-day however that Top and Ned got no further
than Dover, Ned being now so dreadfully ill that they will probably have to
return to London.

(Quoted in Henderson, *William Morris*, 97)

It seems that Mrs Zambaco had stipulated that Edward leave his wife or
consent to a double suicide, for which she had chosen Holland Walk,
Kensington, as a fitting site. Failing this, she tried to drown herself in
the Paddington canal near Browning's house. Rossetti, who is the chief
relayer of this scandal, delights to tell Brown of 'bobbies collaring Ned
who was rolling on the stones with her to prevent it, and God knows
what else.' Some versions of the scourging of Mrs Zambaco from
England's shores hold that Burne-Jones chased her all the way to France
– or even Greece! – but returned home only to find her in contention
with Georgiana in the drawing-room at the Grange, where she had been
introduced by C. A. Howell, who 'looked after' Rossetti. All parties
maintain that when Ned saw Marie with Georgiana, he fainted, falling
against the mantelpiece and giving his forehead a permanent scar. P.
Henderson mentions a letter from either Burne-Jones or Marie which
Mrs Aglaia Coronio lent to Mackail when he was writing the life of

Morris and which shows that the affair between Edward and Marie went on until at least 1872. Henderson concludes that 'At this time [1868-72?] Morris and Georgie must have drawn particularly close together in understanding and sympathy.' Together they were, perhaps, a kind of mutual rescue party.

In the midst of his anguish over Jane, Morris may have toyed with the notion of suicide. In 'On the Edge of the Wilderness' (*Poems By the Way*) he created a pretty account of how he was dissuaded from the attempt. In this poem a number of girls or *Puellae* argue chorally with a man called *Amans* or 'He Who Loves.' On the edge of a wasteland – i.e., the opposite of an Earthly Paradise – appropriate for self-slaughter, the girls challenge him:

> What wilt thou do within the desert place
> Whereto thou turnest now thy careful face?
> Stay but a while to tell us of thy case.
>
> Abide! abide! for we are happy here.

Amans says he is too near his journey's end to give up, especially since he believes his 'love' is also wandering in the waste because of him – 'Let me depart, since ye are happy here.' To this the girls quickly reply that his 'love,' forgetting him, is enjoying parties in London conservatories (or some such overheated Edens):

> Nay, nay; but rather she forgetteth thee,
> To sit upon the shore of some warm sea,
> Or in green gardens where sweet fountains be.
>
> Abide! abide! for we are happy here.

His next objection to surviving his calamity they reject categorically:

> Forget the false forgetter and be wise,
> And 'mid these clinging hands and loving eyes,
> Dream, not in vain, thou knowest paradise.
>
> Abide! abide! for we are happy here.

They ask him if he thinks that in their land he will never see a face or hear a voice that will restore his faith in his own attractiveness. All women are not like his betrayer.

> Stay! take one image for thy dreamful night;
> Come, look at her, who in the world's despite
> Weeps for delaying love and lost delight.
>
> Abide! abide! for we are happy here.

To this *Amans* answers enigmatically,

> Mock me not till to-morrow. Mock the dead,
> They will not heed it, or turn round the head,
> To note who faithless are, and who are wed.
>
> Let me depart, since ye are happy here.

Amans' charge that some of the girls are faithless while others are wives (whom he obviously wouldn't dream of using to console himself) receives a quick riposte':

> We mock thee not. Hast thou not heard of those
> Whose faithful love the loved heart holds so close,
> That death must wait till one word lets it loose?
>
> Abide! abide! for we are happy here.

That there is a form of love which can not only be felt by a woman, whether single or married, for her lover but which can save him from death is a revelation which dampens *Amans'* death-wish. He even seems to hear the 'sweet voice' of such a one

> . . . cry from far,
> That o'er the lonely waste fair fields there are,
> Fair days that know not any change or care?
>
> Let me depart, since ye are happy here.

To which the girls, now confident of success, reply:

> Oh, no! not far thou heardest her, but nigh;
> Nigh, 'twixt the waste's edge and the darkling sky.
> Turn back again, too soon it is to die.
>
> Abide! a little while be happy here.

At last he capitulates:

> How with the lapse of lone years could I strive,
> And can I die now that thou biddest live?
> What joy this space 'twixt birth and death can give.
>
> Can we depart, who are so happy here?

'On the Edge of the Wilderness' seems to say pretty clearly that Morris was discouraged from ending his life, literally or figuratively, in the late 1860s by the brilliant little world of women he knew, with Aglaia Coronio and Georgiana Burne-Jones at their head; also, that one 'image' from this group wept for 'delaying love and lost delight' – a woman who, 'in the world's despite,' could hold the heart of him she loved so close that his death could never be caused by depressive whims but would come only in her own good time by her own '*Nunc dimittis.*' The closer *Amans* had come to the death of body or, worse, spirit, the greater appeared the beauty and glory of such faithful, succouring love. On this theme Morris, speaking out of his own experience perhaps, wrote the delightful parable 'Of the Three Seekers' (*Poems By the Way*). Looking for the best thing life has to offer were three knights who met as prearranged at the end of a year's search. The first was dressed in silk, the second 'in iron and steel,/But the third was rags from head to heel.'

> The first said: 'I have found a king
> Who grudgeth no gift of anything.'
> The second said: 'I have found a knight
> Who hath never turned his back in fight.'
> But the third said: 'I have found a love
> That Time and the World shall never move.'

When, however, the three friends go to the king for 'good cheer,' they find him turned into a miser, while the once brave knight, to whom they turn next, has shut himself up in a castle where he nurses a morbid fear of death. Only the ragged knight's lady, glad to have him in her arms once more, receives his friends with unstinted 'cheer.' For us the interesting portion of the poem is the dialogue between the reunited lovers.

> 'Where would'st thou wander, love,' she said,
> 'Now I have drawn thee from the dead?'
> 'I go my ways,' he said, 'and thine
> Have nought to do with grief and pine.'
> 'All ways are one way now,' she said,
> 'Since I have drawn thee from the dead.'

The lover protests that his 'old hurts' still smart and he cannot believe she has recovered from the 'pain' in which he earlier found her.

> 'There is no pain on earth,' she said,
> 'Since I have drawn thee from the dead.'

He reminds her that the worst pain of all, the parting of death, is inevitable –

> 'Yet first a space of love,' she said,
> 'Since I have drawn thee from the dead.'
> He laughed; said he, 'Hast thou a home
> Where I and these my friends may come?'
> Laughing, 'The world's my home,' she said,
> 'Now I have drawn thee from the dead.
> Yet somewhere is a space thereof
> Where I may dwell beside my love. . .
> Come, tell my flowery fields,' she said,
> 'How I have drawn thee from the dead.'

Here the refrain of the lady whom 'Time and the World shall never move' causes the ragged knight to sing of the resurrection, the release from fear, the conviction of immortality, that love brings:

> 'No fear my house may enter in,
> For nought is there that death may win.
> Now life is little, and death is nought,
> Since all is found that erst I sought.'

The love described is that which Morris had envisioned since childhood but had not found in Jane. It is impossible to tell whether the saviour-woman of these lyrics is Georgiana, some other actual person, or a creation of the poet's pitifully starved desires. All we can say is that she is not Jane and that for Morris as for every other human being there can be no fruitful ideal without some basis in reality. The remaining poems written to this 'unknown' may, like the others, be discussed without reference to Georgiana though it is almost impossible to keep her out of one's mind. An image frequently recurs in *A Book of Verse*, that book so painstakingly written out by Morris for Georgiana in 1870 and so lovingly illuminated by him with sprays, branches and whole trees full of delicate leaves, blossoms and reddening fruits. It is that of the poet wandering 'hand in hand' with a woman whom he kisses from time to time in a garden, a country landscape, or on the seashore, as in 'From the Upland to the Sea':

> Then we wander hand in hand
> By the edges of the sea,
> And I weary more for thee
> Than if far apart we were,
> With a space of desert drear
> 'Twixt thy lips and mine, O love!
> Ah, my joy my joy thereof!

There is a recurrent thought too which suggests that if these lovers are never to be united in life, they may at least look forward to union in death. One of the earliest expressions of this thought occurs as the nymph's song to Hylas in *Jason* (1867). It carries one back even further: to Morris's severe rheumatic attack of 1864 and the 'desertion' of his Palace of Art after Georgiana's illness was added to his own as a conclusive block to the two families enlarging and occupying Red House together. Jane Morris embroidered the first stanza of 'A Garden By the Sea' along the top edge of the beautiful coverlet she made for Morris's bed here at Kelmscott, but I cannot feel, as she must have, that the poem was written with her in mind.

> I know a little garden-close
> Set thick with lily and red rose,
> Where I would wander if I might
> From dewy morn to dewy night,
> And have one with me wandering.

The rest of the poem is dark-toned but not in a key that suggests the trouble with Jane.

> Still have I left a little breath
> To seek within the jaws of death
> An entrance to the happy place,
> To seek the unforgotten face,
> Once seen, once kissed, once reft from me
> Anigh the murmuring of the sea.

My guess is that the poem was written about 1865 when Georgiana was convalescing from scarlet fever by the seaside and commemorates a visit which Morris, himself still an invalid, paid to the Burne-Joneses near Hastings.

The 'once kissed' face reappears in the ironical 'Love Fulfilled' of *A Book of Verse*. In this poem, addressed throughout to himself, Morris seems, by an almost superhuman act of will, to have renounced all hope of attaining the fruit of longing – and thus to have won the right to long, however painfully, to his heart's content.

> Hast thou longed through weary days
> For the sight of one loved face?
> Hast thou cried aloud for rest,
> Mid the pain of sundering hours; . . .
> O rest now; and yet in sleep
> All thy longing shalt thou keep.
>
> Thou shalt rest and have no fear
> Of a dull awaking near,
> Of a life for ever blind,
> Uncontent and waste and wide.
> Thou shalt wake and think it sweet
> That thy love is near and kind . . .
>
> Sweetest that thine heart doth hide
> Longing all unsatisfied . . .

Then, still talking to himself in the solemn form of the second person, he rejoices to think that his deep passion, concealed but otherwise cherished, will not only keep him intensely alive but will be a distinct improvement over the hidden hand-holding and fugitive kissing. These had given love a forlorn instability:

> Thou rememberest how of old . . .
> How thou might'st not measure bliss
> E'en when eyes and hands drew nigh.
> Thou rememberest all regret
> For the scarce remembered kiss . . .
> Then seemed Love born but to die,
> Now unrest, pain, bliss are one,
> Love, unhidden and alone.

Actually, if the lady of this poem is Georgiana, the wife of Morris's best friend, any resolution of the tangle other than the 'enjoyment' of complete abstinence would have been unacceptable to the poet. Intimacy would have ruined his two most treasured friendships and made quite impossible the equanimity, straightforwardness, and generosity he was all his life – and never more desperately than now – striving to achieve. Yet love-making with someone who could hardly have been Jane seems to have occurred soon after 1870.

In 'Thunder in the Garden' (*Poems By the Way*) we have, remarkably, a rather wonderful garden and hand-holding poem in which union is unpostponed and complete, with love slaying time and pain and death quite literally. This is such a rare mood, perhaps such a rare fact, in Morris's life that several stanzas must be quoted. This poem of 'the ending of wrong' not only resolves the tension created by a storm but, as it were, all the tensions created during Morris's strained existence. When the poem begins, the lovers are holding hands indoors for a storm is brewing. Suddenly the woman 'Changed all with the change of her smile,'

> For her smile was of longing, no longer of glee
> And her fingers, entwined with mine own,
> With caresses unquiet sought kindness of me
> For the gift that I never had known.
>
> Then down rushed the rain and the voice of the thunder
> Smote dumb all the sound of the street
> And I to myself was grown nought but a wonder,
> As she leaned down my kisses to meet.

                    *   *   *

> It was dusk 'mid the thunder, dusk e'en as the night,
> When first brake out our love like the storm,
> But no night-hour was it, and back came the light
> While our hands with each other were warm.
>
> And her smile, killed with kisses, came back as at first
> As she rose up and led me along,
> And out to the garden, where nought was athirst,
> And the blackbird renewing his song.
>
> Earth's fragrance went with her, as in the wet grass,
> Her feet little hidden were set;
> She bent down her head, neath the roses to pass,
> And her arm with the lily was wet.
>
> In the garden we wandered while day waned apace
> And the thunder was dying aloof;
> Till the moon o'er the minster-wall lifted his face.
> And grey gleamed out the lead of the roof.

> Then we turned from the blossoms, and cold were they grown:
> In the trees the wind westering moved;
> Till over the threshold back fluttered her gown,
> And in the dark house was I loved.

In 1870 *The Atlantic Monthly* published a sonnet of Morris's called 'Rhyme Slayeth Shame' which may be a postlude to 'Thunder in the Garden.' It suggests that the poet's life is now changed to something close to what he can call 'My Life' and renews the theme of love beyond death. May republished this in Volume XXIV of her father's works, from which I quote it.

> If as I come unto her she might hear,
>   If words might reach her when from her I go,
>   Then speech a little of my heart might show,
> Because indeed nor joy nor grief nor fear
> Silence my love; but her gray eyes and clear,
>   Truer than truth, pierce through my weal and woe;
>   The world fades with its woods, and naught I know
> But that my changed life to My Life is near.
>
> Go, then, poor rhymes, who know my heart indeed,
>   And sing to her the words I cannot say, –
>   That Love has slain Time, and knows no today
> And no tomorrow; tell her of my need,
> And how I follow where her footsteps lead,
>   Until the veil of speech death draws away.

The description of 'her grey eyes and clear,/Truer than truth' has made many people think of Georgiana's and of Graham Robertson's description of them in *Time Was*:

Eyes like those of Georgiana Burne-Jones I have never seen before or since, and, through all our long friendship, their direct gaze would always cost me little subconscious heart-searchings, not from fear of criticism or censure, but lest those eyes in their grave wisdom, their crystal purity, should rest upon anything unworthy.

The last volume of *The Earthly Paradise* being in the press, Morris spent the rest of 1870 illuminating MS. poems for Georgiana and dressing up for her certain translations from the Icelandic sagas which he had lately been working on with his teacher Eríkr Magnússon. To her he sent, either with *The Eyrbyggja Saga* or separately, an *envoi* to it which Lady Burne-Jones finally passed on to May Morris as late as 6 September 1910. It is a poem to Georgiana, entirely different from the printed envoi, and seems to refer to a vague hope which Morris held around 1870. 'This' seems to refer to the subject matter of the saga.

And though this seems so far from me,
Though sunk in dreams I still must be
Self-made about myself – yet now
Who knows what out of all may grow;
Who knows but I myself at last
May face the truth, with all fear cast
Clean forth of me; real Love and I
Set side by side before I die.

(Quoted in Henderson, *William Morris*, 116)

Here 'real Love and I/Set side by side' seems to echo a phrase like 'My changed life to My Life is near' from 'Rhyme Slayeth Shame.'

If Morris was having thoughts like these while composing the later poems of *The Earthly Paradise*, it would be odd if they did not creep into some of them. I think they did. For instance, 'The Ring Given to Venus' tells how a brown-skinned goddess – in fact, she is made of bronze and is similarly hard in every way – seeks to keep a man from marrying his betrothed, a blonde girl who shone among the young people gathered for her wedding

Like some piece of the pale moonlight
Cut off from quietness and night . . .

In the grounds of a palace so fair and beautifully decorated with jewelled tapestries that it was nothing less than 'A paradise midst whispering trees,' the young wedding guests toss a ball back and forth while they dance in 'a cloister of delight.' The wedding over, the groom, fearing the ball may damage his 'spousal ring,' slips it for the moment on the fair 'fourth finger' of the statue of a long-outmoded pagan deity who stands on the edge of the ball-ground holding out her 'open hand/As erst on Ida triumphing . . .' This 'Queen Venus,' ample but lovely was 'a marvel for the life/Wherewith its brazen limbs were rife.' The bridegroom's mistake was to mock the long-vanquished goddess:

'O cold and brazen goodlihead,
How lookest thou on those that live?
Thou who, tales say, wert wont to strive
On earth, in heaven, and 'neath the earth,
To wrap all in thy net of mirth,
And drag them down to misery
Past telling – and didst thou know why?
And what has God with thee then,
That thou art perished from midst men
E'n as the things thou didst destroy . . .'

Implacably the goddess closes her bronze fingers on the ring and that night in the form of a 'cloudy column' blocks the groom's path to the bridal chamber, crying

> *'I love thee well,*
> *And thou hast loved me ere to-night,*
> *And longed for this o'ergreat delight,*
> *And had no words therefor to pray.*
> *Come, have thy will, and cast away*
> *Thy foolish fear, thy foolish love . . .*
> *Now thou with ring hast wedded me:*
> *Come, cast the hope away from thee*
> *Wherewith unhappy brooding men*
> *Must mock their threescore years and ten;*
> *Come, thou that mockest me! I live;*
> *How with my beauty canst thou strive?*
> *Unhappy if thou couldst! for see*
> *What depth of joy there is in me!'*

After being kissed and embraced by the brown Venus, our hero fell senseless. Tricked so dreadfully, he resorted to an astrologer to recover his ring and enough self-respect to possess his true bride. After he has witnessed an impressively described procession of the ancient gods, including Venus, through a 'drear, unhallowed place,' he finds she has dropped before him the ring which enables him to consummate real love.

Apparently there was an earlier versification of this tale told in a spirit almost of fun with little about a midnight procession of shadowy figures through a waste land, or about a statue that made quite realistic love, or an astrological search for a way to break the phantom's power. In a version that May knew, the sequestered betrothal-ring was simply returned by a great black bird who dropped it at the groom's feet. In other words, Morris changed the whole tenor of the old story, taken from William of Malmesbury's *De Gestis Regum Anglorum*, to make it relevant to a situation in which a malignant brown 'witch' sets her beautiful face against the 'real love' of a young man for a pure-eyed, moonlit girl. The seed is here, I think, for a whole series of poems and romances (those toward the end of Morris's life) in which a tender, quiet blonde is actually persecuted by a large-limbed brunette. In 'The Ring Given to Venus' the shy girl plays a very small role but her character is developed in a pair of *Earthly Paradise* stories which make her out to be an enchantress herself – a 'white witch' – or at least an angel-like guardian of her lover's life. The tales I have in mind are those about Bellerophon and Ogier the Dane.

The small epic of Bellerophon is made to count as two tales by dividing it into 'Bellerophon at Argos' and 'Bellerophon in Lycia', but they are related and unified because they tell of two queens who love the hero, one to his undoing, the other to his salvation. Actually they are sisters and look somewhat alike but inwardly they are opposites. When Bellerophon comes to Argos after unwittingly killing his brother, King Proetus makes him a battle-captain, thus giving him the chance to fulfil his childhood dream of 'Bringing the monsters of the world to nought.' However, he is so busy resisting Queen Sthenoboea's solicitations that he has little time to exhibit heroic prowess. Physically her majesty was, as they say, every inch a queen, but her 'full lips' never trembled, her eyes held only a scornful 'empty stare,' her 'breast' seemed innocent of 'any thought,' and she seldom moved the limbs 'a God might well have loved.' Here Morris gives us a much fuller inner portrait than is usual with him. Pity she knew

> As the last folly wise folk turn unto.
> For pain was wont to rouse her rage, and she
> Was like those beasts that slaughter cruelly
> Their wounded fellows – truth she knew not of,
> And fain had killed folk babbling over love;
> Justice she thought of as a thing that might
> Balk some desire of hers, before the night
> Of death should end it all: nor hope she knew,
> Nor what fear was, how ill so'er life grew . . .
> But she was one of those wrought by the gods
> To be to foolish men as sharpest rods
> To scourge their folly; wrought so daintily
> That scarcely could a man her body see
> Without awaking strife 'twixt good and ill
> Within him; and her sweet, soft voice would fill
> Men's hearts with strange desires, and her great eyes,
> Truthful to show her to the cold and wise
> E'en as she was, would make some cast aside
> Whatever wisdom in their breasts might hide,
> And still despite what long ill days might prove,
> They called her languid hate the soul of love.

This must surely be a picture of Jane, overwrought by her overwrought husband, but a passage worth quoting as Morris's bitterest outburst so far against the woman who had spoiled his life by making it almost impossible for him to live the warm, affectionate, fearless, deathless, creative days he had always expected love to further. When Bellerophon definitely rejects Sthenoboea's advances, the furious queen persuades Proetus to send this Joseph to the Lycian king, her father, to be put to death for trying to rape her. Then, having fashioned for herself such a hell as 'from it never any path did go/To lands of rest,' she committed suicide, shrieking like Gudrun, ' "*I have loved one man alone,/And unto him the worst deed have I done . . .*" '

The way is now clear for Bellerophon's more heroic – actually, more dreadful – adventures in Lycia, which have, however, a happy end because there the hero meets Sthenoboea's sister, the Princess Philonoë, who spends her time saving his life from King Jobates's manifold attempts to kill him in accordance with the request of Proetus. Tender and timid as Philonoë is, she woos Bellerophon forthrightly – in order to protect him – from the moment he arrives in Lycia, asking him the first time they ever speak together whether he thinks ' "the world without thy life can thrive,/More than my heart without thy heart can live?" ' It is no wonder that Bellerophon, who enjoyed possibly like Morris himself, being 'buttered up' by women, moved quickly from pity for her to sweet content to burning love till 'dead and passed away were fear and shame, /Nor might he think that he could never die.' These feelings were, for Morris, the glorious guarantee and seal of 'real love.' From here on Bellerophon conquers one after another, the frightful Solymi, the unspeakable Amazons, and the ghastly Chimaera, pausing between feats to embrace in a paradisial garden Philonoë's 'slim and perfect daintiness' with words like ' "Lo now, if I depart," ' – that is, leave dangerous Lycia, as she urges – ' "I lack the safeguard of thy faithful heart." '

> 'Rest in mine arms, O well-beloved,' said he;
> 'I faint not, neither shall death come on me
> While thus thou art: nay, nay, I think if I,
> Hacked with an hundred swords should come to lie,
> Yet without thee I should not then depart.'

Such speeches make us think, perhaps, of those lines in 'On the Edge of the Wilderness' in which the girls tell *Amans* that there is a kind of 'faithful love' that holds the beloved heart 'so close/That death must wait till one word lets it loose.' Death will come to all, of course, and Bellerophon urges his laggard soldiers not to seek to live forever, but while they breathe to live vividly – ' "never death in life for me, O King!" ' A good life consists of good states of mind and with these every kind of fear, every minute without hope of a widening existence, is incompatible. Real love, says Bellerophon, is the only catalyst for the courage and hopefulness necessary to support a man's inner health through life, and help him to rank with those who ' "on the earth make heaven . . ." ' Of no other heaven can we really know though we may, if we like, extrapolate one from some earthly deed or vision inspired by love. After Philonoë saves Bellerophon from the last death-trap baited by Sthenoboea, the hero can finally be joined to the saviour-woman:

> And even as a man new made a god,
> When first he sets his foot upon the sod
> Of Paradise, and like a living flame
> Joy wraps him round, he felt, as now she came,
> Clear won at last, the thing of all the earth
> That made his fleeting life a little worth.

I think we must agree that in the Bellerophon poems Morris managed to convey what he meant by the role of love in human life by contrasting the characters and deeds of a pair of sisters who bear a resemblance to women he knew. Since there is almost a sense of 'Q.E.D.' at the end of the story, it may be something of a relief to turn to a more fairy-tale handling of the theme as is found in 'Ogier the Dane.' This story was never forecast for *The Earthly Paradise* but probably about 1869 Morris saw it as filled with the seeds of delightful allegory. When Ogier was in his cradle six 'fay ladies gave him various gifts, as to be brave and happy and the like; but the sixth gave him to be her love when he should have lived long in the world ...' The sixth fairy, Morgan the Fay, is not described except that she is said to be still fairer than the others, including the fifth, who was herself 'grey-eyed.' Morgan simply says that when Ogier's earthly life

> 'Is drunk out to the dregs, and war and strife
> Have yielded thee whatever joy they may,
> Thine head upon this bosom shalt thou lay;
> And then, despite of knowledge or of God,
> Will we be glad upon the flowery sod
> Within the happy country where I dwell ...'

We need not linger over this tale, but it is pleasant to note that the supernatural girl has no trace of malice in her. When Ogier, Charlemagne's chief prop and the saviour of France, is wrecked in old age on a desert island and dying of starvation, Morgan carries him unconscious to her own paradisal island of Avallon. Here is an innermost garden by the sea which Ogier, slowly recovering, mistakes for Eden till he falls dazzled by a fountain-side.

> It was as though he slept, and sleeping dreamed,
> For in his half-closed eyes a glory gleaned
> As though from some sweet face and golden hair,
> And on his breast were laid soft hands and fair,
> And a sweet voice was ringing in his ears,
> Broken as if with flow of joyous tears!
>   'Ogier, sweet friend, has thou not tarried long?
> Alas! thine hundred years of strife and wrong!'

Ogier is pained by the proposal to renew his life in a garden 'Wherein guilt first upon the world befell.' Yet Morgan –

> Within her glorious eyes such wisdom dwelt
> A child before her had the wise man felt –

convinces him that 'Despite the laws of God' men can be drawn from death and live immortally mortal. The other heroes Ogier finds in Avallon,

> Love knew they, but its pains they never had,
> But with each other's joy were they made glad;
> Nor were their lives wasted by hidden fire,
> Nor knew they of the unfulfilled desire
> That turns to ashes all the joys of earth . . .

So flitted the days until Ogier's once beloved land of France is endangered by a fierce enemy, whereupon Morgan herself begs him to go again to the rescue. Not for a moment does he weary of Avallon. It is the fairy mistress who sends him back to earth and she imposes no taboos which might make it impossible for him to return to her. The trouble with Ogier's return to France is that he has to forget Avallon, even to the point of falling in love in the miserable way of mortals. In spite of memories, now revived, of 'The bitter pain of rent and ended love,' the saviour of his country promises, once the war is won, to wed the widowed Queen of France, a woman as beautiful

> As any woman of the world might be,
> Full-limbed and tall, dark-haired; from her deep eyes,
> The snare of fools, the ruin of the wise,
> Love looked unchecked . . .

Morris can hardly bear to think of the danger of his hero falling into 'the fire that erst his heart had burned,' or growing 'content to live and die /Like other men . . .' He asks the reader not to chide him for dwelling on Ogier's dangers 'Because the thought of Avallon still clings/Unto my heart' and he wants to get him back to that most credible of earthly paradises as quickly as possible. One of Morris's most famous songs, later included – beautifully illuminated – in the *Book of Verse* he made for Georgiana in 1870, occurs now. A duet of two young voices in a garden, it suggests that the sense of immortality, of Avallon, is made up of a series of mortal moments so jewel-hard in their beauty that they cannot be cracked by death – yet who knows?

> HAEC.
> In the white-flowered hawthorn brake,
> Love, be merry for my sake;

1. Dante led by Beatrice through the Earthly Paradise. Woodcut facing opening of 'Il Paradiso' by Dante in an edition printed at Brescia, May 31 1487.

2. William Blake's 'The Young Poet's Dream, L'Allegro.'
Courtesy of the Trustees of the Pierpont Morgan Library, New York City.

3. Tibetan Mandala Thangka. At the centre of the mandala is the female deity Cunda associated with Vairocana, the white Buddha of the centre. 18th century. Author's collection.

4. Tibetan Thangka. Avalokitéshvara, the Boddhisattva of compassion, surrounded by attendant deities in his heavenly palace. 18th century. Author's collection.

5. 'The Earthly Paradise.' Illustration by Burne-Jones for *The Golden Legend*, Kelmscott Press, 1892.

6. Plaque of Morris on one of the cottages in Kelmscott village by George Jack.

7. From an edition of the *Cantica Canticorum* blockbook. (*The Song of Songs* as related to the Blessed Virgin Mary). Netherlands, *c.* 1470?

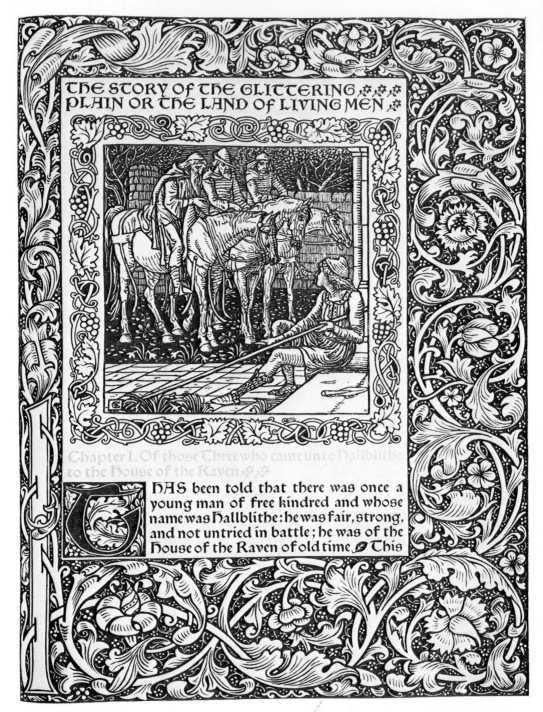

8. 'Is this the Land?' Illustration by Walter Crane for *The Story of the Glittering Plain*,
Kelmscott Press, 1894.

9. Detail from 'Allegory of Good Government' by Ambrogio Lorenzetti in the Palazzo Publico, Siena.

10. Detail from 'The Last Judgment: the Paradise' by Fra Angelico (1387–1455), San Marco Museum, Florence.

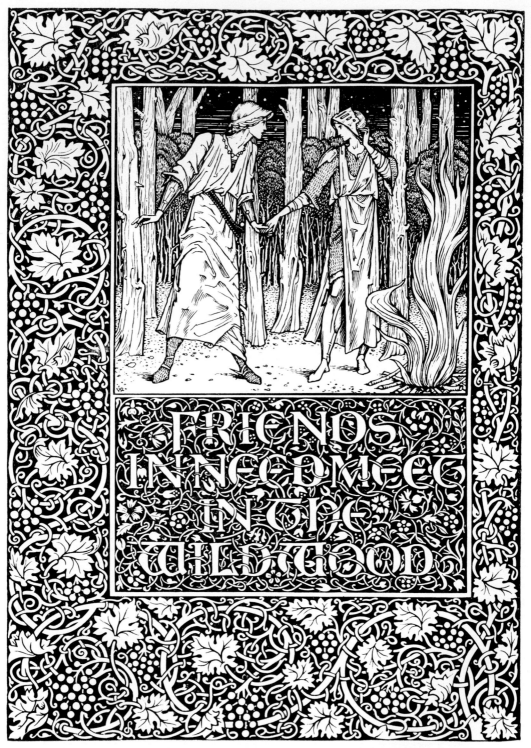

11. 'Friends in Need Meet in the Wildwood.' Illustration by Burne-Jones for
The Well at the World's End, Kelmscott Press, 1896.

> Twine the blossoms in my hair,
> Kiss me where I am most fair —
> Kiss me, love! for who knoweth
> What thing cometh after death?

ILLE.

> Nay, the garlanded gold hair
> Hides thee where thou art most fair;
> Hides the rose-tinged Hills of snow —
> Ah, sweet love, I have thee now!
> Kiss me, love! for who knoweth
> What thing cometh after death?

At this point Morgan, France being saved, manifests herself on the banks of the Seine to rescue Ogier from the dark Queen of France, saying, ' "Come, love, I am not changed" ' to you ' "who some faint image of eternity/Hast gained through me ..." ' She hopes he may ' "remember what we are:/The lover and the loved from long ago," ' to which

> He stammered out, 'O love! How came we here?
> Have I not been from thee a weary while?
> Let us return . . .

She took him by the hand and

> All was grown a dream,
> His work was over, his reward was come,
> Why should he loiter longer from his home?

As I suggested above, 'Ogier the Dane' seems to combine a parable of true love with a mystic affirmation that the good life properly led on earth is practically indistinguishable from heavenly life and perhaps just as 'immortal.' No one could have led Morris to this insight except Georgiana. Hand-holding with her and the conviction of a heavenly existence together were already twin-lamps in the darkness.

There is only one more tale of *The Earthly Paradise* which I wish to tie, however tenuously, to Morris's experience of Geogiana Burne-Jones: 'The Fostering of Aslaug.' Here the blonde heroine is neither a foil for, nor the foiler of a treacherous brunette. The whole tenor of the tale is so different from most of the other stories that the heroine can be compared, it seems to me, only to Psyche, whose adventures had occupied Morris ever since the conception of a series of Earthly Paradise tales. He seems to have kept refining her story until she lost every vestige of blot that could have kept her from emerging as a symbol of the unblemished soul. In the published *Paradise* she no longer plans the fate of her wicked sisters, is no longer severely rebuked by Cupid for betraying her promise, or scratched and cursed by Venus for rivalling her foam-born beauty. By 1864 or '65 Burne-Jones had completed about seventy illustrations of her story. Among these are so many 'nakeds' of Psyche, as he called them, that we can see how perfectly at one he was with Morris in identifying nudity with purity, body with soul. They projected a richly illustrated edition of this tale which, substantially as they planned it, has lately appeared in A. R. Dufty's *The Story of Cupid and Psyche by William Morris* (1974). The history of the writing and illustrating of the story has been well covered in J. R. Dunlap's *The Book That Never Was* (New York, 1971). Psyche in English is 'Soul,' in Latin, *Anima*, a power practically equatable with the life-force. Woman-as-Anima stands, according to Jung, for the unconscious life which must be brought to light if we are to live fully and freely. She is the Sacred Spirit in matter which must be liberated in each man if he is to live deeply and usefully. The Anima is the animator, connected with rebirth, regeneration, transformation and, somehow, immortality. She is also a healer, physician, and saviour. That her face is filled with, to use Blake's words, mercy, pity and peace does not mean that she is a zombie. Quite the contrary. She is, as Jung would say, the 'Archetype of Life itself,' the blended sum of all the archetypal figures which haunt the human unconscious, preserving and maintaining life for millennia. Such figures are gods and their synthesis a great God or Goddess. Gods, especially female, are creators who treasure life and stimulate the ineffable experiences which we refer to loosely as numinous, mystic or religious. This life-giving fighter in the human underground must once, and for untold centuries, have been a fact of the environment – a priestess in charge of agriculture and all forms of fertility, a matriarchal queen, a war leader who organised the defence of her peoples' homes and lands. A Sheba or Boadicea. It is no wonder, then, that it was the Roman Anima, so much more evocative of this mysterious omnipotence, omniscience and all-pervading love than the Greek Psyche, that Morris sought – in the depths of his being (where we have thrust this pagan goddess), in actual women and, when baulked in his search, in artistic creations founded on human figures who glow with this deity's peculiar charisma. She takes a predominant role in the prose romances written toward the end of Morris's life. In the meantime he first projected this resurrecting dream in recognisable form in 'The Fostering of Aslaug.' It is my belief that the real-life model behind the heroine Aslaug is Georgiana Burne-Jones.

There is a portrait of Georgiana drawn in black chalk by Rossetti about 1860, the year of her marriage. She looks pensive but mentally alert, the incredible grey eyes slightly lowered. Another, painted by F. J. Poynter in 1870, the year which saw the height of Morris's marital troubles and also her own, shows the beautiful eyes raised but the expression on her face is very melancholy. A more elaborate but unfinished picture in oils, showing her seated at her piano with her adolescent children on either side, was made in 1884 (when she was forty-four) by her husband. All show her, though pensive and possibly on the petite side, full of an energy probably too tightly controlled, a leadership too wilfully held in check, a diffused pity hating cruelty and eager to bind up wounds. If the beautiful nude figure that represents Psyche in Burne-Jones's woodcuts for 'Cupid and Psyche' [which he later turned into lovely pastels like *Cupid Discovering Psyche* (the Yale University Art Gallery, c. 1871) and oils like *Pan and Psyche* (the Fogg Art Museum, c. 1872–4)] was based on Georgiana's, the translucent grace of her body must have equalled the confounding truthfulness of her eyes. Figure and face, body and soul, she was a model not so much of Psyche the myth as of Psyche the Spirit or Anima and could fully furnish a mainstay for a jumpy sensitivity like Morris's.

Aslaug is the daughter of a pair of lovers whom Morris's Icelandic studies had led him as early as 1868 to regard as the world's paragons, not least perhaps because their 'utter love,' as he wrote, was 'defeated utterly.' Child of the perfect passion of Sigurd and Brynhild, Aslaug's own perfect power of love and fearless courage cannot be broken by the bitterest misfortune. It is of the essence of Morris's Anima-stories that the girl be tested for the role by prolonged persecution and 'God-like despair that makes not base.' After her parents' death the three-year-old Aslaug fell into the clutches of a sour crone who persuaded her evil husband to murder the child's guardian for a jewel he wore. Then they batter what we may call the gold-and-diamond child as much as they dare, but some mysterious glow in her body and spirit holds them back. Besides, no amount of swingeing can bring her to speak, and her dumbness combined with intelligence somewhat awes the wretches. However, when she is alone in the woods near the sea she talks to herself about her parents, surmising that her father may have put into her head the image of a 'steel-clad maiden ... Asleep within the ring of flame/Asleep and waiting till love came.' She decides that the flowers in the grass were not made for murders, that she 'was not made for misery,' and that love may come even to her, somehow, in this lovely land with its lake for bathing.

> While she spake
> Her hands were busy with her gown,
> And at the end it slipped adown
> And left her naked there and white
> In the unshadowed noontide light,
> Like Freyia in her house of gold ...

This is the Indian-like ritual undressing and bathing of the goddess figure, which is, for whatever reason, indispensable to Morris and never absent – any more than is the torturing old witch – from such a tale. After the ritual bath Aslaug becomes a truly hieratic figure, commanding worship. When she returns to the hovel, she finds Vikings in search of provender who

> . . . open mouthed upon her stare,
> As with bright eyes and face flushed fair
> She stood; one gleaming lock of gold,
> strayed from her fair head's plaited fold,
> Fell far below her girdlestead,
> And round about her shapely head
> A garland of dog-violet
> And wind-flowers meetly had she set . . .

Quickly they run back to the dragon-boat to tell their master Ragnar Lodbrok of the miracle of the fay who had suddenly appeared in the hovel of the 'bler-eyed crone' –

> 'Yet surely of the gods I deem,
> So fair she was . . . this dream
> Of Freyia on midsummer night . . .'

Half in jest Ragnar tells his men to bring this nature-goddess aboard the boat,

> but when her foot
> First pressed the plank, to his heart's root
> Sweet pain there pierced, for her great eyes
> Were fixed on his in earnest wise . . .

In the slant sun she 'flashed as in a golden cloud' and suddenly Ragnar had found his queen. Following the marriage, he dreams of wandering through a dreadful 'Childe Roland' waste land strewn with bones of men until he comes to a charmed circle of fire. From this emerge Brynhild and Sigurd who give him a white lily from which

> 'Great light upon the world did fall,
> And fair the sun rose o'er the earth,
> And blithe I grew and full of mirth;
> And no more on a waste I was . . .'

He and Aslaug end the tale at this point with a kiss and Aslaug fulfills her fate of leaving

> to unborn men
> A savour of sweet things, a tale
> That midst all woes shall yet prevail
> To make the world seem something worth . . .'

That Morris heroines before Aslaug, or perhaps most English girls, even mid-Victorian ones, were fond of forest bathing and running naked among flowers does not detract from the ceremonial quality of this episode.

The Scandinavian goddess of love and fertility, Freyia, has a house of gold, and the ritual of immersion may have been added to the legends about her from Tacitus's description of a goddess of fertility whom he called Nerthus, or Mother Earth. During Nerthus's springtime festival no one dared draw sword from scabbard.

The story that Freyia, the goddess of love and re-birth, the animator, presided over the resurrection of Baldur, a god of radiant beauty, and a transformed world was probably Morris's invention. Moreover, there is little doubt that this Anima-figure was based on Georgiana Burne-Jones. It takes a lot of synthesizing to create from within and without, from myth and familiar faces, the deity and ceremonials needed to sustain a sensitive and pain-plagued life.

In many of Morris's annals about the Anima the evil crone who tortures the Soul is a dark, handsome, full-limbed woman, and this antagonism can be traced back to the tension between the Jane- and Georgiana-personae mentioned earlier in this chapter. Morris did not operate in a vacuum. The 'fairy-tale' characters he drew were always fresh-moulded for a purpose, worked out along psychological lines.

Toward the end of 1870 Morris felt himself rather lost, as he wrote, 'at having done my book: I find I liked working at it better than I thought. I must try and get something serious to do as soon as may be.' One of Morris's main reasons for writing *The Earthly Paradise* was to relieve his anguish over failing to hold Jane's love. At the time of their marriage and throughout most of the years at Red House, he had possessed it or whatever it was she was able to feel which resembled passion and marital affection. But we have seen how for various reasons – dislike of Morris's imperious and noisy rages, hatred of the workshop clatter about the Queen Square house, discouragement with that constant proliferation of his interests with which she could not keep up, boredom with an atmosphere of all-work-and-no-play, distaste for coition and pregnancy, a growing fondness for studio parties with Rossetti as cicisbeo – she suddenly broke off sexual relations, entirely and definitively, with her astonished husband about 1867. He could get no reason from her and was driven half-wild, as we have seen, with frustration and despair. Jane's conduct, which hardly ruffled her usual complacency, perhaps because long premeditated, appears unbelievably cruel and mean – the act of a truly petty mind – but we are destined, I fear, never to understand it any better than her husband could. For some reason, which we cannot fathom any more easily than Jane's behaviour, Morris frequently speaks as if the fault were his, as if he had wronged her in some way, or violated an unfathomable taboo laid down by a deity or supernatural creature privileged to torment him with a sense of 'sin.' If we remember Morris's generous, capacious, reasonable, unspiteful nature – and also what he had expected from love – we can see that he was practically defenceless against such conduct. His chief resource lay in his ability to turn his pain into poetry. The second line of defence was the endless work demanded of him by his many talents and the increasing business of the Firm of household artists or interior decorators which he had founded – to make Red House as 'worthy' of Jane inside as it was without! – in 1861. Though we have by no means come to the end of the Jane trouble, it is clear that the poet had won considerable relief from pain by the time he finished *The Earthly Paradise* in 1870. There was still, however, the morning emptiness, the evening ache, to be outlived.

Fortunately, Morris was being weaned from his torturous love for Jane by a woman who sought, or so at least some of his lyrics and Earthly Paradise poems suggest, to give him as much consolation, pity, peace and protection as she could. In gratitude, and clearly out of burgeoning love, Morris began practising an art new to him but capable of occupying his taste, his hands and his mind with happy work – thoughts of Georgiana – for hour after hour. He produced hand-written and painted books and by 1810 had completed five or six. Failing to follow *The Earthly Paradise* with the composition of a contemplated poem on Tristram and Iseult – which would necessarily have described a long series of furtive adulteries between King Mark's best friend and King Mark's wife! – he began to write out and illuminate for Georgiana Burne-Jones a selection of his poems (*A Book of Verse*), several translations he was making from Icelandic sagas with Erríkr Magnússon, and Omár Khayyám's *Rubáiyát*, Fitzgerald's translation of which had only just been discovered by Rossetti. These are beautifully hand scripted on vellum with small floriated capitals in gold and exquisitely chosen colours, the generous margins often decorated with tiny female figures (from one to two inches tall) swathed in lovely medieval gowns and playing on various old-fashioned musical instruments. These talented girls are surrounded by wreaths or thickets of delicate flowers and fresh greenery. Such 'painted' books, beginning with *A Book of Verse*, dedicated to Georgiana and always described as an exquisite token of his friendship – usually 'love' – for her, were certainly an ingenious way of keeping her image before him through long hours of pleasant if exacting hand-work.

There is nothing odd about Morris writing to share his delight in *The Rubáiyát* with Georgiana, who had been such a help to him since 1868 or earlier. Perhaps they had read it together and the handwritten book with the gorgeously painted borders was meant to commemorate the 'rest' and splendour of those hours. A little odder, perhaps was his deep desire to share with her his new-found interest in Icelandic literature. In fact, there seems to have grown up in his mind a profound identification of the woman with the literature, which would probably have surprised Georgiana in spite of the fact that he often talked to her of his Icelandic studies and translations. Perhaps the fact that he had got help and consolation, strength and wisdom, from both exactly when needed for his sanity's sake welded them together in his passionate gratitude to a degree we can hardly conceive. Icelandic translations written out and decorated for Georgiana include a leather-bound volume of the first draft of 'The Lovers of Gudrun,' not 'painted' but stamped outside with sprays of pomegranate and inscribed to 'Georgie from W.M. April 15th, 1870,' *The Story of the Dwellers of Eyr* (the second calligraphic copy) and three short sagas (of *Hen Thorir, The Banded Men*, and *Haward the Halt*) which he had bound together and inscribed with decorated initials and a large floriated 'G.B.J.' at the foot of page one. Partially completed and illustrated short sagas probably intended to keep Georgiana abreast of his Icelandic interests included thirty-five chapters of *The Story of the Volsungs and Nieblungs* and about fifty chapters of the *Heimskringla Saga*, which he called *The Story of the Ynglings*. These she may never have seen, along with *The Kormak Saga*, which was completely finished in Morris's fine handwriting and decorations.

These stories consist for the most part of family histories coolly told but suggesting adequately enough the passion overriding reason, the treacheries, jealous murders, bloody ambushes known as battles, etc. which made up much of the domestic life of Iceland's early settlers. Perhaps Morris did want to call to Georgiana's attention the awful pain caused by faithless wives and the stoic bravery of heroes who, when ambushed, went on fighting long after they had had a leg sliced off at the knee. Were these tales of treacherous women and maimed men who battled to the death supposed to make her sorrier than ever for the dark fate that had overtaken her friend? Actually, the delicate beauty of the painted books bears practically no relation to the domestic turmoil and bloodshed of the text (the Ynglings were doomed to commit parricide, which the younger generation did with monotonous gusto until the family was wiped out). I think that Morris decorated the margins of such tales, however inappropriately, with these lovely girl musicians set in bowers of fruit, flowers and greenery – tiny goddesses of abundance, concord, and peace – to keep Georgiana's mind and perhaps his own, off the gory details. Were these girls abstracted, as it were, from Georgiana and her beloved piano? Did Morris want her to understand that the tragedy of at

least one 'family history' had been soothed and softened and turned back
to happy creativity by the blessing of a fairy minstrel, here endlessly pictured?

Actually, Morris was far from totally recovered from the agony Jane
and Rossetti had caused him, and his preoccupation with Icelandic literature – it began in 1868 – was, I think, an instinctively cultivated form of
self-preservation. The translations were punctuated by two trips to Iceland, in 1871 and 1873, climaxed in a poem many have called Morris's
greatest, *Sigurd the Volsung*. Meantime, Georgiana continued to play
her helpful role and was now thought of by the poet as his 'love
beloved,' as in 'Earth the Healer,' which seems to have been written
before one of the Icelandic voyages:

> So swift the hours are moving
> Unto the time un-proved:
> Farewell my love unloving
> Farewell my love beloved!

The second 'love' is not likely to have been Jane. On returning from his
second journey to Iceland, Morris wrote to Aglaia Coronio to tell her
how being again in 'the terrible and tragic' land had 'killed . . . querulous
feeling' in him and 'made all the dear faces of wife & children, and love,
& friends dearer than ever to me . . .' Georgiana and Iceland, restorers of
inner strength, each dearer now because of the other! The mingling of
thoughts about them appears first in *A Book of Verse* (1870) in 'Meet-
ting in Winter.' Here the poet is still dreaming about the once 'unhoped
kiss' which he has now obtained.

> Round thine eyes and round thy mouth
> Passeth no murmur of the south,
> When my lips a little while
> Leave thy quivering tender smile,
> As we twain, hand holding hand,
> Once again together stand.

In the wintry Northland of this poem she is

> Kind and cold-cheeked and mine own,
> Wrapped about with deep-furred gown.

> *   *   *

> And our horses' bells shall cease
> As we reach the place of peace . . .
> O my love, the night shall last
> Longer than men tell thereof
> Laden with our lonely love!

But Iceland and her literature also helped Morris in his 'stormy days,' when his Red House paradise and its presiding deity had been lost. The ways were varied, really, and one of them had philosophical implications which deserve attention. What was it that Morris, as he so often put it, went forth – or North – for to see?

VIII The Uses of an Anti-Paradise of Fire and Ice, 1868-1876

When they were at Oxford, Burne-Jones gave Morris *Northern Mythology* by Benjamin Thorpe. This was the beginning of an ongoing passionate interest, and by the time Morris met Eríkr Magnússon and began a serious and comprehensive study of Icelandic literature, he had read Thorpe's *Yuletide Stories*, Amos Cottle's *Mythic Songs of the Edda*, P. H. Mallett's *Northern Antiquities*, and Dasent's *Popular Tales from the Norse* along with his translations of the *Gisli* and *Njála* stories. Something in these stories and sagas drew him irresistibly to read more. They seemed, along with Georgiana's strength and support, to ease the despair of losing Red House and its exotic centrepiece, and to keep open the way back to life and its paradisal possibilities. In the emotionally troubled times after 1865 these stories of adverse fate faced without complaint set up deep reverberations in Morris's psyche which he felt he must pursue in search of fuller self-understanding. As soon as he and Magnússon began to study the language, Morris decided he must translate all the sagas – or at least have his teacher make literal versions of them in English which he could then turn into a somewhat medieval-flavoured Norse-English. These 'translations' seemed to turn the Icelandic tales into prose-poems of his own which both revealed the nature and relieved the intensity of the hidden strains of failure and jealousy which as Morris implies, sometimes threatened his sanity. Since Morris endured many different stresses, it is not possible to give just one reason why he turned to the sagas for relief and healing. Through rewriting the events in these stories, he could clarify and 'act out', as we say, certain repressions and frustrations. But the sagas brought him much more: insight into how a brave man faces tragedy, handling with dignity 'the fated Love that draws the fated Death', as he wrote in 'To the Muse of the North' in *A Book of Verse* (1870). There was also such catharsis in reliving the ancient woes that the Muse of the North seemed a physician of the mind – so close to him and sympathetic that she might have been a cosmic version of Georgiana herself:

> O Mother, and Love and Sister all in one,
> Come thou; for sure I am enough alone
> That thou thine arms about my heart shouldst throw,
> And wrap me in the grief of long ago.

Between 1869 and 1876 there was a veritable explosion of Morris 'translations' from the sagas to which Magnússon introduced him. Analysis of a few of these may help to clarify what instigated Morris's passion for Icelandic sagas. The following lines are quoted admiringly by Mackail (I, 264) from a manuscript of Morris's translation of *The Erbyggja Saga*. Here he turns from the saga to apostrophise the Icelandic story-teller:

> Tale-teller, who 'twixt fire and snow
> Had heart to turn about and show
> With faint half-smile things great and small
> That in thy fearful land did fall,
> Thou and thy brethren sure did gain
> That thing for which I long in vain,
> The spell, whereby the mist of fear
> Was melted, and your ears might hear
> Earth's voices as they are indeed.
> Well ye have helped me at my need!

The words 'helped me at my need' provide the clue to Morris's attraction to the sagas, and his needs were many.

Not long after beginning to study Icelandic with Magnússon, Morris used the central episode of the *Laxdaela Saga* as the basis of an *Earthly Paradise* story – 'The Lovers of Gudrun.' Without being supernatural, Gudrun has essentially the same fay-like attraction and the same imperious cruelty which bedevilled so many of the heroes in the second half of Morris's collection. According to the 'Argument', ' "The Lovers of Gudrun" shows how two friends loved a fair woman, and how he who loved her the best had her to wife, though she loved him little or not at all ...' Her perverse spite makes sure that one kills the other and then is punished by the customary family vengeance. Other sagas contain triangle-situations which magnetised Morris from the time of the height of his troubles with Jane, 1868–'70. Sometimes the jealousy of the rivals is deadly, but at other times there is a faltering or equivocation that springs from submerged motives (often called 'witches' curses') which might puzzle Freud himself. And in these stories we keep stumbling on passages tinged with the fire or freezing fog of Morris's personal dilemma. It may be that Morris gravitated to the barbarous and often horrible Icelandic tales as a means of neutralising murderous fantasies about Rossetti and Jane. We may take a quick look at two stories of jealousy which may have helped him drain off an anger that might have otherwise proved fatal to all three principals. No stories like these are found in *The Earthly Paradise*. Perhaps Morris was reluctant to reveal such fantasies as in any way coming from himself.

The first tale Morris ever read with Magnússon in 1868 was almost immediately 'translated' and published as *The Saga of Gunnlaug Worm-tongue* in the *Fortnightly Review* for January, 1869. This is the story of two warrior-poets, one red-headed, one with black hair, who love the same girl, Helga. She is 'vowed, but not betrothed' to Gunnlaug, called the Worm-tongue because he is 'somewhat bitter in his rhyming'. Helga is pledged to 'bide' three winters for Gunnlaug while he travels abroad 'to shape himself in the ways of good men'. When he does not return in three years, a rival poet, Raven, wins Helga in marriage, though at her wedding 'the bride was but drooping ...' Afterward, Raven 'fared ill in his sleep', reporting to Helga:

> 'In thine arms, so dreamed I,
> Hewn was I, gold island!
> Bride, in blood I bled there,
> Bed of thine was reddened.
> Never more then mightst thou ...
> Bind my gashes bloody –'

Helga says she will not weep for this, for black-haired Raven has evilly beguiled her, and on Gunnlaug's return she deserts him. When Gunnlaug meets her, he too breaks into song:

> 'Worst reward I owe them,
> Father thine, O wine-may,
> And mother, that they made thee
> So fair beneath thy maid-gear;
> For thou, sweet field of sea-flame,
> All joy hast slain within me. –'

Gunnlaug and Raven soon fall to fighting for Helga, Gunnlaug cutting off one of Raven's legs, Raven traitorously murdering Gunnlaug when the latter brings him a helmet full of water. Helga, married to a third man, dies plucking red threads from a cloak given her by Gunnlaug. It seems unnecessary to stress what might be called resemblances between the two poets who kill each other and Morris and Rossetti.

When it came to fantasising the murder of Jane, if that is what Morris was doing in 'Of the Wooing of Hallbiorn the Strong, a Story from *The Land-Settling Book of Iceland*, Chapter XXX,' he turned the bitter original into a spirited poem with ballad-like echoes. Hallgerd marries Hallbiorn but seems to have been long in love with Snaebiorn. When it comes time to leave her home she will not budge from the seat where she sits silently combing her long gold hair in the sun. While her husband pleads with her to come away, the shaft of sunlight slips from her head to her knees, lower and lower.

> The sunbeam lay upon the floor;
> She combed her hair and spake no more.
> He drew her by the lilly hand:
> 'I love thee better than all the land.'
> He drew her by the shoulders sweet:
> 'My threshold is but for thy feet.'
> He drew her by the yellow hair:
> 'O why wert thou so deadly fair?
> 'O am I wedded to death?' she cried, . . .'
> 'Sharp sword,' she sang, 'and death is sure,
> But over all doth love endure.'
> She stood up shining in her place
> And laughed beneath his deadly face.
> Instead of the sunbeam gleamed a brand,
> The hilts were hard in Hallbiorn's hand:
> The bitter point was in Hallgerd's breast
> That Snaebiorn's lips of love had pressed.
> Morn and noon, and nones passed o'er,
> And the sun is far from the bower door.
>
> *(Poems By the Way)*

This time the incensed lover, Snaebiorn, lops off the husband's foot in revenge but himself dies ' "fulfilled of bitter lack." '

The Story of Kormak was translated in or soon after 1870 but was not published until a hundred years later. *Kormak* (London, 1970) is a curiosity among Icelandic tales of love and jealousy, and it may shed some light on Morris's motives and states of mind in the days when he was drawn to translate the story and write it out in lovely calligraphy.

Kormak, a great warrior-poet like Gunnlaug, loves Steingerd from the moment he sees her. Though at this moment he can see little but her feet, he immediately makes a poem, or sings a stave, as Morris says, something he does in all seasons as the story unfolds. The poem to Steingerd's feet is given by Morris as,

> Ah, how my heart now holdeth
> That heaven-bright land of gems!
> Her light feet laid upon me
> Great love in little space.
> But those feet of the fair-coifed woman
> Shall flit to bear me ruin
> Full oft before all endeth,
> If aught I know at all.

Steingerd is quickly wooed and won in spite of her father's opposition, but a witch curses Kormak's love, saying he shall never have any joy of Steingerd. The marriage is set but the eager bridegroom does not turn up for the wedding! After this she is twice married though not to Kormak, who has many opportunities to wed her. A great warrior, he fights many duels with the successful men or their relatives but kills no one. Once he spends a night with Steingerd but 'with the panel of the bed between them . . .' He blames the witch's curse for all his failures to ful-fulfil the passion served out in his poems. Finally, still singing songs in honour if his sweetling's beauty, he dies in a Viking attack on Scotland.

Kormak is a different kind of Icelandic love. If it was jealous ven-geance which attracted Morris to the sagas in the first place, the theme was here in abundance, but the fact is that none of Kormak's duels suc-ceeded. There is something bemused about him, as there is about Mor-ris, as he stumbles through both the ecstasy and tragedy of his life with-out being able to distinguish one from the other. That he is spell-bound and cursed in the enjoyment of his 'sweetling' reminds us of Morris too, who often seems to have borne his agony as a spell laid on him by a hostile fairy-power as punishment for an unknown 'sin'. It seems quite natural for someone who had read all of Scott by the age of seven to welcome the witches and trolls who abound in the Icelandic sagas and Morris did not often avoid or minimise their role. Many of Morris's favourite saga heroes, including Grettir, Kormak and Sigurd, are be-devilled by the spells and potions of revenants, trolls and 'wise wives.' They move about as if in trance because they are in trance. If this was also true of Morris, or true to his perception of his plight, we have here another of the homologues which drew him to Icelandic literature.

The great love-saga of the North, the *Völsunga*, was almost bound to be the favourite of a man who tended to see life at that time (1870) in terms of blood-brotherhood betrayed, of paradise ruined by something as mys-terious and malignant as witchcraft, of bitter resentment uncrowning a glorious soul. This great saga offered little opportunity for Morris to indulge in vicarious vengeance, but it frequently impinged on his ex-perience. And so Morris tells his readers that in this saga 'we awhile/ With echoed grief life's dull pain may beguile.' In a way the terrible tale may have steadied his mind, lowered the temperature of his own resentments, and soothed him like 'the sweet voice/of the bells' that sometimes pierces 'amid the clatter of the town' when the wind drops. These phrases come from Morris's 'Prologue in Verse' to the *Völsunga*. He credits the saga with effects it could hardly ever have had on anyone but himself. If the saga seemed to him to say,

> 'Be wide-eyed, kind; curse not the hand that smites;
> Curse not the kindness of a past good day,
> Or hope of love; cast by all earth's delights
> For every love,'

we can only count this a blessing, for it shows a gradual relaxing of tensions which might have boded harm to Jane and Rossetti (the black-locked Gunnar of the saga, who not only tricked Sirgurd into winning Brynhild for *him* but later had the hero murdered in spite of a pact of friendship sealed in blood). It is hard to see how the saga enforces the valuable moral of the verses quoted above, but fortunately it worked that way for Morris. The self-apostrophe that follows, if written with Georgiana in mind, can be more easily understood:

> 'through weary days and nights,
> Abide thou, striving howsoe'er in vain,
> The inmost love of one more heart to gain!'

The year this translation was published, 1870, was also the year when Morris practised his calligraphic wizardry and beautiful illumination on *A Book of Verse* for Georgiana, in which the 'Prologue to the Völsung Tale' has a prominent place. This prologue ends with a famous couplet

> Of utter love defeated utterly,
> Of grief too strong to give Love time to die!

That love had no time to die suggests that, living on, it naturally sought a refuge in 'one more heart.'

For several years Morris toyed with the idea of turning the saga into an English epic. Perhaps he wanted to produce a version of it which would justify the judgements and emotions expressed in 'A Prologue in Verse.' Another among the themes of that prologue not found in the saga itself was the hope of men 'the Gods to stay'

> When at that last tide gathered wrong and hate
> Shall meet blind yearning on the Fields of Fate.

These lines refer to *Ragna Rök*, the German *Götterdämmerung*, when Loki, the Fenris Wolf and the Midgard Serpent will destroy Odin and the Aesir, defeating man's blind yearning for an Earthly Paradise. The poet seems to be saying that he will pit his remaining hope for a bit of paradise against all the 'wrong and hate' with which the world seethes. Apparently when writing Sigurd, his prose version of the *Völsunga*, Morris had come to see himself as the noble, loving, trusting 'brother' who had him murdered. All this needed to be made explicit, he thought, and the anguish caused by Jane, the 'utter love defeated utterly,' presented, not as his private tragedy but as 'the best tale pity ever wrought' as the 'Iliad of the North' matured steadily between 1870 and '75, and finally Morris could keep his hand from a Norse-English epic no longer.

In the *Völsunga* Sigurd has no burning ambition to work for an Earthly Paradise. Morris believed that this urge is born of a deep sexual passion which makes each lover insist on having a society kind and just and beautiful enough to be worthy of the other; which makes both demand a country 'blithesome' enough to bring up children in; which fills the parents' minds with a vision that they must work at tirelessly if they are to be true to the wonderful awakening within them. Usually each lover attributes this vision and the energy to realise it to the 'inspiration'. Certainly this was the principal Morrisian tenet on the subject of 'utter love.' However, there is little about such love in the *Völsunga*: it is so brilliantly present in *Sigurd* because Morris put it there. To be sure, the Icelandic Brynhild seems to have won Sigurd's love not only by her perfect beauty but by her unsurpassable wisdom – ' "Sure no wiser woman than thou art ... may be found in the wide world; yea, yea, teach me more yet of thy wisdom!" ' What she teaches him is a series of runes – runes of war by which he may become great, sea-runes to get him home safely from raiding parties, word-runes to make sure that 'no man/Pay back grief for the grief thou gavest,' ale-runes to keep another man's wife from betraying 'thine heart that trusteth,' etc., etc. She also warns him never to fight indoors lest he be burnt in his house nor to overlook the wiles of friends who break plighted troth – and other folk clichés which he neglects at the cost of his own life and Brynhild's. In spite of Sigurd's sincere self-betrothal to the Sleeping Beauty he had rescued by riding through a wall of roaring fire, he is tricked by a 'hurtful' drink into marrying the Niblung princess Gudrun and winning Brynhild for Gudrun's brother Gunnar by reriding the flames in the latter's likeness. The amnesiac drink and the shape-shifting are the work of the pitiless Niblung witch-wife and queen, Grimhild. It was hard for many readers of the *Völsunga* to agree with Morris and Magnússon that this saga was 'The Iliad of the North' because the crude bewitchments do not correspond to known psychological states or motives. Consequently, Morris softened or slurred over the enchantments in his *Sigurd*, except for the magic potions which Grimhild dispensed so freely. In fact, he often blew up the description of Grimhild's brews from a word or two to half a dozen lines:

> Night-long had she brewed that witch-drink and
>   laboured not in vain.
> For therein was the creeping venom, and hearts of
>   things that prey
> On the hidden lives of ocean, and never look on day;
> And the heart of the ravening wood-wolf and the
>   hunger-blinded beast
> And the spent slaked heart of the wild-fire the
>   guileful cup increased:
> But huge words of ancient evil about its rim
>   were scored ...
>
>   (*Sigurd*, Bk. III)

But the question is, how did Morris transform the *Völsunga* into 'the best tale pity ever wrought?' One of the first and most obvious things to notice is the substitution of a real love-vision of a better world for the runic clichés inserted in the *Völsunga* from the *Sigdrifasmál*. Brynhild tells Sigurd how, when Odin punished her for being a disobedient Valkyr by condemning her to wed with 'the children of sorrow,' she had thought,

> 'Shall I wed in the world, shall I gather grief on
> the earth?
> Then the fearless heart shall I wed, and bring the
> best to birth,
> And fashion such tales for the telling, that Earth
> shall be holpen at least,
> If the Gods think scorn of its fairness, as they sit
> at the changeless feast.'
>
>   (Bk. II)

It seems that 'the wall of the wildfire wavering' around the sleeping girl had been fashioned to help her find a fearless husband who would help build a world which can never come into being without 'daring deeds' and 'the eager hearts of love':

> 'Be wise, and cherish thine hope in the freshness
> of the days,
> And scatter its seed from thine hand in the field
> of the people's praise . . .'
>
>   (Bk. II)

From the top of Hindfell, where stands the golden palace lately surrounded by fire, the new-born lovers have a vision of the whole world as a place whose happiness, safety, and beauty are entrusted to their personal efforts. Indeed, it is this knightly, rather than Viking view of his heritage that Sigurd adopts from the time he 'reasons' with Morris's Brynhild. Woe to ' "the fashioners of tears!" ' ' "unpeace to the lords of evil" ' –

> 'And I would that the loving were loved, and I would
> that the weary should sleep,
> And that man should hearken to man, and that he that
> soweth should reap.'
>
>   (Bk. III)

Even when among the Niblungs – that is, before Grimhild has fed him 'the cup of evil' which causes him to forget Brynhild – Sigurd fights only for the vision that comes from love, and is duly acclaimed:

> Yea, they sing the song of Sigurd and the face without
>   a foe,
> And they sing of the prison's rending and the tyrant
>   laid alow,
> And the golden thieves' abasement, and the stilling
>   of the churl,
> And the mocking of the dastard where the chasing
>   edges whirl;
> And they sing of the outland maidens that thronged
>   round Sigurd's hand,
> And sung in the streets of the foemen of the war-
>   delivered land;
> And they tell how the ships of the merchants come free
>   and go at their will,
> And how wives in peace and safety may crop the vine-clad
>   hill;
> How the maiden sits in her bower, and the weaver sings
>   at his loom,
> And forget the kings of grasping and the greedy days
>   of gloom;
> For by sea and hill and township hath the Son of
>   Sigmund been,
> And looked on the folk unheeded, and the lowly people
>   seen.
>
>   (Bk. III)

However deeply Sigurd has looked into the wrongs of the deprived and brought comfort to the downtrodden, once he has drunk the cup of forgetfulness, he loses his high sense of purpose and lends himself to the cruel magic by which, in the guise of Gunnar, he wins Brynhild for his new brother-in-law. The subsequent righting of his befuddled wits brings him his last period of glory in Morris's epic:

> It was most in these latter days that his fame went
>   far abroad.
> The helper, the overcomer, the righteous sundering
>   sword;
> The loveliest King of the King-folk, the man of
>   sweetest speech,
> Whose ear is dull to no man that his helping
>   shall beseech;
> The eye-bright seer of all things, that wasteth
>   every wrong,
> The straightener of the crooked, the hammer of
>   the strong . . .
>
>   (Bk. III)

But Brynhild cannot win back a sparkle of her lost joy; she can love none but the best, quarrels dreadfully with Gudrun, and at last demands that Gunnar, not merely Sigurd's relative by marriage but his blood-and-earth-sworn brother, kill the betrayer. 'Swart-haired' Gunnar is a man of 'measureless pride' mixed with jealousy, envy, and guile, whence springs a nameless ambition for which his vicious mother soon finds a title: 'sole King in the world-throne, unequalled, unconstrained ...' By murdering Sigurd and stealing the treasure which, as an untried boy, he had won from the dragon Fafnir, Gunnar thinks to please Brynhild and fulfill his vile dream of super-kingship. Actually, Brynhild kills herself after the Niblungs have butchered 'the redeemer, the helper, the crown of all their worth.' Now

> They are gone – the lovely, the mighty, the hope of
> the ancient earth:
> It shall labour and bear the burden as before that
> day of their birth:
> It shall groan in its blind abiding for the day that
> Sigurd hath sped,
> And the hour that Brynhild hath hastened, and the
> dawn that waketh the dead ...
>
> (Bk. III)

Another Earthly Paradise has been lost as soon as born but the utter lovers have prepared the way for the Dusk of the Gods and the dawn of a better if not absolutely paradisal time.

In the *Völsunga* little is made of black-locked Gunnar's lust for gold, power and 'Sigurd's Brynhild,' but Morris plays it up, perhaps because while he was writing *Sigurd*, Rossetti was still making trouble as cicisbeo and do-nothing member of the Firm, refusing to sell his interest in the company for a penny less than the letter of the law required. Thankfully the villainy of the Niblungs is ended when Gudrun's second husband, Atli, who is also a power-maniac, lures the Niblungs to their utter destruction, leaving Gunnar to die harping and singing (the singing is added by Morris) in an adder-pit. Here Morris expands five or six lines of the saga to almost as many pages, giving the snakes chilling names but reserving his finest epithets for the worm who could stay awake through Gunnar's soporific poetry until he had stung him thoroughly:

> And the crests of the worms have fallen, and their
> flickering tongues are still,
> The Roller and the Coiler, and the Greyback, lord of ill,
> Grave-groper and Death-swaddler, the Slumberer of
> the Heath,

Gold-wallower, Venom-smiter, lie still, forgetting
    death,
And loose are coils of Long-back; yea, all as soft
    are laid
As the kine in midmost summer about the elmy glade;
– All save the grey and Ancient, that holds his
    crest aloft,
Light-wavering as the flame-tongue when the evening
    wind is soft . . .

               (Bk. IV)

So far, the love stories of the North that Morris translated or paraphrased have been tales in which sexual jealousy leads to murder,
whether of a wife, lover or husband. The *Völsunga* surpasses the other
sagas in many ways, especially in the double-edged jealousy which would
not allow either Gunnar or Brynhild to let Sigurd live. From the hopelessly self-centred Gudrun of the *Laxdaela* to the generally magnanimous
Brynhild, most of the tragedies are caused, wholly or in part, by women
who go out of their way to set their lovers at each other's throats. Two
of the tales in *Three Northern Love Stories* (1875), translated at various
times after *Gunnlaug the Worm-Tongue* of 1869, may be said to have
'happy endings' but a fourth (accounted for in the subtitle *And Other
Tales*), 'The Tale of Hogni and Hedinn,' is a paradigm of the turmoil
and slaughter which women stir up among men, usually those who have
for years been the dearest of friends. Though not in itself a love story,
this tale of the acts of Freyia – a Northern 'Venus Descordia' like those
Burne-Jones painted about this time – gives us our best clue to Morris's
fascination with 'Northern love,' a realm dominated by big, incredibly
lovely and strangely prepotent women who fill the lives of sworn- or
foster-brothers with year after year of nightmarish strife which promises
at any moment to turn into crime. Filling the desperate years between
1869 and '75 with vicarious participation in these shattering tragedies
may have helped Morris to hold on to his sanity and forego acts of
violence which might have erupted from his fierce fits of temper. The
sagas built no '*shadowy isles of bliss/Midmost the beating of the steely
sea,/Where tossed about all hearts of men must be,*' but their echoed
furies could beguile one's own fury. And they had another effect, quite
unlooked-for. They could persuade us, so Morris says in his verse prologue to the *Völsunga*, to 'curse not the hand that smites.' For Morris
there was something so moving in the hero's pain, and especially in his
ability to bear pain with stoic bravery, that the inflicter of pain could
almost be overlooked. To the Muse of the North he prayed to have 'a
part/In that great sorrow of thy children dead/That vexed the brow,
and bowed adown the head' but did not wring from the spirit one faint-
hearted complaint. He seems to beg the Muse to wrap him in 'the grief

of long ago' that he may realise how little his pains are by comparison. Kiartan of Laxdale, Gunnar of Lithend (in the *Njàl Saga*), Sigurd Fafnirsbane – these were heroes with brighter prospects and sadder disillusionments than his own, yet,

> . . . while yet they dwelt on earth
> Wearied no God with prayers for more of mirth
> Than dying men have; nor were ill-content
> Because no God beside their sorrow went
> Turning to flowery sward the rock-strewn way,
> Weakness to strength, or darkness into day.

Let Venus or Freyia do her worst, they seemed to say, she could not do worse to man than she did in 'The Tale of Hogni and Heddin.' After selling her body to four dwarf goldsmiths for a collar she fancied, she saw it confiscated by Odin with no chance of getting it back

'Unless forsooth thou bring to pass that two kings, each served of twenty kings, fall to strife, and fight under such weird and spell, that they no sooner fall adown than they stand up again and fight on: Always unless some christened man be so bold of heart . . . that he shall dare go into that battle, and smite with weapons these men: and so first shall their toil come to an end, to whatsoever lord it shall befall to loose them from the pine and trouble of their fell deeds.'

The two kings whom Freyia finds to hack at each other forever are Hogni and Heddin, so alike in daring and prowess that 'they swore themselves foster-brethren, and should halve all things between them.' Yet Freyia, with the help of the usual amnesiac drink, persuades Hedinn to murder Hogni's wife by cutting her in two with his dragon-boat as she lies on the beach. Naturally the erstwhile brothers with their servant-kings are soon in the thick of a battle with lasts both night and day for 143 years. At that time Christianity reached the North and King Olaf of Norway sent a knight to loose them from their 'woeful labour and miserable grief of heart' by killing them all outright and forever. However, the *Skáldskapurmál*, the source of this tale, relates that this nightmare will continue until Ragner Rök, the Doom of the Gods. The original mythmaker did not equate this event with the coming of Christianity.

If this bloody tale caused Morris to toss in his sleep, it also probably helped to steady him when awake. If the saga material 'amidst all its wildness and remoteness' displays 'a startling realism,' and 'close sympathy with all the passions' that move men today, how considerable is its warning against supranatural women moving in our midst and setting foster-brothers on courses of horrible destruction! Too late to prevent distress, but not too late to prevent tragedy, Morris discovered this rich literature of domestic discord from which he drew the moral: 'Be wide-eyed, kind; curse not the hand that smites ...'

Besides the Northern *femme fatale* and the jealous lovers, besides the witch and her demented prey, there was another breed of Icelanders whose response to trouble fascinated Morris and helped him 'at his need.' These were the great 'outlaws' like Gisli, Grettir, and Gunnar of Lithend (*Njál Saga*). It is not difficult to understand how Morris who had so little in common with the social, economic, political and esthetic values of his time – values fundamentally unjust and even inhuman – found it easy to identify with the famous Icelandic outlaws whose motives are usually high but misunderstood. They are often envied for their courage, the probity of their lives, and ruined by spiteful wives and deadly witches. What a clutch of parallels – what new 'friends in need'!

As well as *The Story of Burnt Njál* (1861) George Dasent had translated *The Story of Gisli the Outlaw* (1866), but left for Morris and Mágnússon to translate was the greatest of outlaw tales. Like *Gunnlaug, The Story of Grettir the Strong* appeared in 1869, scarcely a year after the beginning of their coöperation. The translators called it the best of Icelandic sagas after the *Völsunga* and the *Njála*: fuller than the tale of Gisli; less frightful that that of Egil; as dramatic as the story of Gunnlaug; more consistent than that of Gudrun of Bathstead, and more a work of art than 'the unstrung gems of *Eyrbyggja*.' Mostly, however, they admired *Grettir the Strong* for its 'eager interest in human character.' In the 'Preface' we are called on to appreciate the uncompromising realism with which the acts and the words of the great outlaw reveal the inner man. Even as a child he would not be deflected from his life's work, which seemed to be laying ghosts and killing those Viking-pests known as 'Bearserks.' He would do no 'milksop's work,' and accordingly strangled the goslings and maimed a horse entrusted to his care. At fourteen he killed a 'house-carle' in a quarrel over a sack of meal and sang a contemptuous stave (he was, of course, a poet from the cradle) about the death:

> 'Over the battle ogress ran
> The red blood of the serving-man;
> Her deadly iron mouth did gape
> Above him, till clean out of shape
> She tore his head and let out life:
> And certainly I saw their strife.'

(Ch. XVI)

After this deed he was outlawed from Iceland for three winters, during which time he laid the foundation of a remarkable reputation for throttling ghosts (who caused much property damage as well as uproar when 'riding the roofs' of medieval Scandinavia. He also killed a boatload of Bearserks single-handed. When he returned to Iceland, a man of great fame, he reached the height of his glory by beheading the monstrous revenant called Glam the Thrall, a troll who stole men's sheep and cracked every bone in the shepherd's bodies. No worse fate, however, could have befallen Grettir than Glam's dying curse that everything he did after that would turn to woe and mishap, manslaying and outlawry, as the frightful eyes of the ghost slowly drove him to his death.

Grettir is not merely the greatest man in Iceland; he is also the most 'luckless.' He makes enemies without intending to and is outlawed by Thorir of Garth for burning his sons, a deed Grettir never did. Refusing to stay away from Iceland, he has a price put on his head and is driven from one lair to another. All the while he carries women and children through ice-floes to church and rids the common people of a Grendel-and-Dam-like pair of trolls who feed on human bodies. 'Mighty' is his life but 'troublous' and after nineteen years of outlawry (within one year of official pardon) the last troll-wife, or pagan witch, in Iceland weaves spells which cause him to wound himself with an axe. The wound turns gangrenous and gives a posse of enemies the chance to murder the half-dead outlaw-hero.

In the 'Preface' to *Grettir* Morris (I think it is his hand and his alone here) delights to underscore the fact that

the sagaman never relaxes his grasp of Grettir's character, and he is the same man from beginning to end; thrust this way and that by circumstances, but little altered by them; unlucky in all things, yet made strong to bear all ill-luck; scornful of the world, yet capable of enjoyment, and determined to make the most of it; not deceived by men's specious ways, but disdaining to cry out because he needs must bear with them; scorning men, yet helping them when called on, and desirous of fame; prudent in theory, and wise in foreseeing the inevitable sequence of events, but reckless beyond the recklessness even of that time and people, and finally capable of inspiring in others strong affection and devotion to him in spite of his rugged self-sufficing temper . . .

Grettir's character so conceived strongly suggests Morris's own personality. It seems to have been this deep affinity with the traits and tribulations of the Icelandic 'outlaws' which, more than anything else, drew Morris to their literature and later to the island itself. From childhood had often felt out of sympathy with, set apart from, and opposed to the

world in which he lived. He refused to travel up to London for Welling-
ton's funeral, to rejoice at modern 'progress' as represented by the
Crystal Palace exhibition of 1851, or to find anything but fierce cruelty
in the rumours of city-life which filtered into Epping Forest. One of the
most characteristic of his juvenile poems, 'The Night-Walk,' begins:

> Night lay upon the city
>   Dull clouds upon the night
> O! London without pity!
>   O! ghastly flaring light!
>
>   *   *   *
>
> It fell on faces, bloated
>   With many hideous crimes,
> On some, whose thoughts had floated
>   Away to long past times.
>
>   *   *   *
>
> It fell on hungry faces
>   Thin lips, despairing frown,
> Truly a dismal place is
>   That grim, gold-pavèd town.
>
>   (Sup. I, 525)

Through the wet London streets walks a woman with frightened eyes
and clenched teeth past

> 'The fearful, dusky houses
>   They hemmed me in alway,
> The angry, terrible horses
>   They met me yesterday.'
>
>   (Sup. I, 526)

She is trying to escape to the country to die in 'an old, old garden
where', says the boy poet,

> I think the leaves will bury her,
> The snowy lillies look on her,
>   They look as if they love her,
> The bee will look as he goes by,
> The sun will look when he is high;
>   No sound will ever move her.
>
>   (Sup. I, 529)

In our so-called civilisation, this woman was ragged and persecuted – an
an outcast or outlaw – but her eagerness for the beauty of the earth was
never stilled nor her rejection of the world of trolls and bearserks who
had rejected her. Morris was not so unlucky as this poor girl, but was
just as scornful of the cruelty of people and the horror of their houses.

In due time he would gain the strengths of the essentially just and noble 'Icelandic outlaw.' The street-girl is, then, Morris as a youthful truant moving through ugliness and wrong toward an ancient Icelandic stance.

For these old outlaws, dogged by bad luck when trying to do good, often deserted by friends and wives, laid under the fatal weirds of the revenants and troll-women of whom they are trying to rid society, Morris felt a deep kinship. When translating *Grettir* he wrote two sonnets addressed to the outlaw hero. The first lines of the one published as a superinscription to the translation would have fitted the London outcast of years before:

> A life scarce worth the living, a poor fame
> Scarce worth the winning, in a wretched land,
> Where fear and pain go upon either hand,
> As toward the end men fare without an aim
> Unto the dull grey dark from whence they came . . .

The second, which May published in *The Collected Works*, (VII, xix), brings us closer to the object of Morris's empathy – the eager life which struggles against pain and fate to affirm the conviction of an unquenchable goodness and joy in the earth; a worth in day-to-day living even when the victim is surrounded by enemies both human and supernatural.

> Grettir, didst thou live utterly for nought?
> Among the many millions of the earth
> Few knew thy name or where thou hadst thy birth.
> And yet, that passing glow of fame unsought,
> That eager life in ill luck's meshes caught
> That struggles yet to gain a little mirth
> Amidst of pain –

That 'eagerness' is exactly the passion with which 'great men' endow small things with value, giving promise to every phase, of experience however unpromising that phase appears to be. At the end of this second sonnet Morris writes, 'Speak, Grettir, through the dark: I am anear.' The first poem ends with lines which emphasise the role Grettir played in the poet's beleaguered life in 1870:

> Nay, with the dead I deal not; this man lives,
> And that which carried him through good and ill,
> Stern against fate while his voice echoed still
> From rock, now he lies silent, strives
> With wasting time, and through its long lapse gives
> Another friend to me, life's void to fill.

After Grettir, Morris's favourite outlaw was Gunnar of Lithend in the *Njála*. Gunnar married Hallgerd (her third marriage), a beautiful woman described as 'bitchy,' though adjectives describing most of the cardinal sins including 'murderous' would have been more appropriate for a woman who from birth had 'a thief's eyes.' She was forever engaged in bitter quarrels and she cultivated vendettas in which deaths occurred at regular and frequent intervals. By contrast, Gunnar, though the most famous and fearsome warrior of his time, was a magnanimous, peace-loving man, brave and generous like Kiartan or Sigurd. Like them, he was also guileless, a virtue hopelessly and dangerously out of place in a land where insatiable greed and uncontrollable tempers put 'the hallowed peace of the Thing' in constant jeopardy. A man like Gunnar who loved the earth he farmed not only for its fruitfulness but for its wild beauty is something of a rarity in the sagas. One feels that if his mischief-making wife had left him alone, he might have been quite happy in a constructive, Morrisian way. But Hallgerd's feud with Njál's wife drew him into condoning or taking vengeance until blood-suits made him an outlaw. He intended, as was usual, to leave Iceland by an agreed day, but on the way to the coast his horse tripped and threw him.

He turned with his face up towards the Lithe and the homestead at Lithend, and said, 'Fair is the Lithe; so fair that it has never seemed to me so fair; the corn fields are white to harvest, and the home mead is mown; and now I will ride back home, and not fare abroad at all.'

By staying on the land he loves, Gunnar makes himself the legal prey of his enemies. On hearing that he is alone at Lithend, they get together a posse to destroy him. Since Gunnar is the best bowman in Iceland, they cannot get at him until one manages at the cost of his life to cut Gunnar's bowstring. The great outlaw is twice wounded though 'he never once winced either at wounds or death.'

> Then Gunnar said to Hallgerd, 'Give me two locks of
> thy hair, and ye two, my mother, and thou, twist them
> together into a bowstring for me.'
> 'Does aught lie on it?' she says.
> 'My life lies on it,' he said; 'for they will never
> come to close quarters with me if I can keep them off
> with my bow.'
> 'Well!' she says, 'now I will call to thy mind that
> slap on the face which thou gavest me; and I care never
> a whit whether thou holdest out a long while or a short.'
>
> (*Burnt Njál*, tr. Dasent, Ch. 76)

After his death Gunnar's friends 'cast a cairn' over his body, arranging it so that he sat upright – not supine in death – and soon afterward 'this token happened at Lithend, that the neat-herd and the serving girl were driving cattle by Gunnar's cairn. They thought that he was merry and that he was singing inside the cairn.' Restored to the womb of the earth he loved and sitting ready for new life, Gunnar's spirit could well be expected to rejoice. Shortly after this his favourite son Hogni and Njál's son Skarphedinn had an even more eerie experience:

The moon and stars were shining clear and bright, but every now and then the clouds drove over them. Then all at once they thought they saw the cairn standing open, and lo! Gunnar had turned himself in the cairn and looked at the moon. They thought they saw four lights burning in the cairn, and none of them threw a shadow. They saw that Gunnar was merry, and he wore a joyful face. He sang a song, and so loud, that it might have been heard though they had been further off.

(Ch. 77)

The saga gives the words of Gunnar's happy death song, stressing that the brave man would 'sooner die than yield an inch.' 'After that the cairn was shut up again.'

We can imagine how the story of this heroic man stirred Morris. Gunnar was much wronged by his wife and delivered by her to his enemies. Yet complaining not and rejoicing after death in his beloved earth, he sang a loud, clear song regretting nothing. When Morris was in Iceland in 1871, it was Gunnar's cairn which inspired the best poem composed on the journey, 'Gunnar's Howe Above the House at Lithend.'

> Ye who have come o'er the sea
> to behold this grey minster of lands,
> Whose floor is the tomb of time past,
> and whose walls by the toil of dead hands
> Show pictures amidst of the ruin
> of deeds that have overpast death,
> Stay by this tomb in a tomb
> to ask of who lieth beneath.
> Ah! the world changeth too soon,
> that ye stand there with unbated breath,
> As I name him that Gunnar of old,
> Who erst in the haymaking tide
> Felt all the land fragrant and fresh,
> as amidst of the edges he died.
> Too swiftly fame fadeth away,
> if ye tremble not lest once again
> The grey mound should open and show him
> glad-eyed without grudging or pain. . . .

> Little labour for ears that may hearken
> to hear his death-conquering song,
> Till the heart swells to think of the gladness
> undying that overcame wrong.
>
> (*Poems By the Way*)

Unlike Grettir with his uncontrollable temper, his bad luck with revenants and troll-wives and his nineteen years of unmerited outlawry, Gunnar led a somewhat normal life though no witch could have been more deadly than handsome Hallgerd or any outlawry have left him at the end more naked to his foes. Gunnar's love of the earth may not have surpassed Grettir's but as a farmer, his contact with the soil was a source of strength and gladness, reaching beyond the grave. This Grettir lacked. Both men grew patient in adversity, uncomplaining, unwarped, un-soured, harbouring no spite, renouncing vendettas but inspired by the gleam in field and sky to live and, if necessary, die without yielding an inch. In lives like these Morris found the traits he admired and needed. Although they lived in medieval times, these Icelandic heroes lacked the panache, the jousting, the mysterious Grail-questing of Arthur's knights. More ordinary, even hum-drum, the Icelanders fought a brutal climate and a poor soil for their lives while attempting to deal with their violent human passions – patiently and without complaining. To Morris the sagas seemed both realistic and wise, full of the love of earth, and touched with magnanimity. Their characters spoke directly to him – 'Speak, Grettir, through the dark: I am anear,' looking for 'Another friend to me, life's void to fill.' What Gunnar said to Morris as he stood by the 'howe' made him believe that the old outlaw could help the youth of his day to build a world of patient, brave, big-hearted men.

> O young is the world yet meseemeth
> and the hope of it flourishing green,
> When the words of a man unremembered
> so bridge all the days that have been,
> As we look round about on the land
> that these nine hundred years he hath seen.
>
> (*Poems By the Way*)

After the move to Kelmscott Manor in southwest Oxfordshire in 1871, Jane's relations with Rossetti continued to upset Morris more than he had expected. So he sought a new means of relief. He probably felt that the soil and scenery of Iceland had had much to do with fashioning the heroes he admired. Iceland must be congruous to his nature and experience: a place where bravery was perfect but seldom triumphed, where longing was deep but hardly ever attained its goal, where love was utter but utterly defeated, where the hand was unfaltering but always failed.

Yet, as Morris said in a lecture on the Norse chieftains, 'in all the stories of the North failure is never reckoned a disgrace, but it *is* reckoned a disgrace not to bear it with equanimity, and to wear one's heart on one's sleeve is not well thought of. Tears are not common ...' (Sup. II, 450) The real religion of the Norsemen is 'the worship of courage.' A journey to Iceland with visits to the scenes whose names reverberated helpfully through the nightmares he still suffered might help him to shake off his shamefully lingering hopes and passions. There perhaps he would be cured of 'plagues and evil spirits' (Luke vii, 21), by a power such as that which the multitudes had gone 'out into the wilderness to behold' (Luke vii, 24) or, as Morris always put it, went 'out for to see.'

He knew it was no Earthly Paradise he was going to find, no '*shadowy isle of bliss/Midmost of the steely sea*,' but he probably had no idea that he was embarking for an Eden turned upside down; an infernal mandala or anti-paradise undermined by fire and crushed by ice. On the other hand, by the time he made his first trip to Iceland in 1871 Morris knew pretty well what he was looking for. He wanted to make a pilgrimage to the shrines of the saints of that 'religion of courage' which had helped him so much in the last three years to stand up to the pain he was 'never meant to bear.' As he said in the preface to *Howard the Halt* printed in 1891, 'a journey to Iceland to the traveller read in its ancient literature is a continual illustration ... of the books which contain the intimate history of its ancient folk' (vi). Morris's itinerary led straight to Laxdale, to the lairs of Grettir and the country of Njál and Gunnar. By now his turmoil over Jane was ebbing but it was still there and the quaint idea of taking a joint-lease of Kelmscott Manor with Rossetti in 1871 was the least effective way of finding equanimity Morris could have hit on. The Earthly Paradise which he had 'collared' for himself on the Upper Thames was immediately undermined and it seems that he went to Iceland to test his courage to bear pain to the utmost.

Sacred centres of literary pilgrimage he would, of course, find, but the properties and proportions of everything Icelandic were to be more monstrous, fire-reddened, and rock-bound than anything he had imagined. To be sure, Morris had read enough about Iceland to have an inkling of all this. But he had not expected the gigantic chaos, the mournfulness, the dreadful wastes. He had hardly discovered his new summer home which he called Kelmscott Manor – 'a heaven on earth' – when he found himself describing the coast of Iceland, seen from the Danish mail boat *Diana*:

a terrible shore indeed: a great mass of dark grey mountains worked into pyramids and shelves, looking as if they had been built and half-ruined; they were striped with snow high up, and wreaths of cloud dragged across them here and there, and above them were two peaks and a jagged ridge of pure white snow ...

This description comes from *Journals of Travel in Iceland 1871, 1873*, which was later handscripted for Georgiana, the one friend who could understand and sympathise with what the others of the Morris circle talked of as a whimsical caper. The *Journals* was first published by May Morris in 1911 as Volume VIII of the *Works*. Nearly all the following quotations in this chapter come from this book. 'Most strange and awful the country looked to me . . . in spite of my anticipations.' 'Doleful,' 'dismal,' 'ghastly,' full of 'ink-black' peaks and 'saw-toothed' ridges – these are among his favourite epithets for the land he had been dreaming of!

This was the landscape of hell, a capsised Eden, but since it was the country which had nourished his heroes and developed their religion of courage, it could only be treated as a challenge and accepted for what it was – the wilderness he had come out for to see, as he wrote in 'Iceland First Seen':

> Ah! what came we forth for to see
> that our hearts are so hot with desire?
> Is it enough for our rest,
> the sight of this desolate strand,
> And the mountain-waste voiceless as death
> but for winds that may sleep not nor tire?
> Why do we long to wend forth
> Through the length and breadth of a land,
> Dreadful with grinding of ice,
> and record of scarce hidden fire,
> But that there 'mid the grey grassy dales
> sore scarred by the ruining streams
> Lives the tale of the Northland of old
> and the undying glory of dreams?
>
> *   *   *
>
> No wheat and no wine grows above it,
> no orchard for blossom and shade;
> The few ships that sail by its blackness
> but deem it the mouth of a grave;
> Yet sure when the world shall awaken,
> this too shall be mighty to save.
>
> *(Poems By the Way)*

The 'undying glory of dreams' may not seem the most accurate description of the sagas, but it is possible to see how they, along with the story of the seismically distorted island which produced them, 'shall be mighty to save.' Iceland, so inhospitable to life whether vegetable, animal or human, was nevertheless a mother; the wife of Odin, the blinkered deity who loved to watch the drama of life best when it was played under the most difficult conditions and endured through failure to a characteristically tragic end. More than other mothers, then, she had to tempt and prod her children to struggle forward to inevitable defeat. Such drama had become for Morris a wondrously helpful dream when he watched the actors fight on and on in the face of adverse 'Fate.' For such drama is truth and allegory combined. If 'fight on' is phrased as 'work on,' 'create,' 'do,' 'never give up,' we can see that a poor country like Iceland, 'whose plunder all gathered together/was little to babble about,' gave its people the sharpest possible goad to live deeply, concoct glorious debâcles, and immortalise them in sagas which wrap our personal defeats 'in the grief of long ago.' Iceland has gifts, even exaltation, for sufferers from the most common human dilemma. Addressing her, Morris tells Iceland to cry aloud from her wastes that she is not like lands reared on riches that wane or dogmas that die. Cry,

> 'I abide here the spouse of a God
> and I made and I make and endure.'

Then, toward the close of 'Iceland First Seen' he apostrophises the country he is about to set foot on:

> O Queen of the grief without knowledge,
> of the courage that may not avail,
> Of the longing that may not attain,
> of the love that shall never forget,
> More joy than the gladness of laughter
> thy voice hath amidst of its wail:
> More hope than of pleasure fulfilled
> amidst of thy blindness is set;
> More glorious than gaining of all
> thine unfaltering hand that shall fail . . .

> *(Poems By the Way)*

Morris immediately set out on his literary itinerary, paying little attention to the geysirs with their 'stinking steam' which most visitors went to Iceland to see; people who won Morris's scorn by never having 'heard the names of Sigurd and Brynhild, of Njál or Gunnar or Grettir or Gudrun' – those heroic characters who had saddened his sad life further, yet made it great to live. Of the geysirs Morris wrote, 'I was quite ready to break my neck in my quality of pilgrim to the holy places of Iceland' but not to be scalded to death or 'wake up boiled . . .' Not that many shrines gave outright pleasure. Gudrun's Bathstead was 'a very sad place . . . my heart sickened.'

Just think, though what a mournful place this is – Iceland I mean . . . how every place and name marks the death of its short-lived eagerness and glory . . . I don't doubt the house stands on the old ground. But Lord! what littleness and helplessness has taken the place of the old passion and violence that had place here once – and all is unforgotten . . . Yet it is an awful place . . . a piece of turf under your feet, and the sky overhead, that's all; whatsoever solace your life is to have here must come out of yourself or these old stories, not over hopeful themselves.

Morris's spirits were not raised when his party visited a lair where Grettir had hidden. However, seeing the place did raise his already unrivalled admiration for the outlaw.

. . . the lava goes along the river for some way, looking dark grey and dreadful among the grey green pastures and yellow green marshes. We ride along the slopes still heading up the valley, and presently we see ahead of us a spur rushing at right angles out from the mountains, a great ruin spoiling the fair green slopes; it is a huge slip of black shale, very steep, and crested by thin jagged rocks, like palings set awry . . . under these palings on the top of the grey ruin was Grettir's lair . . . It was such a savage dreadful place, that it gave quite a new turn in my mind to the whole story, and transfigured Grettir into an awful and monstrous being, like one of the early giants of the world.

The party also visited 'half-ruined and deserted, . . . the stead of Fródá haunted once by those awful ghosts of the pest-slain and the drowned in Eyrbyggia . . .' The scenery of the *Njála* was tamer and richer. Bergthorsknoll was where Njál, his wife and a little grandson, lying covered by a great oxhide, had been burned to death for a crime they had had no hand in. The place consisted of 'three mounds something the shape of limpets rising from a bright green home mead with a turf wall all around it.' Beyond was marsh land 'all channelled with innumerable ruts, getting greyer and greyer in the distance . . .' The flat, green meadows of Lithend that Gunnar died for because he could not bring himself to forsake their beauty, interested Morris most of all: 'these meadows were Gunnar's great wealth in the old days, but they are now sadly wasted and diminished by the ruin of black sand and stones the always shifting streams of Markfleet . . . have brought down on it.' However, Gunnar's Howe 'is most dramatically situated to remind one of the beautiful passage in the *Njála* where Gunnar sings in his tomb: the sweet grassy flowery valley with a few big grey stones about it has a steep back above . . . but down the hill the slope is shallow, and about midways of it is the howe.' From the top of the howe are fine views of the fertile hill called the Lithe and the great ice-topped mountain of Eyjafell.

From here one can also see up into the 'terrible valley east of the Lithe,' the Thorsmark, a terrestrial inferno. A local Icelander agreed to guide Morris and his party through the Thorsmark. Having forced their way into the valley by fording half a dozen icy streams, they found themselves between red volcano-burned cliffs that overhung much more than seemed possible; 'they had caves in them just like the hell-mouths in 13th-century illuminations' and clefts through which 'you would see a

horrible winding street with stupendous straight rocks for houses on
either side . . .' 'The great mountain-wall which closes up the valley, with
its jagged outlying teeth, was right before us now, looking quite impassable . . .' The explorers seemed trapped in a kind of anti-Happy Valley,
its River of Paradise supplanted by the foaming, black-bordered Markfleet, and nothing more than a solid stone to indicate a temenos-centre.
When the others of his party decided on a bit of a climb, Morris, soon
outstripped and feeling tired and a little downhearted with the savagery
of the place, sat down

on the bare shale of the steep slope that overlooked the valley . . . below was the
flat black plain space of the valley, and all about it every kind of distortion and
disruption, and the labyrinth of the furious brimstone-laden Markfleet winding
amidst it lay between us and anything like smoothness: surely it was what I
'came out for to see,' yet for the moment I felt cowed, and as if I should never
get back again: yet with that came a feeling of exaltation too, and I seemed to
understand how people under all disadvantages should find their imaginations
kindle amid such scenes.

What a Happy Valley, what a River of Paradise, what a scrambled mandala, what a smooth seat for an epoch of rest! And yet . . .

Spiritually, this was his journey's end though its physical end was
Thingvellir or Thingvalla, which played a part in most of the Icelandic
stories retold by Morris. The Hill of Laws was itself a kind of sacred
centre surrounded by the burning mountains, chaotic cliffs, and black-
sand valleys which make the whole of Iceland into a mock-mandalic
structure. Here 'a deep rift in the lava,' dark and 'dreadful-looking,' surrounded a little island which sloped upward from the rift to a small
mound high on the hill. This was the heart of the Hill of Laws, as 'the
HILLS OF LAWS is the heart of Iceland . . . The whole island is not a
large church for the ceremony' of democratic justice to have grown up
in, but 'Grim Goatshoe, who picked it out for the seat of the Althing,
must have been a man of poetic insight.'

Morris had now pilgrimaged to the shrines of his long suffering saints
and discovered why their religion of bravery could not be shaken by continued and inevitable defeat. They had needed no Earthly Paradise to
rest in, no Heavenly one to even scores, because they had learned perforce how to make a kind of heaven of hell. They could not easily be
small or dispirited when living in a kind of inferno where, if life was to
go on, every struggle had to be titanic, every affection hardy, every act
imaginative, every defeat a victory. Life endured to the utmost cannot be
dull and may be the secret of exaltation.

The desire to understand more about this mystery led Morris back to
Iceland a second time in the summer of 1873. Before going he revised his
journal of the 1871 trip and gave a handsome transcript of it to Georgiana. On his arrival at Reykjavik on 18 July he wrote to Jane saying he

wished he were already back in England, for travelling in Iceland was no common ordeal – 'how wild and strange everything here is.' He apologises for 'this shabby letter! but how can I help it, not knowing whether I am on my head or my heels?' and declares, 'It is all like a kind of dream to me, and my real life seems set aside until it is over.' (*Letters*, 57) Apparently his thoughts were once again busy with the problem of how what is 'terrible and tragic' in human life can be transfigured and immortalised by what is terrible and awful in scenery. When unable to support her children easily, Nature or Earth demands of them more work and creativity, more determination and deeds, than normally. This means great mistakes will be committed – even tragedies – but where so much energy is called into play, no act, no joy, no sorrow, will be wholly lost. The deeds inspired by Earth's hard commands are commemorative: they heal or embalm the stark courage demanded, turning unforgettable efforts into unforgettable tales. Thinking along these lines, Morris evolved, with the indispensable help of Iceland and her literature, a belief in Earth as Healer and Keeper which went far beyond the love of nature that had been part of him since boyhood. Even turned upside-down, Earth keeps, though distorted, a beauty, a determination, a power of healing, an urge to commemoration, sometimes a period of rest – mandalic blessings still emanating powerfully from the heart of ruin. Soon after returning to England and immediately visiting the Burne-Joneses at the Grange with 'as joyous a meeting as you may imagine,' Morris wrote to Aglaia Coronio, telling her that

The journey was very successful, & has deepened the impression I had of Iceland, & increased my love for it, though I don't suppose I shall ever see it again: nevertheless . . . the glorious simplicity of the terrible & tragic, but beautiful land with its well remembered stories of brave men, killed all querulous feeling in me, and have made all the dear faces of wife & children, and love, & friends dearer than ever to me . . .

Do you know I feel as if a definite space of my life had passed away now I have seen Iceland for the last time: as I looked up at Charles' Wain tonight all my travel there seemed to come back on me, made solemn and elevated, in one moment, till my heart swelled with the wonder of it: surely I have gained a great deal and it was no idle whim that drew me there, but a true instinct for what I needed.

(*Letters*, 58–9)

Morris's feelings about his Icelandic experience, both literature and travel, are poignantly expressed in a poem he wrote in 1876 or perhaps earlier. It is called 'Earth the Healer, Earth the Keeper,' and is one of his finest poems. Each of the nineteen quatrains is clearly and often powerfully phrased and the poem as a whole indicates that the poet has reached a decisive moment in the development of his thought on the subjects of nature, sagas, love and work. The first four stanzas seem to speak of a high-hearted departure for Iceland, full of courage and joy renewed, 'For they have called who love us,/Who bear the gifts that heal.' Presumably 'they' who beckon are the wraiths of Morris's Icelandic heroes like Grettir who brought him friendship out of the dark and healed him by sharing with him their calamities, injustices, and unconquerable love of life. With their help he can now build a satisfying life without depending on either of the women close to his heart – the one who has spurned him; the other whom he cannot overtly love. The opening stanzas, like all the others are addressed to himself:

> So swift the hours are moving
> Unto the time unproved:
> Farewell my love unloving,
> Farewell my love beloved!
>
> What! are we not glad-hearted?
> Is there no deed to do?
> Is not all fear departed
> And Spring-tide blossomed new?
>
> The sails swell out above us,
> The sea-ridge lifts the keel;
> For They have called who love us,
> Who bear the gifts that heal:
>
> A crown for him that winneth,
> A bed for him that fails,
> A glory that beginneth
> In never-dying tales.
>
> (*Poems By the Way*)

Now the long misery over Jane is ended and his hand grips the sword of deeds, but without a desire for vengeance. His life before he loved Jane had been cursed by terrors born of thinking himself unlovable and doomed to early death, and his life to follow is not likely to be particularly joyous whether or not he hears her spectre haunting the house with 'empty laughter' and 'friendless care.' Once he had feared to lose her; now, though enjoying inner peace, he is almost afraid to keep this tangler of the net. Love does not come and go blindly except for the blind, who must reap what they have sown in folly. But Morris's long pain, his failure with Jane, have not killed his power to love and work and enjoy. The often impressive stanzas summing up this sorry domestic life, which has not broken and cannot break him, unroll as follows:

Yet now the pain is ended
And the glad hand grips the sword,
Look on thy life amended
And deal out due award.

Think of the thankless morning,
The gifts of noon unused;
Think of the eve of scorning,
The night of prayer refused.

And yet. The life before it,
Dost thou remember aught,
What terrors shivered o'er it
Born from the hell of thought?

And this that cometh after:
How dost thou live, and dare
To meet its empty laughter,
To face its friendless care?

In fear didst thou desire,
At peace dost thou regret,
The wasting of the fire,
The tangling of the net.

Love came and gat fair greeting;
Love went, and left no shame.
Shall both the twilights meeting
The summer sunlight blame?

What! cometh love and goeth
Like the dark night's empty wind,
Because thy folly soweth
The harvest of the blind?

Hast thou slain love with sorrow?
Have thy tears quenched the sun?
Nay even yet to-morrow
Shall many a deed be done.

This twilight sea thou sailest,
Has it grown dim and black
For that wherein thou failest,
And the story of thy lack?

The last six stanzas are perhaps the most puzzling, being a short lyric expression of all Morris has learned from his long intimacy with Iceland's heritage. He can let the old grieving go because, like the deep if often blind passions of the Northmen stranded on their fearful island, it was 'born of the Earth the kind.' Earth has arranged that 'sad tales' and moments of 'joy abiding' – and deeds which can be an insight and inspiration to those who come after – may never perish. They are kept, as in the sagas, as a 'tiding,' as 'good news,' for those who will need them. The 'soul' as well as the 'life' of the artist, including his very name, shall pass away, but not the 'deed' flung from the forge of Earth's creativity working through him. Though 'men call you dead,' you will remain 'a part and parcel of the living wisdom of all things,' flourishing in the ever larger, richer, fuller life of this earth. (Consult Mackail II, 350) The final stanzas say:

> Peace then! for thine old grieving
> Was born of Earth the kind,
> And the sad tale thou art leaving
> Earth shall not leave behind.
>
> Peace! for that joy abiding
> Whereon thou layest hold
> Earth keepeth for a tiding
> For the day when this is old.
>
> Thy soul and life shall perish,
> And thy name as last night's wind;
> But Earth the deed shall cherish
> That thou to-day shalt find.
>
> And all thy joy and sorrow
> So great but yesterday,
> So light a thing to-morrow,
> Shall never pass away.
>
> Lo! lo! the dawn-blink yonder,
> The sunrise draweth nigh,
> And men forget to wonder
> That they were born to die.
>
> Then praise the deed that wendeth
> Through the daylight and the mirth!
> The tale that never endeth
> Whoso may dwell on earth.

The Victorian poets, both before and after Morris, as well as many of the great Romantics, apotheosised Nature, but none in quite this Morrisian idiom, blending Nature-bred failure with Nature-bred healing, grief with the relief of grief-stricken poetry, pain with the bravery to bear pain, death with the imperishable deeds of thought and creation. Earth as 'healer' and 'keeper' is the indwelling life of all things, driving, shaping, finding work for all before finding death for all. A few lines of Swinburne's 'Hertha,' published in 1871, come to mind. Earth says,

> I am in thee to save thee,
>   As my soul in thee saith;
> Give thou as I gave thee
>   Thy life-blood and breath,
> Green leaves of thy labour, white flowers of thy thought,
>   and red fruit of thy death.

This is closer to Morris than the many attempts made from Tennyson to Meredith, to soften the growing loss of a wholly benevolent deity proposing and disposing a perfect plan cut off from human understanding and forever impenetrable to human foresight.

For Morris, after his experience in Iceland, man's life was in the living of it. He must endure anguish to the utmost, and perhaps this is possible only when his desired Earthly Paradise is sacrificed for an anti-paradise of ice and fire – a state more in accord with man's nature as a creature who dreams, endeavours, is usually defeated, and yet endures, winning Earth's approbation by every deed she wrings from him. The height of man's life is to make it a saga and a good one, for then the Norse gods (powers of Nature, spirits of Earth) realise that he is playing the game they have set him. For a moment they pause to look down and admire the exalted if bloody entertainment. This is man's reward – this and his realisation that his work – the game – will not be entirely lost for all who endure on an earth which, it is said, will survive the chaotic battle of *Ragna Rök* to bloom afresh for those whose religion is bravery. Baldur will come and go again without much change overall, but deeds, work, cannot be entirely lost. There is just a thumbnail chance of infinitely slow and faint improvement. This is the essence of the Icelandic experience taken in its totality. Such an experience might help all of us 'at our need,' that is, when tempted by despair to give up planning, devising and creating for the dawn that will follow the next Ragna Rök – for one more glimpse of the beautiful home-field as Gunnar saw it when thrown from his horse and decided to fight on for it to the death. This is the only decision that will minimise fear – fear of not being lovable, of losing the beloved, of falling short of the self-set goal, of succumbing to self-pity, of knuckling under to death. Fear – a word once frequent in Morris's life but no longer. The sagamen had given him the quality he longed for:

> The spell, whereby the mist of fear
> Was melted, and your ears might hear
> Earth's voices as they are indeed.
> Well have ye helped me at my need!

And they had given him back, surprisingly, in one of Earth's voices, perhaps the stillest, smallest and most chastened, the courage to work in a still, small, chastened way for a momentary flash of Paradise, on Earth, not for himself but for all, before the end.

IX Paradise Reintegrated at Kelmscott Manor and Among the Cotswolds 1871-1880

In May, 1871, when he was working on his Icelandic translations, Morris found Kelmscott Manor. It was on the upper Thames in the south-western corner of Oxfordshire. Morris's first preserved letter about his discovery was sent on 17 May 1871 to D. J. Faulkner, book-keeper of the Firm in his spare time.

> I have been looking about for a house for the wife and kids, and whither do you guess my eye is turned now? Kelmscott, a little village about two miles above Radcott Bridge – a heaven on earth; an old stone Elizabethan house like Water Eaton, and such a garden! close down on the river, a boat house and all things handy. I am going there again on Saturday with Rossetti and my wife: Rossetti because he thinks of sharing it with us if the thing looks likely . . .
>
> (*Letters*, 41)

Morris had known and loved the Thames above Oxford since college days and may have rowed as far upstream as Kelmscott without seeing its old gables because of the tightly clustered willows and the tall elms drawn up in parade-drill between the Manor and the stream.

The Thames had many literary associations which young Morris must have been aware of though he had many personal reasons, too, for loving the river. The year Morris went up to Oxford (1853) Matthew Arnold published 'The Scholar-Gipsy,' whose sombre but unruffled, withdraw-ing spirit suggests the Thames itself, slipping along – and away. It is said that a few undergraduates of Morris's day read the poem about the stu-dent who deserted Oxford to live with the gipsies, though only Morris was to be accused of marrying one. And perhaps the undergraduates enjoyed the apostrophe to Glanvil's strayed scholar:

> O born in days when wits were fresh and clear,
>   And life ran gaily as the sparkling Thames;
>   Before this strange disease of modern life,
>   With its sick hurry, its divided aims,
>   Its head o'ertax'd, its palsied hearts, was rife . . .

If Morris by chance steeped himself in these thoughts and read Arnold's companion poem 'Thyrsis,' they could have encouraged him, when the time came, to see himself as 'the idle singer of an empty day.' However, by the time he found Kelmscott, Morris was more attuned to the famous couplet in old Denham's 'Cooper's Hill' which describes the river as

> Though deep, yet clear: though gentle, yet not dull:
> Strong without rage: without o'erflowing, full.

Lucid but not placid, smooth but gracefully determined, gleaming in tranquillity – these stereotyped descriptions of England's famous river sound like phrases Morris would have enjoyed applying to himself in the period when he was longing 'to keep the world from narrowing on me, and to look at things bigly and kindly!' (*Letters*, 51). It is also likely that he knew Peacock's 'Genius of the Thames' (1810), which contrasted the turbulent enormity of the Mississippi, St Lawrence, Ganges, Niger and Amazon with the humane dimensions and unbroken peacefulness of the Thames –

> But now, through banks from strife remote,
> Thy crystal waters wind along,
> Responsive to the wild bird's note
> Or lonely boatman's careless song.

This was not great riverine poetry, and Morris improved on it in the lyrics for June and August in *The Earthly Paradise*.

He often said he had dreamed of Kelmscott long before he ever saw it, and the preamble to the June stories tells how a picnic party from Oxford set out for a holiday on 'their chief river,' pushing far upstream.

> What better place than this then could we find
> By this sweet stream that knows not of the sea,
> That guesses not the city's misery,
> This little stream whose hamlets scarce have names,
> This far-off, lonely mother of the Thames?

This sounds as if the holiday-makers may have rowed to Lechlade or above, passing Kelmscott unknowingly.

> Here then, O June, thy kindness will we take;
> And if indeed but pensive men we seem,
> What should we do? thou wouldst not have us wake
> From out the arms of this rare happy dream
> And wish to leave the murmur of the stream,
> The rustling boughs, the twitter of the birds,
> And all thy thousand peaceful happy words.

The August lyric is specifically located, and seems to tell of a holiday with Jane at Dorchester, some forty miles downstream from Kelmscott though little more than half that distance by road. The picnic spot seems to have been an elevated field marking the spot where Sinodun Hill, (according to Morris once a Roman earthwork) was cut in two by the early English to form the pair of domes which overlook Dorchester from the Berkshire side of the river. The original poem contained four stanzas and I quote them all to give a notion of how lovingly Morris had memorised Thames-side topography for miles around Oxford.

> In this sweet field high raised above the Thames
> Beneath the trenched hill of Sinodun
> Amidst sweet dreams of disembodied names
> Abide the setting of the August sun,
> Here where this long ridge tells of days now done;
> This moveless wave wherewith the meadow heaves
> Beneath its clover and its barley-sheaves.
>
> Across the gap made by our English hinds,
> Amidst the Roman's handiwork, behold
> Far off the long-roofed church; the shepherd binds
> The withy round the hurdles of his fold,
> Down in the foss the river bed of old,
> That through long lapse of time has grown to be
> The little grassy valley that you see.
>
> Rest here awhile, not yet the eve is still,
> The bees are wandering yet, and you may hear
> The barley mowers on the trénched hill,
> The sheep-bells, and the restless changing weir,
> All little sounds made musical and clear
> Beneath the sky that burning August gives,
> While yet the thought of glorious Summer lives.
>
> Ah, love! such happy days, such days as these
> Must we still waste them, craving for the best,
> Like lovers o'er the painted images
> Of those who once their yearning hearts have blessed?
> Have we been happy on our day of rest?
> Thine eyes say 'yes,' – but if it came again,
> Perchance its ending would not seem so vain.

This poem seems to record the memory of a young lovers' quarrel over the 'best' way to spend a day of rest – Jane satisfied with rest itself, Morris dissatisfied without loving caresses.

However, apart from memories of picnics with school mates and an unscholarly gipsy-girl, perhaps Morris had a deeper reason for liking the country around Kelmscott. It is flat, marshy, often mistily melancholy, its broad willow- and elm-fenced fields fading away into tiny blue uplands in the north or little escarpments in the south. Here the Thames, perhaps twenty-five or thirty yards wide, 'inlays the vale with silver,' though it seldom feels like a valley – perhaps only when one is standing on the Golden Ridge at Faringdon. Such country reminded Morris poignantly of the Essex flatlands around the River Lea where he had passed what he always remembered as an ecstatic childhood. This 'romantic land' is commemorated in 'Frank's Sealed Letter' (*Oxford and Cambridge Magazine* for April, 1856).

what people called an ugly country . . . that spreading of the broad marshlands around the river Lea; but . . . it seemed very lovely to me then; indeed I think I should not have despised it at any time. I was always a lover of the sad lowland country. I walked on, my mind keeping up a strange balance between joy and sadness for some time, till gradually all the beauty of things seemed to be stealing into my heart, and . . . all the songs of birds ringing through the hedges, and about the willows; all the sweet colours of the sky, and the clouds that floated in the blue of it; . . . the tender fresh grass, and the sweet young shoots of flowering things, were very pensive to me . . .

Much later, in *News from Nowhere* (1880), he resketched this Essex country restored to its pristine glory in the rehabilitated England that was to be:

'eastward and landward . . . it is all flat pasture, once marsh, except for a few gardens, and there are very few permanent dwellings there, scarcely anything but a few sheds and cots for the men who come to look after the great herds of cattle pasturing there. But however, what with the beasts and the men, and the scattered red-tiled roofs and the big hayricks, it does not make a bad holiday to get a quiet pony and ride about there on a sunny afternoon of autumn, and look over the river and the craft passing up and down, and on to Shooter's Hill and the Kentish uplands, and then turn round to the wide green sea of the Essex marshland, with the great domed line of the sky, and the sun shining down in one flood of peaceful light over the long distance.'

(Ch. X)

These descriptions (barring the red tiles) could equally well fit the Kelmscott countrside – including the boats that seem to be moving (except when the river is in flood) on the surface of the meadows, and the orange-and-lavender sunsets edging indigo skies.

And then Kelmscott Manor itself! Morris described the manor as 'a heaven on earth' and the children referred to it as 'our Earthly Paradise.' After his return from the Icelandic voyage of 1871, Morris wrote to a friend about the 'little place deep down in the country' where his family would spend the summer months – 'a beautiful and strangely naif house, Elizabethan in appearance . . . on the S.W. extremity of Oxfordshire, within a stone's throw of the baby Thames, in the most beautiful grey little hamlet called Kelmscott.' (*Letters*, 45) In a letter of about the same date (August, 1871) he wrote to Georgiana's sister, Mrs Alfred Baldwin, mother of Stanley Baldwin, that his 'own little old house by Lechlade . . . is sweet and innocent' in comparison with modern villas with red geraniums. and 'though it has a sadness about it, which is not gloom but the melancholy born of beauty I suppose, it is very stimulating to the imagination. I am going down there on Saturday ...' (*Letters*, 46) In February 1872 he wrote a letter to Georgiana which shows how the 'retreat' was growing on him: 'I have come down here for a fortnight to see spring beginning, a sight I have seen little of for years, and am writing among the gables and rook-haunted trees, with a sense of the place being almost too beautiful to live in.' (*Letters*, 46) In October 1872 he wrote to his other intimate correspondent, Aglaia Coronio, about having to leave Kelmscott after a short weekend:

It was such a beautiful morning when I came away, with a faint blue sky and thin far away white clouds about it: the robins hopping and singing all about the garden. The fieldfares, which are a winter bird and come from Norway are chattering all about the berry trees now, and the starlings, as they have done for two months past, collect in great flocks about sunset, and make such a noise before they go off to roost. The place looks as beautiful as ever though somewhat melancholy in its flowerless autumn gardens.

(*Letters*, 49)

These are among Morris's first recorded impressions of the spot; his 'harbour of refuge' that was to grow more precious to him steadily until the day he died.

If one ponders the peculiar magic which catalysed one of the most famous love-affairs ever carried on between a man and a house, it is helpful to think of scenic mandalas. During the first years at Kelmscott Morris seemed half-sunk in a sweetness of embracing arms. A dream had emerged from the depths into daylight. What was it that Morris took in with the first oblique glance of his 'wandering' sharp eyes? Besides the river, the boat-house, the 'beautiful old barns' and the expanses of tree-hedged fields that stretched south to the very low hills and east and west to the domed horizon (Kelmscott Village lay to the north), there was the walled-in complex of house, gardens, and orchard. The dry-stone walls of local oolite, from seven to nine feet high and nicely coped, enclosed a large square containing the house, trees, lawns and gardens. Here were all the elements of a rectangular mandala, brought to life in the semblance of a walled Elizabethan garden sectioned by hedges of yew or wattle, with straight paths lined with peonies, roses and lilies. The garden was studded with a number of trees; mulberry, ash, and evergreen as well as apple and pear – all making a glaucous sea. From the south-west corner of the garden rose the gables and chimneys of the warm grey house, its mullioned windows wreathed with grape and ivy. All rather Baconian, but also resembling the brightly coloured miniatures in *Roman de la Rose* or even the engravings, popular between the fifteenth and seventeenth centuries, representing Solomon's Shulamite or the Christian Virgin in the shape of an *ortus conclusus*. These allegorical gardens, undoubtedly familiar to Morris, almost invariably contain a secular-looking though probably holy building, palatial in shape, which would seem to be Solomon's dwelling – or God's. They were often built, like Kelmscott, as a part of the garden wall, suggesting that the garden itself is to be regarded as a redeemed Eden and the house as the body of the Shulamite or Mary. Thus there is an old tradition in Western art in which either a house or garden – sometimes both – has been symbolised by a woman called the *anima loci* or even *mundi*. One wonders whether this ancient idea stirred in the depths of Morris when he first saw Kelmscott. It was not long before he began to look forward to his excursions to the country as times when 'the old house will hold me in her arms once more.'

It is something of a puzzle that Rossetti was chosen to share the amenities (and of course the rent) of Kelmscott. While Morris never seemed to blame his old friend and mentor for his 'failure' with Jane, there seems no doubt that Rossetti was dancing continual attendance on Jane during the critical years of *The Earthly Paradise* time, squiring her to studio parties in London and writing love letters of considerable warmth. One written to her at Bad-Ems, perhaps in answer to a letter of hers, maintains that the more Morris 'loves you, the more he knows that you are too lovely and noble not to be loved: and, dear Janey, there are too few things that seem worth expressing . . . for one friend to deny another the poor expression of what is most at his heart.' (R. C. H. Briggs, 'Letters to Janey,' *The Journal of the William Morris Society*, I, 4, Summer 1964) Others dating from January and February of 1870 are full of love and worship – and also frustration. They have much to say of a thawing-out of 'the chilling numbness that surrounded me in the utter want of you, but it comes too late'; of the fact that 'No one else seems alive at all to me now, and places that are empty of you are empty of all life'; and of his realisation that 'to be with you and wait on you and read to you is absolutely the only happiness I can find or conceive in this world, dearest Janey.' We know that Morris writes of Jealousy more than once in the most anguished of *The Earthly Paradise* tales, and he may have been deeply shaken when in April 1870 Jane and Rossetti spent a couple of weeks at Scalands near Robertsbridge 'together and alone.' However, he never in any overt way accused Rossetti for his loss of Jane. For his failure to stir her from what seems to have been an almost congenital passivity and introverted depression he blamed only himself. Also, he may have believed, on the basis of long personal experience, that Rossetti, for all the tropical heat of the 1870 poems, may never really have roused her from her customary prostration. He may even have suspected that con-

tinued insomnia combated by massive doses of chloral chased by whis-
key must have made Rossetti a sorry lover. Besides, he had never ceased
to admire Rossetti as a friend of poetic and artistic genius who had once
encouraged him with unstinted praise to write, paint and design. Morris
was also aware of his one-time mentor's ever-sharpening guilt about the
suicide of his wife Lizzie Siddal in 1863 and his desecration of her grave
to obtain from the corpse's tangled hair poems he had laid as a last tribute about her once-golden head. These he used to pad out the *Poems* of
1870. In addition, being volatile and quick-tempered, Morris may have
begun to feel it a moral duty to act with ever greater patience and
magnanimity in proportion to the weight of the provocation. For all
these reasons, abetted perhaps by Jane's urging and a genuine need to
economise, he invited Rossetti to share Kelmscott, and often said later
that the primary reason for taking the old house in the first place was the
restoration of Rossetti's health. This was hardly true.

They first inspected the house in late May, 1871. Early in July Morris
set off on his first voyage to Iceland for reasons none of his friends could
fathom. One of these reasons, however minor, must have been his reluc-
tance to welcome to Kelmscott the London sophisticate for whom life in
the 'dozy' village and wind-swept house was sure to be a subject of complaint. Rossetti, however, descended with *éclat* on Jane and the girls a
week or so after Morris's departure, bringing animals – which Morris
hated – and furniture from his London establishment in Cheyne Walk.
He immediately made the Tapestry Room his studio and settled down to
enjoy the happiest days of his life. When Morris returned, he found Rossetti in full possession of the house, not to mention Jane and the children.
In a letter of 25 November 1872 to Aglaia Coronio Morris speaks of the
'blessing & help last year's journey was to me; what horrors it saved me
from.' (*Letters*, 51) The mistake he had made in inviting Rossetti to
Kelmscott had struck home in a matter of months. The old wound,
apparently healed, opened deeper than ever.

On 11 August 1871 Morris had written to Jane that he 'often thought
of the sweet fresh garden at Kelmscott and you and the little ones in it,
and wished you happy.' Whatever he found on his return, he did not or
could not stay for more than a few days at a time in the house he had
dreamed of and now longed to live in. He had to look after the work of
the Firm in London, of course, but above all, it seems, he needed his
long-tried and usually effective source of relief from pain: writing poetry.
In fact, he had been driven to this therapy almost from the moment of
his return. On 2 October, while at Kelmscott, Rossetti wrote to a friend:

Morris has been here twice since his return, for a few days at first and just now
for a week again. He is now back in London, and this place will be empty of
inmates by the end of this week, I guess. Morris has set to work with a will on
a sort of masque called 'Love is enough,' which he means to print as a moderate

quarto, with woodcuts by Ned Jones and borders by himself, some of which he has already done really beautifully. The poem is, I think, at a higher point of execution perhaps than anything that he has done, having a passionate lyric quality such as one found in his earliest work and of course much more mature balance in carrying out. It will be a very fine work.

(Quoted, Henderson, *William Morris*, 127–8)

This morality play or interlude written in a medieval style has never been popular but E. L. Lucas suggests that it may be one of the few overlooked treasures of English literature. (*Eight Victorian Poets*, 1930, 106) Our interest is in its reflection of Morris's inner life. May Morris says it reveals more about his personal life than anything else he wrote but I find it hard to agree. It was stimulated partly by Rossetti's 'Cup of Cold Water.' a short-short-story said to have been written in 1871, possibly when Morris was in Iceland, as the 'cartoon' for a projected painting. It is doubtful whether the picture was even sketched, but the story seems to have circulated. With the hindsight of fifteen years, Rossetti tells a tale which suggests that in medieval times (Oxford of 1857) a forester's daughter (Jane) was dying with love for a king who, though returning her passion, could not break his troth to a princess (Lizzie Siddal). The king, 'with wide eye fixed and his proud and scarcely quivering mouth half-hidden in his beard,' had enacted a dream of 'passion and wrongdoing and despotic will' in his soul, but 'cast it out.' (See *Dante Gabriel Rossetti ... Unpublished Verse and Prose*, ed. P. F. Baum, 1831, 75) Then he pleaded successfully with the girl to lower her sights and marry his friend, a knight who loves her and whom the king prefers to all men.

The young King of a country is hunting one day with a young knight, his friend; when, feeling thirsty, he stops at a Forester's cottage, and the Forester's daughter brings him a cup of water to drink. Both of them are equally enamoured at once of her unequalled beauty. The King, however, has been affianced from boyhood to a Princess, worthy of all love, and whom he had always believed he loved until undeceived by his new absorbing passion; but the Knight, resolved to sacrifice all other considerations to his love, goes again to the Forester's cottage and asks his daughter's hand. He finds the girl has fixed her thoughts on the King, whose rank she does not know. On hearing it she tells her suitor humbly that she must die if such be her fate, but cannot love another. The Knight goes to the King to tell him all and beg his help; and the two friends then come to an explanation. Ultimately the King goes to the girl and pleads his friend's cause, not disguising his own passion, but saying that as he sacrificed himself to honour [i.e., in marrying the Princess] so should she, at his prayer, accept a noble man whom he loves better than all men and whom she will love too. This she does at last.

(Quoted in Henderson, *William Morris*, 50–1)

Morris's first attempt to counter this fantasy may have been a novel of contemporary life, never finished, about two brothers who fell in love with the same girl. He sent portions of the manuscript to Georgiana 'to see if she could give me any hope,' but 'she gave me none, and I have never looked at it again.'

Morris's real answer to Rossetti was *Love Is Enough* (1872), which he sweated over for a year after his return from Iceland. It was not published until the end of 1872 for he had trouble making it 'march' at first. However, by May it was moving toward completion and perhaps Morris felt that he had avenged 'The Cup of Cold Water.' About this time, too, troubled by conscience and chloral, Rossetti was devastated by Robert Buchanan's republication, this time in pamphlet form, of his magazine article 'The Fleshly School of Poetry.' Pilloried for brothel-sensualism which was making London 'a great Sodom and Gomorrah waiting for doom' Rossetti was afraid that Jane would be alienated by the notoriety poured on him – and on poems like 'Nuptial Sleep,' which she knew had been written to her. Suddenly, libelled himself, 'The Cup of Cold Water' probably seemed a rather poor joke, and Morris's unexpectedly vigorous repudiations turned the cup upside down. On the night of 2 June 1872, having returned to London, he attempted suicide by taking an overdose of chloral. However, his doctor, George Hake, pulled him round and, after deciding he did not need to be sent to an asylum, took him off to Scotland to recuperate.

By late September Rossetti was back at Kelmscott, and Morris (letter of 8 October) was writing to Aglaia that

I have been backwards and forwards to Kelmscott a good deal this summer & autumn; but shall not go there so often now as Gabriel is come there, and talks of staying there permanently: of course he won't do that, but I suppose he will stay some time: he is quite well and seems very happy. . . .
The weather has been lovely here this autumn, but doesn't seem to have suited me very well. I have been queer several times, and am not very brilliant today – As to my mental health – I have had ups and downs as you may very easily imagine: but on the whole I suppose I am getting less restless and worried, if at the same time less hopeful; still there is life in me yet I hope.

(*Letters*, 47–8)

On 24 October he wrote that he had been suffering from 'a fit of low spirits, – for no particular reason that I could tell ...' Later, on 25 November he elaborated on this statement at considerable length:

When I said there was no cause for my feeling low, I meant that my friends had not changed at all towards me in any way and that there had been no quarrelling: and indeed I am afraid it comes from some cowardice or unmanliness in me. One thing wanting ought not to go for so much: nor indeed does it spoil my enjoyment of life always, as I have often told you: to have real friends and some sort of aim in life in so much, that I ought still to think my self lucky: and often in my better moods I wonder what it is in me that throws me into such rage and despair at other times. I suspect, do you know, that some such moods would have come upon me at times even without this failure of mine. However that may be, though, I must confess that this autumn has been a specially dismal time with me. . . . my intercourse with G. [Georgiana Burne-Jones] has been a good deal interrupted; not from any coldness of hers, or violence of mine; but from so many untoward nothings: then you have been away so that I have had nobody to talk to about things that bothered me: which I repeat I have felt more than I, in my ingratitude, expected to. Another quite selfish business is that Rossetti has set himself down at Kelmscott as if he never meant to go away; and not only does that keep me from that harbour of refuge (because it is really a farce, our meeting when we can help it) but also he has all sorts of ways so unsympathetic with the sweet simple old place, that I feel his presence there as a kind of slur on it: this is very unreasonable though when one thinks why one took the place, and how this year it has really answered that purpose: nor do I think I should feel this about it if he had not been so unromantically discontented with it & the whole thing which made me very angry and disappointed. There, dear Aglaia, see how I am showing you my pettinesses! *please* don't encourage me in them; but you have always been so kind to me that they will come out. O how I long to keep the world from narrowing on me, and to look at things bigly and kindly!

I am going to try to get to Iceland next year, . . . I know there will be a kind of rest in it, let alone the help it will bring me from physical reasons. I know clearer now perhaps than then what a blessing & help last year's journey was to me: what horrors it saved me from.

My poem is out now.

(Letters, 50–1)

The poem referred to is *Love Is Enough,* which he wrote to tide him over the crisis of 'horror' he had encountered on his return from Iceland. It seems to have served its purpose for he was able, amongst his complainings, to assure Aglaia that there was no reason at all for her to 'be alarmed for any domestic tragedy . . .' It may have had another unintended effect too: by showing its poet far less mean-spirited than the cold-water thrower, it may have been one of the forces that unhinged Rossetti again in 1874. We know that Rossetti had followed the early stage of its composition with interest and admiration. And now, though the painter had stormed back from Scotland in such an apparently possessive mood, might it not be hoped that the poem's publication in November would make him more humble and bearable about the house if he really did intend to stay much longer?

To understand how the poem (said even by Mackail to be unreadable) may have moved Rossetti – himself a sensitive poet – we should take a brief glance at its climax. *Love Is Enough* tells of a three year period

(1868–71?) when King Pharamond wandered deliriously in search of true love only to have his ideal woman come to him on bended knees. At this point what is called 'THE MUSIC' of the poem breaks out in praise of a rose-wreathed cup filled with wine brewed by Love himself. This is no cup of cold water meant to misrepresent truth and compound trouble. It is, in fact, the only drink capable of enlarging the heart through both pleasure and pain.

> LOVE IS ENOUGH: *ho ye who seek saving,*
> *Go no further; come hither; there have been who*
> *have found it,*
> *And these know the House of Fulfilment of Craving;*
> *These know the Cup with the roses around it;*
> *These know the World's Wound and the balm that*
> *hath bound it . . .*

Eros himself concludes the Morality with words that might have been spoken by Earth the Healer, Earth the Keeper, when he says that for all the misery love causes, believe

> That from these hands reward ye shall receive.
> – Reward of what? Life springing fresh again? –
> Life of delight? – I say it not – Of pain?
> It may be – Pain eternal? Who may tell?
> Yet pain of Heaven, beloved, and not of Hell.

Eros then tells his follower (Morris) not to shudder at crimes committed against him but to forgive, 'Have faith, and crave and suffer . . .' Live by love for you can live by nothing else, though love be treacherously

> . . . filched away; the world an adder-den,
> And all folk foes; and one, the one desire –
> – How shall we name it? grown a poisoned fire . . .
> So turneth love to hate, the wise world saith,
> – Folly – I say 'twixt love and hate lies death,
> They shall not mingle: neither died this love,
> But through a dreadful world all changed must move . . .

Then Eros describes Morris's ordeal even more specifically, distinctly underscoring the gravamen of the Morality Play: from such long trouble the kingly man will gain insight, wisdom, the power to lose love yet keep it, to forsake love for love's sake, thereby holding its essence forever.

> Through flame and thorns I led him many days
> And nought he shrank, but smiled and followed close,
> Till in his path the shade of hate arose
> 'Twixt him and his desire . . .

> – Lo, saith the World, a heart well satisfied
> With what I give, a barren love forgot –
> – Draw near me, O my child, and heed them not!
> The world thou lovest, e'en my world it is,
> Thy faithful hands yet reach out for my bliss,
> Thou seest me in the night and in the day,
> Thou canst not deem that I can go astray.

Finally, Eros speaks directly of Morris and Jane, once more using the image of a cup – the one Tristan shared with Iseut:

> No further, saith the world, 'twixt Heaven and Hell
> Than 'twixt these twain. – My faithful, heed it well! . . .
> But how shall tongue of man tell all the tale
> Of faithful hearts who overcome or fail,
> But at the last fail nowise to be mine.
> In diverse ways they drink the fateful wine
> Those twain drank mid the lulling of the storm
> Upon the Irish Sea, when love grown warm
> Kindled and blazed, and lit the days to come,
> The hope and joy and death that led them home.
> – In diverse ways; yet having drunk, be sure
> The flame thus lighted ever shall endure,
> So my feet trod the grapes whereby it glowed.

Those responsible for Morris's distress and turmoil in love have been forgiven with a magnanimity which changed him from victim to beneficiary. But his anguish was not over.

Rossetti was now back at Kelmscott after his 'holiday' in Scotland. For sleeping quarters he took the White-panelled Room, which had a fireplace with a lovely old grey surround, rustically carved with a shield and festoons of fruit. Rossetti coloured it dark green and veined it with white to imitate marble! He did most of his drawing and painting in the next best room at Kelmscott, the Tapestry Room on the first floor. The walls of this room were hung with tapestries from Brussels dated about 1600. They represent scenes from the life of Samson and were in the house when Morris leased it. He thought that in their pleasantly faded condition, all brown and yellow and bluish-grey with nothing but the deep-blue armour of the Philistine soldiers untouched by time, they struck a 'romantic' note that no other décor could equal. Rossetti, on the other hand, complained continually about the villainous execution of the abominable scenes supposed to represent *The Marriage in Timnath*, *The Water-Miracle of the Jawbone*, *The Betrayal and Blinding of Samson*, and *Samson in the Temple of Dagon*. Rossetti wanted to make a bonfire of the lot and, it is said, accused Morris of liking them merely because the unshorn Jewish hero reminded him of his unkempt self. Indeed, the profile of Samson tugging at the temple column does recall certain photographs of Morris. On the other hand, Morris is said to have got back at Rossetti by telling him that the tapestry he hated most, *The Blinding*, ought to distress him, for the job had been bungled, leaving Samson quite well aware of what was going on. All this bickering, added to Morris's intense distaste for his old friend's sleeping and eating habits – he is said never to have taken his chloral until dawn began to break (the time when Morris was often rising) and to have breakfasted late in the day off a mountain of greasy bacon topped with half-fried eggs which bled disgustingly down its sides – not only kept Morris away from his 'haven' of country beauty but hardened a growing determination to get rid of Rossetti once and for all. However, it took another year and a half to achieve this.

Meantime, Rossetti worked on his pictures of Jane, retouching the old ones and painting new ones so melancholy and minatory that it is easy to think of them as part of a campaign to drive Morris from his sweet country refuge. *La Pia de' Tolomei* (begun 1868) was not fully finished till 1880. The *Pandora* in sanguine kept at Buscot Park had been finished in 1869, but the finest version in oils was not completed until 1871. *Desdemona's Death-Song*, now known only through letters and sketches, was planned in March 1872 but was not completed until '81, if then. The picture that Rossetti had chucked over was *Proserpine*. Between 1871 and '77 he painted eight versions of *Proserpine*, each differing slightly from the others. The one now in the Tate was, for the most part executed in 1873. We see Proserpine in her moment of realisation, just after biting into the pomegranate, when she knows she has ruined her life. The pomegranate is a Greek betrothal pledge, and she will have to marry Pluto, the rich but tyrannical lord (Morris) of the Underworld (Kelmscott), where she will have to live in darkness for all but a few short periods of the year (i.e. when she can break out to rejoin Rossetti?). The various faces of Jane on the *Proserpine* canvases express everything from a furtive sneer to frightened despondence to deathly despair. In the upper right-hand corner of most of the versions is a poem to Proserpine written by Rossetti in Italian, which he anglicised himself. It is not so moving as many of the poems he wrote for his pictures. The pomegranate is a ' "drear/Dire fruit," ' of course, and, alas, ' "how far away,/The nights that shall be from the days that were" ' spent with Rossetti – ' "Woe's me for thee, unhappy Proserpine!" ' Possibly it was this picture that made Morris decide to put up with no more insults in paint of the kind that began with *Sir Tristran* in 1867. All of these, *La Pia*, *Pandora* and *Desdemona's Death-Song* (for which he had finally to use a model with more combable hair), as well as sketches like *The Ms at Ems* and *Jane Dozing Over a Copy of 'Guenevere'* were attacks on Morris as a vain, cruel, foolish cuckolded, bloody-minded husband while they showed Jane as an aggrieved and tortured wife but resentful too and dangerous in her larger-than-life-sized roles as Pandora punishing her frustrator, or Proserpine meditating revenge on her half-spouse in hell.

Before he started work on *Proserpine, Pandora* (1871) modelled on Jane had been Rossetti's favourite among his pictures. The poem for *Pandora* was one of his best.

> What of the end, Pandora? was it thine,
> The deed that set these fiery pinions free?
> Ah! wherefore did the Olympian consistory
> In its own likeness make thee half divine?
> Was it . . . all men might see
> In Venus' eyes the gaze of Proserpine?
>
> What of the end? These beat their wings at will,
> The ill-born things, the good things turned to ill, –
> Powers of the impassioned hours prohibited.
> Aye, clench the casket now! Whither they go
> Thou mayest not dare to think; nor canst thou know
> If hope still pent there be alive or dead.

The echo of 'Sooner strangle an infant in its cradle than nurse an unacted desire' is loud, and Swinburne's outburst – 'The design is among his mightiest in its godlike terror and imperial trouble of beauty, shadowed by smoke and fiery vapour of winged and fleshless passions crowding round the casket in spires of flame-lit and curling cloud round her fatal face and mourning veil of hair' (A. C. Swinburne, *Essays and Studies,* 1875) – is understandable if somewhat incoherent. The watercolour version of Pandora (1870), now in the Princeton Art Museum, is softened a bit by the light-coloured gown but the cat's eyes under the overpowering black hair are remorseless. More merciful, oddly enough, is the effect of the dramatically dark oil of 1871 (now in a private collection). The version I know best, the first finished study (1869), has been kept at Buscot Park, Berkshire, since 1885 or '86. Done in coloured chalks with red ('sanguine') predominating, it seems to be exploding in a spray of bloody droplets. Pandora's husband had a name, Epimetheus, meaning 'he who looks only after leaping.'

Taken together, Rossetti's 'Janes', passively sullen or aggressively alarming, comprised not an army of tutelary Red House heroines, but a 'monstrous regiment' of melancholiacs whose seemingly inexorable advance shook Morris badly after his return from Iceland in 1871. It is likely that these paintings more than anything else, catalysed his decision to rid Kelmscott of Rossetti and his works. After all, an enemy of sorts was using Jane, his own wife, against him in a campaign of what looked like, and was perhaps intended to be, psychological warfare. Now he, Morris, would use Jane, but without hatred – that dangerous futility – toward either her or Rossetti, to get his life back on an even keel so that his personality and talents could flourish unhindered. After a second trip to Iceland, in 1873, to refresh both body and soul, to recall the religion of bravery amidst the fire and ice that gave it birth, and to tap once more the power of Earth the Healer, Earth and Keeper, Morris came back to England to set his manor in order.

On returning from Scotland to Kelmscott in September 1872, Rossetti had written to his brother William that 'all, I now find by experience, depends primarily on my not being deprived of the prospect of the society of the one necessary person.' Here was the exposed nerve as Morris, forced to review the *Poems* of 1870, well knew –

> O love, my love! If I no more should see
> Thyself, nor on the earth the shadow of thee,
>   Nor image of thine eyes in any spring, –
> How then should sound upon Life's darkening slope
> The ground-whirl of the perished leaves of Hope,
>   The wind of Death's imperishable wing? –
>
> (From 'Love-sight')

and now, patient, large-hearted man though he was, Morris began to play upon this weakness for the sake of his own rights. He knew that Rossetti had attempted suicide in 1872 partly through fear of losing Jane after Buchanan had attacked him as a lustful satyr, but he did not know what Jane thought of satyriasis. He was no longer so sure of her frigid temper as he might have been had he read Rossetti's long unpublished poem, 'The Steel's Temper That Is Cold':

> Her glances rested on me with a show
>   Of kindness and complacence, but too cool
>   And compassed; 'twas as if the line and rule
> Had marked: 'Thus far, no farther, shalt thou go.'
> A feeling came on me, some little woe
>   But more of pity; for I felt how dull
>   And hollow are the precepts of that school
> Which gibbets love and hate and makes a row
> Of poor half-passions virtue. In her laugh
> There was an aching jingle, and for whom
>   This laugh was meant she herself knew not . . .
>
> (*D. G. Rossetti . . . Unpublished Verse and Prose*, 1931, 60)

Other poems unprinted before 1931 and probably dating from 1871–73 show that Rossetti's thoughts still turned to suicide whenever his hope of finding 'that unknown link/To bind her soul to mine' failed. Only some kind of unbreakable bond with Jane could solder him to life and every event that threatened to separate them seemed a form of persecution directed against his life.

Rossetti told Dr Hake in the summer of 1872 that the seine-fishing they were watching 'is an allegory of my state. My persecutors are gradually narrowing the net around me until at last it will be drawn tight.' It is not likely that he counted Morris among his enemies. However, after surrendering Kelmscott for a year and a half (1873 and part of '74) to Rossetti and his family (and sometimes Jane), Morris did draw a kind of net about his one-time friend. First, on 16 April 1874, he wrote to Rossetti telling him that he was giving up his share of the Kelmscott tenancy. The Rossetti clan had been monopolising the manor for months and Morris was not prepared to take any blame for his threat – 'You have fairly taken to living at Kelmscott, which I suppose neither of us thought the other would do when we first began the joint possession of the house.' Since it is unlikely that Morris was ready to give up his 'harbour of refuge,' this letter was probably intended to drive Rossetti from 'the sweet simple old place.' where his presence was 'a kind of slur.' (*Letters*, 51) At the same time Morris was planning to dissolve the Firm of Morris, Marshall, Faulkner and Co., and reorganise it under his sole management. Rossetti, like the other members who had contributed little or nothing to the art-work or management of the Firm for years, was to be dropped – a prospect that was probably 'leaked' to him before the other 'sleeping partners.' Finally, Morris took Jane and the children on a tour of Belgium in late July. Shortly afterwards, Rossetti's condition, which had been worsening throughout the summer of 1874, frightened his family into calling Dr Hake to Kelmscott. The persecution symptoms were now so alarming, especially vis-à-vis the townspeople, that the friendly physician advised him to leave the manor for good, and again took him into his personal care for the duration of the crisis.

After the reorganisation of the Firm, held up until 1875 because of litigation started by Brown and Rossetti, Morris never saw his partner again, or mentioned him in his letters, even when he died in 1882. Jane made short visits to Rossetti at Aldwick Lodge, Bognor, in 1875 and '76 so that he could work on his picture of her known as *Astarte Syriaca* (1877). This is in many ways his most startling and alarming treatment of Jane's form and features. Were the lips not so pursed and 'deep-freighted,' the figure with its unfathomable fixed eyes and powerful bare arms could represent any *femme fatale* from Salambô to Dolores Our Lady of Pain, any *belle dame sans merci* from Faustine to Salome. The picture reminds R. Wilkinson (*Pre-Raphaelite Art and Design*, 1970, 161) of visions that might have haunted Strindberg, while A. C. Benson wrote as early as 1904 that Astarte's

two attendants with their torches and upward glance, seem to testify to some dark, unholy power, the cruelty that is akin to lust. The strange sights that she has seen in grove and shrine seem to have fed her beauty with lurid and terrible royalty, where she reigns in a dark serenity which nothing can appal.

(Quoted in Surtees, *Rossetti, Text*, 146)

It is hard, nevertheless, to believe in these 'raptures and roses of vice' when the poem Rossetti wrote for the picture tells us so clearly that,

> Torch-bearing, her sweet ministers compel
> All thrones of light beyond the sky and sea
> The witnesses of Beauty's face to be:
> That face, of Love's all-penetrative spell
> Amulet, talisman, and oracle, –
> Betwixt the sun and moon a mystery.

Although this picture was frightening to some, it never frightened Morris. So far as is known he never saw it. For now all his spare time could be given to exploring, enjoying and touching up the beauties of Kelmscott.

Morris loved the old house because it had 'grown up out of the soil and the lives of those who lived on it ...' (Sup. I, 371). Ellen in *News from Nowhere*, leading the dreamer 'up close to the house,'

laid her shapely sun-browned hand and arm on the lichened wall as if to embrace it, and cried out, 'O me! O me! how I love the earth, and the seasons, and weather, and all things that deal with it, and all that grows out of it, – as this has done!'

(Ch. XXXI)

This speech follows another of Ellen's in which she echoed Morris's longing for the kind of miracle one cannot live without. ' "Yes, friends," ' she said, ' "this is what I came out for to see; this many-gabled old house built by the simple country-folk of the long-past times, regardless of all the turmoil that was going on in cities and courts ..." ' Again she exclaims, ' "The earth and the growth of it and the life of it! If I could but say or show how I love it!" ' In the Cotswolds the claim that the houses themselves are growths of the soil like trees and flowers, that they are autochthons of a seamless piece with the earth, is literally true because they are built of the same kind of stone, perhaps the very stone, on which they stand. This is a peculiar limestone composed of granules of calcium carbonate called oolite which, when freshly dug, varies in tone from orange-tinted buff to pale cream. This stone flourishes both beneath the shallow soil and on the soil, the lime in it flavouring both the wind and water of the Cotswolds, giving the region its uniqueness – once derided, but since Morris 'discovered' it, much prized.

The comparative softness of the rock is responsible for the formation of the wolds into smoothly moulded undulations without harsh contours or angularities. In the north the hills have such a wide sweep and amplitude that the eye ranges far before a curve is completed and another begins. In the south the folds of the hills are more intricate, the valleys more ravine-like, but the landscape still keeps its gracious, sweetly-flowing lines in true affinity with the arc of the skies above them.

> (E. Brill, *Portrait of the Cotswolds*, 1971, 11)

Under the sky the roofing tiles for churches, farm-houses, barns and cottages come from the soil too but from special Cotswold surface quarries. The stone is dug in autumn and left exposed through the winter so that it will split easily along clay layers into which water has seeped and frozen. There is also thin-layered rock which can be quarried for tiles without such 'frosting.' This stone roofing is pearly-grey in colour mottled with tufts of brown moss which turn bright green after just a sprinkle of rain. As Morris said of Kelmscott:

The roofs are covered with the beautiful stone slates of the district, the most lovely covering which a roof can have, especially when, as here and in all the traditional old houses of the countryside, they are 'sized down'; the smaller ones to the top and the bigger toward the eaves, which gives one the same sort of pleasure in their orderly beauty as a fish's scales or a bird's feathers.

> (Sup. I, 366)

As for the house itself, Morris never tired of admiring the low three-storied building built about 1570 and the higher block of rooms with larger windows and pedimented gables which may have been added, he thought, between 1630 and 1640 (1670?). The whole house 'is built of well-laid rubble stone of the district,' now a warm grey, 'the wall of the latter part being buttered over, so to say, with thin plaster which has now weathered to the same colour as the stone of the walls.' (Sup. I, 366) He counted over like treasure the many mullioned windows with drip-moulds and transoms, the handsome gables and beautifully grouped chimney-stacks. Standing in a square of grass 'a little aloof from the N.E. angle of the building,' he rejoiced to see its walls, like those of other old buildings of the district, "batter," i.e. lean a little back. This is so invariable that it is hardly possible to suppose that it was done to save material, the resulting gain in which would have been inconsiderable, or by accident; and we must suppose that it is an example of traditional design from which the builders could not escape. To my mind it is a beauty, taking from the building a rigidity which would otherwise mar it; giving it (I can think of no other word) a flexibility which is never found in our modern imitations of the houses of this age.

From this square place also one gets a good view of the farm buildings which stand to the South of the house; a very handsome barn of quite beautiful proportions, and several other sheds, including a good dove cot, all built in the same way as the house, and grouping delightfully with it.

(Sup. I, 367)

On the north side of the house there are two bold 'projections' running from the ground to the roof, one on the older part of the house and the other, 'copied' from it, on 'the later addition ...' These projections or 'excursions' (to use the Elizabethan word) 'with their elegantly shaped gables, handsomely moulded,' add 'much,' he said, 'to the general beauty of the house.' (Sup. I, 367) Morris was correct in thinking that these twin 'projections,' or tiny wings, were built at different times, but they are so perfectly matched in gable shapes and drip-moulds (window-heads) and soar in such sisterly affection that it is difficult to notice the difference in age. Much dwindled, they seem to be Tudor 'oriels' or 'oryalles,' timidly suggesting a feature of sixteenth-century architecture introduced into England by the imported artists of Henry VIII. At Kelmscott these oriels were, in a few cases, just capacious cupboards without windows, or hide-away alcoves, rather than extensions of the rooms they adjoined. In Henry's palaces they were always used as extensions as they are at Kelmscott today. In 1882 Morris wrote, 'It has come to be to me the type of the pleasant places of the earth, and of the homes of harmless simple people not overburdened with the intricacies of life ...' (Mackail I, 225)

All these architectural simplicities (or refinements) Morris could enjoy while wandering through his garden, which was as carefully and more lovingly planned than the decoration of many a client's house. In 1879 Morris gave a lecture entitled 'Making the Best of It' (*Hopes and Fears for Art*, 1882). He told his listeners that in flat country a garden 'is often the very making of a homestead.' He was of the opinion that all gardens should be enclosed by a wall of 'live hedge or stones set flatwise (as they do in some parts of the Cotswold country), or timber or wattle, or, in short, anything but iron.' Inside its walls he wanted the garden-space, if large enough, divided, as at Kelmscott, by 'old clipped yew hedges' and the flower beds 'boxed' in a way that made the garden seem, if not a part of the house, 'at least the clothes of it, which I think ought to be the aim of the layer-out of a garden.' (Sup I, 367) After more than a century of great domains laid out to imitate the vagaries of nature at its most capricious, Morris stood uncompromisingly for a return to the small walled or 'encloséd' garden of Elizabethan days.

And now to sum up as to a garden. Large or small, it should look both orderly and rich. It should be well fenced from the outside world. It should by no means imitate either the wilfulness or the wildness of Nature, but should look like a thing never to be seen except near a house. It should, in fact, look like a part of the house. It follows from this that no private pleasure-garden should be very big, and a public garden should be divided and made to look like so many flower-closes in a meadow, or a wood.

Morris was quite willing to lecture on the flowers which make the best clothes for a house. He has a lot to say against double ones:

. . . choose the old columbine where the clustering doves are unmistakeable and distinct, not the double one, where they run into mere tatters. Choose (if you can get it) the old china-aster with the yellow centre, that goes so well with the purple-brown stems and curiously coloured florets, instead of the lumps that look like cut paper, of which we are now so proud. Don't be swindled out of that wonder of beauty, a single snowdrop; there is no gain and plenty of loss in the double one. More loss still in the double sunflower, which is a coarse-coloured and dull plant, whereas the single one, though a late comer to our gardens, is by no means to be despised, since it will grow anywhere, and is both interesting and beautiful, with its sharply chiselled yellow florets relieved by the quaintly patterned sad-coloured centre clogged with honey and sweet with bees and butterflies.

The double rose, he admits, was 'a gain to the world,' but enough is enough:

The full colour it had gained, from the blush rose to the damask, was pure and true amidst all its added force, and though its scent had certainly lost some of the sweetness of the eglantine, it was fresh still, as well as so abundantly rich. Well, all that lasted till quite our own day, when the florists fell upon the rose – men who could never have enough – they strove for size and got it, a fine specimen of a florist's rose being about as big as a moderate Savoy cabbage. They tried for a strong scent and got it – till a florist's rose has not unseldom a suspicion of the scent of the aforesaid cabbage – not at its best. They tried for strong colour, and got it, strong and bad . . . But all this while they missed the very essence of the rose's being; they thought there was nothing in it but redundance and luxury; they exaggerated these into coarseness, while they threw away the exquisite subtility of form, delicacy of texture, and sweetness of colour, which blent with the richness which the true garden rose shares with many other flowers, yet makes it the queen of them all – the flower of flowers.

And then a final bit of advice about colour in gardens:

... I think the best and safest plan is to mix up your flowers, and rather eschew great masses of colour – in combination I mean. But there are some flowers (inventions of men, *i.e.* florists) which are bad colour altogether, and not to be used at all. Scarlet geraniums, for instance, or the yellow calceolaria, which indeed are not uncommonly grown together profusely, in order I suppose, to show that even flowers can be thoroughly ugly.

Morris's letters about his garden, full of happiness and free of didacticism, positive or negative, make more delightful reading than his lectures. One May he wrote to Georgiana (?):

The fields are all butter-cuppy. The elms are mostly green up to their tops: the hawthorn not out, but the crabs beautiful, and also that white-beam (I think they call it) with the umbelliferous flowers. In the garden we have lots of tulips out looking beautiful; the white bluebells and some blue ones: some of the anemones are in blossom and they all soon will be: they are very lovely. Apple-blossom for the most part only in bud, but that cherry-tree near the arbour opposite my window is a mass of bloom. The heartseases are beautiful; a few of the Iceland poppies are out: the raspberries are showing for blossom.

(Quoted in Mackail I, 237)

Other pleasant flower descriptions carry us out of the garden to the banks of the Thames, where Morris enjoyed the unenclosed wild flowers whenever a fierce North-easter was not making his 'boat go like a Japanese tea tray.'

Altogether a very pleasant river to travel on, the bank being still very beautiful with flowers; the long purples and willow-herb, and that strong-coloured yellow flower very close and buttony, are the great show: but there is a very pretty dark blue flower, I think mug-wort, mixed with all that, besides the purple blossom of the house-mint and mouse-ear and here and there a bit of meadow-sweet belated. As to the garden it seems to me its chief fruit is – blackbirds. However, they have left us some gooseberries, and I shall set to work this morning to get some before their next sit-down meal. As for flowers, the July glory has departed as needs must, but the garden looks pleasant though not very flowery. Those sweet sultans are run very much to leaf, but the beds in which they and the scabious are look very pretty, the latter having very delicate foliage. There are two tall hollyhocks (O so tall) by the strawberries, one white, one a very pretty red ...

(Undated letter quoted in Mackail I, 238)

In the autumn of 1972 the hollyhocks here at Kelmscott, maroon, red, pink, apricot, yellow and white, grew to fifteen feet and assailed the first-floor windows with a will which would have pleased Morris.

The reference to blackbirds in the last quotation makes one think of the many birds who orchestrated most of Morris's river and garden

excursions. The valley of the upper Thames has often been described as
'a land of birds.' (Mackail I, 234) One passage from a late-summer letter
(again undated) must stand for others just as pleasant:

> The birds were very delightful about us; I have been of late so steeped in
> London that it was a quite fresh pleasure to see the rooks about, who have been
> very busy in this showery weather. There was no lack of herons in these upper
> waters, and in the twilight the stint or summer snipe was crying about us and
> flitting from under the bank and across the stream: such a clean-made, neat-
> feathered, light grey little chap he is, with a wild musical little note like all the
> moor-haunting birds.
>
> (Quoted in Mackail I, 234)

Anyone who has visited Kelmscott will remember the 'Song for the Bed'
embroidered in wool by May Morris and a sister of W. B. Yeats on a
linen valance which runs around three sides of Morris's oaken bed with
patterned 'ceiling,' solid back, and gorgeously carved foot posts. The personified bed, heart of the personified house which so often held the poet
in its arms, claims to be 'warm/Midst winter's harm', so let him rest
and dream ahead to the spring

> When all birds sing
> In the town of the tree
> And ye lie in me
> And scarce dare move
> Lest earth and its love
> Should fade away
> Ere the full of the day.

The last couplet may refer to Morris's fear of death, never entirely forgotten, though by now, largely because of Kelmscott, it had softened into ap-
prehensions of 'dying before his time.' Kelmscott was the most satisfying
form of analgesic for physical tiredness, fidgets, disappointment, fear, grief
and even back-ache he had ever dreamed of. Trees, birds, flowers, the river,
the house – these were the elements of an unbelievable assuagement, the
beloved source of many 'epochs of rest' which continually freshened the
springs of life. At the end of *News from Nowhere* (Ch. XXXI) we have
all the motifs of the Kelmscott symphony of peace.

My companion gave a sigh of pleased surprise and enjoyment; nor did I wonder,
for the garden between the wall and the house was redolent of the June flowers,
and the roses were rolling over one another with that delicious superabundance
of small well-tended gardens which at first sight takes away all thought from
the beholder save that of beauty. The blackbirds were singing their loudest, the
doves were cooing on the roof-ridge, the rooks in the high elm-trees beyond

were garrulous among the young leaves, and the swifts wheeled whining about the gables. And the house itself was a fit guardian for all the beauty of this heart of summer.

Soon after coming to his manor in the southwest corner of Oxfordshire Morris discovered that the 'Kelmscott Peace,' with its trees, birds, rivers and architectural beauty, stretched, as it had since Elizabethan days, for miles around, especially throughout the region to the north and west known as Cotswold. This area had not been penetrated by the industrial ugliness, polluting man and nature, which Morris despised and dreaded. In fact, the Cotswolds had been standing practically unchanged since the period of their prosperity as the woollen centre of England. The trade in wool, woven or unwoven, flourished especially during the sixteenth and seventeenth centuries, at which time the 'Cotswold vernacular' in architecture reached its greatest perfection in Gloucestershire and western Oxfordshire, with some spillover into Worcestershire, Wiltshire and Berkshire. The village churches show signs of Saxon and Norman building as well as of fourteenth and fifteenth century English work, but it was only in Tudor and Stuart times that domestic building – manor-houses, farmhouses and cottages – achieved the miniature beauty which Morris loved and led others to prize. The many gables and dormers which give the Cotswold villages and towns so much of their peculiar distinction are due to the fact that the houses often measure no more than fifteen feet from ground to eaves. Since there was no space for upper-storey windows under the eaves, the walls were built up into windowed gables while the steep-pitched roofs were pierced with dormers. The variation created by setting dormers between or among gables is a distinctive beauty of the native style. But when a roof is pierced with several identical dormers or saw-toothed into three or four indistinguishable gables – a practice extended in our day to whole streets of identical 'Cotswold' houses – the effect is just as monotonous and boring as that of any typical builders' explosion. This modern Cotswold architecture, especially during the last three decades, does not even use the classic material of the district; it uses artificial stone, a mixture of crushed limestone and cement moulded into blocks somewhat larger than bricks. Their grey pallor lacks the warmth of the natural stone, or goes far beyond it to garish shades of dyed yellow. These cement bricks are cheaper and easier to handle than quarried stone and can be built up into a more or less Cotswold-shaped house by semi-skilled workmen. Other new houses are of brick or stucco and are roofed, not with the local stone slates which Morris so admired but with red, blue, or brown asbestos slates or tiles. Sometimes one finds old stone-roofed houses which have been stuccoed over and painted white, pink, or yellow. Morris always insisted that in this 'stone-country . . . every house must be either built, walls and roof, of grey stone or be a blot on the landscape.' (*News from Nowhere*, Ch. XXVII) A bearable compromise between the old and recent building is found in the row of Kelmscott Council Houses, built of artificial stone but faced on the road side with old stone, rock-hard, rescued from pulled-down cottages. Morris would have liked the result of this tasteful ingenuity. However, few of the Cotswold villages, hamlets and towns are any longer so pleasantly homogenised as when he came to the district.

In Morris's time many old cottages were – as they still are – so small as to be half-lost among trees except when they were joined together to snake up a hillside, grey-brown and sinuous, like those of Arlington Row at Bibury or a similar row at Snowshill. Even the large farm-houses and manors were often so sequestered in foliage that one could travel for miles through Wolds divided into farms by hedges of stone, hawthorne or beech but apparently desolate until one spotted in the midst of a clump of trees the tower or spire of an ancient church that marked the presence of a village. In fact, especially under a darkening sky, the countryside is often lonely and distinctly melancholy which may have been a reason why Morris grew so fond of it. One remembers Sidney Smith's conclusion that the Cotswolds were a region of 'stone and sorrow.' What struck Morris, however, was a sense of sturdy imperturbability, composure, solace and sanctuary – qualities he could never get enough of – and he praised the whole countryside shamelessly in letters and lectures. He wanted people to know what a relatively unspoiled portion of England still existed where Earth the Healer was much in evidence, especially in the architecture which had sprung from her womb. Time and again he attributes the beauty of Cotswold buildings to a guiding principle taken from Ruskin: that beauty is a necessary by-product of the workman's delight in doing a congenial task. He believed that the unpretentious, always gracious structures of the region, including churches, manors and farm-houses, had needed 'no grand office architect.' (Sup. I, 371) They were the creation of village masons working with 'some thin thread of tradition, a half-anxious sense of delight of meadow and acre and wood and river; a certain amount (not too much let us hope) of common sense, a liking for making materials serve one's turn, and perhaps at bottom some little grain of sentiment.' Morris felt he must share all this beauty with an unhappy world, echoes of whose 'still, sad music' troubled him severely in his periods of country isolation. He could not have foreseen how quickly his praise was to lead the developer, the estate-agent, the giant lorry, the flocks of tourists from abroad, to invade and upset the aesthetic and ecological balance he treasured.

Who could resist the following invitation to the Cotswolds, taken from a little essay called 'Under an Elm Tree; or, Thoughts in the Countryside'?

Midsummer in the country. Here you may walk between the fields and hedges that are, as it were, one huge nosegay for you, redolent of bean flowers and clover and sweet hay and elder-blossom. The cottage gardens are bright with flowers, the cottages themselves mostly models of architecture in their way. Above them towers here and there the architecture proper of days bygone, when every craftsman was an artist and brought definite intelligence to bear upon his work. Man in the past, Nature in the present, seem to be bent on pleasing you and making all things delightful to your senses; even the burning dusty road has a taste of luxury as you lie on the strip of roadside green, and listen to the blackbirds singing, surely for your benefit, and, I was going to say, as if they were paid to do it; but I was wrong, for as it is they seem to be doing their best.

(Quoted in W. H. Hutton's By Thames and Cotswold, 1908, 13)

Morris called Bibury on the Coln, some twelve miles northwest of Kelmscott, with its now famous Arlington Row of miniature old dwellings, 'surely the most beautiful village in England.' To this May adds (XVIII, xxv) that surely Minster Lovel, also in the Coln Valley, about two miles below Burford, 'must have run it very close in the mind of my father':

It is the epitome of English beauty in landscape, so small, so elegant in detail, sweet and tender in colour, and in its smallness nothing trivial or obvious. Years ago, crossing a rather ragged piece of waste upland and emerging from a by-way on to the highway, there, in the deep valley, emerald-green and clothed but not smothered with stately timber, we came upon our first sight of Minster Lovel, which impressed itself on my memory the more because of some quiet exclamation to which Father's delighted surprise moved him. The sparse buildings of the village are set in odd sloping corners and along the water, a scattered gathering of humble cottages in the wide river-meadow, bounded at one end by an arched bridge and a mill with a broad pond, and at the other by the church and the melancholy and romantic ruins of a stately mansion-house. Nothing could be more complete, more sweetly composed, more like a great painter's design for a background landscape.

From Bibury Morris frequently journeyed north to the other end of the Cotswolds in Worcestershire to see another 'most beautiful' village, Broadway. Who could fail to be intrigued by such praise? In 'Gossip' (Sup. I, 364) he says that from Kelmscott 'on the plain of the Thames Valley ... the ground rises up ... gradually with little interruption of the rise, till the crest of the ridge is gained which lies between Oxfordshire and Worcestershire, culminating in the Broadway Beacon some thirty miles from Kelmscott.' Standing near the Beacon, he describes how 'just below on either side [of] the Broadway lie the grey houses of the village street ending with a lovely house of the fourteenth century' while 'all about lie the sunny slopes, lovely of outline, flowery and sweetly grassed, dotted with the best-grown and most graceful of trees: 'tis a beautiful countryside indeed, not undignified, not unromantic, but most familiar.' This quotation comes from a lecture called 'The Prospects of Architecture in Civilisation,' given in 1881 and published the next year in *Hopes and Fears for Art*. It precedes his description of an old cottage of the town which is necessarily lovely, he says, because built by one who loved his work:

And there stands the little house that was new once, a labourer's cottage built of the Cotswold limestone, and grown now, walls and roof, a lovely warm gray, though it was creamy white in its earliest day; no line of it could ever have marred the Cotswold beauty; everything about it is solid and well wrought: it is skilfully planned and well proportioned: there is a little sharp and delicate carving about its arched doorway, and every part of it is well cared for: 'tis in fact beautiful, a work of art and a piece of nature – no less: there is no man who could have done it better considering its use and its place.

Who built it then? No strange race of men, but just the mason of Broadway village: even such a man as is now running up down yonder three or four cottages of the wretched type we know too well: nor did he get an architect from London, or even Worcester, to design it . . .

Obviously, there is a moral here for a world 'now growing uglier day by day, and there the swiftest where civilisation is the mightiest . . .'

Morris elaborates this moral in other lectures included in *Hopes and Fears* such as 'The Art of the People' (1879), always illustrating his point by contrasting modern buildings with old Cotswold examples. Speaking of 'those treasures of architecture that we study so carefully nowadays,' he asks,

. . . what are they? how were they made? There are great minsters among them, indeed, and palaces of kings and lords, but not many; and, noble and awe-in-spiring as these may be, they differ only in size from the little grey church that still, in some parts of the country at least, makes an English village a thing apart, to be seen and pondered on by all who love romance and beauty. These form the mass of our architectural treasures, the houses that every-day people lived in, the unregarded churches in which they worshipped.

And, once more, who was it that designed and ornamented them? The great architect, carefully kept for the purpose, and guarded from the common troubles of common men? By no means. Sometimes, perhaps, it was the monk, the ploughman's brother; oftenest his other brother, the village carpenter, smith, mason, what not – 'a common fellow,' whose common, every-day labour fash-ioned works that are today the wonder and despair of many a hard-working 'cultivated' architect. And did he loathe his work? No, it is impossible. I have seen, as we most of us have, work . . . so delicate, so careful, and so inventive, that nothing in its way could go further. And I will assert, without fear of con-tradiction, that no human ingenuity can produce work such as this without pleasure being a third party to the brain that conceived and the hand that fashioned it. Nor are such works rare. The throne of the great Plantagenet, or the great Valois, was no more daintily carved than the seat of the village mass-john, or the chest of the yeoman's good-wife.

In his address to the second annual meeting of SPAB (Society for the Protection of Ancient Buildings) in June 1879, Morris again affirmed his belief that 'the little grey weather-beaten building, built by ignorant men, torn by violent ones, patched by blunderers, that has outlived so many hopes and fears of mankind, and yet looks friendly and familiar to them,' (Sup. I, 123) can never become an offence to the 'beauty and majesty' of streets that may be raised in 'the future times of perfect art,' should such time ever come. These examples of the beauty inherent in buildings made with joy in the labour must be *protected* by the Society newly founded for just that purpose. Often one has to explore a dozen densely built, right-angled streets before finding that old 'inventiveness' and 'individuality' which, coming from the country's 'very heart, was given as freely to the yeoman's house, and the humble village church, as to the lord's palace or the mighty cathedral: never coarse, though often rude enough, sweet, natural and unaffected ...' These phrases are taken from Morris's lecture, 'The Lesser Arts' (in *Hopes and Fears*). He urged his listeners to get beyond the 'smoky world' into the country to see for themselves the full sympathy that once existed between the works of man and the land. We must learn to prize and emulate what our fathers did for England, for

... the land is a little land; too much shut up within the narrow seas, as it seems, to have much space for swelling into hugeness: there are no great wastes overwhelming in their dreariness, no great solitudes or forests, no terrible un-trodden mountain-walls: all is measured, mingled, varied, gliding easily one thing into another: little rivers, little plains, swelling, speedily-changing up-lands, all beset with handsome orderly trees; little hills, little mountains, netted over with the walls of sheep-walks: all is little; yet not foolish and blank, but serious rather, and abundant of meaning for such as choose to seek it: it is neither prison, nor palace, but a decent home.

The towns Morris cared for most usually had churches which he grew to love. Stretching north of Kelmscott, he writes in 'Gossip' (Sup. I, 364), is a

string of pretty inland villages, or rather two strings, the westward comprising Little Faringdon, Broughton Poggs and Filkins; the eastward, Langford, Broadwell, and Kencott. Of these Langford with its church partly thirteenth-century, partly pre-conquest, Broadwell with its lovely thirteenth-century tower and spire, and the curious little church of Boughton Poggs are specially interesting.

These churches motivated many of his excursions into the countryside and served to illustrate his favourite tenet that those who work for the joy they find in work can 'do no otherwise ... than give some gift of beauty to the world ...'

'I myself am just fresh from an out-of-the-way part of the country near the end of the navigable Thames, where within a radius of five miles are some half-dozen tiny village churches, every one of which is a beautiful work of art. These are the work of the Thames-side country bumpkins, as you would call us – nothing grander than that.'

(Quoted in Mackail II, 20)

There are within a five-mile radius of Kelmscott, at least a dozen hand-some old churches, some quite tiny, which include as well as the three al-ready praised (in Langford, Broadwell and Broughton Poggs) those of Kelmscott itself, Little Faringdon, Clanfield, Lechlade, Black Bourton, Inglesham, Bampton, Filkins and Kencot. In 'Gossip' (Sup.I, 355) Morris has kind words for the little church in Kelmscott.

The church, at the N.W. end of the village, is small but interesting; the mass of it, a nave with a tiny aisle, transept and chancel, being Early English of date, though the arches of the aisle are round-headed; a feature which is imitated from Faringdon Church and repeated at Little Faringdon and Langford. There are remains of painting all over the church, the North transept having been painted with figure subjects of the life of Christ in trefoil head panels. The East window has a painted glass image of St. George (in whose honour the church is dedicated) of the time of Edward IVth. Most of the windows (which are insertions of the early fourteenth century) have their inner arches elegantly cusped, a characteristic feature of these Oxfordshire churches. A very beautiful bell-cot formed by two trefoil arches crowns the eastern gable of the nave, and composes pleasantly with the low-pitched roofs over a clerestory, which in the fifteenth century took the place of the once high-pitched ones. The church . . . is fortunate in having escaped the process of stripping and pointing which so many of our village churches have undergone at the hands of the restoring wiseacres.

This description shows how the buildings Morris loved impressed them-selves indelibly on his consciousness. Actually, Kelmscott Church had escaped the 'restorers' through the efforts of Morris himself, working through the Society for the Protection of Ancient Buildings ('Anti-Scrape'), which he founded in 1877. He made a less successful appeal for funds to protect Inglesham Church, which stands at the 'ingle' where the Coln joins the wispy Thames some five miles above Kelmscott. This old church, as Morris wrote to Georgiana in August 1880, is 'a lovely little building about like Kelmscott in size and style, but handsomer and with more old things left in it.' (*Letters*, 138) He held that its two-bell bell-cot is 'one of the prettiest among several examples in the neighbourhood'

Inglesham Church . . . is more than picturesque. It is a very remarkable example of early Gothic architecture, seldom equalled, and never surpassed among buildings of its size for refinement and beauty of design; it contains interesting fittings of more than one date, and is archaeologically very interesting. It has never been 'restored,' and thus has escaped the process which has obliterated so much of the history of our ancient Churches. It is now in urgent need of substantial repairs . . .

(Sup. I, 160)

When he could not raise enough money to protect this little church, Morris used his own. Today the cross in front of the church and the grave-stones around it are listing picturesquely but inside, the old box-pews of oak are still in place and usuable, the screen stands fast and the old prayers and responses painted in view of the congregation can still be read. A little brass plate, kept well polished, records the church's debt to Morris.

In addition to these miniature churches, there are in the immediate neighbourhood of Kelmscott others, all very old, with external carvings which intrigued Morris. Inside Inglesham itself is a rather crude version of the Virgin and Child with God's pointing finger emerging from a cloud to the upper right. This Saxon sculpture once adorned the outside of the church. St Stephen's in the adjoining parish of Clanfield shows the blissful martyr standing under a canopy, two-thirds of the way up a corner of the sturdy square tower. He holds in his hands a platter piled with buns which represent the stones that killed him. The Anglo-Saxon Church of St Matthew at Langford has sculptured figures on the South porch. Morris would have appreciated annother example of this Gothic tradition – found in Kelmscott on the cottages erected by Mrs Morris for the poor of the village. (See Plate 6.) Here a stone plaque, carved by George Jack of Morris & Co., has been set into the wall. It shows Morris sitting near a garden-house or gazebo in the grounds of the manor with a wool-barn in the background. (Neither of these buildings is still standing.) His back to a tree trunk, he is listening to birds singing 'in the town of the tree' – not St Francis, but clearly, as Bernard Shaw called him, St William of Kelmscott. To this day the cottages are known as 'the house where Mr Morris is,' and, resting by his work-satchel, he attracts more interest than St Stephen with his platter of stones.

The spired churches within Morris's five-mile radius are St Mary's of Bampton, St Peter's and St Paul's of Broadwell, and St Lawrence's of Lechlade – all larger, more impressive and usually more elegant than any of the churches mentioned so far, though all, large and small, were built about the same time with traces of Saxon workmanship, sturdy Norman construction, and additions and alterations dating from England's three chief building centuries. Like the still more magnificent churches of Fairford, Cirencester and Burford, these seem something more than 'the work of Thames-side country bumpkins,' but who knows? Of each can be said what Morris said of Broadwell – 'a remarkably beautiful church, conspicuous for its lovely thirteenth-century spire of the same character (and perhaps built by the same hands) as those of Oxford Cathedral, Witney, and Bampton ...' (Sup. I, 162) He would have liked Bampton even better than Broadwell but for some shocking restoration: 'There is Norman work in it, and transition; and a fine decorated nave with a beautiful western doorway. The tower and the spire is very pretty; much the same date as Broadwell but handsomer.' (*Letters*, 300) It is possible that the spired church Morris loved best was St Lawrence's of Lechlade – always associated with Shelley's 'Stanzas in Lechlade Churchyard.' The meditations in this poem were never far from the 'poet upholsterer's' own thoughts. These continued to be, though not so heart-breakingly as in the past, 'formless and wailing,' while Shelley's were characteristically gentle and beckoning. Shelley welcomes the coming of evening which

> . . . twines its hair
> In duskier braids around the languid eyes of day,

though silence and twilight are 'unbeloved of men.' For a moment a touch of setting sun turns Lechlade's spire into a fiery pinnacle, clothing it, now grown 'dim and distant' in the dusk, with 'hues of heaven' while

> Around [its] lessening and invisible height
> Gather among the stars the clouds of night.

'The dead are sleeping in their sepulchres,' but

> Thus solemnised and softened, death is mild
> And terrorless as this serenest night;
> Here could I hope, like some enquiring child
> Sporting on graves, that death did hide from
> human sight
> Sweet secrets, or beside its breathless sleep
> That loveliest dreams perpetual watch did keep.

Near Kelmscott there are several more imposing churches, of minster or near-cathedral size. Burford has an impressive spire while Fairford and Cirencester have towers of striking design. In a letter he wrote to Georgiana in September 1881 Morris tells her that in Cirencester there is 'a grand church ... mostly late Gothic, of the very biggest type of parish church, romantic to the last extent, with its many aisles and chapels: wall-painting there and stained glass and brasses also ... I could have spent a long day there ...' (*Letters*, 151) Burford's spire is perhaps the tallest and most graceful in the Cotswolds. It was at Burford, in the autumn of 1876, when Morris found the great church at the mercy of 'restorers', that he first conceived the idea of organising an association to protect old buildings from such depredation. Since restoration of what has perished is obviously impossible – and it is also impossible to change the present state of any building without making it look modern – Morris wanted his association to be 'set on foot to keep a watch on old monuments, to protest against all "restoration" that means more than keeping out wind and weather, and, by all means, literary and other, to awaken a feeling that our ancient buildings are not mere ecclesiastical toys, but sacred monuments of the nation's growth and hope' (*Athenaeum*, 10th of March 1877; Sup. I, 107) When SPAB was well launched, Morris reminded the Society on 3 July 1889 that historical buildings are our only accurate record of the art of daily life as lived by our ancestors. He reinforced his statement with his own definition of romance as 'the capacity for a true conception of history, for making the past part of the present' by reliving it with the indispensable help of architecture *as it was*, not as we think it was or wish it had been. Possibly the first time he clarified this argument, even to himself, was in the controversy he carried on with Mr Cass, the vicar, over renovations at Burford church. The vicar's last word was, says Mrs Gretton in *Burford*, ' " This church, sir, is mine, and if I choose to, I shall stand on my head in it." ' By laughing long and heartily at this misericord-like picture of a vicar preaching upside down, Morris cooled the ecclesiastic's passion to give his edifice a 'Victorian look.'

More sacred to Morris than most great churches was Great Coxwell tithe barn – four miles away in Berkshire – a great minster-like structure of the thirteenth century, 'unapproachable in its dignity, as beautiful as a cathedral, yet with no ostentation of the builder's art.' Its stone-slate roof is set, as Mackail said, on a 'forest' of great oak timbers which fan out as they rise to give an effect of vaulting which, with the external buttressing, reminds one of a cathedral. Morris always praised it as 'one of the finest buildings in England or in the world.' (Mackail I, 233) He was much pleased to learn that the fifteenth-century lord of the manor in charge of the farm on which the barn stands was named William Morris and had a wife called Jane. In the parish church of St Giles he found early-Tudor brasses of 'Willm Morys, Sütyme fermer of cockyswell on whose soule jhū have mercy amen' and of 'Johane the wyf of Willm Morys,' also to be recommended to Christ's forgiveness, along with a small brass of their three children. The delight which these brasses gave Morris – he 'rubbed' them carefully with a result that any visitor to Kelmscott can see in the north-south attic – is pleasant proof of the improved relations within the Morris family only a few years after Rossetti's departure.

Clearly, not only Kelmscott Manor but the village and the whole Cotswold country with its flowered cottaged and churches became for Morris as the years went by a Paradise Recovered, a Utopian region, something as close to Heaven on Earth as he could imagine. All his life he had been seeking an environment that would still his fidgets, allay his panics, arrest his frenzies. He had sought such sedation in Epping Forest, New College Cloisters, and the beauty of Jane. Now, not only in his own house but in a whole area of England, he had found his refuge and nepenthe. Here was the philosopher's ataraxia, the pilgrim's rest, 'das Land wo die Citrönen blumen.' He could seldom talk or write about the district without becoming lyrical.

we came to the valley which the tiny Coln cuts through, . . . very beautiful, the meadows so sweet and wholesome. Two fields were grown all over with the autumn crocus, which I have not seen wild elsewhere in England . . . we spent our time with the utmost recklessness, so that by then we had had tea at a nice little public by the bridge, and were ready to start down the Coln towards Fairford, it was 6.30, and getting towards twilight. However, we saw the first two villages well enough and had some inkling of the others: the scale of everything of the smallest, but so sweet, and unusual even; it was like the background of an innocent fairy story. We didn't know our way till we had reached the last of the Coln villages, and kept asking and knocking at cottage doors and the like, and it was all very delightful and queer. Our trap put us down at St. John's Bridge, and we trudged thence into Kelmscott on a night so dark that even Kelmscott lights made a kind of flare in the sky.

(*Letters*, 151–2)

Naturally, Morris wanted to keep all as it was, to 'protect' the whole region against poachers, patchers, restorers, improvers, uglifiers, modern builders. The sight of Welsh blue slate, red tiles or galvanised iron replacing the uniquely beautiful stone roofs of the district became agony to him, as a letter of August 1895 to Georgiana shows.

It was a most lovely afternoon when I came down here, and I was prepared to enjoy the journey from Oxford to Lechlade very much: and so I did; but woe's me! when we passed by the once lovely little garth near Black Bourton, I saw all my worst fears realised; for there was the little barn we saw, being mended, the wall cut down and finished with a zinked iron roof. It quite sickened me when I saw it. That's the way all things are going now. In twenty years everything will be gone in this countryside, which twenty years ago was so rich in beautiful building: and we can do nothing to help or mend it. The world had better say, 'Let us be through with it and see what will come after it!' . . . Now that I am grown old and see that nothing is to be done, I half wish that I had not been born with a sense of romance and beauty in this accursed age . . .

(*Letters*, 374)

Morris seems to have been quite unaware of the extent to which he himself was responsible for bringing change to the district – mostly in the form of art-worker groups, but they were not necessarily 'protective' like himself. How he would have shrivelled in spirit could he have foreseen the results of the 'Cotswold Craze' which has lasted from the twenties to our own day and has so often been blamed, rightly or wrongly, on him! Meantime, he was quite ready to have all the works of industrialism swept from the earth in order to see 'what will come after it.' He had a dream of a future that would follow the revolutionary sweep-away, which he embalmed in a utopian romance called *News from Nowhere* (1890). In his dream, the scenery stretches along the Thames from the neighbourhood of Kelmscott House in Hammersmith, Morris's London home, to Kelmscott Manor. He finds hay-meadows blooming 'like a gigantic tulip-bed' in the atmosphere of a 'fairy garden.' (Ch. XVIII) Best of all, he finds everybody living ' "comfortably and happily, and not just a few damned thieves only, who were centres of vulgarity and corruption wherever they were, and who, as to this lovely river, destroyed its beauty morally, and had almost destroyed it physically, when they were thrown out of it." ' (Ch. XXIII) In Nowhere, ugliness and noise and confusion have disappeared for the people of the new dispensation (c. A.D. 2000), ' "Like the mediaevals, . . . like everything trim and clean and orderly and bright . . ." ' (Ch. X) They seem to have been 'born out of the summer day itself.' Since the revolution there has been a spontaneous upsurge of aesthetic pleasure in work, which sprang

'from a kind of instinct amongst people, no longer driven desperately to painful and terrible overwork, to do the best they could with the work in hand – to make it excellent of its kind; and when that had gone on for a little, a craving for beauty seemed to awaken in men's minds, and they began rudely and awkwardly to ornament the wares which they made . . . All this was much helped . . . by the leisurely, but not stupid, country-life which now grew . . . to be common amongst us. Thus at last and by slow degrees we got pleasure into our work; then we became conscious of that pleasure, and cultivated it, and took care that we had our fill of it; and then all was gained, and we were happy. So may it be for ages and ages !'

(Ch. XVIII)

The stretch of the river which pierces into Cotswold country interests the dreamer more than any other, for he can see how beautiful all buildings have become again in that countryside where 'every house must be either built, walls and roof, of grey stone or be a blot on the landscape.'

Finally, the dreamer arrives at a house toward which, 'almost without my will, my feet moved . . .' Ellen, the heroine of *News from Nowhere*, was with him as, 'again almost without my will, my hand raised the latch of a door in the wall . . . over which a few grey gables showed.' The 'many-gabled old house' amid its luxuriant gardens, relic of the unhappy past but not representative of it, was worthy of the new dispensation, 'the time of art,' and the inhabitants of Nowhere took great care of it. ' "It seems to me," said Ellen, "as if it had waited for these happy days, and held in it the gathered crumbs of happiness of the confused and turbulent past." ' (Ch. XXXI) When everything is so supremely right – the beautiful place, the lovely girl, the journey accomplished – consciousness is immersed for a moment in an air-bath of omniscience, omnipotence, all-loving bliss, qualities usually associated with 'the idea of the divine.' To enjoy such a gleam in the dark, however briefly, is to replace our customary insufficiency with a moment of that indescribable experience usually called 'mystic.' This gleam can also be described as the grail of our searching, a eucharistic meal which induces trance while feeding the starved spirit. Morris comes as near as he ever did to describing such an experience when, whilst exploring the house with Ellen, they come to what was and still is known as the Tapestry Room.

> We sat down at last in a room . . . still hung with old tapestry, originally of no artistic value, but now faded into pleasant grey tones which harmonised thoroughly well with the quiet of the place, and which would have been ill supplanted by brighter and more striking decoration.
>
> I asked a few random questions of Ellen as we sat there, but scarcely listened to her answers, and presently became silent, and then scarce conscious of anything, but that I was there in that old room, the doves crooning from the roofs of the barn and dovecot beyond the window opposite to me.
>
> My thought returned to me after what I think was but a minute or two, but which, as in a vivid dream, seemed as if it had lasted a long time . . .
>
> (Ch. XXXI)

This immortal doze makes us think of the scene on shipboard when Pericles after years of strained searching finds his daughter Marina: he immediately – falls asleep! In *News from Nowhere* Ellen wakes the narrator saying, ' "Come, I must not let you go off into a dream again so soon. If we must lose you, I want you to see all that you can see first before you go back again." ' He responds in terror, ' "Lose me? . . . go back again?" ' Elsewhere he says that

> suddenly the picture of the sordid squabble, the dirty and miserable tragedy of the life I had left for a while, came before my eyes; and I had, as it were, a vision of all my longings for rest and peace in the past, and I loathed the idea of going back to it again.
>
> (Ch. XIX)

Now the dreamer must leave 'the present rest and happiness of complete Communism' described in the 'utopian romance' because he cannot make his hosts feel he is really one of them. He cannot rid himself of the pollution of the world of industrial cruelty and commercial fraud by flight – he can purify himself only by doing all he can to end injustice.

He is too sick and spectre-like to live among the healthy and lovely. He describes himself as a 'scare-crow amidst these beauty-loving people' – a 'being from another planet.' He cannot become new-born. It is as if he wore a 'cap of darkness' which kept him from being clearly perceived by the Utopians themselves. Finally, at a harvest dinner held in Kelmscott Church itself, a pang shoots through him 'as of some disaster long expected and suddenly realised,' and he fades entirely from the sight of those flower-people, including Ellen. The trouble was that the more he saw of what man could become, the louder 'the still, sad music of humanity rumbled in his ears.' To soften that music was an inescapable duty and conscience drove him from Nowhere forever, as in real life Morris's conscience drove him from Kelmscott again and again.

The Cotswolds, with Kelmscott as their spiritual if not geographical centre, played an incalculable role in Morris's life. Here, when he could escape from his artistic, educational and political work, was the firmest based, the least illusory, Earthly Paradise he ever found. Here was his Great Good Place, an Elysium where he could go to renew his energy and courage, This good place gave him epochs of rest from time to time and the soothing penetration of the Kelmscott peace, which came close to that peace which passeth understanding.

In 1879 Morris wove with his own hands a tapestry, now here in Kelmscott Manor, that was much more than an experiment which might help the Firm. It was a symbol of the perfect peace of mind, the perfect protection of all the spirit prizes, which Morris had so long been seeking. A miniature Earthly Paradise dotted with grapes and roses and consisting of four great acanthus swirls which, like rococo armour (even having the colour of high-lighted blue-green steel) guard two love-birds perched near the centre of the composition. The acanthus swirls guard them from two birds of prey (at the bottom) which are testing the strength of the ingenious defence. Here is a mandalic structure, complete with a temenos or sacred centre protected by a wreath of acanthus circles set within a square made by the flowered border. There is, however, no sacred building nor are there guardian goddesses – just the wondrously meshed swirls spring from Earth the Healer, Earth the Keeper. A very original mandala rising from long-agitated depths at last stilled and filled with perfect joy. This tapestry was called *Grape and Acanthus* and later, when Morris's friends had laughed at the great swirls, *Cabbage and Grape* or *Rose and Cabbage*. Later examples of the swirling acanthus fortress surround the fertility figures in the *Flora, Pomona* and *Woodpecker* tapestries.

Henry James's story called 'The Great Good Place' tells of a house in the country. The phrases and titles used to describe this house apply equally well to Kelmscott; for instance, 'The Great Want Met.' Dane, the hero of James's tale, often tried, like Morris, to find fitting similes for the place which (in a dream) provided a refuge from 'the mere maniacal extension and motion' of modern living. Sometimes it seemed to him like 'a sacred silent convent' crossed with a 'bright country-house'. In *News from Nowhere* 'large country-dwellings were used as book-filled homes for groups of the most studious men of our time.' (Ch. X) Sometimes more secular comparisons came to Dane's mind – 'a sublimated German "cure" ' (like Bad-Ems, perhaps) or Independence Hall or even 'a sort of kindergarten' run by a great mild indivisible mother who stretches away into space and whose lap's the whole valley . . .' Always it was a refuge of enfolding arms and a gentle welcoming breast into whose hushed depths Dane let himself happily sink. Everywhere was the fragrance of flowers and a gentle peace – 'the queerest deepest sweetest sense in the world – the sense of an ache that had stopped.' Here 'the vision and the faculty divine' of the exhausted and discouraged artist revived, the 'inner life woke up again . . .' From 'the paradise of his own room . . . high up, he looked,' as Morris often did from the Tapestry Room windows, 'over a long valley to a far horizon . . .' There was hypnosis 'in the way an open window in a broad recess let in the pleasant morning; in the way the dry air pricked into faint freshness the gilt of old bindings . . .' 'What had happened was that . . . the deep spell worked and he had got his soul again . . .' At last Dane felt 'the need for action . . . again, the stir of the faculty that has been refreshed and reconsecrated,' and woke up. 'The Great Good Place' describes Morris's Cotswold-Kelmscott experience almost perfectly and in terms close to those he himself used.

At the end of *News from Nowhere* a black cloud met and engulfed Morris as he fled from Kelmscott Church, realising that the people of the new dispensation were no longer aware of his scarecrow existence. Fortunately the cloud carried him back to his bed in 'dingy Hammersmith' and he could continue working with increased hope in the eventual triumph of a cause he had been fighting for, for almost a decade. This was Morris's long effort to win for all men, and especially workingmen, a paradisal period of rest from the unreal life of mechanised labour forced on them by the 'infallible maxims' of counting-house economics. In his ears kept ringing Ellen's admonition to go on, 'with whatsoever pain and labour needs must be, to build up little by little the new day of fellowship.' (Ch. XXXII) Rested by his 'vision,' he did continue the struggle after 1890, but less strenuously. He needed more and more often to return to his Kelmscott-Cotswold-Nowhere for periods of peace, rest, dreams, and something approaching mystic ecstasy which refreshed the springs of life damaged by periodic attacks of rheumatic fever, incipient diabetes and lecturing for the Cause in foul weather. To get a clear notion of his Socialist-paradise phase we must go back to the early '80s and before.

Meanwhile those interested in Morris's example and wisdom for our time may ponder what nature and periodic country retirement (a word used either jokingly or with fear or horror by most of us nowadays) can mean to a person who cannot live with tragedy without trying to turn it into some kind of triumph.

x Paradise for All Through 'Aesthetic Socialism' 1882-1890

It must have seemed to Morris when he was at Kelmscott Manor that much of the still sad music which drifted into his *ortus conclusus* was caused by the industrial blight – the Great Uglification (Carroll's Victorian word for a Victorian fact) – which was settling yearly over more and more of England. He could never cease asking himself why the country must keep growing uglier and uglier: the things men labour to make, the dwellings they live in (if 'live' is the right word), the clothes they wear, the food they gulp (how could any sane man *eat* it?), their very features. London is a 'horrible muck-heap' while other cities of England, like Manchester, for instance, get 'nastier and shabbier every time I come there.' (*Letters,* 303) Even the houses of the rich are 'brutally vulgar and hideous' while the poor live in sweltering dog holes 'for whose wretchedness there is no name.' Actually, they compete against each other 'for something less than a dog's lodging and a dog's food.' (This and the following quotations from Morris are from B. N. Schilling's *Human Dignity and the Great Victorians,* 1946.) To look at a crowd of English people is depressing for the over-all colour is 'a dirty sooty black-brown-drab with a few spots of discordant and ill chosen bright hues due always to the feminine part of it ... the shape of our garments ... is for the most part so hideous that it seems to be an indication of our degradation in the scale of life.' Actually the clothing of the poor 'has been known to grow so foul that the dirt becomes an integral part of its substance, providing an additional defense against the weather.' Looking at these filthy, ignorant, brutalised creatures, 'burned and grimed until one mistakes them for black slaves' – 'bent and beaten, and twisted and starved out of shape' – Morris could not help thinking of the bitterly ironical fact that when artists picture God, they celebrate his omnipotence by pointing to his ability to create 'the race of those ungainly animals.'

From boyhood Morris, who would not visit the Crystal Palace Exhibition, suffered from a sensitivity to ugliness that was unusual in a person of any age – the penalty for his unusual love of beauty. In a letter to Cormell Price written when Morris was twenty-one and staying in Normandy, he describes elements of beauty and ugliness dramatically juxtaposed in the way that always aroused his fury:

O! the trees! it was all like the country in a beautiful poem, in a beautiful Romance such as might make a background to Chaucer's Palamon and Arcite;

how we could see the valley winding away along the side of the Eure a long way, under the hills: but we had to leave it and go to Rouen by a nasty, brimstone, noisy, shrieking railway train that cares not twopence for hill or valley, poplar tree or lime tree, corn poppy, or blue cornflower, or purple thistle and purple vetch, white convolvulus, white clematis, or golden S. John's wort: that cares not twopence either for tower, or spire, or apse, or dome, till it will be as noisy and obtrusive under the spires of Chartres or the towers of Rouen, as it is under Versailles or the Dome of the Invalides; verily railways are ABOMINATIONS . . .

(Letters, 13–14)

This reminds us of his sickening encounter with a 'zinced iron roof' in 'the once lovely little garth near Black Bourton'. In one of his last letters Morris rejoices that there is 'no eyesore' in the garden at Kelmscott and none to be feared now that 'Hobbs has been thatching his sheds all about; this is a great gain to me, who am always shaking in my shoes before the advent of zinced and iron sheets.' *(Letters,* 381)

Fear of England growing always and everywhere more ugly haunted Morris like the fear of contagious disease. What was the source of the infection? Why did the sickness spread? Could the blight never be reversed and the creeping horror stopped? Believing in man's natural goodness, his innate love of beauty, his strong impulse to create and enjoy, Morris never thought of blaming 'the condition of England' on original sin with penitential wailing as the antidote. At an early age he had already decided, following Ruskin, that the 'system' was to blame, that is, capitalism with its machine production of 'cheap things and nasty,' which 'necessarily results in utilitarian ugliness in everything which the labour of man deals with.' (Quotations from Ruskin are also found in Schilling, *ibid.*) This work without beauty is irksome to the body, degrading to the spirit, ruinous to civilisation. Like Ruskin, Morris believed that capitalism had warped human nature, destroying man's natural dignity and burying it under 'rattling, growling, smoking, stinking' industrial centres which are ghastly heaps of 'fermenting brickwork, pouring out poison at every pore.' The problem was to deliver the Giant Albion from under these mountains of industrial detritus. Englishmen's hope and faith in life and in an improved future, must be restored. A hundred physicians, sometimes called unkindly, medicine-men, each with a diagnosis of the illness and a prescription for its cure, crowded round. The most famous were Owen, Fourier, Carlyle, Ruskin, Arnold, Marx, and now Morris in the days after finishing *Sigurd the Volsung* (1876), which he considered to be his last important poem.

For years Morris had read books by Carlyle and Ruskin and Arnold but had not felt called on to rush to the patient's bedside. As early as 1856 Hugh, the hero of 'Frank's Sealed Letter,' realised that the world wanted help; I was strong and willing and would help it. I saw all about me men without a leader, looking and yearning for one to come and help them. I would be that leader . . . I had much work to do, trying to help my fellow-men . . . I threw myself heart and soul into that work, and joy grew up in my soul . . .

But Morris-as-Hugh was a dream. In 1856 he told Cormell Price that he could live by 'love and work, these two things only. . . . I can't enter into politico-social subjects with any interest, for on the whole I see that things are in a muddle, and I have no power or vocation to set them right in ever so little a degree.' (*Letters*, 17) Eighteen years later (1874), in a letter to Mrs Alfred Baldwin, Georgiana's sister, he was still insisting that bettering conditions was not his line: 'if people lived five hundred years instead of three score and ten they would find some better way of living that in such a sordid loathsome place' as London has become, 'but now it seems to be nobody's business to try to better things – isn't mine you see in spite of all my grumbling . . .' (*Letters*, 61–2) However, we can detect in this letter an itch to begin lecturing Englishmen on the things they need if they are ever to have 'civilisation' in place of what they call by that word. The alternative to change is collapse or worse. As he continues to Mrs Baldwin:

but look, suppose people lived in little communities among gardens and green fields, so that you could be in the country in five minutes' walk, and had few wants, almost no furniture for instance, and no servants, and studied the (difficult) arts of enjoying life, and finding out what they really wanted: then I think one might hope civilisation had really begun. But as it is, the best thing one can wish for this country at least is, meseems some great and tragical circumstances, so that if they cannot have pleasant life, which is what one means by civilisation, they may at least have a history and something to think of . . .

(*Letters*, 62)

Six months later (August 1874) he elaborated on this theme in a letter to the Hon. Mrs George Howard of Naworth Castle:

this blindness to beauty will draw down a kind of revenge one day: who knows? Years ago men's minds were full of art and the dignified shows of life, and they had but little time for justice and peace; and the vengeance on them was not increase of the violence they did not heed, but destruction of the art they heeded. So perhaps the gods are preparing troubles and terrors for the world (our small corner of it) again, that it may once again become beautiful and dramatic withal: for I do not believe they will have it dull and ugly for ever. Meantime, what is good enough for them must content us: though sometimes I should like to know why the story of the earth gets so unworthy. . .

(*Letters*, 64)

Morris's scheme for social reform can be found in a well developed form as far back as 'The Story of the Unknown Church' of January, 1856. Furnishing and decorating Red House had started not only a Firm which developed into 'a big job ... no less than the regeneration of popular art as it used to be called,' but also the Arts and Crafts Movement with its gospel of salvation by craftsmanship. However, forced to leave Red House before it was ready for thorough enjoyment, and driven from one temporary residence in Queen Square, Bloomsbury, to another at Horrington House in Turnham Green, it was not until Morris found Kelmscott Manor that he came to understand fully the role a beautiful house can play in a man's inner life. Once when he had to leave Kelmscott for a time in 1880, he wrote to Georgiana:

> I can't pretend not to feel being out of this house and its surroundings as a great loss. I have more than ever at my heart the importance for people of living in beautiful places; I mean the sort of beauty which would be attainable by all, if people could but begin to long for it. I do most earnestly desire that something more startling could be done than mere constant private grumbling and occasional public speaking to lift the standard of revolt against the sordidness which people are so stupid as to think necessary ...
>
> (*Letters*, 139)

As early as 1877 he had begun to give lectures intended to help his countrymen make the best of their homes, however small and hopeless-looking. His advice was based on two decades of craftsmanship in every field, combined with a theory of simplicity in the use of decoration which he had worked out at Kelmscott Manor.

There is a notion that Kelmscott was for Morris merely a knock-about weekend place over which he took no decorative pains. The opposite is true. His taste, which was good from the beginning, had matured during fifteen years of decorating other people's houses, though usually against his grain. To keep the workmen of the Firm busy he had, when his client would not take his advice, to follow the client's wishes, no matter how conventional, fussy, overcrowded, and sombre the result. Kelmscott, when he found it, showed how beautiful a modestly decorated house, with small handsomely shaped rooms, could be. There were echoes of the old décor in the Elizabethan and Jacobean carved chests, cupboards, chairs, and bed which Morris seems to have found there; in the White-panelled Room's fireplace surround festooned with carved leaves and fruits which set off a heraldic shield above and feathered serpents at either side; and in the Tapestry Room, whose walls had been covered at some time between 1600 and 1860 with Belgian tapestries. In *News from Nowhere* he speaks of there being 'but little furniture, and that only the most necessary and of the simplest forms,' but there must have been many beds – and what a bed Morris's simple taste required! The generous windows, mullioned and in some rooms transomed, were a treasured feature of the house, letting in views of trees, lawns and flowers in great picturesque swatches. That the house was bare of creature comforts or even modest luxuries; a mere mat on which to wipe the mud of week-end boots, is sheer myth.

Consider Rossetti's painting of 1874 called *Marigolds* or *The Bower Maiden*, 'painted from Little Annie (a cottage girl and house assistant at Kelmscott),' which is now in the Nottingham Castle Museum and Art Gallery. The wall behind the servant girl, who is placing a blue vase of marigolds on the mantle of the fireplace in the Green Room, seems to be covered with the 'Vine' wallpaper of 1873 and furniture is plentiful. The wallpaper, the maid's work-cap, the kitten playing with a ball of yarn, all suggest a house very much lived-in and loved – certainly no bare barn. Either before this date or later, Morris himself tried his prentice-hand at designing, firing and installing around the fireplace brazier blue tiles of varied patterns. At the present time there are enough tables, chairs, cabinets and mirrors said to have been here since the early seventies, to furnish several rooms. Should any more proof of the comforts of Kelmscott be needed, it can be found in *Letters to Marco*, quoted below from W. H. Hutton's *By Thames and Cotswold* (1908, 64):

'I never saw an old house so lovingly and tenderly fitted up and cared for as this one; the perfect taste and keeping of the furniture and hangings, and the way in which the original beauties of the house had been preserved was indeed a lesson to be remembered. The window seats had cushions in them, the floors were beautifully clean, the old boards by no means disguised or disfigured with stain or varnish, and with right sort of mats and carpets where wanted. Some fine old tapestry belonging to the house still hung on the walls in one room, and the furniture throughout was simple in character and not overcrowded. . . . Morris took us up into the attics, where he delighted in descanting on the splendid old woodwork displayed in the trussing and staying of the roof timbers. We paid a visit to the garden, which was kept up with some skill and taste, and on one hedge, a clipt yew, was the form of a dragon which Morris had amused himself by gradually developing with the clipper.'

This was Morris's 'Fafnir Hedge,' still flourishing but now reverted to a tamer shape than that of the garden-dragons once fairly typical of Cotswold scenery. Since it is likely that Mrs Morris, while bringing from Kelmscott House to Kelmscott Manor favourite bookshelves, engravings, candlesticks, rugs and finely written manuscripts, nevertheless kept the house looking pretty much as it had at the time of her husband's death, we may also quote from Hutton's description (65) of Kelmscott in the early days of the present century:

Now Mrs. William Morris lives there, and the house gives as beautiful an example of reverential homely inhabiting of an old dwelling-place as one may wish to see. The whitewashed ceilings and walls hung with bright stuffs of Mr. Morris's own designing, the characteristic Jacobean tapestry, the gloomy four-poster bed with curious carvings, . . . the yews, the single dahlias, and the trim walks in the garden — all combine to make a perfect picture. Perhaps there is not such another house in England. There are many large houses that bear their antiquity nobly, but here is an old yeoman's dwelling in which at a thought one may fancy one's self in the days of great Elizabeth.

This was the house, then – very simply furnished and under decorated when compared with what the Firm could have done had Morris unleashed it. Kelmscott Manor impressed Morris 'more than ever' with 'the importance for people of living in beautiful places . . .' and inspired him with a message which, while owing something to Carlyle and Ruskin, was essentially his own medicine for his country's sickness. Between 1877 and 1883 when he became a Socialist, and for the rest of his life, he gave talks, lectures, sermons on his personal gospel of remaking the life of man by making houses lovely.

From childhood Morris had a high-strung, restless, fussy nature, easily excited into fits of frenzy and ungovernable rage, and he was always seeking alleviation: guardian goddesses, Egyptian Helens armed with sedatives. No one was ever more determined to lead a happy life in spite of inner unease and outer disaster. The therapy he worked out for himself was perfected at an early age and served him the whole of his life. It was to live in a home made pleasant – even beautiful – by one's own effort. Morris had discovered such a house, (preferably not very large and, if necessary, as small as a single room) and never tired of telling his audiences about its fourfold effect: it restored lost energies, soothed exasperated nerves, offered consolation, and acted as an analgesic for minor aches and pains. We can imagine that the second of these uses – that of stilling fidgets, assuaging fear, dulling the hundred alarms of neurasthenia – was for Morris the most prized. He wanted to be happy, and for a man poised precariously on the crumbling top of the 'Celtic slide' into melancholia, keeping a balanced hold on happiness became necessarily his chief problem. He called it the art of living, and this art became for him the aim of Art itself. In a pamphlet called 'The Aims of Art,' published in *Signs of Change* (1888), the mid-point of his Socialist agitation period, Morris interrupts his comments on society to explain the psychology of creating art and enjoying beauty.

In considering the Aims of Art, that is, why men toilsomely cherish and practise Art, I find myself compelled to generalise from the only specimen of humanity of which I know anything; to wit, myself. Now, when I think of what it is that I desire, I find that I can give it no other name than happiness.

I want to be happy while I live; for as for death, I find that, never having experienced it, I have no conception of what it means, and so cannot even bring my mind to bear upon it. I know what it is to live; I cannot even guess what it is to be dead. Well, then, I want to be happy, and even sometimes, say generally, to be merry; and I find it difficult to believe that that is not the universal desire: so that, whatever tends towards that end I cherish with all my best endeavour.

From here he goes on to explain his theory that human life is dominated by two states of mind which he calls 'the mood of energy and the mood of idleness.' These words are shorthand for, first, the state of mind which insists on and delights in work, especially the creative work which fulfils the multiple purposes outlined above, and, second, the state of mind which, in times of necessary rest from such work, relaxes physical, mental and emotional strain of every kind through enjoyment of the beautiful products of the work-mood, whether made by oneself or others. Also, the memory of work done (a feeling of jolly pride) or the dreamy period of planning work to be done (with its feeling of hope) can satisfy the mood of idleness and lead back to energy and accomplishment. Morris stresses that 'pleasure in work' should not be thought of as confined to the production of works of art only; it has been and 'should be a part of all labour in some form or other: so only will the claims of the mood of energy be satisfied.' 'Therefore the Aim of Art is ... to make man's work happy and his rest fruitful. Consequently, genuine art is an unmixed blessing to the race of man, yielding 'eager life while we live, which is above all things the Aim of Art.' This pamphlet was written in Morris's high-Socialist days and he regrets the passing of beauty, resulting in the 'obliteration of the arts' and the demise of man's true motivation to work. Unfortunately man inhabits a world clanking with machines set in motion by the profit motive in its rawest form. Nevertheless, 'I do not think that anything will take the place of art; not that I doubt the ingenuity of man, which seems to be boundless in the direction of making himself unhappy, but because I believe the springs of art in the human mind to be deathless ...' Men will not give up that happiness, or work-ecstasy, so often touched with momentary hints of supernal glory that it comes closer than any other experience to that satisfaction for which we feel we have been born.

Long before publishing the *Signs of Change* Morris had clarified his psychology of creative effort with its moods of happy work and happy rest. He was now famous not only as a poet but as a practitioner of what he called 'the lesser arts of life' in the home, theorist of beauty, examiner at the School of Art, South Kensington, and political activist for the Liberals in the Anti-Turk campaign. In 1877 he began to lecture about the interrelations of work, art, justice and peace. The lectures given between 1877 and 1881 were collected and published as *Hopes and Fears*

for *Art* in 1882. 'Making the Best of It' (c. 1879) is perhaps the most interesting of these lectures, for here, before the dogmatic generalisations
and echoed platitudes of his Socialist period, Morris is preaching his own
gospel on how to make a house into a healing container for the flagging
or battered spirit. Not everyone can find a Kelmscott or 'have the good
luck to dwell in those noble buildings which our forefathers built, out of
their very souls, one may say; such good luck I call about the greatest that
can befall a man in these days.' Consequently,

I shall . . . be chiefly speaking of those middle-class dwellings of which I know
most; but what I have to say will be as applicable to any other kind; for there
is no dignity or unity of plan about any modern house, or but little. It has neither centre nor individuality, but is invariably a congeries of rooms tumbled
together by chance hap. So that the unit I have to speak of is a room rather than
a house.

After explaining how machines and the division of labour set in motion
by 'the soulless drive for commercial profit' have degraded 'that field of
the arts whose harvest should be the chief part of human joy, hope and
consolation,' Morris tells his audience that

my extravagant hope is that people will some day learn something of art, and so
long for more, and will find, as I have, that there is no getting it save by the
general acknowledgement of the right of every man to have fit work to do in a
beautiful home. Therein lies all that is indestructible of the pleasure of life; no
man need ask for more than that, no man should be granted less . . .

While waiting for beautiful homes to become the norm, men can try to
'make the best of it,' that is, 'make the best of the chambers in which
they eat and sleep and study, and hold converse with their friends . . .'
Here Morris goes into detail about the right height for ceilings in relation to the shape and size of rooms; about painting the underside of
joists and beams in patterns; about colours to use on walls; about letting
a considerable amount of flooring show around the edges of a rug; about
not varying the colour in parquet-work; about avoiding the 'mean,
miserable, uncomfortable and showy' fireplaces of the time with their
'wretched sham ornament, trumpery of cast iron and brass . . . huddled
up with rubbish of ashpan, and fender, and rug . . .'; about not using too
much movable furniture, etc., etc. '. . . all rooms ought to look as if they
were lived in, and to have, so to say, a friendly welcome ready for the incomer.' 'A drawing-room ought to look as if some kind of work could be
done in it less toilsome than being bored.' By this time Morris had decided it was his particular job to turn the most makeshift room into as
much of a bower in paradise as possible. It would be years, he feared,
before men would enjoy the full rest, consolation, and analgesia which
their homes, if tastefully arranged, could offer. This, then, was his life's

work – to 'make endurable those strange dwellings – the basest, the ugliest, and the most inconvenient that men have ever built for themselves, and which our own haste, necessity, and stupidity, compel almost all of us to live in.'

When he gave this lecture Morris was still talking to people of the middle class and it was for them that he had by this time (c. 1879) devised a dozen handsome wallpapers, a half-dozen chintzes, and about the same number of damasks, double-woven woollens and pretty rugs. Though he was deeply worried by the fearful sufferings of the poor, he was faced with the frustrating fact that, as he insisted his works must be handmade, he could not afford to throw these life-lines to those who needed them most. What a pity! Yet, driven from within, he went ahead with his ideas for decorative patterns, for dyeing, and for weaving silks, serges, carpets and tapestries on his own looms. In his hundreds of designs his chief idea seems to have been to bring the outdoors indoors. Seeing most English dwellings as he saw those of London's East End – 'the mere stretch of houses, the vast mass of shabbiness and uneventfulness, sits upon me like a nightmare' (*Letters*, 236) – he demanded that we 'turn this land from the grimy backyard of a workshop into a garden.' He had many practical ideas for improving 'these horrible brick encampments' to turn them into garden-suburbs. '. . . I want the town to be impregnated with the country . . . I want every homestead to be . . . a lovely house surrounded by acres and acres of garden. . . . I want the town to be . . . in short, a garden with beautiful houses in it.' But he realised that within the foreseeable future people starved for natural beauty were much more likely to get it – or something like it – from his papers, chintzes, rugs, tiles, and stained-glass windows. If only men could be happy in their work (a claim he would soon make for successful Socialism), that happiness would produce a 'Noble, *popular* art' which would 'make our streets as beautiful as the woods, as elevating as the mountainsides: it will be a pleasure and a rest, and not a weight upon the spirits to come from the open country into a town . . .' (Lecture on 'The Lesser Arts' in *Hopes and Fears for Art*.) His desire to turn rooms into garths and whole houses into indoor pleasaunces lay at the bottom of all his papers and textiles. '. . . I insist,' he told his pupils, 'on plenty of meaning in your patterns; I must have unmistakable suggestions of gardens and fields and strange trees, boughs and tendrils . . .' (XXII, 195–6) In fact, he wanted a sense of growth, 'strong and crisp,' in the vegetal elements of all patterns: 'Take heed . . . that the lines do not get thready or flabby or too far from their stock to sprout firmly and vigorously; even where a line ends it should look as if it had plenty of capacity for more growth if so it would.' (XXII, 99) While accepting the common notion of his time that wallpapers should be flat, he often managed to suggest, with a dark ground, lighter leaves and brilliant flowers, a certain depth if not perspective, for he wanted 'to be reminded, however simply, of the close vine-trellis that keeps out the sun by the Nile side; or of the wild-woods and their streams ... or of the many-flowered summer meadows of Picardy ...' (XXII, 178)

Such was Morris's ideal and also his accomplishment in the household arts which were, with their light, bright, firm yet subtly intertwined leaf and flower designs, to transform many a dismal Victorian interior into a Persian garden. He consciously aimed at an effect both brilliant and subdued, exciting yet soothing, and he usually had remarkable success in creating what would have been every man's 'due share of art, the chief part of which will be a dwelling that does not lack the beauty which Nature would freely allow it, if our own perversity did not turn nature out of doors.' Actually, what deprived every man of his 'due share' was a money problem. Only the rich could afford what was meant for all. In order to keep the workmen of the Firm constantly employed, he *had* to sell to the wealthy and to them alone, a compulsion which weighed so heavily on him that he despaired of ever seeing his therapy-for-the-times have a chance to work unless the economy-of-the-times was simply turned upside down. Unless there was, perchance, a second *Ragna Rök*? Unless there was a new instauration with 'equality of condition,' including income, which would leave every man free to do work he loved in a beautiful house. He wanted unqualified opportunity for everyone to realize in this life every potential of the Earthly Paradise adumbrated in the poems, glass, papers, chintzes, tiles, and tapestries of William Morris. However, the current organisation of toil degraded men into less than beasts and 'they will some day come to know it, and cry out to be made men again and art only can do it and redeem them from this slavery; and I say once more that this is her highest and most glorious end and aim ...' ('The Beauty of Life,' in *Hopes and Fears*) When Morris thought of gathering up these pre-Socialist lectures in the form of *Hopes and Fears for Art* (1882), he wrote to Georgiana that the book would treat of a 'subject, which seems to me to be the most serious one that a man can think of; for 'tis no less than the chances of a calm, dignified, and therefore happy life for the mass of mankind.' (*Letters*, 134)

Morris's *Hopes and Fears* offered a vague blueprint for a utopia of craftsmen busily employed at work they loved in shops that were rooms in the workers' own simple but handsome dwellings. They were making goods to satisfy the needs of people they knew, who in exchange were making goods to satisfy and please them. This solution for the terrible poverty and growing ugliness which afflicted industrial England has often been called Morris's Aesthetic Socialism. The vision excited Morris to move the workshops of the Firm in 1881 from London to a kind of Garden Factory at Merton Abbey on the river Wandle not far away in Surrey. He had hoped to move it to Brockley near Chipping Campden in his beloved Cotswolds but that was too far from the materials and clientele available in London. Mackail (II, 35) wrote of Merton:

> The works stood on about seven acres of ground, including a large meadow as well as an orchard and vegetable garden. They were old-fashioned, though still in good repair. The riverside and the mill pond are thickly set with willows and large poplars; behind the dwelling-house a flower garden, then neglected, but soon restored to beauty when it came into Morris's hands, runs down to the water. The workshops, for the most part long wooden two-storied sheds, red-tiled and weather-boarded, are grouped irregularly round the mill lade. Beyond the meadow are the remains of a mediaeval wall, the sole remaining fragment of Merton Abbey.

Conditions at Merton, with Morris carrying armfuls of flowers back to his daughter Jenny in London, have something Ruskinian about them, and correspond to those Morris imaged in his lecture 'A Factory as It Might Be' – well designed, set in fine gardens, with no litter, pollution, or smoke, though to what extent it ever became a social centre with restaurant, library, school, stage, concert hall, adult education classes and four-hour work days we cannot be sure. In the attic at Kelmscott is a great flowered porcelain pitcher in an Oriental idiom, which holds about six litres. This and others like it were used to serve tots of beer to Merton workmen during the day. According to May (Sup. II, 130–9) most of the work at Merton, as in Morris's ideal factory, was 'of the nature of art; therefore all slavery of work ceases under such a system, for whatever is burdensome about the factory would be taken turn and turn about, and so distributed would cease to be a burden, would in fact be a kind of rest from the more exciting or artistic work.' Morris boldly asserted that men working under such conditions, 'having manual skill, technical and general education, and leisure to use these advantages, are quite sure to develop a love of art, that is to say, a sense of beauty and an interest in life, which, in the long run must stimulate them to the desire for artistic creation, the satisfaction of which is of all the pleasures the greatest.' Some of the Merton workmen are on record as thinking of the factory as a heaven on earth.

Finally, Morris convinced himself that the work conditions and pay-scale he had brought into existence at Merton could be spread over England by the Socialism which was coming into existence in the 1880s. In fact, he found in such craftsmen's paradises England's only hope of justice, dignity and joy for all, and in the 'scientific Socialism' of the Democratic Federation (soon to be called the Social Democratic Federation) an iron-clad guarantee that this hope could be realised. In 1883, soon after its birth under the leadership of H. M. Hyndman, Morris joined the Democratic Federation, the first English Socialist party, his heart full of new hope for the destiny of the human race.

He was prepared to serve the Cause in any way, however humble, by running errands or writing or lecturing. Chosen to convert workingmen to the Party by speech-making because he had acquired a reputation for lecturing on art and social change, he found himself confronted with an unexpected chore: that of mastering socialist theory. Morris, who liked ideas to be clear-cut and capable of being presented in the form of pictures, had a hard time 'reading economics.' In 1885 he broke with the Social Democratic Federation, and after being driven out of the Socialist League in 1890 he formed his own Hammersmith group. W. B. Yeats, who attended a number of the Hammersmith group meetings, wrote, 'I did not read economics, having turned Socialist because of Morris's lectures and pamphlets, and I think it unlikely that Morris himself could read economics.' (*Autobiographies*, 1955, 146) What headaches reading the economists, those past-masters of abstraction – the very antitheses of picture-makers – caused Morris we can only imagine. His acutest pain must have come from reading Marx, who, it has been said, devised 'a mythology founded on the maladies of language.' What the economists had to say which could be intermingled with his own gospel of salvation by craftsmanship can be gathered from lectures given between 1884 and 1887 and collected as *Signs of Change* in 1888. Here Morris's ideas that man is essentially a maker who is most effectively fulfilled through creative work, and that capitalism is morally reprehensible, unspeakable and unforgiveable because it forces men to do stultifying jobs for starvation wages or deprives them of work altogether, were liberally used to flavour the Marxist clichés. With the exception of his lectures on 'Feudal England' and 'The Hopes of Civilisation,' Morris had little to say about class-war, the liquidation of capitalism, the people's ownership of the means of production, the dictatorship of the proletariat or the resultant state's quick withering away. All he could really use of Marx was his interpretation of history though he must have been revolted by the German's obtuse inability to see man as anything but an economic animal or his story as anything but a dog-dance motivated by the desire to snap up bones tossed from Dives' table – or the shin bones of Dives himself. As Herbert Read wrote in *Poetry and Anarchism* (1938, 25), Marx does not recognise 'art as a primary factor in human experience, or art as a mode of knowledge or as a means of apprehending the meaning or quality of life.' The so-called 'pure economics' of *Das Kapital* with its tortuously elaborated theories, left Morris's mind, which was always in search of intellectual clarity bolstered by attractive imagery, half-sunk in a morass of abstract words twisted around the stumps of submerged ideas.

In 1893 *Socialism, Its Growth and Outcome* was published; a book made up from a series of articles which had appeared in *Commonweal*, the Socialist League newspaper which Morris had edited and financed. It is said that in a passage called 'Socialism from the Root Up' Morris merely added a few thoughts and a tang of his own language to what was really the work of E. B. Bax. However, some parts of the book are definitely Morris's own thought, especially where the writing does not follow Marx. According to Morris, Bax, who had been 'steeped in the Marxite pickle over at Zurich,' wanted sitting on. Writers like Fourier Morris could easily understand and a passage like the following (305–6) must have come from his pen:

Fourier was right in asserting that all labour could be made pleasurable under certain conditions. These conditions are, briefly: freedom from anxiety as to livelihood; shortness of hours in proportion to the stress of the work; variety of occupation if the work is of its nature monotonous; *due* use of machinery, i.e. the use of it in labour which is essentially oppressive if done by hand; opportunity for every one to choose the occupation suitable to his capacity and idiosyncrasy; and lastly the solacing of labour by the introduction of ornament, the making of which is enjoyable to the labourer.

Morris continually echoed Ruskin's thesis that beauty is the result of man's joy in his work. Therefore nothing that any man can do is so important, valuable, or quickly embraced as work in which he finds pleasure. Morris had been saying things like this to small groups for years before he became a Socialist and spoke directly to large numbers of workmen. Work must satisfy the worker's 'natural and rightful desire for pleasure' or 'the greater part of his life must pass unhappily and without self-respect. ... The chief duty of the civilised world today is to set about making labour happy for all ...' This is a characteristic passage from 'The Art of the People' published in *Hopes and Fears for Art* in 1879. Socialism's job is to exalt work from servitude and joyless toil into altar-service through the joyous creation which is art. This is a far more important duty of Socialism than bringing about the changes in crime, property, marriage, and working hours which the movement emphasised in Morris's day.

More than any other friend or thinker, Bruce Glasier understood the psychological, aesthetic, and ethic profundity of Morris's emphasis on joyous work and saw how clearly he differed from other Socialist theorisers in this central concern. As he was the Baptist of Salvation by Craftsmanship in Scotland, much that he had to say of Master Craftsman Morris is worth quoting.

Perhaps the most distinctive as well as the most prophetic part of his teaching was his exaltation of work. No other writer, ancient or modern, that I know of, has so glorified work for its own sake. If ever man can be said to have believed in work as the greatest human pleasure and as the highest form of worship, it was he. In this respect his teaching stands out almost as uniquely from the teaching in prevalent Socialist literature as from that of literature generally. Both Carlyle and Ruskin had, it is true, proclaimed the nobility of work; but there was in their axioms a preceptorial and disciplinary note. Work with them has still something of the Old Testament penitential curse upon it. With Morris there is no such detraction. Ever and ever again he dwells upon the idea that work is the greatest boon of life, not simply because work is necessary for the sustenance of life – what is necessary may yet be painful and irksome – but because it is in itself a good and joyous thing; because it is the chief means whereby man can express his creative powers, and give to his fellows the gifts of his affection and diligence.

Underneath much of the prevalent teaching of Socialism, especially that of Marxist propagandists, as in the teaching of the Book of Genesis, there lurks the notion that work is from its very nature an oppressive and hateful obligation, to be borne at least as a burden, as a price to be paid for the privilege of life. One feels when reading many of the leading expositions of Socialism that we should want, were such a thing possible, to free the workers not only from the present conditions of work, but from work altogether. In other words, there clings to Socialist teaching the idea – the Capitalist idea, it might be called – that work is in its nature a servitude and oppression, and that the ideal of complete social emancipation would be that we should all be able to live without work – live, that is to say, as 'ladies and gentlemen' without having to do any work at all!

So far from regarding work in that light, so far from looking upon work as being in itself an evil, an undesirable or penitential task, Morris held work to be the highest, the most God-like of all human capacities. Without work life would cease to have any meaning or yield any noble happiness at all.

(*William Morris and the Early Days of the Socialist Movement*, 1921, 146–7)

Glasier noted (149) that in *News from Nowhere* men work without special reward for their labour:

'No reward of labour!' exclaimed Hammond. 'The reward of creation. The wages which God gets, as people might have said long agone. If you are going to be paid for the pleasure of creation, which is what excellence in work means, the next thing we shall hear of will be a bill sent for the creation of children.'

Morris is at his dullest when simply underwriting Bax's version of Socialist doctrine on 'the assumption by the community of all the means of production and exchange, to wit, the land, the mines, the railways, the factories, etc. and the credit establishments of the country.' (Bax and Morris, *Socialism*, 280) The idea that the expropriating capitalists were to be expropriated by bloody revolution appealed to him in moments of despair – in day-dreams of *Ragna Rök* – but the book written by Morris and

Bax says, 'It is a matter of course that we do not intend to see this done by catastrophe ...' (280) However, as Marx had rejected entirely the 'Utopists' like Owen, Saint Simon and Fourier, it had become standard Socialist doctrine that 'Communism can never be realised till the present system of society has been destroyed by the workers taking hold of the political power.' (217) That bloodshed and civil war were played down so much by Bax and Morris in 1893 was partly due to the fact that in January of that year Keir Hardie had persuaded the representatives of dozens of trade unions, trade councils, labour leagues, and Fabian-type organisations to form a new political party, parent of the present Labour Party, to work for certain 'Socialist' ends through the traditional British ballot. It began to look now as if the middle-of-the-roaders would succeed. If 'the means of production' could be got into the hands of the people by the ballot, the violence of Morris's dreams of revolt contained in the poems, stories and romances of the 1880s would be washed away leaving Morris free to confess, 'once for all, what I have often wanted to say of late ... that the idea of taking any human life for any reason whatever is horrible and abhorrent to me.' In the manifesto of the Hammersmith Socialist Society Morris deprecated 'spasmodic and desperate acts of violence' on humanitarian and tactical grounds while proclaiming that 'it may be necessary to incur the penalties attaching to *passive* resistance, which is the true weapon of the weak and the unarmed,' far more likely to embarrass tyranny than violence. In a lecture on 'Communism' given in 1892 and printed as *Fabian Tract No. 113*, 1903, Morris said that 'Some of us ... once believed in the inevitableness of a sudden and speedy change' but now see that, however the workers are 'to get hold of ... the executive power of the country, ... the organisation and labour which will be necessary to effect that by means of the ballot-box will, to say the least of it, be little indeed compared with what would be necessary to effect it by open revolt.' (Sup. II, 350)

Still, a question about communism which had always bothered Morris remained: how was the government of a country owned by the People to be organised and administered? What about 'the dictatorship of the proletariat' when all are 'equal in condition' and society is actually classless? Marx had always warned against detailed speculation about the conditions of the classless future, but it was precisely a 'picture' of that future which a mind like Morris's could not do without. Morris could not have believed that property could be transferred from private to collective ownership overnight, and *News from Nowhere* tells of a period of mixed economy (such as Lenin later, for want of foresight, was forced to adopt for a time). In Morris's romance this mixed economy led, not to State Socialism, with all the horrors of centralisation, bureaucracy, and government interference in private life that Morris feared Communism might bring, but to a Paradise of Craftsmen. Morris imagined a revolution without prolonged violence, so that men were able to escape the period of state coercion and proceed almost at once to the decentralised period when, the state having 'withered away,' they were free to get on with their chosen work. They kept machinery that did distasteful work but eliminated the machines which disfigured the landscape or prevented men from doing forms of work in which the spirit delights. In *William Morris, the Man and the Myth* (1964), Page Arnot says that much of *News from Nowhere* 'answers to the indications given by Marx in his notes on the "Gotha Programme".'

In a higher phase of communist society, after the enslaving subordination of individuals under division of labour, and therewith also the antithesis between mental and physical labour, has vanished; after labour, from a mere means of life, has itself become the prime necessity of life; after the productive forces have also increased with the all-round development of the individual, and all the springs of co-operative wealth flow more abundantly – only then can the narrow horizon of bourgeois right be fully left behind and society inscribe on its banners: 'from each according to his ability, to each according to his needs!'

(Arnot, note on 117)

This passage from Marx's *Critique of the Gotha Programme* gives an idea of why Morris 'suffered agonies of confusion of the brain over reading the pure economics' of the great thinker. It appears from this quotation that in 'the higher phase of communist society' the state has not exactly 'withered away.' If LeBlanc's idea of social and economic justice summed up in the cliché 'From each according to his ability; to each according to his needs' can only *begin* in 'the higher phase' of communism, we are still dismally far from Morris's dream of tiny communes loosely banded together, a dream which stands in opposition to Marx's vision of a great, even global state, based on heavy industry and girded for continual 'jumps forward' on to ever dizzier heights of mechanised development. Marx's exploitation of LeBlanc's cliché under the name of Freedom worried Morris greatly. Morris always demanded 'the opportunity for every one to choose the occupation suitable to his capacity and idiosyncrasy'. With heavy industry forever expanding through tighter central control, how can men ever get rid of State or World Socialism? The size and power of the bureaucracy implicit in the Socialist cliché is staggering. Who, if not a bureaucracy operating with something like absolute power, can determine what each man's talent is or what will be necessary to satisfy his needs? Can any bureaucratic set-up, however benevolent, satisfy the imperiously vital adjustments always present in any process of self-development? For himself, said Morris, and for his whole vision of craftsmen's commonwealths, freedom from coercion in

these adjustments is a matter of life and death. Once a People's bureaucracy has been set up to employ the People and use the People's collective
wealth for the People's collective good, will you not have a tyranny of
the People over the People more complete and harder to get rid of than
any tyranny the world has seen? It is easy to imagine what Morris would
think of the communism of Marx and Lenin as practised in Russia
today. Yeats and others have reported Morris's declaration that if any
man were ever to thrust him into a Fourierist phalanstery or labour
squad, 'I will lie on my back and kick.' (*Autobiographies*, 147) And
Marx's sneer at 'the idiocy of rural life' must have horrified Morris.

In spite of Marx's constant warning that communists should not try to
envisage the classless future but get on with liquidating capitalists,
Morris could never stop creating pictures of the time to come. In his
lecture 'How Shall We Live Then?' (given in 1889 but never printed
until 1971, ed. P. Meier, 16) he stresses that, while believing some direction of workmen will be needed,

I am very far from thinking that it would be either necessary or desirable to
prescribe to people what occupation they should follow; I am assuming only
that opportunity will be afforded for people to do what they can do well, and
that the work as far as the relations of men go will be voluntary; nature will be
the compeller . . .

To Dr John Glasse Morris wrote on 23 May 1887 that '. . . I have an
Englishman's wholesome horror of government interference and centralisation which some of our friends who are built on the German pattern
are not quite enough afraid of, I think.' Actually Morrisian Socialism
seems to have owed little to Marx except catchwords and phrases:

. . . no one who knew him personally, or was familiar with the general body
of his writings, could fail to perceive that these Marxist ideas did not really
belong to his own sphere of Socialist thought, but were adopted by him because
of their almost universal acceptance by his fellow Socialists, and because he did
not feel disposed to bother about doctrines, which, whether true or false, hardly
interested him.

(Glasier, *William Morris*, 143)

Glasier also tells (32) of an episode in Morris's first lecture visit to Glasgow when a local comrade named Nairne put him through 'the cate-
chism a bit, after your Scottish Kirk-Session fashion' by asking, ' "Does
Comrade Morris accept Marx's theory of value?" '

Morris's reply was emphatic, and has passed into the movement as one of the
best remembered of his sayings: 'I am asked if I believe in Marx's theory of
value. To speak quite frankly, I do not know what Marx's theory of value
is, and I'm damned if I want to know.' Then he added: 'Truth to say,

my friends, I have tried to understand Marx's theory, but political economy is not in my line, and much of it appears to me to be dreary rubbish. But I am, I hope, a Socialist none the less. It is enough political economy for me to know that the idle class is rich and the working class is poor, and that the rich are rich because they rob the poor. That I know because I see it with my eyes. I need read no books to convince me of it. And it does not matter a rap, it seems to me, whether the robbery is accomplished by what is termed surplus value, or by means of serfage or open brigandage. The whole system is monstrous and intolerable, and what we Socialists have got to do is to work together for its complete overthrow, and for the establishment in its stead of a system of co-operation where there shall be no masters or slaves, but where everyone will live and work jollily together as neighbours and comrades for the equal good of all. That, in a nutshell, is my political economy and my social democracy.'

It was wild talk like this of 'working jollily together' that led Engels to call Morris a *Gemütssozialist*, almost as bad as that humanitarian Leroux who was always advocating a literal equality that would give birth to 'a religion of humanity.' (L. W. Eshleman, *A Victorian Rebel*, 1940, 358) Later Glasier, recalling how 'Morris, when he first met us in Glasgow, had flatly declared his indifference to Marx's theory of value, or any other dogmas of political economy,' says that he himself catechised the master about a magazine report which said that Morris attributed his Socialist convictions to Marx. Morris replied (p. 142) that

'. . . it is quite true that I put some emphasis on Marx — more than I ought to have done, perhaps. The fact is that I have often tried to read the old German Israelite, but have never been able to make head or tail of his algebraics. He is stiffer reading than some of Browning's poetry. But you see most people think I am a Socialist because I am a crazy sort of artist and poet chap, and I mentioned Marx because I wanted to be upsides with them and make believe that I am really a tremendous Political Economist — which, thank God, I am not! I don't think I ever read a book on Political Economy in my life — barring, if you choose to call it such, Ruskin's 'Unto This Last' — and I'll take precious good care I never will!'

Another of Morris's friends, Bernard Shaw, later (in 'Morris As I Knew Him,' Sup. II) held that Morris had been quite right to take this view of Marx for

As a matter of fact Marx's theory of value and the explanation of surplus value he founded on it are academic blunders; and the dialectic, though it may have been a convenient instrument of thought a hundred years ago for a German university student soaked in Hegelianism, can now only make Communist thinking difficult and uncongenial. Morris put all that aside instinctively as the intellectual trifling it actually is, and went straight to the real issues on which he was quite simple and quite right.

Shaw goes on to describe Morris's views on a fair society.

people who do not do their fair share of social work are 'damned thieves,' and that neither a stable society, a happy life, nor a healthy art can come from honouring such a thieving as the mainspring of industrial activity. To him the notion that a British workman cannot arrive at this very simple fundamental conclusion except through the strait gate of the Marxian dialectic, or that the dialectic can be anything to such a one but a most superfluous botheration, was folly.

Glasier (144) was sure that Morris's 'Socialism was Utopian rather than Scientific,' by which

... I mean that his Socialism was not derived from any logical inferences from economic analyses of industrial history, but from his whole conception of life. He did not concern himself so much with the science of wealth, or rather money-making, as with the art of living. While ordaining absolute equality of wealth conditions for all as essential to the realisation of the Co-operative Commonwealth, he regarded all readjustments of economic conditions as a means to an end rather than as ends in themselves. The great object of Socialism was to place all men and women on a footing of equality and brotherhood in order that they might one and all have the utmost possible freedom to live the fullest and happiest lives.

It is certain that when he joined the Democratic Federation in 1883 Morris had never heard of Marx and it is possible that he never read more than the historical portion of *Das Kapital* (there was a French translation of Volume I in 1883 and an English version of the whole published in 1886). In many of his lectures he refers to class struggle, exploitation of the workers, revolution, and common ownership of the means of production, but these notions did not necessarily come from Marx and were used chiefly to fill out his vision of how every man was to find joy in work through the restoration of handicrafts and the creation of beauty. As Schilling says, there is more Pre-Raphaelitism than Marxism in this ideal, and Marx and Engels, those sombre dialecticians in whose vocabulary art is an unknown word and humanitarianism a nasty one, seem to repudiate men like William Morris outright in *The Communist Manifesto*. Probably they were right to do so, for it is not clear that Morris understood what they meant by the People's collective ownership and dictatorial administration of the means of production. Glasier quotes (145) a letter Morris wrote in 1884 after visiting Edward Carpenter's little farm at Millthorpe:

I went to Chesterfield and saw Edward Carpenter on Monday, and found him sensible and sympathetic at the same time. I listened with longing heart to his account of his patch of ground, seven acres: He says that he and his fellow can almost live on it: they grow their own wheat and send flowers and fruit to Chesterfield and Sheffield markets: all sounds very agreeable to me. It seems to me that a very real way to enjoy life is to accept all its necessary ordinary details and turn them into pleasure by taking interest in them: whereas modern civilisation huddles them out of the way, has them done in a venal and slovenly manner till they become real drudgery which people can't help trying to avoid. Whiles I think, as a vision, of a decent community as a refuge from our mean squabbles and corrupt society; but I am too old now, even if it were not dastardly to desert.

This was written more than a year after he had joined the Democratic Federation.

'Equality of condition,' living in agreeable houses, protecting the environment, enjoying work and thereby creating beauty – these were the indispensable ingredients of the life Morris wanted for all men. They were 'my Socialism.' His democratic faith took for granted innate good will and good taste in men and women. He was a dreamer really, but a practical one who used every means his fertile mind could invent for bringing paradise to earth. He tried every avenue that might lead to the sacred centre of a mandalic arrangement of the elements of experience. His Socialist nostrum called for every man to create his own mandala, peaceful, solacing, curative, by the joyous work of mind and hands. This was his personal remedy for disappointment, heart-break and periodic illness. He *knew* that it worked for him and felt, as he wrote in 'The Prospects of Architecture in Civilisation,' published in *Hopes and Fears for Art*, that

from simplicity of life would rise up the longing for beauty, which cannot yet be dead in men's souls, and we know that nothing can satisfy that demand but Intelligent work rising gradually into Imaginative work; which will turn all 'operatives' into workmen, into artists, into men.

Morris treasured at Kelmscott a picture by the younger Breughel, patterned after one by his father, which depicts the cultivation of a tulip-filled garden, itself a formal mandala, as one of the most important of human activities. All who are not working in the garden are dancing in the upper left-hand corner of the picture in front of a street of houses which slopes gradually upward and in other ways reminds us of Arlington Row! The picture hangs over the mantelpiece of the White-panelled Room where I have written most of this book and has always seemed to me a perfect symbol of Morris's Utopian and Aesthetic Socialism. Here people, the sexes and classes mingling, all goaded from within, seek and find happiness in work which surrounds them with beauty.

What makes Morris's paradise of workers seem impossible is the same complicated and recalcitrant human nature which ruined Morris's love-life. Just as Jane failed to give him the sympathetic companionship he needed, workmen, even when freed from the fear of periodic unemployment and the crushing burden of 'mechanical toil,' usually failed to develop the good taste and joy in work and fellowship that Morris looked for.

Morris's disappointment with his fellow workmen and Socialists, usually well concealed, broke out dramatically on an occasion when Bruce Glasier made what Morris considered to be a disparaging remark (51–2) about a picture by Burne-Jones.

Then the heavens burst open, and lightning and thunder fell upon me. Hardly had I completed my sentence than Morris was on his feet, storming words upon me that shook the room. His eyes flamed as with actual fire, his shaggy mane rose like a burning crest, his whiskers and moustache bristled out like pine-needles. . . .

He poured forth an amazing torrent of invective against the whole age. 'Art forsooth !' he cried, 'where the hell is it? Where the hell are the people who know or care a damn about it? This infernal civilisation has no capacity to understand either nature or art. People have no eyes to see, no ears to hear. The only thing they understand is how to enslave their fellows or be enslaved by them, grubbing a life lower than that of the brutes. Children and savages have better wits than civilised mankind to-day.'

Glaiser realised that he himself had been the unwitting catalyst of a prophetic outburst against 'the scarlet woman of civilisation' or, rather, the ungrateful recalcitrance of human nature itself. In the summer of 1889, W. S. Blunt who spent the season at Kelmscott, wrote that Morris was

in a mood of reaction from his socialistic fervour. He was . . . disgusted at the personal jealousies of his fellow-workers in the cause and at their cowardice in action. He never got over the pusillanimity they had shown at the Trafalgar Square meeting two years before, when a few hundred policemen had dealt with thousands of them as though they had been schoolboys. Morris was too loyal and too obstinate to abjure his creed, but the heart of his devotion to the cause of the proletariat had gone. In some ways our two positions were the same. We had both of us sacrificed much socially to our principles, and our principles had failed to justify themselves by results, and we were both driven back on earlier loves, art, poetry, romance.

(*My Diaries*, 1888–1914, 1-vol. ed., 1932, 23)

To this Blunt adds, 'My talks with him that summer confirmed me in my resolution politically to retire into my shell . . .' (25) When deposed from his editorship of the *Commonweal* in 1890 by the anarchist element in the Socialist League which he had organised after his 1885 'secession' from the Social Democratic Federation, Morris wrote to Glasier that he was feeling 'sick of things in general. The humbug which floats to the top in all branches of intelligence is such a damned greasy pot-scum.'

The Hammersmith Branch of the League stood by him, however, holding its meetings in the grounds of Kelmscott House, and constituting his last tie to the Socialist movement.

When he was editor of *Commonweal* Morris wrote for this paper a long poem called *The Pilgrims of Hope* (1886), a story called *A Dream of John Ball* (1886–7), which appeared in book form in 1888, and a utopian romance called *News From Nowhere* (1890; book form, 1891). He also wrote during this period two semi-historical novels which have a Socialist flavour: *The House of the Wolfings* (1888) and *The Roots of the Mountains* (1889). All have scenes of revolt against assorted oppressors from the Romans to the bourgeois-backed police and soldiers who broke the Paris Commune of 1870. For Morris Socialism meant the practice of handicraft or other creative labour, with free choice of work as its industrial qualification, 'equality of condition as its economic goal, and the habitual love of humanity as its rule of ethics.' (Letter from Morris to the Reverend Mr George Bainton, 2 April, 1888). In spite of this 'love of humanity' and his often expressed aversion to bloodshed, Morris seems to have despaired, especially from 1885 to 1890, of getting what he wanted by peaceful agitation. The more desperately he longed for an arts and crafts Utopia, the more necessary it seemed to destroy the present industrial and commercial system root and branch. This meant revolution, including perhaps the destruction of the arts themselves as then practised, though 'not necessarily . . . a change accompanied by riot and all kinds of violence . . . by a group of men who have somehow managed to seize on the executive power for the moment.' ('How We Live and How We Might Live,' in *Signs of Change*, 1885) Elsewhere he says that 'the hope in me has been that matters would mend gradually, till the last struggle, which needs must be mingled with violence, would be so short as scarcely to count.' (Letter of c. 1882 quoted in Mackail II, 25) Neither of these statements was calculated to reassure the timid, even when he added, as a note of hope, that 'Destruction is, alas! one of the forms of growth.' ('Architecture and History,' 1884, in *Lectures on Art and Industry*, XXII, 299) Morris seems to be declaring his allegiance to a war *à l'outrance* but not one *à la Marx*. He says far too much about the purpose of the struggle and has far too specific a vision of the end result for Marx's taste: the fellowship of workers, the handicraft happiness everywhere, the four-hour day allowing every man eight hours for his chosen work, the rebirth of art through the creation of lovely things. Did Marx and Engels hang back from particularising the triumphs of communism because they would not face the question of whether the changes they preached could produce true creativity? This question they never answered.

Some years ago K. Litzenberg in an essay called 'The Social Philosophy of William Morris and the Doom of the Gods' (*Essays . . . by Members of the English Department of the University of Michigan*, 1933) suggested that a more likely source for Morris's concept of destruction and rebirth other than the Marxist dialectic might be the *Ragna Rök* of the Icelandic Eddas. These words can be translated as the Gods' Dusk or Twilight or Doom. The fearful battle of Odin, Thor, Heimdall *et al* against Loki, the Fenris Wolf and the Midgard Serpent in which each side destroyed the other, marks only a token 'end of all things'. Rather, it prepares a Great Change to happy days for a race reborn – 'an end for-ever of all who were once afraid' (*Sigurd the Volsung*, Bk. I) and a last-ing 'epoch of peace' and spontaneous prosperity under the governance of Baldur the Bright. This god, slain by mischance, will return from Hell to an earth 'all green,' with the troubles of mankind healed at last. According to Morris the old gods had to perish for they had made a 'strifeful, imperfect earth, not blindly indeed, yet foredoomed.' Though they did what they could to remedy the dread and misery they had allowed to brood over life,

at last the great destruction breaks over all things, and the old earth and heavens are gone, and then a new heavens and earth. What goes on there? Who shall say, of us who know only of rest and peace by toil and strife? And what shall be our share in it? Well, sometimes we must needs think that we shall live again : yet if that were not, would it not be enough that we helped to make this unnameable glory and lived not altogether deedless? This seems to me pretty much the religion of the Northmen. I think one would be a happy man if one could hold it, in spite of the wild dreams and dreadful imaginings that hung about it here and there.

(Quoted in Mackail I, 334)

Mackail called these lines Morris's summary of Northern Mythology, and indeed this Doom of the imperfect Old Gods, accomplished 'at a stroke' and immediately followed by a Great Change, a Fresh Dispensation, a New Earth, seems a more likely source for Morris's 'revolution' than Marx's insistence on destroying the 'civilised world' in order to guarantee nothing more specific than the possibility of a condition of life which would allow improvement! In *News from Nowhere* we have Morris's fullest account of how the Change came about, but the transition is so swift that we have entered into an 'unnameable glory' of arts and crafts, of happy workmen in garden cities, before we know or can discover what happened.

Nevertheless, Morris frequently boiled violently against the entrenched injustice and encroaching ugliness of the industrial system and felt it must be wiped from the earth. Sometimes he called for the use of *force majeur*, but he found so much indifference and apathy among the tens of socialists and thousands of workmen of his time that he was driven to captain fictional campaigns against the oppressors. But his Socialist poems, stories and romances did more than satisfy his desire to exhibit the often really clever battle-strategies of Morris as 'lost leader.' They contained some of his profoundest thoughts on Socialism: the reasons for its set-backs, conditions needed for successful co-operation, visions of the future to be won. At the same time they had the effect of moving ideas from the hazy field of speculation into the exciting arena of fact.

The Pilgrims of Hope (1885–1886) is a poem in thirteen parts which brings a country-bred husband and wife to London and finally to Paris, not to enable the pair to escape Marx's 'idiocy of rural life,' but to cheer depressed people by sharing with them their sense of earth's fruitful promise to all. They have heard of 'the growing' hope of the proletariat which bids them,

> 'Rise up on the morrow
> And go on your ways toward the doubt and the strife;
> Join hope to our hope and blend sorrow with sorrow
> And seek for men's love in the short days of life.'
>
> (XXIV, 371)

But they awake the morning after leaving the country to find themselves trapped like animals among the pitiless-faced houses of London:

> My heart sank; I murmured, 'What's this we are doing
> In this grim net of London, this prison built stark
> With the greed of the ages, our young lives pursuing
> A phantom that leads but to death in the dark?'
>
> (372)

However frightened and shaken in hope, they decide to do what they can to ensure the 'rights of the wretched, the days of the poor.' The first London pageantry that greets them is a parade of soldiers bound for a far-off war, but their eyes are riveted in horror by 'the London holiday throng':

> Dull and with hang-dog gait they stood or shuffled along,
> While the stench from the lairs they had lain in last
>   night went up in the wind,
> And poisoned the sun-lit spring: no story men can find
> Is fit for the tale of their lives; no word that man
>   hath made
> Can tell the hue of their faces, or their rags by
>   filth o'er-laid:
> For this hath our age invented – these are the sons
>   of the free,
> Who shall bear our name triumphant o'er every land
>   and sea.
> Read ye their souls in their faces, and what shall
>   help you there?

Joyless, hopeless, shameless, angerless, set is
                                 their stare.

                    *   *   *

Sick unto death was my hope, and I turned and looked
                                 on my dear,
And beheld her frightened wonder, and her grief
                                 without a tear . . .

                                                        (375)

They are then comforted when they go to a 'Radical spouting-place'
and hear a talk about a future people's army bringing a dawn of peace
and joy to a tortured world.

Some thirty men we were of the kind that I knew full well,
Listless, rubbed down to the type of our easy-going hell.
My heart sank down as I entered, and wearily there I sat
While the chairman strove to end his maunder of this
                                 and of that.
And partly shy he seemed, and partly indeed ashamed
Of the grizzled man beside him as his name to us he named.
He rose, thickset and short, and dressed in shabby blue,
And even as he began it seemed as though I knew
The thing he was going to say, though I never heard
                                 it before.
He spoke, were it well, were it ill, as though a message
                                 he bore,
A word that he could not refrain from many a million of men.
Nor aught seemed the sordid room and the few that were
                                 listening then
Save the ball of the labouring earth and the world which
                                 was to be.
Bitter to many the message, but sweet indeed unto me,
Of man without a master, and earth without a strife,
And every soul rejoicing in the sweet and bitter of
                                 life:
Of peace and good-will he told, and I knew that in
                                 faith he spake,
But his words were my very thoughts, and I saw the
                                 battle awake,
And I followed from end to end; and triumph grew in
                                 my heart
As he called on each that heard him to arise and
                                 play his part
In the tale of the new-told gospel, lest as slaves
                                 they should live and die.

                                                        (383)

Becoming a Communist agitator himself, the narrator loses his London job and is thrown into prison, but later, out of prison, makes a convert when he gives a speech on 'The Great Revolution in France.' This new friend gets his message but steals his wife. All three, however, go to Paris to fight for the Commune of 1870, where they find Socialism 'real, solid and at hand.' It seemed to the narrator that here the promise made him by earth when he was a country lad had at last been kept:

> O earth, thou kind bestower, thou ancient fruitful place,
> How lovely and beloved now gleams thy happy face!

(403)

But he speaks too soon, for when flesh and blood are pitted against 'the modern war machine,' his wife and friend are killed on the barricades and he is badly wounded. He recovers and finally with his young son (born when he and his wife were in London), returns to his native English village. There he will bring up the boy strong in body and mind, and teach him to be a Socialist. By the time he was forced out of the Socialist League (1890), Morris had decided that the best activity for all Socialist groups was 'to make Socialists,' educating them in Morris's theory and practice of handicrafts. And the best environment for such education was rural communities where people had access to Earth the Healer, Earth the Keeper.

In Paris the strayed English sympathisers had been able to do little to forward Socialism except to die. At home the mass of the people, poor, lethargic, untaught, could not be relied on to promote the Cause by widespread organisation or shows of solidarity, as Morris had seen in the 'Black Monday' demonstration of the unemployed in Trafalgar Square on 8 February, 1886. Country-bred Englishmen had made their collective power felt against thievish slavers more effectively in the days of a poor 'hedge-priest' of the Middle Ages, whom Morris now proceeded to celebrate in a thoughtful story for *Commonweal* called *A Dream of John Ball*. Many elements of Morris's *Oxford and Cambridge Magazine* and *Earthly Paradise* stories begin to crop up again in this tale. Throughout his writing from now on, and especially in the romances of the '90s, certain themes will receive greater prominence; for example, scenic mandalas spread about architectural temenoi or sacred centres, armed struggles against organised evil, and small blond heroines with grey eyes who are tortured by tall dark witches but are bright enough to preserve themselves for the arms of the conquering hero.

John Ball opens with three pages of architectural dreaming:

Sometimes I am rewarded for fretting myself so much about present matters by a quite unasked-for pleasant dream. I mean when I am asleep. This dream is as it were a present of an architectural peep-show. I see some beautiful and noble building new made, as it were for the occasion, as clearly as if I were awake; not vaguely or absurdly, as often happens in dreams, but with all the detail clear and reasonable. Some Elizabethan house with its scrap of earlier fourteenth-century building, and its later degradations of Queen Anne and Silly Billy and Victoria, marring but not destroying it, in an old village once a clearing amid the sandy woodlands of Sussex ... Or sometimes 'tis a splendid collegiate church, untouched by restoring parson and architect, standing amid an island of shapely trees and flower-beset cottages of thatched grey stone and cob, amidst the narrow stretch of bright green water-meadows that wind between the sweeping Wiltshire downs, so well beloved of William Cobbett. Or some new-seen and yet familiar cluster of houses in a grey village of the upper Thames over-topped by the delicate tracery of a fourteenth-century church ...

(Ch. I)

These architectural visions of the night lead to a delightful dream of a recently built medieval town with its new cherub-spire, dazzling white, '... a certain unwonted trimness and handiness about the enclosures of the garden and orchards, puzzled ...' On the houses around the church was 'much curious and inventive carving,' deft, neat, even beautiful. 'Half a stone's throw from the east end of the churchyard wall was a tall cross of stone, new like the church, the head beautifully carved with a crucifix amidst leafage.'

Round this cross soon gathered a great press of villagers and armed men to listen to a sermon by John Ball urging them to resist the renewed enslavement threatened that very day by the local lords and their mercenaries. God wills, he says, that all shall be happy here as well as hereafter.

'Forsooth, ye have heard it said that ye shall do well in this world that in the world to come ye may live happily for ever; do ye well then, and have your reward both on earth and in heaven; for I say to you that earth and heaven are not two but one ... Forsooth, brothers, fellowship is in heaven, and lack of fellowship is hell: fellowship is life, and lack of fellowship is death: and the deeds that ye do upon the earth, it is for fellowship's sake that ye do them, and the life that is in it, that shall live on and on for ever, and each one of you part of it, while many a man's life upon the earth from the earth shall wane.

'Therefore, I bid you not dwell in hell but in heaven, or while ye must, upon earth, which is part of heaven, and forsooth no foul part.'

(Ch. IV)

This pre-battle sermon leads our dreamer to ponder the beauty of the priest's concept of Paradise reaching from earth to heaven and back, rooted in the indissoluble fellowship of self-respecting men and God-guided saints and angels. At the same time, as a modern man, the dreamer cannot help remembering how men fight and lose the battle, and the thing that they fought for comes about in spite of their defeat, and when it comes turns out not to be what they meant, and other men have to fight for what they meant under another name . . .

(Ch. IV)

However, the 'rascal hedge-priest,' on his way to death in London, seems to foresee such a failure and has an answer:

'Yea, forsooth, once again I saw as of old, the great treading down the little, and the strong beating down the weak, and cruel men fearing not, and kind men daring not, and wise men caring not; and the saints in heaven forbearing and yet bidding me not to forbear; forsooth, I knew once more that he who doeth well in fellowship, and because of fellowship, shall not fail though he seem to fail today, but in days hereafter shall he and his work yet be alive, and men be holpen by them to strive again and yet again; and yet indeed even that was little, since, forsooth, to strive was my pleasure and my life.'

(Ch. IV)

After the townsmen have won a pitched battle against the lords who were trying to bring their necks under the yoke of villeinage, John Ball and the dreamer take a meal with Will Green, a yeoman whose terrible long-bow was 'reckoned to kill through cloth and leather at five hundred yards.' He had played a large part in the victory. They eat in a strangely beautiful room furnished with a stout oak table and a quaintly carved sideboard covered with shining pewter pots and earthen bowls. The salt-cellar of Fellowship seems to be the sacred centre of a mandala-like room whose walls

were hung with a coarse loosely-woven stuff of green worsted with birds and trees woven into it. There were flowers in plenty stuck about the room, mostly of the yellow blossoming flag or flower-de-luce, . . . and the table was all set forth with meat and drink, a big salt-cellar of pewter in the middle, covered with a white cloth.

(Ch. VIII)

Here there is talk of the march to be made on London and the future of the Fellowship. That night the priest and the dreamer continue the discussion standing in another mandalic interior – inside the church with the new spire.

We entered the church through the south porch under a round-arched door carved very richly, and with a sculpture over the doorway and under the arch, which, as far as I could see by the moonlight, figured St. Michael and the Dragon.

(Ch. IX)

The nave was lighted only by moonlight, but the dreamer

could see all the work on the great screen between the nave and the chancel which glittered bright in new paint and gilding: a candle glimmered in the loft above it, before the huge rood that filled up the whole space between the loft and the chancel-arch.

(Ch. IX)

Except for a few oak benches, nicely carved and moulded,

the floor of the nave, which was paved with a quaint pavement of glazed tiles, was quite clear, and the shafts of the arches rose out of it white and beautiful under the moon as though out of a sea, dark but with gleams over it.

The priest let me linger and look around, . . . and then I saw that the walls were figured all over with stories, a huge St. Christopher with his black beard looking like Will Green, being close to the porch by which we entered, and above the chancel arch the Doom of the Last Day, in which the painter had not spared either kings or bishops, and in which a lawyer with his blue coif was one of the chief figures in the group which the Devil was hauling off to hell.

(Ch. IX)

John takes the dreamer into the chancel, lighted chiefly by a lamp which 'burned on the high altar before the host, and looked red and strange in the moonlight that came through the wide traceried windows unstained by the pictures and beflowerings of the glazing.' Everywhere was 'rich and fair colour and delicate and dainty form,' and here the dreamer from the nineteenth century is forced to tell the priest, in answer to his questions, that the revolt of 1381 will fail after initial success because his brave but unschooled followers will not know what to do with their victory. However, villeinage will slip from the hands of the nobles ' "till there be, and not long after ye are dead, but few unfree men in England; so that your lives and your deaths both shall bear fruit." ' (Ch. X)

However, the dreamer from Hammersmith has to tell John that days worse for England's poor than those of villeinage will follow – days when men shall be free but free only to sell their bodies to machines which will quickly wear out both body and soul for the enrichment of the already rich. In fact, it will be five or six hundred years before anything like John's Fellowship of men, saints and angels engaged in works of love will be realized on earth. John thinks that this future fiendish slavery will end in a revolt like his own, and this time the revolt will be successful because of the tremendous increase in the numbers of workmen. The Morris-persona is persuaded to agree because not just a husband and wife as in *The Pilgrims of Hope*, not just the Comrades of 1870, not just the Fellowship of four English counties as in this dream, will be on the march, but the whole English working class, now educated for Socialism. Meantime he and John have held a fascinating dialogue on the meaning of death, in which the dreamer concluded 'that though I die and end, yet mankind yet liveth, therefore I end not, since I am a man; and even so thou deemest, good friend; or at the least even so thou doest, since now thou art ready to die in grief and torment rather than be unfaithful to the Fellowship . . .'

(Ch. IX)

It is significant that Morris had to go back in time to find an illustration of his idea that when men live as members of a society of man which survives through every oppression and catastrophe, '. . . the individual somehow lives always in the undying collectivity.' The priest's visitor from the sceptical nineteenth century says he cannot imagine death but as 'living in some new way.'

In *The House of the Wolfings* (1888) we have 'Socialism' founded not on Comradeship or Fellowship but on Kindredship, an early form of relation in which men of the same tribe find it hard to distinguish themselves from each other or from the animals among whom they live and from whom they often claim descent, on the male side at least, as with the Wolfings, the Bearings, the Hartings, and the Elkings of this tale. There are also divisions of the Kindred of the Mark who display boars, snakes, hawks, salmon and trees on their banners. Some of Morris's ideas about the exogamy and totemic organisation of the Goths he describes may have been found in a book by Engels, published in 1883, called *The Mark*. It was intended to teach workingmen how the system of private property developed replacing 'the old common property of all free men.' The full title of Morris's book, *The House of the Wolfings and All the Kindreds of the Mark*, is an indication of the theme: 'kindreds' holding common property which they are willing to defend with their lives. Among the people of Mirkwood 'collective ownership of the means of production' is not a slogan but an everyday fact. While moving back in time – the story tells of a successful attempt by the Goths to resist the Roman yoke in the latter days of the Empire – the story moves ahead of *The Pilgrims of Hope* and *John Ball* by involving greater numbers of people – in a psychologically profounder way – in the struggle for freedom to live communally and do self-chosen work to satisfy each other's genuine needs.

Here the mandalic imagery becomes truly impressive. All branches of the kindreds, or as many as possible, lived under one roof in what was called the House of the group, 'and had herein the place and dignity; nor were there many degrees amongst them as hath befallen afterwards, but all they of one blood were brethren and of equal dignity.' (XIV, 5) A few thralls, usually spoils of war, were lodged in cots about the House, but were often adopted through a system of rites into blood-kinship. The word 'House' in the title must be taken quite literally and is described as very high, long and handsome, 'not built of stone and lime but framed from the goodliest trees of the wild wood squared with the adze, and betwixt the framing filled with clay wattled with reeds.'

As to the house within, two rows of pillars went down it endlong, fashioned of the mightiest trees that might be found, and each one fairly wrought with base and chapiter, and wreaths and knots, and fighting men and dragons; so that it was like a church of later days that has a nave and aisles; windows there were above the aisles . . .

(XIV, 6)

The folk slept in these aisles warmed in winter by three great hearths spaced out along the nave under the pierced crown of the roof from the man's door 'anigh the gable' at one end of the enormous hall to the women's door at the other end. Near the man's door was a dais in front of which was

the noblest and greatest of the hearths; . . . and round about the dais, along the gable-wall, and hung from pillar to pillar were woven cloths pictured with images of ancient tales and deeds of the Wolfings, and the deeds of the Gods from whence they came. And this was the fairest place of all the house and the best-beloved of the folk . . .

(XIV, 7)

The dais indicated the sacred centre, which was more specifically marked by a lamp:

over the dais there hung by chains and pulleys fastened to a tie-beam of the roof high aloft a wondrous lamp fashioned of glass; yet of no such glass as the folk made then and there, but of a fair and clear green like an emerald, and all done with figures and knots in gold, and strange beasts, and a warrior slaying a dragon, and the sun rising on the earth: nor did any tale tell whence this lamp came, but it was held as an ancient and holy thing by all the Markmen, and the kindred of the Wolf had it in charge to keep a light burning in it night and day for ever; and they appointed a maiden of their own kindred to that office . . .

This lamp which burned ever was called the Hall-Sun, and the woman who had charge of it, and who was the fairest that might be found was called after it the Hall-Sun also.

(XIV, 7–8)

The Hall or House, often spoken of as 'a God,' the symbol of majestic deeds and domestic joys – of all that the Folk could conceive of as sacred – dominates the story.

The narrative itself is simple enough. Thiodolf, the war-duke of the Wolfings, whose hall-seat is the chair on the dais, has been for years the lover of a beautiful forest-dweller, 'a daughter of the Gods' and 'a Chooser of the Slain' – a Valkyr like Brunhild. Her name is Wood-Sun and by Thiodolf she has had a daughter, the present prophetess Hall-Sun. On the eve of the Roman attack on the Markmen, both Hall-Sun and her mother feel that Thiodolf will be killed. Wood-Sun persuades him to wear a magic hauberk made by the dwarfs which will make him invulnerable. Alas, the armour will not make him or his followers invincible, and he foresees that ' "this mail is for the ransom of a man and the ruin of a folk." ' However, Wood-Sun persuades him to wear it by expressing the intensity of her love and by revealing to him that he was not born a Wolfing nor had he been formally adopted into the tribe. Nevertheless, he has always felt great solidarity with this people (as Morris with his workmen?) and is so intensely distressed to feel, when encased in the magic armour, that he ' "loved them not and was not of them …" ' that he throws it away. When Wood-Sun asks, ' "If thou diest today, where then shall our love be?" ' he immediately replies, ' "It shall abide with the soul of the Wolfings." ' This oversoul will endure forever, and those who have lived and died as parts of the whole will be 'ever reborn and yet reborn,' remaining part of the eternal soul. This idea of immortality, the most interesting by-product of Morris's growing impatience with Socialism, is founded on 'the melting of the individual into the society of the tribes' (Letters, 302) One result of this joining together is the unanimity achieved in democratic debate. Morris lovingly describes a debate at the early medieval Folk-Thing held in the Doom Ring – another mandalic configuration. He felt that this kind of debate was the only satisfactory way to reach a decision which would be acted upon with the full co-operation of everyone (as opposed to the endlessly derisive Socialist debates). Discussions at the Folk-Thing were conducted with a serious sense of purpose and dignity, qualities which Morris so desperately missed in the squabbles of the Social Democratic Federation and of the Socialist League. No wonder the Mark-men repulsed the Romans so decisively. They protected their sacred House with the magic green lantern from fire and crushed the would-be enslavers and exploiters. If the Socialists ever expected to get anywhere, they must look back to these primitive gleams of solidarity, bravery, beauty and justice. Morris summed up the purpose of *The Wolfings* in the poem he wrote for the book's title-page:

> Whiles in the early winter eve
> We pass amid the gathering night
> Some homestead that we had to leave
> Years past; and see its candles bright
> Shine in the room beside the door
> Where we were merry years agone
> But now must never enter more,
> As still the dark road drives us on.

E'en so the world of men may turn
At even of some hurried day
And see the ancient glimmer burn,
Across the waste that hath no way;
Then with that faint light in its eyes
A while I bid it linger near
And nurse in wavering memories
The bitter-sweet of days that were.

As soon as he had finished *The House of the Wolfings* Morris began a much longer novel called *The Roots of the Mountains* in which he re-played all the themes of *The Wolfings* but with great elaboration. The idyllic woodland life is now supplemented by agricultural, pastoral and craft activities. Co-operative democracy is still practised at the Folk-Thing on the Speech-mound located at the centre of a Doom-ring of monoliths. The fiend-like cruelty of the enslaving foreigners (Huns?) is elaborated and there are many architectural symbols. Now for the first time in these Socialist tales, Morris appears as the war-leader who saves the Folk by brilliant battle strategems which involve him in love affairs with three beautiful women at the same time – a complication which points ahead to the 'romances' written after *News from Nowhere* (1890). The Great House of *The Roots* stands in Burgstead, a kind of early-medieval arts and crafts centre where the homes are

all built fairly of stone and lime, with much fair and curious carved work of knots and beasts and men round about the doors; or whiles a wale of such-like work all along the house-front. For as deft as were the Woodlanders with knife and gouge on the oaken beams, even so deft were the Dalesmen with mallet and chisel on the face of the hewn stone; and this was a great pastime about the Thorp. . . . and facing east was the biggest house of the Thorp . . . Its door-posts and the lintel of the door were carved with knots and twining stems fairer than other houses of that stead; and on the wall beside the door carved over many stones was an image wrought in the likeness of a man with a wide face, which was terrible to behold, although it smiled: he bore a bent bow in his hand with an arrow fitted to its string, and about the head of him was a ring of rays like the beams of the sun, and at his feet was a dragon, which had crept, as it were, from amidst of the blossomed knots of the door-post wherewith the tail of him was yet entwined. And this head with the ring of rays about it was wrought into the adornment of that house, both within and without, in many other places, but on never another house of the Dale; and it was called the House of the Face.

(XV, 8–9)

This is the home of Face-of-God, our Morrisian saviour-hero. When the story begins he is betrothed to a girl called, prematurely, 'Bride.' However, she cannot awake him to the full sense of life, bravery and creative leadership he needs, and he goes wandering off among the mountains which overhang the 'fair and lovely' Dale which, so far, has seemed 'the Blessing of the Earth.' (11) Longing for he knows not what, Face-of-God finds it in a mountain-woman as awesomely beautiful as a goddess or as 'the fairest and the noblest of all the Queens of ancient story.' (39) Though not so impressive as the House of the Face, her home (like Queen Elizabeth's Lodge at Chingford in Morris's boyhood) is 'dight very fairly with broidered cloths.'

The hangings on the walls, though they left some places bare which were hung with fresh boughs, were fairer than any he had ever seen, so that he deemed they must come from far countries and the City of Cities: therein were images wrought of warriors and fair women of old time and their dealings with the Gods and the Giants, and Wondrous Wights; and he deemed that this was the story of some great kindred, and that their token and the sign of their banner must needs be the Wood-wolf, for everywhere was it wrought in these pictured webs.

(40)

We know from this sacred-centre décor that Face-of-God has found what he needs in its *anima loci*, the girl who 'was to him as if one of the Ladies of the Heavenly Burg' – a Valkyr from Valhalla. She was also called, anticlimactically, Sun-beam. However, at this very moment the third heroine enters the sacred centre '. . . of some five-and-twenty winters, trimly and strongly built; short-skirted she was and clad as a hunter, with a bow in her hand and a quiver at her back . . .' (41) This is Bow-may, the greatest archer of these descendants of the old House of the Wolfings. Even on snow-shoes, she goes 'lightly and scantily clad, as one who heeds not the weather, or deems all months midsummer.'

The Wolves have been driven from their home in Silverdale high into the mountains above Burgdale by a savagely cruel invading race of Dusky Men. The goddess-like Mountain-woman and Bow-may, her close kin, have decided to ask Face-of-God to lead them and the Dalemen against these Turks or Huns before it is too late. Bow-may protects her chosen leader at all times and in the last great battle saves his life. Now and again she augments her services as messenger from the Mountain-woman to the hero;

she turned about to him and took his head between her hands, and kissed him well favouredly both cheeks and mouth; and she laughed, albeit the tears stood in her eyes as she said: 'Now smelleth the wood sweeter, and summer will come back again. And even thus will I do once more when we stand side by side in battle array.'

(XV, 83–4)

In contrast to *The Wolfings*, which took place in a vague period before dyeing became common, *The Roots of the Mountains* contains several gorgeous descriptions, often called Pre-Raphaelite, of colourfully dressed or half-dressed women similar to those Morris described in *The Earthly Paradise*. Face-of-God's calf-love, the Bride, is, like Sun-beam and Bow-may, something of a soldier in the old Germanic tradition, but I imagine Morris found little in that tradition to justify the following elaborate picture:

> But just as the Alderman was on the point of rising to declare the breaking-up of the Thing, there came a stir in the throng and it opened, and a warrior came forth into the innermost of the ring of men, arrayed in goodly glittering war-gear; clad in such wise that a tunicle of precious gold-wrought web covered the hauberk all but the sleeves thereof, and the hem of it beset with blue mountain-stones smote against the ankles and well-nigh touched the feet, shod with sandals gold-embroidered and gemmed. This warrior bore a goodly gilded helm on the head, and held in hand a spear with gold-garlanded shaft, and was girt with a sword whose hilts and scabbard both were adorned with gold and gems: beardless, smooth-cheeked, exceeding fair of face was the warrior, but pale and somewhat haggard-eyed: and those who were nearby beheld and wondered; for they saw that there was come the Bride arrayed for war and battle, as if she were a messenger from the House of the Gods, and the Burg that endureth for ever.
>
> (178)

The Dusky Men, who were 'pure evil,' are totally destroyed in a great fire devised by Face-of-God – his most brilliant stratagem. After their destruction there is a 'Brides of Burgstead' celebration, which Morris obviously enjoys. Seventeen brides from the Burg including Sun-beam, with others coming from up and down the vale, are all armed to prevent men from carrying on their business for a day – in memory, perhaps of an early era of militant Amazons who kept men in their place. Sun-beam bears only a sword called Dale-warden, 'girt to her side by a girdle fair-wrought of golden wire,' but some of the other brides are more elaborately and elegantly armed. They remind one of the Illustrious Women who were to guard William Morris from evil at Red House, just as Bow-may defended Face-of-God with her peerless archery.

Forsooth they were a lovely sight to look on, for no fairer women might be seen in the world; and the eldest of them was scant of five and twenty winters. Every maiden was clad in as goodly raiment as she might compass; their sleeves and gown-hems and girdles, yea, their very shoes and sandals were embroidered so fairly and closely that as they shifted in the sun they changed colour like the king-fisher shooting from shadow to sunshine. According to due custom every maiden bore some weapon. A few had bows in their hands and quivers at their backs; some had nought but a sword girt to their sides; some bore slender-shafted spears, so as not to overburden their shapely hands; but to some it seemed a merry game to carry long and heavy thrust-spears, or to bear war-axes over their shoulders. Most had their flowing hair coifed with bright helms;

some had burdened their arms with shields; some bore steel hauberks over their linen smocks: almost all had some piece of war-gear on their bodies; and one, to wit, Steed-linden of the Sickle, a tall and fair damsel, was so arrayed that no garment could be seen on her but bright steel war-gear.

(398–9)

Besides the imaginary liquidation of the oppressor-class in a fearsome battle, there is little of Socialist interest except the ever-widening solidarity from Comradeship through Fellowship and Kindredship to what we have here: a union of many kindreds, 'the men of Burgdale and the Sheepcotes, and the Children of the Wolf and the Woodlanders,' into 'one Folk, for better or worse, in peace and in war, in waning and waxing . . .' (411) All men of goodwill, (as is indicated in the title, *The Roots of the Mountains, Wherein Is Told Somewhat of the Lives of the Men of Burgdale, Their Friends, Their Neighbours . . . and Their Fellows in Arms*) can band together to pulverise exploiters, who take 'no delight save in beholding torments and misery,' and in whose enthralled peons Face-of-God sees all the 'Sorrow of the Earth.' After that 'all days shall be good and all years.' As in *The Wolfings* Morris prefaces this novel with a poem intended to recall an old way of life. Those who suffer from industrialism may wish to think about it and perhaps use certain aspects to change their own lives. The poem is really about an 'Epoch of Rest' beyond price but not beyond recovery. The past history of man is not any more hopelessly lost than each man's own past; we can find in both a quality of country peace connected with a grey old house set in a garden close which is surrounded by an orchard encircled by a meadow, all edged about by a river or forest. An earlier version of the poem in *The Roots* is given by May Morris (XV, xxxi–ii):

> Bright morn, and on the iron road
> You hurry past some fair abode . . .
> And all is there – and all is gone.
> But as it goes how fain were I
> To be afoot and saunter by
> The field and homestead! and turn back
> And take the sun-burnt stile-barred track
> Unto the water meadow green
> Whereof e'en now a glimpse was seen
> To tell us of the river's way
> Betwixt the willows wind-blown grey;
> E'en thus-wise have I tried to do
> Within these leaves I give to you.
> I saw a thing and deemed it fair
> And longed that it might tarry there
> And therewithal with words I wrought
> To make it something more than nought.

Kelmscott seems to be the centre of this numinous mandalic experience as Red House was in *The Wolfings*. Both of his beloved dwellings, or the mere thought of them, quickly carried Morris into an imaginary past so clear to his mind's eye that he could extrapolate from it the outlines of a good future for mankind. In his Socialist poems and tales one notices an ever-widening conception of the numbers of people involved – Comradeship, Fellowship, Kindredship, Folkship. The Socialism suggested in *News from Nowhere* is world-wide.

By 1890 Morris had fought many imaginary battles against cruelty and exploitation in *The Pilgrims of Hope, John Ball, The Wolfings*, and *The Roots*. At the same time he had given dozens of outdoor lectures, often to tiny and uncomprehending groups in the industrial towns and cities of England and Scotland, trying to explain to workingmen the theoretical origin (Marxist) and the real cure (Morrisian) of their plight. It has often been said that his death in 1896 at the age of sixty-two was brought on by overexposure to the heart-breaking ugliness of workers' hovels and the health-breaking vagaries of British weather. There may be considerable truth in this for he died of diabetes, which could have been aggravated during the '80s by the shocks of wind, rain, cold, irregular diet and apathetic or hectoring audiences which reduced him to almost insupportable periods of exhaustion. Socialist and Communist groups today often extol his political lectures (few when compared to those on house décor) far above anything else he ever wrote, but Morris knew better. When he wrote the closing scene of *The Roots*, in which the hero leads his bride home through the mandalic scenery surrounding the House of the Face, he knew, as he wrote to Jenny in October 1889, that I 'must have a story to write now as long as I live' (XV, xii) and that these stories probably would be his most considerable literary achievement. Surely they would be his best succour during years of ill health, no matter how much congenial designing and production of lovely editions at the Kelmscott Press he could manage.

In the passage below Morris describes Face-of-God and his bride Sunbeam walking from the diamond perimeter of a scenic mandala to the sacred centre – home. This fantasy is typical of those which sustained Morris during his last years.

'But hearken, my sweet! . . . we shall sit down for a minute on a bank under the chestnut trees, and thence watch the moon coming up over the southern cliffs. And I shall behold thee in the summernight, and deem that I see all thy beauty; which yet shall make me dumb with wonder when I see it indeed in the house amongst the candles.'

'O nay,' she said. . . .

Spake Face-of-God: 'Then shall we rise up and wend first through a wide treeless meadow, wherein amidst the night we shall behold the kine moving about like odorous shadows; and through the greyness of the moonlight thou shalt deem that thou seest the pink colour of the eglantine blossoms, so fragrant they are.'

'O nay,' she said. . . .

But he said: 'Then from the wide meadow come we into a close of corn, and then into an orchard-close beyond it. . . .

'Short is the way across it to the brim of the Weltering Water, . . . that shall be like wavering flames of white fire where the moon smites . . . There then shall we be in the garden, beholding how the hall-windows are yellow, and hearkening the sound of the hall-glee borne across the flowers and blending with the voice of the nightingales in the trees. There then shall we go along the grass paths whereby the pinks and the cloves and the lavender are sending forth their fragrance, to cheer us, who faint at the scent of the over-worn roses, and the honey-sweetness of the lilies. . . .

'But lo! at last at the garden's end is the yew-walk arched over for thee, and thou canst not see whereby to enter it; but I, I know it, and I lead thee into and along the dark tunnel through the moonlight, and thine hand is not weary of mine as we go. But at the end shall we come to a wicket, which shall bring us out by the gable-end of the Hall of the Face. Turn we about its corner then, and there are we blinking on the torches of the torch-bearers, and the candles through the open door, and the hall ablaze with light and full of joyous clamour, like the bale-fire in the dark night kindled on a ness above the sea by fisher-folk remembering the Gods.'

(403-4)

This moonlit journey through encompassing trees, waters, orchards and gardens to the gleaming centre is one of the best literary mandalas ever written, worthy to stand beside the military forest and flowers and Red Sea with which Marvell surrounded Appleton House.

Clearly Morris, defeated, as he thought, in his efforts to propagate Socialism in real life, succeeded brilliantly on the imaginative level in abolishing slavery, turning people of every class and way of life into a single Folk, cementing this solidarity by mutual aid, constructing the beginnings of a state for the fun of watching it wither away, and getting from the people the best they had to give without building a bureaucracy. But Morris enjoyed a still greater victory among the valleys and mountains of Burgdale. In fact, he discovered a miracle: that the elements of one's personal experience, however unsatisfying, can be rearranged and introduced into dozens of solidly gratifying new lives. The creative artist can live vividly even when confined to his bed so long as the tale of deep love and high deeds goes on unfolding. Never again without a story to write 'as long as I live' – and 'I do not intend to hurry it.' (XV, xii) He had done all he could for Socialism; now, as he felt the years closing in, he must do what he could for William Morris. His last romances, composed between 1890 and his death, have been acclaimed as the crown of his work as a writer.

XI Paradise at the World's End: Therapeutic Dreaming in the Last Years

Almost from birth, Morris had been seeking like everyone, that 'joy! O Lady, joy, by which we live.' He differed from most people however, in possessing an extraordinary capacity for both alarm and hope, vexation and solace, strain and rest. Ugliness worried him sick; beauty brought him back to health. Depression was almost chronic, but was balanced by equally chronic high spirits. From early youth his chief problem – and his chief success – was to devise stratagems for fighting fear, neutralising disappointment, allaying high-strung restlessness. As a boy he instinctively sought therapy by Scott's novels; resting his pony in the hornbeam-circled glades of Epping Forest; wondering at the tapestried walls of Elizabeth's Hunting Lodge at Chingford; boating, swimming and fishing around the enchanted island in the grounds of Water House; steeping himself in 'the sad lowland country' around the river Lea; wandering among the great stone circles of Avebury; finding out all he could about architecture at Marlborough while pilgrimaging to old churches. He found that all these activities stilled his perpetual fidgets and bolstered his uncertain self-confidence. They filled his mind with never-to-be-forgotten shapes of quiet beauty which he could arrange and rearrange into pictures that seldom failed to soothe and heal – and stimulate. The cloistered walks of New College, the Thames, the cathedrals and fields of northern France with the grain growing around fruit trees and mingling with 'purple thistles and blue corn-flowers and red poppies' (*Letters*, 12) – all gave him material he could use to construct Earthly Paradises. Marvellously, Morris found he could master skill after skill which would turn houses into sacred temenoi. In his poetry he created concentric circles of forest, water, orchard and garden around the sacred house at the centre. These mandalic configurations resembled the *pairidaēzas* of ancient Persian monarchs or the royal *chateaux* of the Loire valley described in Scott's novels. Thus Morris could arrange the world in structures that beautifully symbolised protection, equipoise, peace – the peace that passeth understanding. To be able to find, create or imagine such paradisal effects is to build Eden on earth and summon from the depths of unconscious desire an Eve, a White Goddess, the *anima loci*, to perform her dance of life in the sacred centre on a golden flower which is really the heart of the artist. If, on the realistic level, the dancer falls short of her function, all is not lost. New structures can be found or created, new goddesses summoned to ascend. If all prove futile, the whole operation may be conducted with considerable satisfaction on the level of dream and art. This is what Morris did when creating his last paradises in the long prose romances. (See Plate 7.)

The Red House complex was Morris's first mandala, with a beautiful but sluggish dancer at its heart. When Morris had to leave Red House he suffered agonies, enduring both the loss of his creation and rejection by Jane. Slowly, however, with the help of his creative imagination, Georgiana's deep sympathy, courage gained from his immersion in Icelandic myth, and the peace and solace of Kelmscott, he gradually recovered balance, purpose and joy. Much of this joy came from work which yielded genuine satisfaction – that is, which produced beauty. Such work, Morris came to realise, is the only labour which can transform a workman's life from a curse of useless toil into a blessing for the worker and the community. Driven by this conviction, he made his widest cast for paradisal peace. Through socialism he hoped to turn all England into a Great Good Place, a golden hive of busy craftsmen. He ran an exemplary Garden Manufactory at Merton Abbey, gave lectures, edited a Socialist newspaper, and wrote poems, stories and novels filled with propaganda for the Cause. However, his health and patience, if not his faith in the ultimate triumph of Morrisian arts-and-crafts Socialism, crumbled about 1890 with his expulsion from the Socialist League. At this time he completed his 'utopian romance,' published in *Commonweal*, called *News from Nowhere; or, An Epoch of Rest*. In 1890 he founded the Hammersmith Socialist Society for the comrades who remained faithful to his vision of the future. This group met once a week under Morris's chairmanship in a hall fitted up for the purpose in the grounds of Kelmscott House, his Hammersmith home. However, after a severe illness in the spring of 1891, he devoted most of his remaining energy to founding, designing for, and manageing the Kelmscott Press and writing a series of prose romances to ease the increasing irk and painfulness of his decline. Morris suffered from diabetes, and in his day there was no insulin or other useful treatment for this disease.

Morris's first romance was in many ways different from the others written during his last years. It was the first book published – May, 1891 – by the Kelmscott Press, which had been started in January. The romance was called *The Story of the Glittering Plain; or, The Land of Living Men*. Another rather atypical romance, *Child Christopher* (published 1895), is a prose revision of a verse tale written many years before and has little to contribute to the inner story of these last years. *The Glittering Plain* is a revised *News from Nowhere* as opposed to the other romances written after 1890 which were arrangements of the material of Morris's life in stories of high adventure leading to demi-paradisal climaxes. (See Plate 8.)

The differences between *Nowhere* and *The Plain*, written within a year of each other, are mainly superficial, having to do with setting, chronology, and adventures. While they clash on one or two essential matters, they agree on many others. The Glittering Plain is a land of ever-living men, all young and beautiful, and Nowhere is inhabited by a healthy, 'long-lived' people who, with the exception of two or three spry old men, are universally handsome (the disappearance of hard, pointless, joyless labour for starvation wages allowed everyone to develop the lovely faces and physiques which nature intended) and look no older than twenty when they reach forty. As has often been pointed out, Guest, the dreamer from the nineteenth century, never encounters a single ugly, aged or sexually unattractive woman in Nowhere. This also holds true for the women of the Glittering Plain, who are 'exceeding fair of skin and shapely of fashion, so that the nakedness of their limbs under their girded gowns, and all glistering with the sea, was most lovely and dainty to behold.' (XIV, 251) In that land, where it is always summer, they dress in garments of gauze, but the women of Nowhere, where there is said to be some procession of seasons, dress just as lightly. In neither country is there strife or battle; both countries make love rather than war. The dominant mode is 'rest', or, more expansively, an endless series of the 'days of peace and rest and cleanness and smiling goodwill' that Guest had been longing for when *News from Nowhere* began. Work is done in both countries, mostly arts-and-crafts, though cows, horses, and sheep are raised and tended. Houses are built or bowers erected, especially on the Glittering Plain, whose people call their lumber-yards 'timber-bowers.' In both countries there is light farming and weaving, though clothes are almost superfluous. All needs and desires are gratifiable and quickly gratified. The King of the Plain explains that ' "in this land no man hath a lack which he may not satisfy without taking aught from any other. I deem not that thine heart may conceive a desire which I shall not fulfil for thee, or crave a gift which I shall not give thee." ' (261) All wares are fine and beautiful beyond expectation, as when Guest asks for a pipe in Nowhere. First the girlish shopkeeper gives him 'a red morocco bag, gaily embroidered' and crammed with choice Latakia. Then

> She disappeared again, and came back with a big-bowled pipe in her hand, carved out of some hard wood very elaborately, and mounted in gold sprinkled with little gems. It was, in short, as pretty and gay a toy as I had ever seen; something like the best kind of Japanese work, but better.
> 'Dear me!' said I, when I set eyes on it, 'this is altogether too grand for me,

or for anybody but the Emperor of the World. Besides, I shall lose it: I always
lose my pipes.'

(Ch. VI)

The Glittering Plain is a land of glorious semi-nudity where permis-
siveness prevails by day and night, and the women of Nowhere take other
mates *ad libitum*, the chief example being a girl who after a time returns
to her 'husband,' who is very glad to get her back. As 'old Hammond'
tells Guest (Ch. XII), many crimes of violence before the Change came
from ' "the artificial perversion of the sexual passions" ' deriving from
' "the law-made idea" ' of

'the woman being the property of the man, whether he were husband, father,
brother, or what not. *That* idea has of course vanished with private property,
as well as certain follies about the 'ruin' of women for following their natural
desires in an illegal way. . . . Of course that is all ended, since families are held
together by no bond of coercion, legal or social, but by mutual liking and affection, and everybody is free to come or go as he or she pleases.'

In neither Nowhere nor the Glittering Plain do soldiers, sailors, policemen, lawyers or magistrates exist, for there are no laws to enforce.
There is a difference between these Utopias in that the Glittering Plain
is ruled by a benevolent King (with a will of iron) while Nowhere
has Motes or general assemblies to which all may come and which
decide and question of public interest by a majority vote. Neither country has a governing class or prisons or poor houses, nor does the King
of the soldierless, weaponless Plain have any power but to withhold,
now and then, a gift. Hallblithe, the hero of the story, is, along with the
King's daughter, the only unsatisfied person on the island. He has been
lured to the Glittering Plain in the false hope of finding his kidnapped
sweetheart. When he tells the King he can find no 'rest' in his country,
the monarch, not knowing about Nowhere, where people enjoy the 'rest
and happiness of complete Communism' (Ch. XXVIII), asks quite sin-
cerely, ' ". . . where else than in this land wilt thou find rest? Without is
battle and famine, longing unsatisfied, and heart-burning and fear;
within it is plenty and peace and goodwill and pleasure without cease.
Thy word hath no meaning to me" ' In both Earthly Paradises people
are, in old Hammond's words, ' "too happy, both individually and collec-
tively to trouble about . . . what is to come hereafter." ' The Glittering
Plainsmen are sure of living until the unimaginable Dusk of the Gods,
while the Nowherians imagine themselves living on, even when the individual life is interrupted, in ' "the continuous life of the world of men
. . ." ' (Ch. XVIII)

One more feature these romances have in common is Kelmscott Manor itself, though each uses it for a separate purpose. In *News from Nowhere* Kelmscott Manor is kept by the people of the New Age as a symbolic 'guardian for all the beauty of the heart of summer' and a memento of the fact that houses built before the days of commercial and industrial exploitation were not always horrible. As Ellen put it:

'Yes, friend, this is what I came out for to see; this many-gabled old house built by the simple country-folk of the long-past times, regardless of all the turmoil that was going on in cities and courts, is lovely still amidst all the beauty which these latter days have created; and I do not wonder at our friends tending it carefully and making much of it. It seems to me as if it had waited for these happy days, and held in it gathered crumbs of happiness of the confused and turbulent past.'

(Ch. XXI)

It seems to be inhabited, if at all, only by children if one may judge from the 'bunches of dying flowers, feathers of birds, shells of starlings' eggs, caddis worms in mugs,' scattered around 'the strange and quaint garrets amongst the great timbers of the roof, where of old time the tillers and herdsmen of the manor slept . . .'

Everywhere there was but little furniture, and that only the most necessary, and of the simplest forms. The extravagant love of ornament which I had noted in this people elsewhere seemed here to have given place to the feeling that the house itself and its associations was the ornament of the country life amidst which it had been left stranded from old times . . .

(Ch. XXXI)

The Manor was a symbol of Nowhere achieved before its time, though more sombre than Communism's gay houses, or, as Morris had written soon after he found it, having 'a sadness about it, which is . . . the melancholy born of beauty, I suppose . . .'

From existing as a passive relic in *Nowhere*, Kelmscott Manor came back to life in The Glittering Plain as Hallblithe's home. Significantly it is not located on the Plain. When 'accursed and beguiled' (XIV, 265) by the 'dreams' and 'false shows' of the Plain, Hallblithe longed passionately for his home. ' "Oh, if I might but get me back, if it were but for an hour and to die there . . . and not be bandied about by lies for ever." ' (271) He has waking visions (271–2) of his home folk

yoking the oxen to the plough, and slowly going down the acres, as the shining iron drew the long furrow down the stubble-land, and the light haze hung about the elm-trees in the calm morning, and the smoke rose straight into the air from the roof of the kindred. And he said: 'What is this? am I death-doomed this morning that this sight cometh so clearly upon me amidst the falseness of this unchanging land?'

Of course he would have to endure the times of 'famine, longing unsatisfied, and heart-burning and fear' that the Glittering King had warned of, but for reunion with his family and his 'troth-plight maiden' Hallblithe was willing to risk his life. He finally escaped from the changeless land of lying dreams by means of a small boat which he built himself. Once again he could feel pain and weariness – and hope. And then – at last – he recovered his troth-plight maiden of the Rose clan on the way home to Cleveland. Fair 'damsels not less than a score' prepared him for her appearance by singing a poem (313) in the meter of the 'Lines for the Bed at Kelmscott,' written about the time of the publication of *The Glittering Plain*.

> Now waneth spring,
> While all birds sing,
> And the south wind blows
> The earliest rose
> To and fro
> By the doors we know,
> And the scented gale
> Fills every dale.
> Slow now are rooks running because of the weed,
> And the thrush hath no cunning to hide her at need ...
> And O! that at last,
> All sorrows past,
> This night I lay
> 'Neath the oak-beams grey!
> O, to wake from sleep,
> To see dawn creep
> Through the fruitful grove
> Of the house that I love!
> O! my feet in the garden's edge under the sun,
> Where the seeding grass hardens for haysel begun!

And so to bed:

> We shall wend it yet,
> The highway wet;
> For what is this
> That our bosoms kiss?
> What lieth sweet
> Before our feet?
> What token hath come
> To lead us home?
> 'Tis the Rose of the garden walled round from the croft
> Where the grey roof its warden steep riseth aloft,
> 'Tis the Rose 'neath the oaken-beamed hall, where they bide,
> The pledges unbroken, the hand of the bride.

What are we to make of this 'sequel' to *News from Nowhere* in which all the blessings of the Socialist commune, except its neatness, trimness, brightness and busy handicrafts, are mocked by a hero who prefers death to day-dreams of lasting youth, 'light loves,' prolonged comfort, easy achievement, abiding rest, endless peace and benevolent dictatorship? Hallblithe insists that uncertainty, strife, danger, anxiety for those 'hostages to fortune' who come to us in the form of a devoted family, and finally age and death sweetened by the love of children and friends – are all in some mysterious way needed for a deep apprehension of everything beautiful, brave, noble, and 'peaceful' which life can offer. The gods have given us death in order to keep existence from becoming pointless and boring. The old Sea-eagle who journeyed to the Glittering Plain with Hallblithe's help regained youth and girls and days that 'flit no more,' but the young man tells him that he is bound to become weary and bored, longing for what he has lost, though it were only his last human role of ' "a gibbering ghost drifting down the wind of night." '

Then stirred Hallblithe's heart within him and he said: 'O Eagle of the Sea, thou hast thy youth again; what then wilt thou do with it? . . . Where now shall be the alien shores before thee, and the landing for fame . . .? Wilt thou forget the ship's black side, and the dripping of the windward oars, as the squall falleth on when the sun hath arisen, and the sail tuggeth hard on the sheet, and the ship lieth over and the lads shout against the whistle of the wind? Has the spear fallen from thine hand, and hast thou buried the sword of thy fathers in the grave from which thy body hath escaped? What art thou, O Warrior, in the land of the alien and the king? Who shall heed thee or tell the tale of thy glory, which thou hast covered over with the hand of a light woman . . .?'

(256)

Hallblithe does not want Nowhere or the Glittering Plain but only

'the fair woman who shall lie in my bed, and bear me children, and stand by me in field and fold, by thwart and gunwale, before the bow and the spear, by the flickering of the cooking-fire, and amidst the blaze of the burning hall, and beside the balefire of the warrior of the Raven.'

The core of love in Hallblithe's vision of the best life possible is underscored by the lament (266) of the King's daughter, who, for love of Hallblithe, has persuaded her father to lure this hopelessly one-woman man to the plain:

'Yea, why is the earth fair and fruitful, and the heavens kind above it, if thou comest not to-night, nor to-morrow, nor the day after? And I the daughter of the Undying, on whom the days shall grow and grow as the grains of sand which the wind heaps up above the sea-beach. And life shall grow huger and more hideous round about the lonely one, like the ling-worm laid upon the gold, that waxeth thereby till it lies all round about the house of the queen entrapped, the moveless unending ring of the years that change not.'

The Glittering Plain has little in common with the other prose romances written in the 1890s. It is a tale of one more Earthly Paradise, more thrilling perhaps than *Nowhere* and almost free of polemical discussions but in other ways strangely like it. Fed up with the endless jabber about dialectical materialism, with the cowardice when confronted by the police, the sponging, and the growing anarchism of the Socialist League, which had also just fired him from their leadership, Morris seems to have arraigned their dreams, and his own, in an allegory in which the hero challenges the 'lies' which had lured him into a land a-glitter with fairy-gold. He never gave up his belief that life's only satisfactions are to be found in love (of one woman) and work (preferably self-chosen handicrafts). But attempts to penetrate and control the future had lost most of their interest. Morris had wrecked his health working for the Cause. By his example at Merton Abbey and by innumerable lectures he had tried to fight the industrial and commercial uglification of England and to bring about an instant paradise of craftsmen, only to learn that most men, of whatever 'class,' income or background, had no idea what he meant by beauty and no inclination to find out. He wanted to soothe his last years with pleasant work and therapeutic dreams.

Of course, Morris had never given up creating Earthly Paradises. He had simply withdrawn from one earth-work of vision to another. Each of which he was able to enjoy for five or ten years till he found, in the final romances, dream-fortresses that were unassailable by any power weaker than death. In his romances Morris arranged and rearranged his life-experience in patterns that brought happy endings to events that had been fearful, disappointing, bitter, or frustrating. These fantasy variations crowned with joy, in which the hero moves through every kind of trouble straight into the heart of a Great Good Place, and lives to an overripe age with his 'troth-plight maiden,' sweetened Morris's declining years and, in spite of their ambling pace, often make fascinating reading. They are not dreams of the future nor, though based on it, of the past; they furnish creative enjoyment in the present. Perhaps such recastings of the past are a means of reconstituting memories and desires into an actuality that one is happy to live and die with. W. B. Yeats described these last romances – 'the only books I was ever to read slowly that I might not come too quickly to the end' – as

a dream indeed, but a dream of natural happiness. . . . It was his work to make us, who had been taught to sympathise with the unhappy till we had grown morbid, to sympathise with men and women who turned everything into happiness because they had in them something of the abundance of beechen boughs or the bursting wheat-ear . . . All he writes seems to me like the make-believe of a child who is remaking the world, not always in the same way, but always after its own heart . . . He has but one story to tell us, how some man or woman lost and found again the happiness that is always half of the body.

This was, said Yeats, a way of making 'the Cross . . . blossom with roses' and he places Morris 'among the greatest of those who prepare for the last reconciliation . . .' Yeats found more meaning in the final romances than any other critic, but he too was a poet – one with a sensibility which, happily, has never been so flouted and despised as Morris's.

The paradisal aspects of the romances are many, though two in particular immediately come to mind. The landscape is always Edenic: a fountain or palace surrounded by concentric circles of garden, orchard, water and forest. Here is the mandala, that divine configuration of natural forms into a picture of the peace that passeth understanding. At the centre of the sacred palace dances a beautiful girl, usually naked, who is sometimes identified as the spirit of the fountain, sometimes as a goddess of fertility, usually as the life giving source of the quester's soul. The garden of Eden had, at least in Hebrew mythology, two goddesses: first, Lilith, overpowering in her resplendent, sardonic beauty, an angelic witch; and second, Eve, created more to Adam's size and taste though as lovely in her way as Lilith and, for all her humanity, no less an enchantress. In several of the late romances Morris portrays a 'Georgiana-Eve' battling with a 'Jane-Lilith'. The hero must have the right dancer in his lotus-heart – the woman who will give him the tenderness, companionship, care and stimulation he needs to live at the fountain-centre or, as Morris put it, to find the Well at the World's End. Thus the settings, plots, and images of these stories are ancient, symbolic, inward, of no time and no place, yet readily apprehended because they originate in an area of unconscious life only thinly divided from consciousness. They are scenes and characters always poised to spring into life, always in search of an author. When repressed or unreconciled material finds its way into the light, as in these stories, more is involved than, as Bernard Shaw scoffed, a 'startling relapse into literary Pre-Raphaelitism.' As Yeats said, Morris here was like a child remaking the world, reshaping his life into what it might have been, 'not always in the same way, but always after its own heart.' Thus he reconciled miserable contradictions, turned confusion into benediction, and caused the Cross to blossom with flowers.

In Volume XXI of *The Collected Works* May Morris included some 'Unfinished Romances' which show Morris projecting fables about his anguish over Jane. But he was not able to make that distressing memory yield the bliss he was in search of. Both *The story of Desiderius* and *Kil-*

lian of the Closes were broken off after tentative beginnings. In the first (313-4) the mother of Desiderius, a witch-like woman who would destroy the hero's love for a kindly girl, is such a Fury that the story of her malevolence, had it been continued, would have been more of a caricature of Jane than a recasting of injuries which Morris was still trying to forget.

she had seen forty summers but was a stately woman and still very fair; for her face was like the marble image of a good imager, so right and true were all the lines therein and so shapely was the compass of it. Dark smooth and fine was her hair, her lips full and red, her skin smooth and clear of hue, her limbs and all her body excellently fashioned, her eyes great and grey . . . and seeming as if they were the very windows of a true and simple soul. This was her seeming, which was but a painted show: for inwardly she was a fool, false and cruel, of many moods indeed but none of them good, a liar so that no one could say whether any word of hers were false or true; a fawner and a flatterer to make the time pass pleasantly: a friend in the morning, a stranger at mid-day, a foe in the evening: a woman cruel in deeds of set purpose if the mood took her, and always cruel without set purpose, whereas she cared for no soul of man or beast what grief might happen to them either with her or without her.

This woman was no fit inhabitant for the mandalic Roman villa with its pillars of 'marble white and green with gilded chapiters' (315) set in a square. In the midst of the square was

a pool of clear water with a fountain which had been open to the air save for a gay-stained linen cloth hung over it with poles and cores. The floor was of marble wrought with a fair pattern of little squares of many colours . . .

Rescuing the fountain-spirit Pulcheria, now banished to 'the field-house' by her malignant mistress, was an exercise that Morris soon tired of. What satisfaction was there in decapitating Medusa? Nevertheless, murder was often the Jane-persona's fate in the last romances, for Morris never really did forget the misery she had caused. In remoulding his life, he could drop her out entirely, as he sometimes did, but when she was introduced in the romances, he always saw to it that full 'poetic justice' was done. That he never became emotionally reconciled to her is suggested in a letter to Georgiana of August 1881: 'A kind of terror always falls upon me as I near' Oxford, caused mostly by 'all that I remember I have lost since I was a lad and dwelling there . . .' (*Letters*, 150)

A possible alternative to killing the Jane-persona was to represent her love as a temporary blessing, but in this Morris succeeded only once – for a few chapters in *The Well at the World's End*. In *Killian of the Closes* we find the hero (277) rescuing a Jane-like enchantress from pursuing blood-hounds and a furious mounted man in armour. Preceded by shrieks and the howling of hounds, there came runnning forth from the thicket a woman in woeful plight, for she was naked in her smock, and cried out no longer for she was breathless, though even yet she seemed fleet-foot enough. But hard at heel followed her two great sleuth-hounds open-mouthed and eager . . .

These Killian slays just as they rend her smock. Then he quickly disarms the pursuing 'knight.' The next time Killian meets this lady in the forest she uses magic to re-enact the scene with the dogs for his amusement but assures him that the first ghastly pursuit had been all too real. This time she appears to him clad in 'but one strait gown over her smock,' which is said to have been Jane's favoured dress. 'Green was the said gown, and so embroidered with many colours of gold and silk and gems, that it was like a very piece of a meadow of that Maytide.' (285) Killian thinks she may be a creature ' "of the Faery" ' but tells a questioner (289) that on second thought she was not

'like this fashion reputed of the faery kind, that they be as if wrought of blossoms and sunbeams, having nought to do with the wind and weather, and the rough earth of the woodland, and the raggedness of the thicket. For however she is of slender grace, and all carefully fashioned from head to heel, she is tall and well-knit, her arms strong, her limbs brawny and firm; nor is the skin of her made of snow and rose-leaves by seeming, however sweet and fragrant she may be; for her face is tanned by the sun and wind, so that the grey eyes gleam therefrom, and her lips be full red and sweet; and even so tanned or yet more are the hands of her from the wrists down; and her feet to the ankles not much less. So that again I tell thee that she is more like to a fair and dear lady who haunteth the summer woodland for her health and her pleasure, than any wight of strange fashion that hateth the race of Adam.'

At this meeting the woman led Killian out of the beechwood and into a fair meadow in which was a great circle of 'seven oak trees tall and straight of some two hundred years' growth.' There she gave him an emerald ring which enabled him to see 'amidmost the oak trees . . . a full fair fountain of white stone and it hath imagery thereon and is parcel-painted with blue and with gold, and the water is running clear from the four sides thereof, into a goodly basin of work like to the shaft of the fountain . . .' This is the Fountain of Thirst from which she bids him (291) drink,

'and straightway was my thirst gone, but therewith also my vision of what was there before me, and meseemed I was in a wondrous fair garden beset with roses and flowers of the loveliest, and with apple trees most goodly whereon were blossom and fruit growing together side by side. Moreover I heard the sound of harps and fiddles and other string-play, and the voices of folk singing in heavenly fashion; and next I saw folk both men and women, but all young and beauteous . . . and meseemed I had never erst been so full of joy.'

At this point (292) the mandala, compounded of memories of Red House and Malory, was complete and at its centre the half-naked

'Lady stood holding out her two hands to me, and she seemed to me fairer and more lovely than erst, and each thing she did, and every way she moved, more beauteous than the other. So I took her hands and held them in mine and kissed them, either palm. But lo, now another wonder, for all the hot desire I had had toward her was gone, and my heart was altogether at rest; and indeed it seemed to me as if we had both died and entered paradise without pain unwitting.'

This is a dream of Jane plucked from the early days of marriage, evoking her as Tārā dancing on a lotus at the centre of a blessed collocation of emerald trees and ranked ruby gardens which for the yogi, has the peculiar virtue of stilling sexual desire! Actually, the memories of Jane could seldom be arranged into an Indian benediction. But when for a moment they were so arranged, as here, there was no place for the story to go. With the stilling of passion the narrative collapses before it can get started.

The 'Unfinished Romances' edited by May do, however, show Morris developing themes, folkloric incidents and fairy-tale plots which he later used liberally in the completed romances. His first adumbration of what became a favourite romance pattern occurs in a rather silly little poem, 'Goldilocks and Goldilocks,' which Morris wrote about 1890 to pad out *Poems By the Way* (1891). Goldilocks the Swain, to distinguish him from Goldilocks the Maid, goes a-questing for he knows not what. Soon he is lost in a dreary forest and is starving. At this moment he meets in the gloom a maiden

> Face to face, and so close was she
> That their lips met soft and lovingly.

When they find a shaft of light where they can eat *her* frugal lunch, the Swain notes that

> In all the world was never maid
> So fair, so evilly arrayed.

Her feet and shoulders are bare and

> Through her brown kirtle's rents full wide
> Shone out the sleekness of her side.

She tells him how she is kept in this pitiful state by a crone whom she serves with no reward but stripes and torture. Still, she has picked up a bit of the witch's magic, and warns the Swain against her. Nevertheless, when the sorceress emerges from her palace gorgeously clad and, by seeming the 'most wondrous fair/Of all the women earth doth bear,' the foolish lad falls at 'her gold-clad feet,' accepts her caresses and sits on her golden throne. However, he is miserable at the loss of the Maid, and feels his life 'waste and vain,' especially when the day arrives for wedding the Queen. Luckily the 'mirk of midnight' falls suddenly on the midmorn wedding feast and only one person can bring back the sun – Goldilocks the Maid, who had used white magic to cause the crisis. As the price of her sunbeams she demands to sit between the Queen and the Swain at the feast.

> Her gown of green so fair was wrought
> That clad her body seemed with nought
>
> But blossoms of the summer-tide,
> That wreathed her, limbs and breast and side.

She reminds the Swain of the time she saved him from starving and he had left her dainty arms ' "not unkissed/All o'er from shoulder unto wrist." ' When he tries to flee with her from the banquet, the guests turn into shrieking 'swine-herds' and the stately Queen into a foul, one-eyed troll from whom the lovers can escape only by beheading her. Even in death she sends her evil servants, an ice-bear, a dragon, a poison-flood and a 'fire-flaught,' to destroy them, but prayers and counter-magic save them. The last ordeal they have to face is aimed at the Swain's weakness for female beauty, but this time he obeys the Maid and will not succour the apparition that bursts shrieking from the brake:

> A woman bare of breast and limb,
> Who turned a piteous face to him
>
> E'en as she ran: for hard at heel
> Followed a man with brandished steel . . .

When they get to the Swain's home in the land of the Wheaten Shocks, his family agree that the slaying of an 'evil thing,' followed by marriage to an 'angel's child,' is the best possible way a brave man could have chosen to embark on a long and blissful life.

This simple reordering of his life brought about by a tug-of-war between a tall witch and a small enchantress, though never achieved in fact, was something Morris never tired of enacting in his imagination. With variations and slight changes of personnel, it is a constant theme in his last romances.

The Wood Beyond the World, though not printed until 1894, is a mature 'Goldilocks and Goldilocks' in prose. Although the plot is almost the same it seems different because the characters are deeper and more subtle, and several fascinating incidents have been added. The male Goldilocks of the story, Golden Walter, leaves home, not just for adventure but because there was this flaw in his lot, whereas he had fallen into the toils of love of a woman exceeding fair, and had taken her to wife, she nought unwilling as it seemed. But when they had been wedded some six months he found by manifest tokens, that his fairness was not so much to her but that she must seek to the foulness of one worser than he in all ways; wherefore his rest departed from him, whereas he hated her for her untruth and her hatred of him; yet would the sound of her voice, as she came and went in the house, make his heart beat; and the sight of her stirred desire within him, so that he longed for her to be sweet and kind with him, and deemed that, might it be so, he should forget all the evil gone by. But it was not so; for ever when she saw him, her face changed, and her hatred of him became manifest, and howsoever she were sweet with others, with him she was hard and sour.

(XVII, 1)

Once he had decided to leave home, Golden Walter began to see a strange trio of beings, invisible to most people, two of whom riveted and revived his flagging interest in women. The more striking of them is an incredibly magnificent and virulently beautiful queen-like figure; the other, her bond-slave, who is smaller in stature but no less attractive in face and figure, exudes kindliness and sweet temper. The unforgettable pair quickly prove, even to Walter, that his wife has not made a misogynist of him. The third member of the trio is a horrifying Yellow Dwarf. Morris describes the trio as they first appeared to the hero (3–4):

first came a dwarf, dark-brown of hue and hideous, with long arms and ears exceeding great and dog-teeth that stuck out like fangs of a wild beast. He was clad in a rich coat of yellow silk, and bare in his hand a crooked bow, and was girt with a broad ax.

After him came a maiden, young be seeming, of scarce twenty summers; fair of face as a flower; grey-eyed, brown-haired, with lips full of red, slim and gentle of body. Simple was her array, of a short and strait green gown, so that on her right ankle was clear to see an iron ring.

Last of the three was a lady, tall and stately, so radiant of visage and glorious of raiment, that it were hard to say what like she was; for scarce might the eye gaze steady upon her exceeding beauty; yet must every son of Adam who found himself anigh her, lift up his eyes again after he had dropped them, and look again on her, and yet again and yet again. Even so did Walter . . .

The bond-slave reminds us of Goldilocks the Maid; the Mistress, of Goldilocks' tyrant and torturer, while the frightful yellow dwarf (king of a nation of similar horrors), the witch's agent for evil, is the equivalent of the Bear, Dragon, poison-floods and fire-storms rolled into one. There is only one other character, the Mistress's current lover known as the King's Son, who is mostly just another tormentor of the Maid (after whom he lusts) but whose death serves her purpose later on. His feud with Golden Walter over the Maid comes from a previous effort, *The*

King's Son and the Carle's Son. Morris had written sixty-five pages of this story before he threw it aside.

The regal and irresistible mistress-witch is 'as lovely as a goddess of the gentiles,' which is what she turns out to be – an incarnation of the Magna Mater of the savage Bear-tribe of her island, a people to which Walter is drawn by mysterious forces. These Bears form a kind of matriarchal group who must always have an avatar of their deity to call on when abundance is threatened. When she takes Walter hunting with her, the divine creature is usually (50) clad

for the greenwood as the hunting-goddess of the Gentiles, with her green gown gathered unto her girdle, and sandals on her feet; a bow in her hand and a quiver at her back : she was taller and bigger of fashion than the dear Maiden, whiter of flesh, and more glorious, and brighter of hair; as a flower of flowers for fairness and fragrance.

At other times this living idol is dressed (64) somewhat like Jane, who wore a single straight dress, 'guiltless,' according to Henry James, 'of hoops (or of anything else, I should say)':

now was she clad but in one garment of some dark grey silky stuff, embroidered with, as it were, a garland of flowers about the middle, but which was so thin that as the wind drifted it from side and limb, it hid her no more, but for the said garland, than if water were running over her . . .

On this particular occasion Walter, though already in love with the Maid, took the hand she held out to him, 'knelt down before her and kissed it, and abode upon his knees' just like Goldilocks the Swain at first sight of the witch-queen. When he finds his voice he can only stutter ' "that now I see thee unhidden . . . meseemeth there hath been none such since the old days of the Gentiles." ' (64) The idol is infuriated because Walter, now when she stands before him ' "all glorious in my nakedness . . ." (65), does not take her immediately, instead of just kissing her hand. However, she leads him to a seemingly sacred spot in the middle of a mandalic arrangement (66)'

So they crossed the stream by the shallow below the pool wherein Walter had bathed, and within a little they came upon a tall fence of flake-hurdles, and a simple gate therein. The Lady opened the same, and they entered thereby into a close all planted as a most fair garden, with hedges of rose and woodbine, and with linden-trees a-blossom, and long ways of green grass betwixt borders of lilies and clove-gilliflowers, and other sweet garland-flowers. And a branch of the stream which they had crossed erewhile wandered through that garden; and in the midst was a little house built of post and pan, thatched with yellow straw, as if it were new done.

There 'they loved and played together as if they were a pair of lovers guileless . . .'

The Maid, who knows Walter will be lured to the island by the malicious enchantress, has forgiven him in advance. To reject the Mistress would endanger his life and the Maid's and their chance of a happy future. Their task is to escape from false temenoi like this forest pleasaunce and the Lady's golden House of the Wood, both of which, like the gardens in Tasso or Spenser, are mirages. Their fountains at the centre do not splash with the water-of-life and rejuvenation; they are really only jets of sand. In its illusions, lies, lust, and its geographical wall of 'Icelandic' mountains, this Circe-country resembles the Glittering Plain but is far more dangerous. The only genuine mandala which Walter finds there centres on a tall rock, from the foot of which issues truly life-giving water, symbolised by the girl who customarily bathes there. This is the Maiden or bond-slave, whom Walter loves at first sight and who comes here whenever she can escape from the tortures heaped on her by the Mistress, the King's Son and the Yellow Dwarf:

whenas the summer morn was at its brightest, he saw a little way ahead a grey rock rising up from amidst of a ring of oak trees; so he turned thither straightway for in this plain-land he had seen no rocks heretofore; and as he went he saw that there was a fountain gushing out from under the rock, which ran thence in a fair little stream. And when he had the rock and the fountain and the stream clear before him, lo! a child of Adam sitting beside the fountain under the shadow of the rock. He drew a little nigher, and then he saw that it was a woman, clad in green like the sward whereon she lay. She was playing with the welling out of the water, and she had trussed up her sleeves to the shoulder that she might thrust her bare arms therein. (30)

Here is a trustworthy vision of love, peace and bliss.

The Maiden is a 'white' witch (later in the story it is said that her name shall be hallowed little less than that of ' "the Mother of God" ') and she tricks the 'goddess' into murdering the King's Son and committing suicide. After this she leads Walter from the Wood Beyond the World through the mountain barricade to the settlement of the Bears, to whom she announces that she is the new avatar of their Earth Mother, the last having died. She comes to the Bears wearing a dress of flowers with which she had covered herself the day before. By now, of course, these are all faded but she addresses the tribe boldly in their sacred Doom-ring, saying,

'. . . look ye upon me as here I stand, I who have come from from the fairer country and the greenwood of the lands, and see if I bear not the summer with me, and the heart that maketh increase and the hand that giveth.'

Lo then! as she spake, the faded flowers that hung about her gathered life and grew fresh again; the woodbine round her neck and her sleek shoulders

knit itself together and embraced her freshly, and cast its scent about her face.
The lilies that girded her loins lifted up their heads, and the gold of their tassels
fell upon her; the eyebright grew clean blue again upon her smock; the eglantine
found its blooms again, and then began to shed the leaves thereof upon her
feet; the meadow-sweet wreathed amongst it made clear the sweetness of her
legs, and the mouse-ear studded her raiment as with gems. There she stood
amidst of the blossoms, like a great orient pearl against the fretwork of the
goldsmiths, and the breeze that came up the valley from behind bore the sweetness of her fragrance all over the Man-mote.

   Then, indeed, the Bears stood up, and shouted and cried, and smote on their
shields, and tossed their spears aloft.

(107–8)

Having convinced the Bears that she is ' "the very heart of the year's increase" ' and that her feet upon their pastures will make them thrive now
and in the coming years, she leads Walter out of the hills into smiling
country and a splendid city where they become king and queen with the
'assured hope of many days of joy . . .'

   What is the meaning of such a story? Is it more than a sometimes fascinating fairy tale? Morris hastened to assure *The Spectator*, whose reviewer had treated the book as a Socialist allegory, that

I had not the least intention of thrusting an allegory into 'The Wood Beyond
the World;' it is meant for a tale pure and simple, with nothing didactic about
it. If I have to write or speak on Social problems, I always try to be as direct as
I possibly can be. On the other hand, I should consider it bad art in anyone
writing an allegory not to make it clear from the first that this was his intention
. . .

(XVII, xxxix)

Perhaps a reason for his vehement hurry to 'correct what is matter of
fact, and not of opinion' indicates the measure of his current dissatisfac-
tion with Socialism even as practised at Hammersmith and his desire to
be free to get on with more romances in which he had found a form of
creative dreaming which lay well within the scope of his diminishing
physical energy. Perhaps he had come slowly to the point where he
agreed with a famous passage in Goethe's *Truth and Poetry*: 'When a
poet wants to be politically effective, he has to abandon himself to a
party, and when he does this he is lost as a poet; he has to say farewell to
his freedom of thought . . . and pull over his ears the cap of narrow-
mindedness and blind hatred.' Once again Morris seems to take the position he took in his letter to C. Price, July 1856: '. . . I see that things are
in a muddle, and I have no power or vocation to set them right . . . My
work is the embodiment of dreams in one form or another.' (*Letters*, 17)

   What Morris did not reveal in his Spectator letter was that his current dreams probably sprang from a deep need to re-order certain elements and incidents of his life which had not turned out as he wished. The irresistibly beautiful large-limbed witch – who reminds Walter at times of the wife he had fled from – inevitably reminds us of Jane. And her dainty, resourceful, comforting, warm-hearted and lovely servant makes us think of Georgiana. What, if anything, happened in the Jane-Georgiana relationship to make Morris cast Jane, in story after story, in the role of a Black Witch who loves to torture, with everything from pinches to whips, stocks and dungeons, a smaller White Witch who outmagics her in the end, we may never know. It is certain that the two women, after the first years at Red House, fell out and seldom saw each other afterwards. For some reason it gave Morris satisfaction to portray a stately Black Witch, who always begins by luring an adventurous young man, blunt, honest, handsome, irresistible to women, into her toils, but is routed by a small White Witch who not only saves the hero but comforts, cheers, enriches and prolongs his life through a fully sympathetic companionship. Male villains in these pieces are sometimes grotesque, like the malignant dwarf in *The Wood*; yellow, hairy, spiteful, merciless. Or they may be dark, bearded, heavy-set 'knights' exhibiting the same, if not more sinister, psychological perversions. Such portraits seem caricatured out of recognition, but it clearly gave Morris irresistible satisfaction to draw them.

The most important romance using this cast of characters is *The Well at the World's End*. In this story two of the lead figures are doubled, perhaps to show a range of characteristics which Morris could not easily compress. But the Hero (Ralph of Upmeads) and the Maid (Ursula) do not have 'doubles.' These two meet near the beginning of the long tale (written from 1892 to 1896 and known to Morris's friends as 'the Endless'). However, though they are both destined to seek the Well at the World's End, they are soon separated by Ralph's desire for adventure. Almost immediately he finds in a forest, a woman who, 'though she was not to say naked ... had nought to cover her save one short and strait little coat of linen. Yet Ralph deemed her to be of some degree, whereas he caught the gleam of gold and gems on her hands, and there was a golden chaplet on her head.' (XVIII, 49) She is the prisoner of two armed men, one of whom leads her by a rope tied around her neck. Bravery and beginner's luck enable him to kill her persecutors and get a clearer sight of her (51):

in spite of her poor attire, he deemed he had never seen woman so fair. Her hair was dark red, but her eyes grey, and light at whiles and yet at whiles deep; her lips betwixt thin and full, but yet when she spoke or smiled clad with all the enticements; her chin round and so wrought as none was ever better wrought; her body strong and well-knit; tall she was, with fair and large arms, and limbs most goodly of fashion, of which but little was hidden, since her coat was but thin and scanty. But whatever may be said of her, no man would have deemed her aught save most lovely.

Surpassingly beautiful and enticing, large-limbed, etc., in this apparition we have another incarnation of the Black Witch. However, while her reputation for evil is Luciferian, she is nothing like so cruel or wicked as the Enchantress of the Golden House in *The Wood*. That sinister woman pretended to be an avatar of the fertility goddess of the Bears. The woman whom Ralph rescues is in fact a Lady of Abundance, as she is called by most people, while by others a 'goddess of the ancient world,' a 'queen of men,' 'giver of doom' or justice to all, benefactress of the needy, and 'blessed lady-leech' or physician like Morgan the Fay. The local priest tells Ralph, who is worried at first lest she be of that ' "race of ancient devils, the gods of the Gentiles." ' that ' "though she is verily as fair as Venus (God save us), yet is she as chaste as Agnes, as wise as Katherine, and as humble and meek as Dorothy." ' Though she sparkles with energy and apparent youth, old women remember her from their youth – always beautiful, sleek, large-limbed, and incredibly strong as she is now. This longevity is attributed to her courage in adventuring to the Well at the World's End and drinking of its waters. Of this well it is said (11) that for those who drink ' "it saveth from weariness and wounding and sickness; and it winneth love from all and maybe life everlasting." '

The Lady herself tells Ralph she is not so bad as portrayed. Though all men love her, she has during her long life taken only a few lovers. Those she has spurned have become her foes and joined idle jades who, jealous of her in seeking to

'. . . have men deem that my length of days and the endurance of my beauty and never-dying youth of my heart came from evil and devilish sources; and if thou wilt trust my word it is not so, for in the Well at the World's End is no evil but only the Quenching of Sorrow, and Clearing of the Eyes that they may behold. And how good it is that they look on thee now.'

(168)

She has long been waiting and pining for Ralph, though at present she has a husband called the Knight of the Sun. This man, whose dark visage and sour behaviour belie his title, has almost killed Ralph before the Lady tells him of the Well. She has saved the younger man from death and led him to safety through rugged woods to 'a hazel copse, like a deep hedge, into a cleared grassy space where were great grey stones lying about, as if it had been the broken doom-ring of a forgotten folk.' (142) In this partial mandala, they can make sure of each other's sincere love, but for full consummation the Lady of Abundance leads him

through a deserted wilderness to a 'sweetly dight' cave in the face of a
rocky eminence. Before this high perch lies a 'table of greensward' surrounded by a stream which 'ran in a chain of pools and stickles.' Here
too the perfect temenos centre for the *hieros gamos* is wanting, but the
Lady of Abundance, at last feeling safe from the Sun-Knight, hallows
the cave with a prayer: ' "May all blessings light on this House of the
Wilderness and this Hall of the Summer-tide, and the Chamber of Love
that here is!" ' (198) However, it is here that her dark husband finds and
murders her only to perish with one of Ralph's arrows through his eye (a
symbolic enough death, perhaps, for a treacherous, mad painter). Ralph
is left suicidally desolate.

In drawing *The Well* portrait of Jane, Morris was thinking of the
early days at Red House and had momentarily succeeded in forgetting
their sequel except when taking (imaginary) vengeance by the double
murder that brought the Lady and the Sun-Knight to a sudden, irrever-
sible end. All that keeps Ralph on the track of adventure is the memory
of Ursula (the White Witch he had encountered when setting out). In a
dream his murdered 'goddess' tells him of once meeting Ursula:

'a young woman and exceeding fair, as if she were of pearl all over, and as sweet
as eglantine . . . she said that she had a mind to seek to the Well at the World's
End, which quencheth all sorrow; and I . . . went with her into the wildwood,
and taught her wisdom of the way and what she was to do. And again I say to
thee that she was so sweet and yet with a kind of pity in her both of soul and
body, and wise withal and quiet, that I feared her, though I loved her; yea and
still do: for I deem her better than me, and meeter for thee and thy love than
I be . . .'

(195)

When a minstrel describes Ursula's 'eyes set wide apart, grey and deep:
her whole face of sweet aspect, as though she might be exceedingly kind
to one that pleased her; yet high and proud of demeanour also . . . as
though she were come of great kindred,' we can hardly help thinking of
Georgiana. These two, Ralph and Ursula, now both in search of the
Well that quenches sorrow, are destined to meet soon and take up the
quest together. First, however, Ralph must search for her through Goldberg, where the way to the Well begins, and Utterbol, which lies across
the route to it. Goldberg has a widowed queen, young, fair, and wise,
who lives in a High House set among gorgeous gardens. It seems like a
sacred centre – 'a piece of the Kingdom of Heaven for loveliness' (267).
However, she cannot make him forget either the Lady of Abundance or
Ursula, who he now hears has fallen into the cruel, lust-twitching hands
of the Lord of Utterbol. This town is described as a hell on earth peopled
mostly by devils. However, Ralph hastens there and is saved trom the

customary castration of intruders because all women find him irresistible. In the intensely blonde Queen of Utterbol we have another Black Witch, less lovable, goddess-like and intelligent than the Lady of Abundance, but still quite a 'stunner' and possibly, despite her blonde hair, more re-miniscent of Jane:

she was clad all in fine linen and gold, with gold shoes on her feet: her arms came bare from out of the linen: great they were, and the hands shapely, and all very white and rosy: her hair was as yellow as any that can be seen, and it was plenteous, and shed all down about her. Her eyes were blue and set wide apart, her nose a little snubbed, her mouth wide, full-lipped and smiling. She was very tall, a full half-head taller than any of her women: yea, as tall as a man who is above the middle height of men.

(307)

In her rages she is hot-headed and over-masterful, but not overpower-ing. In calmer moods she is, as she herself realises, ' "slothful, ... fool-ish, and empty-hearted and unclean." ' However, she is 'nowise cruel' (309) and even her bondslave whom she beats thinks her ' "no ill woman, but rather something overgood for Utterbol and the dark lord thereof." ' (311) Her chief vice is lust, but she longs for Ralph to love her with kindness and devotion. Possibly she is too stupid to make a good Black Witch. Her unspeakable husband is a short, thick-set, greasy, dark-skinned character who lives by cruelty, deceit and lust. Fortunately Ralph and Ursula are able to slip through the clutches of these doubles of the 'Queen of men' and the Knight of the Sun and get on with the quest for the Well.

Of further adventures little need be said. Many snares beset them on the way, but the Lady of Abundance had taught Ursula how to avoid them. Their encounter with a wise old man puts the powers of the Well they are seeking in clearer perspective than before:

'Son,' said the Elder, 'true it is that the water of that Well shall cause a man to thrive in all ways, and to live through many generations of men, maybe, in honour and good-liking; but it may not keep any man alive for ever; for so have the Gods given us the gift of death lest we weary of life.'

(XIX, 65)

The Elder excuses himself and his people for living so near the Well without ever dreaming of going there. Already they live free of sickness, pestilence, famine, strife and war and hanker after nothing they cannot easily fashion for themselves.

'But for you, guests, it is otherwise, for ye of the World beyond the Mountains are stronger and more godlike than we, as all tales tell; and what ye wear away your lives desiring that which ye may scarce get; and ye set your hearts on high things, desiring to be masters of the very Gods. Therefore ye know sickness and sorrow, and oft ye die before your time, so that ye must depart and leave undone things which ye deem ye were born to do; which to all men is grievous. And because of all this ye desire healing and thriving, whether good come of it, or ill. Therefore ye do but right to seek to the Well . . .'

(66)

When the pair who started their search in the hope of easing their hearts of pain and frustration, arrive at the World's End, they have already found the kind of relief they sought. However, they determine to drink so that increased strength and length of life may help them to serve their fellows and, as the Elder had suggested, ' "deliver them from the thralldom of those that be strong and unwise and unkind" ' in their unparadisal world. Their first sight of the End is from the top of a cliff, which overhangs a shore of forbidding black sand and jutting rocks. The shore holds at bay a beating ocean which is perhaps to be identified with '*the steely sea,/Where tossed about all hearts of men must be*'. To neutralise the sea's fury Morris had, all his life, constructed paradise after paradise. In the black sand

just below the place where they stood, right up against the cliff, was builded by man's hand of huge stones a garth or pound, the wall whereof was some seven feet high, and the pound within the wall of forty feet space endlong and overthwart; and the said pound was filled with the waters of a spring that came forth from the face of the cliff as they deemed . . . but ever the great basin filled somewhat faster than it voided, so that it ran over the lip on all sides, making a thin veil over the huge ashlar-stones of the garth. The day was bright and fair . . . , and all things gleamed and glittered in the sun.

80–1)

Descending to the black sand by a rock-hewn stair, they find a rather sombre inscription reading

YE WHO HAVE COME A LONG WAY TO LOOK UPON ME, DRINK OF ME, IF YE DEEM THAT YE BE STRONG ENOUGH IN DESIRE TO BEAR LENGTH OF DAYS: OR ELSE DRINK NOT . . .

(81)

and nearby a gold goblet inscribed with the words THE STRONG OF HEART SHALL DRINK FROM ME. (82) They drink and then, before beginning their return journey to Ralph's kingdom of Upmeads, they fall peacefully asleep for a time, her head on his breast. Awake and back at the top of the cliff, they wander in an Eden they had not noticed before; a huge mandalic landscape whose sacred centre, a bit off-side, must be the enormous well. There they went hand in hand about the goodly green bents betwixt the sea and the rough of the mountain; and it was the fairest and softest of summer evenings; and the deer of that place, both little and great, had no fear of man, but the hart and hind came to Ursula's hand; and the thrushes perched upon her shoulder, and the hares gambolled together close to the feet of the twain; so that it seemed to them that they had come into the very Garden of God . . .

(87)

On the journey back things go better than could be hoped for, fear having entered the hearts of Ralph's foes from the very moment he drank of the Well. When they come to the land of the Lady of Abundance, her erstwhile subjects, a whole community called the People of Abundance, beg Ralph to become their lord in memory of that great queen beneath whose ' "feet the grass grew greener" ' while ' "flowers blossomed fairer where the shadow of her body fell." ' Ralph consents. He remembers his old passion and knows with gratitude that he is indebted to the Lady of Abundance. For it was through her teaching that Ursula had helped Ralph to become 'a Friend of the Well'. Then the People of Abundance mount a great feast for Ralph and Ursula, who have become more attractive than ever to all of the opposite sex. The girls swarming about Ralph seem to have brought some kind of relief to the author's starved heart, for he dwells on the scene at length.

Then the maidens, made bold by the joy of the feast, and being stirred to the heart by much beholding of this beloved Lord, cast off their shamefacedness and crowded about him, and kissed his raiment and his hands: some even, though trembling, and more for love than fear, prayed him for kisses, and he, nothing loath, laughed merrily and laid his hands on their shoulders or took them by the chins, and set his lips to the sweetness of their cheeks and their lips, of those that asked and those that refrained; so that their hearts failed them for love of him, and when he was gone, they knew not how to go back to their houses . . .

(155)

Finally home at Upmeads, Ralph and Ursula become, like Golden Walter and the Maid, a blessing to their people, and live 'long in health of body and peace of mind.' (244) No one knows their age, and when they change their life, as it is said, in extreme old age, men think them in their late prime. Both die on the same day and are laid in one tomb by their children and grandchildren even to the fourth generation. (See Plate 11.)

These fables of tall dark witches and small blonde witches who supplant them in the heart of a hero whom all women love, and disgruntled villains who are savagely done away with, were not Morris's only romances. He wrote another kind of romance, dominated entirely by the kindly blonde – the witch having only a minor role. In the best known of these stories, *The Water of the Wondrous Isles*, the hero hardly appears before the story is almost completed. Birdalone, as the blonde child is called, is stolen in infancy by a witch, whose only function in the romance is to bring her up in the Forest of Evilshaw by the water, beat her (but not too hard), unwittingly teach her the best of her magic secrets, and accidentally furnish her with a kind of motorboat in which to tour the great lake, the home of the Wondrous Isles. The real friend, teacher, and guardian of Birdalone is a Forest Spirit, Woodwife or Mother of the Earth – a deity of the pre-Christian world who dresses 'in green like to an huntress of ancient days, her feet sandalled, her skirts gathered up into her girdle, so that her legs were naked, . . . a quiver at her back, and a great bow in her hand.' (370) She is a goddess of the Gentiles, which in this romance is glory and an honour as 'the race of Adam' is fallen and sinful. Her name is Habundia, the name of a pagan fairy in *The Romance of the Rose*. Here, however, Habundia suggests 'Our Lady of Abundance,' and not, as in the medieval poem, the 'wild and weird' sprite that tempts a third of sleeping mankind to desert their bodies three times a week to roam the world in search of dream adventures. Indeed, Morris's Habundia is one of his most imaginative conceptions; an Ellen from *Nowhere* raised to the highest pinnacle of existence he could imagine – the Soul of the Earth-life in all the manifold abundance of trees, fruits, flowers, tendrils and curving leafage which he so loved. She is Earth the Keeper, Earth the Healer, come to life in one superlative figure.

Actually, there are two figures of Habundia for she has a double in Birdalone, who exactly resembles her. And was there a third counterpart living at that very moment in The Grange and transmuting the duo of the romance into a sacred female trinity? Birdalone has never had any mirror except the water of the great lake where she swims daily, and on her first encounter with Habundia, both of them naked, the goddess describes Birdalone in minute detail to make her see herself. At the end of this loving catalogue of beauties, Birdalone exclaims that Habundia seems to have been describing herself:

'. . . I will tell thee that it fills my heart with joy to know that I am fair like to thee. For this moreover I will tell thee, that I have seen nought in field or woodland that is as lovely to me as thou art; nay, not the fritillary nodding at our brook's mouth, nor the willow-boughs waving on Green Eyot; . . . nor the white doe rising up from the grass to look at her fawn . . . Yet there is another thing which I must tell thee, to wit, that what thou hast said about the fashion of any part of me, that same, setting aside thy lovely words . . .

(18)

The description reminds one of Burne-Jones's *Andromeda* pictures or the painted version of Psyche in *Psyche and Pan*. Also, the verbal portrait of the head and face make one think of the sweetly melancholy portrait of Georgiana painted by F. I. Poynter in 1870. Excerpts from Habundia's description of Birdalone (17–8) reveal that

'In goodly fashion sits thine head upon thy shoulders . . . The hair of thee is simple brown, yet somewhat more golden than dark; thy legs shapely thin, and thy strong and clean-wrought ankles and feet . . . are with thee as full of thine heart and thy soul and as wise and deft as be thy wrists and thine hands . . . Now as to thy face: under that smooth forehead is thy nose, which is of measure, neither small nor great, straight, and lovely carven at the nostrils: thine eyen are as grey as a hawk's, but kind and serious, and nothing fierce nor shifting. . . . But well are thine eyen set in thy head, wide-apart, well opened, and so as none shall say thou mayst not look in the face of them. Thy cheeks . . . not fully rounded . . . most pitiful kind are they forsooth. Delicate and clear-made is the little trench that goeth from thy nose to thy lips, and sweet it is, and there is more might in it than in sweet words spoken. Thy lips, they are of the finest fashion, yet rather thin than full; and some would not have it so; but I would whereas I see therein a sign of thy valiancy and friendliness. Surely he who did thy carven chin had a mind to a master-work and did no less. Great was the deftness of thy imaginer, and he would have all folk that see thee wonder at thy deep thinking and thy carefulness and thy kindness. Ah maiden! is it so that thy thoughts are ever deep and solemn? Yet at least I know it of thee that they be hale and true and sweet.'

Birdalone's nudity symbolises the soul-made-flesh and we find her continually bathing, swimming or enjoying the forest in her 'darling nakedness' (276, 326). People fear her as 'some goddess of the Gentiles of old time' (112); nature loves her with every greening leaf and opening petal. Her presence, like Habundia's own, stimulates the growth of the soil and of the soul in men. Her crystal body cannot be pierced or harmed, and her tireless movement, as of a dancer, whether in the water, the forest or the waste, creates a fresh sacred centre at every turn.

After memorising the ritual of words and bloodshed needed to arouse the motive power – a great sea-serpent – of the witch's Sending-boat, Birdalone steals away from her cruel kidnapper only to fall into the hands of her vicious sister, who rules the Island of Increase Unsought. She is much better-looking than Birdalone's mistress so long as she has ready access to the elixir which keeps her shapely and makes the island into a garden of groves, fruits and flowers, and even gives strength and beauty to her castle. This lovely land is a Glittering Plain or Wood Beyond the World – a place of illusions. Even with the elixir the Queen cannot correct her stupidity or sharpen her memory and Birdalone is forgotten and allowed to escape from the prison or Wailing Tower. Her escape is aided by three female captives of the Queen. Stolen from their lovers on the eve of marriage, the captives send Birdalone to search for their lost men. This is the motivation of her quest among the islands of the great lake.

The next island she comes to is the Isle of the Young and the Old. She finds an ancient man and two children living in the shadow of a great ruined manor or palace. Learning that the children will never grow any older and that everything is in stasis, Birdalone leaves this island for the next one, the Isle of Queens. Here the fair countryside is entirely deserted, but she goes to a white castle 'all glorious with pinnacles' (92) where she finds a great company of fair women, bright-cheeked and gleaming-eyed, in the act of eating an elaborate meal. But an absolute hush hangs over outstretched hands which never move. It is a scene of death-in-life. Birdalone falls into a deep swoon, and when she recovers she sees a bier set close to the high table. On it lies a crowned and belted corpse with 'a naked sword all bloody' across his breast and his anguished queen kneeling beside him with clasped hands. Pondering the meaning of this spectacle, Birdalone flees to the next island, the Isle of Kings, only to find a similar banquet of regal simulacra in a castle refectory hung with 'terrible pictures of battle and death, and the fall of cities, and towers a-tumbling and houses a-flaming.' (96) Below the crowned kings at the high table lies a dead woman on a golden bier, clad in 'purple and pall, but the bosom of her was bared on one side, and therein was the road whereby the steel had fared which had been her bane.' Once again Birdalone, fearful of losing her sanity, flees, this time to the Isle of Nothing. Though not so frightening as the isles of the dead, this land of 'middling gravel' (99) without 'even the smallest of herbs' or a single vestige of life, even of a worm or beetle, is intensely depressing. Birdalone, exploring everywhere, gets lost in the monotonous ugliness and almost loses her boat. From the Isle of Nothing she reaches the mainland where in the Castle of the Quest she finds the lost lovers of the kidnapped girls on the Island of Increase Unsought. She sends them to the rescue in her magic boat. One of the lovers, forced to become the leman of the forgetful queen, discovers her elixir and brings an end to the enchantments of the island and the stupid tyrant.

Meantime Birdalone, waiting for the lovers' return, has a notable adventure in the Valley of the Greyweathers, great stones said to be 'giants of yore agone,' the first children of Earth, now petrified but capable of returning to life and granting the wishes of people who pray to them. The Valley lies near the Red Hold, a castle of fearful robber-knights, and Birdalone, however impermeable in her purity, undergoes a horrible ordeal. A knight whom she converts by the power of beauty and goodness is beheaded by the terrible Red Knight of the Hold and our heroine is taken captive. In the nick of time her friends return from the great lake to find

a knight weaponed, clad all in red, a very big man, riding on a great bay horse, and behind him a woman going afoot in very piteous plight; for she was tethered to the horse's crupper by a thong that bound her wrists together, so that she had but just room left 'twixt her and the horse that she might walk, and round about her neck was hung a man's head newly hewn off.

(195)

This grisly spectacle gives an impression of Birdalone as a fertility goddess. It is said that in the deep past, idols of the Earth Mother were often decorated with such trophies.

This impression of her role, as conceived by Morris, is confirmed when she retraces her island journey on her way back to Habundia and home. Her footsteps have set in motion the powers of life on the static island of the Young and the Old; the old man has been able to die and the children have not only grown but have multiplied. They are sensible children who are teaching themselves to tend flocks, raise crops, and build shelters. On the Isle of the Kings she finds strange fruit of her terrified stay, being met as she lands by twenty-two lovely and love-sick maidens. Just how the full-grown girls managed to spring from Birdalone's footprints is not suggested, but they make a gay Pre-Raphaelite picture, 'all young' and most 'full fair.'

They were bright and fine of array, and most bore gold and gems on fingers and neck and arms; they were clad in light, or it may be said, wanton raiment of diverse colours, which had only this of their fashion in common, that they none of them hid over-much of their bare bodies; for either the silk slipped from the shoulder of her, or danced away from her flank; and she whose feet were shod, spared not to show knee and some deal of thigh; and she whose gown reached unsheared from neck to heel, wore it of a web so thin and fine that it hid but little betwixt heel and neck.

(298)

They stand in defiant opposition to the castle of dead kings, queen-slayers who amid fearsome tapestries of war torment the nights with 'the sound of clashing swords and clattering shields, and the cries of men in battle.' (299) That the girls cannot find lovers seems to point to the emotional devastation wreaked by war among young women. On the other hand, the many references to their number being precisely twenty-two and to their costumes as scanty even for Morris's taste seem to mock the opening chorus of Gilbert and Sullivan's *Patience* (1881), where we find 'Twenty love-sick maidens' dressed in 'aesthetic draperies.' When Morris's maidens fall in swoons over Birdalone, thinking her a man because she is dressed in armour, we have a truly comic-opera scene. Morris, though no theatre enthusiast, must have seen or heard of *Patience*, in which the poet Bunthorne makes fun of a decorator/poet.

> I do not care for dirty greens
> By any means.

*   *   *

> I am not fond of uttering platitudes
> In stained-glass attitudes.
> In short, my medievalism's affection.

Morris's rugs and chintzes at Kelmscott show a liberal use of a green tone which verges on yellow and there is a four-tiered shelf to display his personal collection of the blue-and-white china (from China!) which he loved and used in many of the houses he decorated. Accordingly Bunthorne's lines about 'A blue-and-white young man ... / A greenery-yallery, Grosvenor Gallery,/Foot-in-the-grave young man' can hardly have amused him. The colour he used is lovely when set off in a pattern by touches of peach and cherry or even when used by itself for window draperies, as in the Green Room at Kelmscott. In 'Making the Best of It' (in *Hopes and Fears for Art*, 1882) Morris goes out of his way to warn his audience not to

fall into the trap of a dingy bilious-looking yellow-green, a colour to which I have special and personal hatred, because (if you will excuse my mentioning personal matters) I have been supposed to have somewhat brought it into vogue. I assure you I am not really responsible for it.

It is true that he talked and lectured more about beauty, art and good taste than any well-known man of his time, and he must have felt that Gilbert's barbs about 'true High Art' and 'high Aesthetic taste' – 'How Botticellian! How Fra Angelican!' – were aimed more or less at him, though he always thought the idea of art-for-art's sake absurd and said so again and again. It is therefore quite possible that the twenty-two girls on the Isle of Kings are a strange little private revenge on Gilbert.

Birdalone solves the solitary longing of the twenty-two girls when she finds on the Isle of Queens a similar number of young men who seem to have been conjured out of the earth by her former visit. They show what the ravages of war do to young men: once 'knights and merry squires,' they are now, like their armour, rusted through, and 'as gangrel men and of ill conditions, thinking nought save our first desires, even those which we share with the wolf and the kite.' (306) From the palace of the dead queens they 'yet hear ... a night-tides, first songs, and then cries and shrieking ...' (303) Like the twenty-two girls, they have been so let down by the old régime of Kings and Queens, itself a phenomenon of death-in-life, that they must build with their own hands – and what could make men and women happier if they only knew it? – a new world of love, peace and craftsmanship.

Birdalone's fertility magic is most noticeable in the Isle of Nothing. Even before the Sending-boat touches shore, she is delighted to see that

now the grass grew thick down to the lip of the water, and all about from the water up were many little slim trees, and some of them with the May-tide blos-

som yet on them, as though it were a fair and great orchard that she was near-
ing; and moreover, beyond all that she saw the thatched roofs of houses rising
up.

(292)

Four young people, two men and two women, clad simply in coats of
white woollen, without hose or shoes, wholly unarmed and wearing gar-
lands of green leaves on their heads, greet her and feed her with milk, a
small loaf of brown bread and cheese. Already they have four babes and
hope for more. They fish, tend cattle, care for their fruit and trees and
build pleasant cottages, trim and clean like themselves. They are creating
a civilisation more credible than Nowhere's because it is uncluttered by
remains of an ugly, despicable, unjust past abolished by bloodshed. Birdalone's heart yearns toward these beauteous beings and when she leaves
them for the witch's cottage which she calls home, they feel that she

must be some Goddess (for of Holy Church they knew nought) who had come
to visit them in her loveliness; and in after-times, when this folk waxed a many
and tilled all the isle and made ships and spread to other lands and became
great, they yet had a memory of Birdalone as their own very Lady and Goddess,
who had come from the fertile and wise lands to bless them, when first they
began to engender on that isle, and had broken bread with them, and slept under their roof, and then departed in a wonderful fashion, as might be looked
for in a goddess.

(296–7)

Birdalone has other adventures, is married and becomes a great lady,
but we remember her as a deity in the flesh, a fertility goddess.

All the small blonde heroines from the Maid Goldilocks through the
Maid of *The Wood* and Ursula of *The Well* to Birdalone have been goddesses or goddess-surrogates with the Lady of Abundance and Habundia
standing by to enforce the point. Morris was not the first author to put
symbolic girls at the centre of his creations. Kālidāsa, Bhavabhuti and
Sudraka had done so in India many centuries before, but Morris's heroines make us think more immediately of the girls in Shakespeare's last
or 'romantic' dramas – Marina, Imogen, Perdita and Miranda. All of
these have been called symbolic figures – 'angelic,' 'divine,' 'a divine temple,' 'goddess-like,' or 'goddess.' (Tillyard in *Shakespeare's Last Plays*,
1938; G. Wilson Knight in *The Crown of Life*, 1952; and Derek Tra-
versi in *Shakespeare: The Last Phase*, 1953). Of one it is said that were
she to 'begin a sect,' it would quench other religions, while all are show-
ered with words like blessed and holy, cherubin and saviour. They are
frequently compared to the goddesses Flora, Juno, Diana, Ceres and
Proserpina, all associated with rebirth, growth and the soil, with endless
resurrection and first-fruits. Symbols of 'great creating Nature,' the 'good

goddess,' these heroines are embodiments of the quenchless spirit of life, growth, healing and renewal in nature. Shakespeare and Morris attempted to compress into believable human figures the Great Goddess of the ancient world who bore a hundred names including Isis, Ishtar, Kybele, 'Diana of the Ephesians.' Most think that our greatest poet attempted the impossible and achieved it. Can something like this be claimed for William Morris?

The last of these romances returns to an earlier pattern in which the leading male is a great warrior and military strategist who rushes about saving the heroine from every kind of baleful fate. The description of the heroine on the brink of womanhood, with her stately-set head, broad forehead, grey eyes and compassionate expression is hardly distinguishable, if we discount her clothing, from the picture of Birdalone drawn by Habundia, the Wood-Mother who is Birdalone's double. Elfhild of *The Sundering Flood*

was that day clad all in black, without any adornment, and her hair was knit up as a crown about her beauteous head, which sat upon her shoulders as the swan upon the billow: her hair had darkened since the days of her childhood, and and was now brown mingled with gold, as though the sun were within it; somewhat low it came down upon her forehead, which was broad and white; her eyes were blue-grey and lustrous, her cheeks a little hollow, but the jaw was truly wrought, and fine and clear, and her chin firm and lovely carven; her lips not very full, but red and lovely, her nose straight and fine. The colour of her clear and sweet, but not blent with much red: rather it was as if the gold of her hair had passed over her face and left some little deal behind there. In all her face was a look half piteous, as though she craved the love of folk; but yet both mirth and swift thought brake through it at whiles, and sober wisdom shaded it into something like sternness. Low-bosomed she was yet, and thin-flanked, and had learned no tricks and graces of movement such as women of towns and great houses use for the beguiling of men. But the dear simpleness of her body in these days when the joy of childhood had left her, and a high heart of good longing was ever before her, was an allurement of love and far beyond any fooling such as that.

(XXI, 112–3)

The real-life model for all these goddesses, full-fledged or surrogate, including the Maid of *The Wood* and Ursula of *The Well*, seems to have been Georgiana Burne-Jones. I think Morris was deeply in love with her by 1868 or '69 and it seems clear enough from the *Memorials* that his tenderness was returned. However, she was the wife of his best friend, and by the time he came to know her well there roared between them a sundering flood, which he externalises as a mighty river pounding from great Icelandic mountains down a gorge 'perilous and awful ... to behold.' The first part of Morris's last romance is staged at this un-bridged gorge. The folk who lived near the opposite banks, twenty feet and more high, could have no communication 'but shouting and crying across the swirling and gurgling eddies of the black water, which them-selves the while seemed to be talking together in some dread and un-known tongue.' (5) From childhood to maturity the lovers of the story, Elfhild and Osborne are separated by this wild river. They have carried on a talking courtship ever since they were thirteen years old. Both are orphans and the wonderful delight they find in looking at and listening to each other across thirty feet of noisy chasm is charmingly invoked. The story is almost four-fifths told before they come within touching dis-tance. After overcoming terrible dangers they are blissfully married and it is said, rather oddly, that 'about both of them there was then and always a sweet wisdom that never went beyond what was due and meet for the land they lived in and the people with whom they dwelt. So that all around them folk grew better and not the worser.' (246)

During the last six years of his life Morris was decidedly unwell, plagued by itching or burning feet, hands and eyes, vexed by growing weakness, periodic faintness and insomnia, all characteristic of diabetes. As well as writing his romances he took up an entirely new art for solace; the production of beautiful books. He devised three type-faces, printed in combinations of black, red and sometimes blue inks, and worked out dozens of marginal decorations, floriated capitals and wood-cut borders. Many of these borders were to have been used later to en-close, usually in a small surround within a larger one, woodcut pictures by Burne-Jones. Morris's Kelmscott Press books were mostly reprints of his favourite English poets from Chaucer to Swinburne, *The Golden Legend,* and some old French history books in Caxton's translation, but also included some of his own poems and late romances. On them he could lavish what remained of his loving energy and lose himself in them as in the handsomely constructed romances. Morris said that 'a book ornamented with pictures that are suitable for that, and that only, may become a work of art second to none, save a fine building duly decorated or a fine piece of literature.' Or again: 'The only work of art that sur-passes a complete Mediaeval book is a complete Mediaeval building.' While writing the romances Morris was designing and overseeing the production of Kelmscott books. Thus he had two kinds of spacious struc-tures in which he could wander away from pain, disappointment, lone-liness, and the death which he felt closing in. He began collecting mediaeval books again (most of his beloved library, including *De Claris Mulieribus,* he had sold to finance *Commonweal*) with their preternatu-rally calm and lovely miniatures in which even battle scenes are hypnoti-cally soothing.

Are these activities of the last years to be condemned as cowardly escapism or alternatively, wondered at as a course of self-prescribed therapy, dictated by a sure instinct which made the last years not only bearable but generally happy? Yeats, who knew him well at this time, declared that Morris was still living, as he always had, the happiest life the Irish poet could imagine – the only one he really envied and would have been glad to have in exchange for his own. 'Escapist literature' applied to Morris's romances has no meaning except that of escaping from depression, desolation and illness into life. A favourite woodcut, Dürer's *Melencolia*, he kept always near him and perhaps the words of James Thomson's *City of Dreadful Night* (1874) describing this picture were often in his ears.

> Her fate heroic and calamitous;
>   Fronting the dreadful mysteries of Time,
> Unvanquished in defeat and desolation,
> Undaunted in the hopeless conflagration
>   Of the day setting on her baffled prime.
>
> Baffled and beaten back she works on still,
>   Weary and sick of soul she works the more,
> Sustained by her indomitable will;
>   The hands shall fashion and the brain shall pore,
> And all her sorrow shall be turned to labour,
> Till Death, the friend-foe, piercing with his saber
>   That mighty heart of hearts, ends bitter war.

In his romances Morris created a world of exciting accomplishment. In that world of purposeful adventure he had always by his side the woman he loved, and he could even derive, in retrospect, some pleasure from transfigured memories of the woman he had once loved. In that world he could be not just a leader of men, for that he was in life, but an always loved and successful leader capable of devising stratagems for ridding society of the silly, the ugly and the unjust. In that world he could overthrow at a stroke the 'modern civilisation' he hated so thoroughly, 'its commonwealth so poor, its enemies so rich, its stupendous organisation – for the misery of life! Its contempt for simple pleasures which everyone could enjoy but for its folly. Its eyeless vulgarity which has destroyed art, the one certain solace of labour.' Its headlong rush 'to end in a counting-house on top of a cinder-heap ...' (See *How I Became a Socialist*.) In the world of his romances he could find around the bend of every twisting country road a mandala of forest encircling orchards encircling gardens encircling a Kelmscott enclosing a fountain of life which could take the shape of the beloved dancer in the inch-space of the heart. In that world he could conquer the Sundering Flood, drink of the Well beyond the World, live long and happily with the woman he loved and pass quietly away, his hand held in hers. (See Frontispiece.)

In his last romances, and in the beautiful Kelmscott books, Morris built structures in which he could take refuge from life's pains and disappointments. These were the most satisfactory and rewarding Earthly Paradises he had ever created, and he had been testing one variation after another of the Edenic theme all his life. (See Plate 10.)

As he approached the end, he treasured up precious memories; once, in November 1895, going down to Rottingdean, the Burne-Joneses' holiday home, when they were not there. Thence he wrote to Georgiana, 'Today has been quite mild and I started out at ten and went to a mountain with some barns on the top and a chalk pit near (where you took me one hot evening in September, you remember) . . . I am getting better here . . .' Morris also spent more and more time at Kelmscott Manor. Georgiana, who had not, for whatever reason, visited there since 1886, went to Kelmscott to see him in 1895. She wrote to her husband, 'I feel the added years in Janey and Topsy and me, so that it seems like visiting something that is not quite real.' From Kelmscott on 27 April 1896 Morris wrote one of his last letters to her.

I cannot say that I think I am better since I saw you a week ago; and I hope I am no worse; only you see down in this deep quiet, away from the excitements of business and callers, and doctors, one is rather apt to brood . . .

However, I am going on with my work, both drawing and writing, though but little of the latter . . . Here everything is as beautiful as it can be: up to now the season is a fine one, the grass well grown and well coloured; the apple-blossom plentifuller than we have ever had it here. The weather with lots of sun . . .

I have enjoyed the garden very much, and should never be bored by walking about and about in it. And though you think I don't like music, I assure you that the rooks and blackbirds have been a great consolation to me. . . . The thing that was the pleasingest surprise was the raspberry-canes, which Giles has trellised up neatly, so that they look like a mediaeval garden . . .

Moreover Hobbs has been rethatching a lot of his sheds and barns which sorely needed it, and used to keep me in a fever of terror of galvanised iron: so that this time at least there is some improvement in the village.

(*Letters*, 382)

Some time before 1891, when *Poems By the Way* was published – perhaps during his severe illness of 1888 – Morris had written in 'Pain and Time Strive Not,'

> What part of the dread eternity
> Are those strange minutes that I gain,
> Mazed with the doubt of love and pain,
> When I thy delicate face may see,
> A little while before farewell?

*　　　*　　　*

> What pity from the heavens above,
> What heed from out eternity,
> What word from the swift world for me?
> Speak, heed, and pity, O tender love,
> Who knewest the days before farewell!

On the first of September 1896 Morris sent to Georgiana in the last note written by his own hand a request to 'Come soon, I want a sight of your dear face.' Did she bring him news of his rôle in the world, of some un-guessed form of eternity, some pity in the scheme of things, extrapolated from their affection in the days before farewell?

He died in London on the third of October following a three-day coma and there is nothing to keep us from believing, if we wish, that his hand was in Georgiana's. She was certainly at the bedside of the man whose work was the embodiment of dreams which continue to sweeten life for the living.

Afterword

Having examined Morris's life, we are left with the question of just what there is in his ideas and work that contains value, wisdom and example pertinent to our modern disorientation. A summary of his situation and attitudes might help to answer this question.

On 26 March 1874 Morris wrote to Georgiana's sister, Mrs. Alfred Baldwin, that if people would only live simply 'in little communities among gardens and green fields' and study 'the (difficult) arts of enjoying life, and finding out what they really wanted: then I think one might hope civilisation had really begun.' (*Letters*, 62) We find out more about these arts of enjoying life in 'the Aims of Art' (*Signs of Change*, 1888). What art can do for one, relieving varied kinds of distress from weariness to heart-break is described so eloquently in this lecture that we can only conclude that Morris's life was continually threatened by or filled with, one sort of misery or another.

From childhood he was pre-occupied with the fear of death, with a kind of frantic time-consciousness and, though brought up in a large family, he suffered considerable loneliness. Even when young he seems to have had visions of groups of people, often assembled around a banquet table, often inhabiting a whole city, who looked alive but were really dead. Death, for him, seemed to lurk in life, a relentless and unforgettable spectre. No one could have more readily understood Victor Hugo's 'We are all under sentence of death but with an indefinite reprieve,' though the first half of the apothegm would have been more decisive for Morris than the second. Often his awareness of death as an unavoidable conclusion capable of striking at any moment made life empty of meaning. It was a brute fact which he could not explain, or mitigate with dogmatic affirmation of a future life, or get out of his mind. Ruskin couldn't

understand how a man who, on the whole, enjoys dinner – and breakfast – and supper – that that extent of fat – can write such lovely poems about misery. There's such lovely, lovely misery in this Paradise.

Yet Morris continually spoke of a 'mist of fear' whose clamminess, when it closed in, brought feelings of anxiety, fatigue, inadequacy, guilt, and approaching death. Unforeseeable depression seemed to be waiting in ambush everywhere. Morris, more constantly aware than most of us of the continual movement of life towards death, sought in every way he could to neutralise and thwart his fear. However he never sought the momentary relief from fear to be found in the numbness of 'cracking a tube' or the exaltation of drug-taking. Over the years he had watched Rossetti's Blessed Damozel turn into that Siren who stands triumphant among the apple-boughs overhanging a pit of dead men's bones:

> In the soft dell, among the apple-trees,
>   High up above the hidden pit she stands,
> And there forever sings, who gave to these,
> That lie below, her magic hour of ease,
>   And those her apples holden in their hands.

So much for chloral washed down with a tumbler of whisky. For the dread of death, which was often, as C. S. Lewis suggests (*Rehabilitations,* 1939, 50), a simple reflex of the passionate thirst for immortality characteristic of the unsatisfied, Morris had the same analgesic as for most of the ills of existence.

In his youth, with England's great love poetry, especially that of Shakespeare, Keats Shelley, and Browning, always chiming in his ears, it was clear to Morris that death has its fiercest enemy and its traditional conqueror, in love. Love is stronger that this bogey, cancels its horror, unlocks its prison, breaks its bonds. All these dungeon-images are creations of a fear which love turns into an affirmation. Love is creation in the beautiful, and conjures up endless vistas of creation. Love says that the world – homes, cities, society, politics, industries, ecology, science – all must be transformed to furnish a worthy setting for the beloved: a place where we are not ashamed to bring up our children. Best of all, love is a joint-stock enterprise carried on by two hand-in-hand against the world at first, then with the world, and finally for the world. Thus love provides the lovers with a life-long quest and clothes them in armour which leaves few chinks for intrusive death. A blessing to all who know them, lovers slip away at last, preferably on the same day, fulfilled as lovers, as parents, as builders, as re-shapers of society in their own hand-in-hand image. For William Morris love didn't work out that way.

Mackail says that 'the house and the household, with all that these words involve, were to Morris, the symbol and the embodiment of civilised human life.' (*Studies of English Poets*, 1926, 181). Yet, for whatever complicated reason, Morris's marriage was a colossal failure and his poetry chronicles a frightful love-frustration. At any time between 1865 and 1875 it might have led to suicide or a double murder. His wound was one of the most grievous that a passionate man who is fully prepared to take delight in the responsibilities of domestic life can suffer. Women friends, especially Georgiana, did much to heal him with unflagging kindness and an understanding which extended to all his artistic efforts and social dreams. No more beautiful gift of grateful love could have been imagined or executed than the profusely illuminated calligraphic masterpieces, *A Book of Verse* and *The Rubáiyát of Omar Khayyám*, which Morris made almost entirely with his own hands for Georgiana. However, their acts of affection could hardly have extended further, as she was his best friend's wife. The closer their tie, the more likely that it would turn into still another frustration flawing emotional wholeness.

Besides Jane, Morris had, by the time her encroaching coldness had frozen them into separate bedrooms, given two more hostages to fortune, their daughters. And then, just as the nightmare of the impassive, self-absorbed wife was dying out, his elder daughter Jenny began to suffer from epileptic seizures. This was in 1876 when she was fifteen. Wilfrid Scawen Blunt says that she had been her father's 'pride as a child for her intellectual faculties' while Bernard Shaw writes ('More About Morris,' *Observer*, 6 November 1949) that the worst and never ceasing sorrow of Morris's life was his conviction that Jenny's illness was 'an inheritance from himself ... Morris adored Jenny. He could not sit in the same room without his arm round her waist. His voice changed when he spoke to her as it changed to no one else.' Shaw thinks that Morris's famous, or infamous rages, which I have not stressed, were themselves epileptic seizures, and perhaps they could have been disturbances of the central nervous system marked by a momentary clouding of consciousness. However, all the stories told of his 'fits' describe them as petulant responses to baffling or thwarting situations, which usually passed off quickly, leaving him apologetic but not broken in health or good temper. When no obvious cause of an outbreak is mentioned, perhaps his marital and erotic frustrations, usually kept well under, could have been the exciting factor. These frustrations are also to be blamed, in part at least, for his strange bouts of depression. '... I have had a fit of low spirits – for no particular reason that I could tell – which is over now for the present I hope.' (*Letters*, 48) However, Morris believed that his side of the family was to blame for Jenny's trouble and was seldom free from worries about her.

Finally, Morris was from an early age disturbed and grieved by the awful working and living conditions of the Victorian poor – an unspeakable injustice which enraged Carlyle, maddened Ruskin, and produced a spate of novels like *Alton Locke, Sybil; or, The Two Nations, Mary Barton, North and South, Hard Times*, and *Felix Holt*. These books will not let their readers forget the horrors of working-class life in the period of England's greatest prosperity. As an artisan and employer of contented workmen, Morris, long before he became a Socialist orator and agitator, had come to empathise with the beaten, broken, sodden, hopeless – or manic – misery of the overworked, underfed poor. Of himself he said, 'If I were to work ten hours a day at work I despised and hated, I should spend my leisure, I hope, in political agitation, but I fear in drinking.'

(Quoted in E. Meynell, *Portrait of William Morris*, 1947, 162) To C. E. Maurice he wrote on 1 July 1883:

in looking into matters social and political I have but one rule, that in thinking of the condition of any body of men I should ask myself, 'How could you bear it yourself? what would you feel if you were poor against the system under which you live?' I have always been uneasy when I had to ask myself that question, and of late years I have had to ask it so often, that I have seldom had it out of my mind: and the answer to it has more and more made me feel that if I had not been born rich or well-to-do I should have found my position *un-endurable*, and should have been a mere rebel against what would have seemed to me a system of robbery and injustice. Nothing can argue me out of this feeling, which I say plainly is a matter of religion to me: the contrasts of rich and poor are unendurable and ought not to be endured by either rich or poor.

(Letters, 176)

Earlier in the same year, 14 March, he had written to *The Manchester Examiner* that

It may well be a burden to the conscience of an honest man . . . to think of the innumerable lives which are spent in toil unrelieved by hope and uncheered by praise; men who might as well, for all the good they are doing to their neighbours by their work, be turning a crank with nothing at the end of it; but this is the fate of those who are working at the building of blind competitive commerce, which still persists in looking at itself as an end, and not as a means.

It has been this burden on my conscience, I do in all sincerity believe, which has urged me on to speak of popular art in Manchester and elsewhere. I could never forget that in spite of all drawbacks my work is little else than pleasure to me; that under no conceivable circumstances would I give it up even if I could. Over and over again have I asked myself why should not my lot be the common lot. My work is simple enough . . . Indeed I have been ashamed when I have thought of the contrast between my happy working hours and the unpraised, unrewarded, monotonous drudgery which most men are condemned to.

(Letters, 166)

As much as the fear of death or the frustration of his loves, this pity for the poor, this nagging of conscience, threatened the balance and control, the feeling of integrity and genial magnanimity, which he prized so highly. When, close to the end, Georgiana thoughtlessly spoke of the hovels of the poor (which he had tried so hard to turn into Cotswold cottages), Morris broke into tears.

Still, plagued by nearly every fear, frustration, disappointment and pain that vexes human beings, he fought back. He was determined to build a heaven in hell's despite. Beauty was his battle-cry and his talents his weapons. Creation was his watchword, and he made houses, poems, stained glass, chintzes, papers, tapestries, rugs, translations and long prose romances, always capturing glimpses of an Earthly Paradise which served very well, after the fashion of Oriental mandalas, as anodynes for distress and sanctuaries in which self-confidence, dignity and hope could grow again.

Towards the end of his life Morris realised that most people have no such armamentarium as his with which to fight neurasthenia, disappointment and frustration, but he had never preached that such a variety of talents and resources were necessary to make an art of life. What is necessary to make one's life bearable and happy is work in 'the lesser arts.' In *News from Nowhere* we see Morris willing to give up science, philosophy and 'high art' as unnecessary for most people's happiness – anxious to give them up because they are, in fact, more likely to do mankind dreadful disservice than to produce the social equality and epoch of rest or unvexed effort he was aiming at. Morris believed that man has an instinctive drive to make things and to make them well – a light in the breast which illumines the path he must take towards self-fulfilment and a fire in the loins which makes him strong to work well and faithfully. Perhaps he simplifies human nature too much – perhaps he is describing only one man: himself. Emerson believed that it is the mark of genius if a man cannot believe his fellow men are essentially different from himself. There were in Morris's time, as there still are, many 'sciences of man,' which Morris brushed aside in favour of his conviction that man is essentially a producer. In his work, spontaneously chosen and drawing on instinctive springs of creative energy, man finds his joy, his solace, his armour against tragedy, and a beauty to sweeten his and all men's lives. He never tired of repeating Ruskin's maxim that beauty is the by-product of joy in work. Only in work which yields joy, and thereby beauty, can man find happiness, fight pain, define his personality, make clear his unique purpose, realise his essence. Obedient to the law of his nature, every man realises that the true purpose of his life is to try to alter the material world where it falls short of the image which has somehow been conceived in the depths of himself. He must struggle to impose his intuited pattern, make something needed by both body and spirit, create something both useful and worthy of survival.

In deadly earnest, with the whole force of his personality, Morris preached this doctrine from the depths of his own experience. A man's work, done with and for love, is his only way of being alive, coping with catastrophe, facing the *nunc dimittis*. He took for granted the notion of his time that there are elements in man's psyche that do not change along with environmental changes – something called 'human nature.' Obviously, his concept of human nature was too simplistic but a similar idea is being celebrated today under names like 'the human-potential movement,' which stresses love, creativity, and beauty as invaluable experiences which enable men to satisfy their desperate need to find meaning in life. Morris's gospel of happy work must be his chief bequest to our time – a way of meeting grief head-on, of firming our too easily shattered personalities, and of finding meaning in life. The search for life's meaning goes on, even in the midst of drug addiction, sexual misery and nerveless irresponsibility. For Morris as for Carlyle, to work was to pray – *Laborare est orare*. Through work one could, if only momentarily, tap the omnipotence, omniscience and all-lovingness associated with the numinous. Creative work yielded glints of ecstasy which made it almost impossible to believe in an end-all.

Though insisting at the beginning ot *The Earthly Paradise* that

> *I cannot ease the burden of your fears,*
> *Or make quick-coming death a little thing,*
> *Or bring again the pleasure of past years,*

Morris's message to later generations, proved on the pulse of his workmanship, was that our fears can be overcome, death is less than life, and the pleasures of past years can be used to extrapolate a hopeful future. Mackail paraphrased him in *Studies of English Poets* (196): 'the whole message and meaning of his life and work' was 'the coming of mankind into its inheritance; life not empty or made for nothing, and the parts of it fitting into one another.' Morris worked unflaggingly at his own work and urged others to get on with theirs – 'not living like fools and fine gentlemen, and not beaten by the muddle, but like good fellows trying by some dim candlelight to set our workshop ready against tomorrow's daylight.' 'Will,' an unforgotten word in his vocabulary, was followed, like the exercise of will itself, by 'Courage' and 'Hope.' On the basis of his life-long experience Morris might have affirmed that the road to Utopia is endless but in travelling that road – in working at our dreams for imposing order on chaos – we will find ourselves.

We know that the people of Nowhere, 'Like the mediaevals,' had to have 'everything trim and clean, and orderly and bright' (Ch. X). The foul 'manufacturing districts' were wiped from the face of the earth and all necessary 'business' was carried on 'with as little as possible of dirt, confusion, and the distressing of quiet people's lives.' It was Morris's notion that every man has a right to:

Money enough to keep him from fear of want or degradation for him and his; leisure enough from bread-earning work (even though it be pleasant to him) to give him time to read and think, and connect his own life with the life of the great world; work enough of the kind aforesaid, and praise of it, and encouragement enough to make him feel good friends with his fellows; and lastly (not least, for 'tis verily part of the bargain) his own due share of art, the chief part of which will be a dwelling that does not lack the beauty which Nature would freely allow it, if our own perversity did not turn Nature out of doors.

(Quoted in Meynell, *Portrait*, 162)

If the attainment of these desirable conditions required a violent, but very brief revolution which disposed of 'the greedy gamblers on the Stock Exchange' and abolished the class system at a blow, Morris was willing at one time to agree to that. He has therefore sometimes been invoked, as in the Berkeley campus riots that began in 1965, as a father-image of the New Left or Neo-Anarchist movement. For a time a badge bearing his bearded face and inscribed 'Popular Art and Revolution,' coloured red, green or yellow, was much displayed by the students. They probably did not understand that Morris wanted revolution so that most machinery could be junk-piled, handicrafts – not 'pop art' – revived, and disagreeable work reduced to four hours a day so that men would have eight hours to work at arts of their own choosing. Morris did not object to automata doing the world's dirty work so long as they left to men the activities that are creative and worthwhile.

Morris also had a low opinion of teachers, 'don' being, after 'British officer,' the most insulting word he could hurl at an enemy. There is no formal education in Nowhere. Morris believed that 'most children, seeing books lying about, manage to read by the time they are four years old.' (Ch. V) Later, when and if they become interested in an intellectual pursuit, they can easily find guidance to the best books to read if they cannot smell these out for themselves. He was quite sure that all good education is self-education. However, he seldom forgot that communes always demand that each member give according to his talents and receive according to his needs. This means dictatorship of some kind and bureaucratic interference in everybody's life until that promised period when – and 'when' is always an unrevealed secret – government will wither away. In Nowhere there is no government and no coercion, perhaps because Morris had a leaning towards anarchism himself – though not towards the Anarchists in his Socialist League – and agreed with Bakunin that *any* state is a 'flagrant' and 'cynical' negation of humanity, presuming like theology that men are bad by nature and the state must set, and keep, them right.

The New Leftists, who see Communist Russia with its bureaucracy, oppression, and neo-imperialism as just another highly organised capitalist society, have as their guru a German philosopher with a Marxist background who claims to have achieved an unlikely synthesis of Marx, Anarchy, Utopianism and Freud, to be realised by the complete destruction of the Affluent Society. New Leftism can hardly be more than an umbrella term sheltering many differing and often warring, factions. Very few of these have alternatives to take the place of the society they would destroy; rather, they seem to think of revolution as an end in itself. Making sure that people are freed from repressions, especially sexual, is enough to keep many of them busy, while the soaring incidence of venereal disease assures them of the success of their 'revolution.' Compared with this babel of tongues, these so-called syntheses of unadjustable gospels, this moaning for destruction, this sexuality divorced from awe, Morris's *Nowhere* is a compendium of inspired common sense. *The Dream of John Ball* contains a meditation on revolution which should never be forgotten:

men fight and lose the battle, and the thing that thy fought for comes about in spite of their defeat, and when it comes turns out not to be what they meant, and other men have to fight for what they meant under another name.

(Ch. IV)

Perhaps the man who put the case for the New Left better than they have for themselves is F. L. Lucas (*Eight Victorian Poets*, 1930, 111):

As men grow tired of their mechanical toys, and lose belief in any future life, they may come to feel the folly of making the world they inhabit so briefly into a hell of hideousness and overcrowding and overwork, when it might be a place, of death indeed and suffering and unhappy love, but also of natural beauty and health and happy labour. An England with a quarter the population and one-tenth the factories of today, no longer earning as 'the world's workshop' the estimable privilege of maintaining so many extra million drudges in an existence they would be better without, might thereafter come to find Morris one of the wisest of his century.

All of us seem to be in need of occupational therapy, of true 'Popular Art,' of a new Arts and Crafts movement like the one fathered by Morris. His conviction that human beings are, above everything else, makers, creators, producers confronting loneliness and death, who can best express, fulfil and defend themselves in and through their work – probably only in and through their work – is perhaps our most valuable legacy from the nineteenth century.

Many people, in their bewilderment, have turned to the East for spiritual help, and Morris profited greatly, without knowing it of course, from the most sophisticated of all the Buddhist and Hindu techniques for self-integration or reconstruction of the damaged or threatened personality. Eastern novitiates paint, or sketch in the sand, pictures called mandalas, patterns predominantly circular (but also enclosing squares) which swirl in revolution upon revolution around a centre, often represented as a temple or sacred point. In the heart of this centre is a fountain of life which may take the form of a dancing woman. The constructor of the mandala creates, as Dr. Jung would say, from the spontaneous spur of his unconscious a portrait which brings him as close as may be to a glimpse of Ultimate Reality – its peace beyond understanding – and this portrait, drawn from the artist's inmost depths, reacts upon its maker as an experience which both solaces and helps him to 'find himself.' This is the real self or mislaid personality, symbolised by the goddess dancing on the lotus at the centre of the sacred spot. To find this centre, with its four-square composure, its indefeasible wholeness, its unvexed joy, was the object of Morris's life-long search for Earthly Paradises. We have seen again and again how this quest enticed him into mandalic topography, whether read of in Scott, uncovered in Epping glades, loved in 'Druid' circles and Oxford cloisters, groped for in early poems and tales, built at Red House, created widely through arts and crafts, found at Kelmscott, practised in calligraphy, sought in Iceland, hoped for in Socialism, created in gorgeous romances. The experience of the mandala – always in some sense a *real* Earthly Paradise – is said to be ineffable, that is, beyond telling. However, G. Tucci finds these words for the wordless adventure:

It is rather an epiphany, a manifestation which appears to the initiate when at the end of his spiritual preparation he comes to be identified with the centre of the *mandala*, the point from which all goes forth and to which all returns . . . The images that the mystic sees come forth from the centre of his own heart, pervade space, and then reabsorb themselves in him. They deify him and almost burn him with their lightning flashes. They are not inert and insignificant images. They calm the stormy sea of the subconscious and they illuminate his darkness. The soul's discord is extinguished and on its agitation there dawns a steady and serene light.

Thus, the reading of the *mandala*, the reliving in one's own consciousness of . . . the spiritual and orderly progression through the various stages that are shown symbolically upon its surface, induces a deliverance . . . This may take place literally, as . . . when the mystic, after having passed through the different parts of the *mandala*, finds himself physically present at the centre and so experiences the *mandala*'s catharsis in himself. Or it may occur mentally when by concentrating his mind on the pattern of the *mandala* he realises in himself the truth which this pattern typifies.

(*The Theory and Practice of the Mandala*, tr. A. H. Brodrick, 1961, 105–6)

On reading Morris carefully, one finds that his poems, stories, patterns and romances contain many pictured mandalas handled, in relation to narrative and psychological climax, with Oriental expertise!

William Morris's life, work, example and ideas hold delight, wisdom and encouragement of a timeless quality for people who are trying to find meaning and joy in their lives.

For Margaret and me the years spent here at Kelmscott, immured on dull days among the flower-patterned papers, rugs, chintzes, tiles and tapestries of the Manor and on bright days among the primulas, paeonies, roses, lilies, begonias, buddleias and hollyhocks of the garden (I say 'immured' because we live in a proper *ortus conclusus*), have seemed to pass

more in timelessness than in time. We cannot imagine that such an
experience will ever really end for us or for others looking for a clue to
'the (difficult) art of living.'

Kelmscott Manor
4 August 1973

Index